Study on the Coordinated Development of Beijing-Tianjin-Hebei

Advisory Group of Experts of
ADB Technical Assistance Project:
TA-9042 PRC

Paths International Ltd

中国财经出版传媒集团
中国财政经济出版社

Introduction

On January 5, 2016, the Asian Development Bank (ADB) contracted with the Chinese Government for a technical assistance project, *Study on the Coordinated Development of Beijing-Tianjin-Hebei* (BTH) (No. 48462-001), which was carried out in Hebei Province. This project was to support Hebei Provincial Government to better implement the *Coordinated Development Plan in the BTH Region*.

After an international tender, a research team led by the Macroeconomic Research Institute of the Hebei Provincial Development and Reform Commission won the bid and formally signed a contract with ADB on July 15, 2016. This project which lasted 15 months and was finished at the end of October 2017. As the implementation agency, Hebei Provincial Department of Finance(HPDF) was responsible for communicating with ADB, governmental agencies, academia and other parties, supervising and promoting the research project, and organizing and coordinating related affairs. This project team consists of three international experts and eight domestic experts.

Since the start of the project, under the management of ADB and HPDF, the team has conducted field researches in Chengde, Zhangjiakou, Baoding, Langfang, Shijiazhuang, Handan, Ganzhou, and Tangshan from November 2016 to March 2017, and carried out special consultations with more than 10 provincial-level business leaders and experts from scientific research departments, universities and colleges. The team also held three large-scale expert consultation workshops for discussing the initial, interim, and final reports, which consist of one summary report and five thematic reports. During the project, the governmental departments gave a lot of support.

On October 21, 2017, ADB held a final report expert discussion workshop in Shijiazhuang. At the workshop, Zhang Junkuo, Deputy Director of Development Research Center of the State Council(DRC), Tang Min, Executive Vice Chairman of China Social Entrepreneur Foundation, Zhang Jing'an, President of China Association of scientific and technological reform, Ma Xiaohe, Former Vice President of Chinese Academy of Macroeconomic Research(AMR.NDRC), Niu Fengrui, Deputy Director of China Society of Urban Economy(CSUE), and Liu Shangxi, director of Chinese Academy of Fiscal Sciences, gave a high evaluation on the final report, and also the ADB project officials attending the meeting. The study passed the experts' argumentation.

ADB Technical Assistance Project, Study on the Coordinated Development of Beijing–Tianjin–Hebei List of Managers

ADB Project Manager: Bo An, Public Management Specialist, Public Management, Financial Sector and Regional Cooperation Division, EARD, ADB

Seung-Min Lee, Financial Sector Specialist, Public Management, Financial Sector and Regional Cooperation Division, EARD, ADB

HPDF Project Officers:

Jin Haizeng Deputy Director General

Wang Lin Division Chief, Foreign Affairs Division

Xu Wei Director, Foreign Debt Management Center

Wang Tieli Vice-Consultant, Foreign Affairs Division

ADB Technical Assistance Project, Study on the Coordinated Development of Beijing–Tianjin–Hebei List of Experts

Team Leader:	Li Lan	Former Director, Macroeconomic Research Institute of the Hebei Provincial Development and Reform Commission
Deputy team Leader:	Zeng Yi	Director, Center for Aging and Human Development Study, Duke University; Chief Scientist, Peking University
Members:	Charles Maxwell Becker	Associate Chair, Research Professor, Department of Economics, Duke University
	Gary Gereffi	Director, Researcher, Center on Globalization, Governance & Competitiveness
	Xiao Jincheng	Former Director, researcher, Institute of Spatial Planning & Regional Economy, NDRC
	Gao Zhi	Director, Macroeconomic Research Institute of the Hebei Provincial Development and Reform Commission
	Chen Zhiguo	Director, Researcher, Department of Social Science, Hebei University
	Luo Jing	Deputy Director, Macroeconomic Research Institute of the Hebei Provincial Development and Reform Commission

Wang Fuhua	Deputy Director, Macroeconomic Research Institute of the Hebei Provincial Development and Reform Commission
Gu Jianqin	Professor, Hebei University of Economics and Business
Zhang Jinjie	Associate Research Fellow, Macroeconomic Research Institute of the Hebei Provincial Development and Reform Commission

Contents

Thematic Report Ⅲ: *Research on Sustainable Development of Less Developed Regions in North Hebei Province* 261

Summary Report

Study on Promoting Coordinated Development in the BTH Region: Focusing on Roles of Hebei Province

Principal Investigator: Li Lan
Investigators: Huang Helin, Liang Shilei, Su Fenghu,
Bai Zhenhua, Wang Guangyu

It is a significant national strategy to promote the coordinated development of the Beijing-Tianjin-Hebei(BTH) Region. As a component of the BTH Region, Hebei Province plays an important part in the aspects of area, population size, resource capacity, economic output and so on. However, it also has many shortcomings in development. It shoulders the historical responsibility in the process of the coordinated development as the major area in the BTH Region. Furthermore,it is an important step in implementing the spirit of the 19th National Congress of the Chinese Communist Party to conduct an in-depth study on the promoting the coordinated development of the BTH Region. The present study also has great practical significance in reducing Beijing's non-capital functions, building the Xiong'an New Area with a high starting point and high standard, and forming a new pattern of coordinated development in the BTH Region.

1. Analysis of the historical development and present situation of the coordinated development of the BTH Region

1.1 Historical development of regional cooperation

Beijing, Tianjin and Hebei Province have been geographically and culturally connected for a long period of time. This regional cooperation has lasted for 30 years. During this period, this inter-regional cooperation has gradually deepened from point to surface,and from shallow to deep.In addition,this regional cooperation has realized a tremendous transformation from initial attempts to consensus, from few fields to the whole area, and from departmental initiatives to government-market joint promotion. In 2014, the coordinated development of BTH Region has become a major national strategy, marking a new era of regional cooperation.

1.1.1 Preliminary exploration of regional cooperation (1981-1985)

In 1981, five provinces and municipalities, including Beijing, Tianjin, Hebei, Shaanxi and Inner Mongolia formed the North China Economic and Technical Cooperation Zone on the basis of the North China Economic Cooperation Zone. The cooperation zone was aimed at solving problems on the cross-regional adjustment of resources through high-level consultation. In the same year, the national government started to implement the land management strategy. As a pilot project, the National Ministry of Land and Resources formulated "The Territorial Planning Outline for the Beijing-Tianjin-Tangshan Region". Under the guidance of the above outline, the BTH Region initiated cooperation in cross-regional infrastructure construction, water conservation, soil pollution remediation and other areas. In 1982, the concept of "capital circle" was proposed in the "Overall Planning Scheme for Beijing Urban Construction" by the Beijing Administration. The inner circle consisted of Beijing, Tianjin and Tangshan, Langfang, and Qinhuangdao in Hebei Province, while the outer circle included Chengde, Zhangjiakou, Baoding and Cangzhou, which were adjacent to Beijing and Tianjin. This scheme has also been identified as the earliest version of the capital's economic zone planning. The BTH Region carried out preliminary cooperation in certain fields and key issues, and gradually developed applicable patterns of cross-regional cooperation, which has provided valuable experience for further cooperation.

1.1.2 First signs of regional cooperation (1986-2003)

In 1986, on the initiative of Ruihuan Li, Mayor of Tianjin, 15 cities in the Bohai Rim region started a joint mayoral meeting for the region, which was considered as the earliest formal mechanism for regional cooperation in the BTH Region. In 1988, Beijing and six surrounding cities, including Baoding, Langfang, Tangshan, Qinhuangdao, Zhangjiakou and Chengde, set up the Beijing-Beijing Economic Cooperation Zone, established a routine mechanism and developed cooperation between enterprises in different regions. In 1995, Hebei Province put forward the strategy of "Opening up the Two Circles" (The inner circle was the Beijing-Tianjin surrounding region, while the outer circle was the Bohai Sea surrounding region), and clarified its position as the main strategy of provincial economic development. In 1996, the concept of "Capital Economic Circle" was first mentioned in the"Beijing Economic Development Strategy Research Report", with Beijing and Tianjin as the core, including seven cities (Tangshan, Qinhuangdao, Chengde, Zhangjiakou, Baoding, Langfang and Cangzhou). In 2001, the "Beijing-Tianjin-Hebei North Urban and Rural Planning for Space Development" was proposed, under the leadership of Professor Liangyuan Wu, with the participation of many experts from Beijing, Tianjin and Hebei Province. The research on the integration of BTH Region reached a new stage. During this period, under the background of rapid economic and social development, the BTH Region increasingly focused on promoting an overall coordinated development. However, due to restrictions in local interests and government assessment mechanisms, the driving force for regional self-development was obviously greater than that of regional cooperation. The excessive competition of resources, industries, projects and markets in these three fields was prevalent, and the substantive promotion of regional cooperation was fraught with difficulties.

1.1.3 Comprehensive upgrade of the consensus of regional cooperation (2004-2013)

In February 2004, the National Development and Reform Commission convened a meeting with the departments of Beijing, Tianjin and Hebei Province on the subject of regional economic development strategy. In this meeting, all related parts reached the "Langfang Consensus". In November, the preparation work for the regional planning of the BTH Metropolitan Area was officially launched. In 2008, "The First Regional Joint Meeting of Development and Reform Commissions in the BTH Region" was held, and the development and reform departments of these three regions jointly signed the "Opinions of Development and Reform Commissions in Beijing, Tianjin and Hebei Province on Establishing a Communication Mechanism to Promote the Development of the BTH Metropolitan Area". In 2010, the "BTH Metropolitan Area Regional Planning" was submitted to the State Council, and a regional development plan was formulated according to the "2+8" model, which included two municipalities(Beijing and Tianjin), and eight cities(Shijiazhuang, Qinhuangdao, Tangshan, Langfang, Baoding, Cangzhou, Zhangjiakou and Chengde). In October 2010, the Hebei government promulgated the "Opinions on Industry Development in Hebei Province's Capital Economic Circle". lu addition, the Hebei government also put forward the official cooperation project with Beijing in six aspects. In 2011, the outline of the 12th five-year plan included the proposal of "building the capital economic circle". With the continuous improvement of China's market system, the endogenous impetus for regional cooperation has gradually increased. The state and the Beijing-Tianjin-Jiading region has reached an intensified consensus of promoting regional integration and accelerated the process. The cross-regional planning of various specific areas has been continuously published. High-level government officials from Beijing, Tianjin and Hebei Province have frequently communicated with each other. However, regional cooperation was still mainly concentrated in the areas of resources, ecology and environmental protection. The cooperation in substantive areas, such as economic development, industrial transfer and resource sharing, coutinued to remain as words on paper.

1.1.4 Opening a new chapter in regional cooperation (2014 to now)

On February 26, 2014, General Secretary Jinping Xi listened to the report on the coordinated development of Beijing, Tianjin and Hebei Province, and emphasized that the coordinated development of the BTH Region is a major national strategy. He also put forward seven specific requirements. In March of the same year, Premier Keqiang Li listed "Strengthening Economic Cooperation in the Bohai Rim and BTH Region" as a major task in 2014 in the report on government work at the second session of the Twelfth National People's Congress. In April 2015, the "BTH Coordinated Development Plan" was promulgated, further clarifying basic starting points of coordinated development, functional orientation of the region, major development goals and breakthrough areas. Since February 2014, the state has put unprecedented emphasis on regional cooperation in the BTH Region. Cross-regional cooperation has been carried out in succession, with substantive progress in all areas. Regional cooperation has entered a new stage of development in an all-round way.

1.2 Major achievements of coor-dinated development

Since 2014, Beijing, Tianjin and Hebei Province have earnestly implemented the Central Government's strategic deployment of promoting the coordinated development of the BTH Region. They have made overall plans and major breakthroughs, and achieved great progress in improving the overall scheme, reducing non-capital functions of Beijing, and making pioneering breakthroughs in key areas and innovations in institutional mechanisms. All these achievements mark a great start of coordinated development.

1.2.1 Strengthen the top-level design and improve the coordinated development of the planning system

On February 26, 2014, General Secretary Jinping Xi chaired a forum on the BTH Region, in which the coordinated development of Beijing, Tianjin and Hebei Province became a major national strategy. The state and the Region set up organizations to implement the strategy and put forward a number of programmatic documents and plans, such as work programs and implementation opinions. Furthermore, the coordinated development planning system was gradually improved, laying a solid foundation for the smooth implementation of various tasks.

The Political Bureau of the Central Committee of CPC deliberated and adopted the "Outline for the Plan for the Coordinated Development of the BTH Region". The country's first five-year regional plan, "The plan for Economic and Social Development of the BTH Region in the 13th-Five-Year Plan

Period" was issued and implemented. Relevant departments of the State Council successively issued 12 special plans for water conservancy, traffic system and ecology, and formulated a series of supporting documents such as the "BTH Cooperative Development Pilot Demonstration Work Plan", which were work programs for making breakthroughs in these key areas. Relevant plans and programs were intensively introduced to improve the planning system, and clarify the functional status and development path of the region. In addition, these documents also pointed out the direction for the cooperation, work division and smooth implementation of coordinated development on the national, provincial and grass-roots level.

The Hebei provincial party committee and the government and took the coordinated development of the BTH Region as a long-term strategic task. Hebei Province was set up as a leading system to promote coordinated development. In order to thoroughly implement the requirements of the national strategy, they successively published government documents of "Opinions on Implementing General Secretary Xi Jinping's Important Speech and Accelerating the Coordinated Development of the BTH Region","Opinions of the CPC Hebei Provincial Party Committee and Hebei Provincial People's Government on Implementing the Outline of the BTH Coordinated Development Plan", and the "Plan for Promoting BTH Collaborative Development". Based on the functional orientation of the "three areas and one base" and national planning, Hebei Province has drafted four functional orientation plans, 27 specific plans and four implementation opinions of national specific plans. All these documents basically formed the planning system of the overall plans, functional orientation plans, specific plans and implementation opinions, which laid a solid foundation for the overall implementation of the "Planning Outline" and promotion of the coordinated development.

1.2.2 Seize the key link to obtain initial achievements in reducing non-capital functions of Beijing

With the support of the central government and efforts of Beijing and Hebei, Hebei Province has made major breakthroughs in undertaking non-capital functions of Beijing. Furthermore, Hebei Province has initiated projects for transferring four major parts of non-capital functions. Moreover, Hebei Province has accelerated the process of major transferring projects. The platform construction of undertaking non-capital functions has made significant progress. The strategy of easing non-capital functions has achieved initial success.

The concentrated transfer of non-capital functions has made major breakthroughs. On April 1, 2017, the Central Committee of the CPC and the State Council decided to establish Xiong'an New Area in Hebei Province, which is located in the northeast of Baoding, which covers three counties (Rongcheng, Anxin and Xiongxian) and the surrounding areas. The new district had obvious geographical advantages, was convenient, and had an unimpeded traffic system, and had plenty of development space and strong resources, as wellas environment carrying capacity. In the future, this would be a green and livable new city, an innovative driving and development leading area, a demonstration area of coordinated development, an open-up zone, and an innovative development zone to implement the new development concept (see Figure 1). The construction of this new district was a historic project to reduce non-capital functions of Beijing, and effectively transfer the population and non-capital functions of Beijing. At present, the government has set up a working committee and a management committee for the Xiong'an New Area. Regional control, city planning, population relocation, major project planning and other tasks would be carried out in an orderly manner.

The projects of undertaking prioritized non-capital functions was orderly promoted. In order to formulate policies and measures for relocating wholesale markets with the Beijing government, Xinfadi-Gaobeidian Agricultural Products Logistics Center, Langfang-Yongqing Garment Center, Baigou-Dahongmen International Clothing Center and many other business centers begun their operations. In 2016, there were already 117 commodity markets moving out of Beijing. The Beijing-Cangzhou Biomedical Industrial Center explored new patterns of regional co-construction, attracting 68 bio-pharmaceutical companies from Beijing. The Langfang Cloud Storage Industrial Center undertook the auxiliary service functions of Beijing, focusing on the construction of a number of ministries and commissions nationwide under the e-government platform, energy enterprise information exchange platform, IDC and other Internet companies such as Baidu and Ali. The construction of the Beijing-Tongzhou Sub-center was fully carried out. Hebei Province took the initiative to connect with Beijing and seek to unify of planning with Tongzhou District of Beijing.

The platform construction of undertaking non-capital functions has made progress. Beijing, Tianjin and Hebei Province has issued guidance on strengthening the platform construction of industrial transfer. The process of platform construction has been gradually accelerated, and the relocation of Beijing's new airport in Hebei Province has been completed. The relevant planning and construction of the project was carried out in an orderly manner. The central government has approved the establishment of the Beijing-Hebei joint administration of coordinated development demonstration zone in Caofeidian.In 2016, 35 projects from Beijing were settled in this zone. Based on the "Three Precise" requirements, Hebei Province further selected and identified 270 platforms on the basis of the strategic cooperation functional areas identified in the planning framework, including 11 provincial-level platforms and 53 municipal-level platforms, and 206 county-level platforms.

1.2.3 Focusing on key areas, construction on traffic system, ecology and industries has achieved breakthroughs

The Central Government and BTH Region take the position of overall planning and timely reform. They took the lead in carrying out regional cooperation in three key areas of transportation, ecology and industry. They promoted the construction and management of transportation facilities in an all-round way, increasingly strengthened the ecological construction, deepened cooperation in industrial upgrading and transfer, and actively promoted the regional coordinated development.

Traffic integration achieved remarkable results. Hebei Province, Beijing and Tianjin work together to renovate "broken roads" and "bottleneck roads", which have made substantial progress. The connecting project of more than 10 highways, such as Beijing-Taiwan express highway, Beijing-Hong Kong-Macao express highway, has been completed. A number of "broken roads" such as Beijing-Shanghai express highway (Cangzhou-to-Jilu section), Rongcheng-Wuhai express highway (Langya to Pocang section) has started operating. Tianjin-Baoding Railway and Beijing-Jixian Intercity Railway were opened to traffic. The Beijing-Zhangjiakou Railway started construction at full capacity. The government also accelerated the construction of the Beijing-Qinhuangdao express highway and Taihang Mountain express highway. And the regional rapid transit system was also gradually improved. The government also accelerated construction of Beijing's new airport. And Beidaihe and Chengde Airports are put into operation. Hebei airport has been incorporated into the management of capital airport group company. The integration operation of regional airports has been accelerated. Expressway ETC charge network of the BTH Region has achieved full coverage, with "one-card access" in 11 municipalities and districts, 642 lines, more than 12,000 buses. By the end of 2017, the regional highway "broken head road" will be completely repaired, the capacity of highway system will be greatly enhanced and the comprehensive transportation network will be gradually improved.

Cooperation on ecological environment protection has been strengthened. Beijing, Tianjin and Hebei jointly carried out ecological co-construction and air defense governance, signed "Cooperation Agreement of the BTH Region Making Breakthroughs in Environ-mental Protection", jointly started ecological protection projects of Beijing-Tianjin sand source management, Beijing-Tianjin ecological water source protection forest, Beijing-Tianjin-Baoding transition zone of plain ecology. These three regions jointly promoted eliminating backward industrial capacity, reducing coal burning, controlling industrial and dust pollution. Hebei Province started the coal limiting policy in 18 counties near Beijing, such as Luanfang and Baoding. Beijing and Tianjin jointly work with Baoding and Langfang, Tangshan and Cangzhou to provide funding, policy and technical support for pollution prevention. The clean-up project of fish tank in Panda Reservoir has been basically completed. Tianjin and Hebei Province has reached an agreement on the horizontal ecological compensation, water quality standards and compensation plans. And the ecological compensation mechanism of diversion project from Luanhe to Tianjin is initially established. The regional ecological environment management and the protection cooperation are gradually strengthened. The environmental quality is significantly improved. In the three years from 2014 to 2016, the BTH Region completed a total of 17.538 million mu[①] of afforestation area. In 2016, the average concentration of PM2.5 in Hebei dropped 35% than that of 2013.

Industrial upgrading and transfer are promoted steadily. Construction of industrial cooperation platforms has been intensified. Hebei Province and Beijing jointly built Caofeidian Coordinated Development Demonstration Zone, Tianjin-Hebei (Tianjin-She County) Circular Economy Industrial Center, Lutheran Jinan and Hebei Coordinated Development Demonstration Zone and other major business centers. The government has accelerated the construction of major cooperation projects. The fourth factory of Beijing Hyundai in Cangzhou has gone into operation. The micro-car industry base of BAIC Automobile Group (North China) has started operation. The "Beijing-Tianjin-Jiading Large Data Corridor" has been launched. And the integrated circuit industry base co-constructed by Shijiazhuang and Beijing has settled in Zhengding New Area. Taking the opportunity of the 2022 Winter Olympic Games jointly hold by Beijing and Zhangjiakou, Beijing, Tianjin and Hebei Province work together to build the eastern Beijing tourism demonstration zone, the northern Beijing ecological (ice and

① 1 mu= 0.0667 hectares.

snow) tourism circle, the southwest Beijing ecotourism zone (including the Western Beijing Baidu leisure resort). The government aims at forming a joint regional tourism brand and accelerating construction of the BTH tourism framework. The BTH Region has gradually deepened the integration of industrial chain, information chain and funding chain. And the process of industrial cooperation has been gradually accelerated. In 2016, Hebei Province introduced 4,100 projects and 382.5 billion yuan from Beijing and Tianjin, accounting for 42% and 51% of total projects and funds from outside the province respectively.

1.2.4 Enhancing innovation-driven development, coordinated innovation has achieved progress

Hebei Province jointly works with Beijing and Tianjin to further deepen the cooperation in regional innovation system, gradually enhance the support capacity of technology platform, accelerate the improvement of regional innovation service system, and promote the efficient allocation of regional innovation resources. All these measures help to build an innovation and development highland that radiates the surrounding area and leads the country.

The pace of joint development of science and innovation platform has been accelerated. The central government has approved the Beijing-Tianjin-Hebei comprehensive innovation reform pilot area declared by Hebei Province and Beijing-Tianjin. Collaborative innovation platforms such as Qinghuangdao Branch Center of Zhongguancun-Haidian Center, Tsinghua University (Gu'an) Pilot Base, Baoding-Zhongguancun Innovation Center have started to operate. And the Big data comprehensive pilot area has been promoted steadily. Hebei Province has also accelerated the construction of key scientific and technological centers, such as Shibaolang comprehensive innovation and reform pilot base, demonstration zone of scientific and technological achievements transformation in southern Beijing, and the modern agricultural science and technology demonstration zone around Beijing. The local government also further enhanced the application and demonstration capabilities of scientific and technological innovation achievements of Beijing and Tianjin in Hebei Province. By 2016, Hebei Province has built 55 technological industrial centers and more than 300 creative units. More than 1,300 high-tech enterprises of Beijing and Tianjin has settled in Hebei Province.

Regional innovation system has been gradually improved. Cooperating with Ministry of Science and Technology and China Merchants Group, the fund supporting transformation of scientific and technological achievements established by Hebei Province has reached 1 billion yuan. Beijing, Tianjin and Hebei Province set up a venture capital fund science and technology transformation. The construction of BTH trading center and other service platforms have also been accelerated. The construction of "Blue Fire Plan" Hengshui base of Ministry of Education has been accelerated. In total of 13 universities and colleges, such as the Chinese Academy of Sciences, Peking University, Tianjin University, have set up workstations in Hebei. Hebei institutions such as Hebei University, Hebei Agricultural University and others have carried out cooperation with Beijing, Tianjin institutions. In cooperation with China Technology Exchange Center and Beijing International Technology Transfer Center, the government established "three centers" and "two platforms" that connect Beijing, Tianjin and Hebei Province. The comprehensive service system for innovation and entrepreneurship has been gradually improved. In 2016, Hebei Province had 550 key scientific and technological projects and built 65 industrial technology alliances. The volume of technology contracts exported to Hebei Province by Beijing and Tianjin amounted to 9.32 billion yuan, which was 2.4 times that of 2013.

1.2.5 Broadening the scope of cooperati-on, and coordinating the promotion of social undertakings

Since the coordinated development has become a major national strategy, Beijing, Tianjin and Hebei Province has focused on improving the preconditions for guaranteeing regional coordination, actively promoting the optimal allocation of public service resources, and vigorously promoting the development of social undertakings, increasing support for the poor areas and the equalization of public services development outcomes in the region gradually.

Cooperation pilot projects have achieved breakthroughs. Beijing and Hebei Province have determined three regions (the Caofeidian district, the new airport economy zone of Beijing, Yanjiao of Langfang) as regional public service pilot areas to deepen cooperation. Beijing and Hebei Province will strengthen cooperation in the fields of employment, entrepreneurship, social security, personnel services, and labor relations. Local governments will jointly accelerate the integration process of pilot regional human communities to promote the rational flow and efficient allocation of essential resources. Beijing, Tianjin and Hebei Province have achieved network-linked drugs qualifications, mutual recognition of bid price. In total of 132 medical institutions of BTH Region have promoted mutual recognition of clinical test results. And the first batch of 27 test items were included in the mutual recognition range. Regional talent qualification has achieved mutual recognition. In the process of three-area flow, people in the fields of professional technical personnel's title promotion, post-employment, talent introduction, training selection, service guarantee enjoy the same treatment. Beijing and Hebei Province open up green channel for off-site employment medical staff reimbursement, to smoothly promote regional social security convergence. Hebei Province launched educational and medical institution cooperation with Beijing and Tianjin to enhance personnel training, medical department construction and education cooperation.

Significant progress has been made in counterpart support. Beijing, Tianjin and Hebei Province urged the relevant state ministries and commissions to promulgate the "Work Program for Cooperation between Beijing and Tianjin and Zhang-Cheng Area in Hebei Province surrounding Beijing and Tianjin". Beijing and Tianjin are paired together to help 21 counties (districts) in Hebei Province and will arrange 4.77 billion yuan for poverty elimination during 2016-2020. Hebei has signed an agreement on cooperation framework for counterpart assistance with Beijing, setting a target of 3.568 billion yuan for helping Zhang-Cheng-Bao region in Hebei Province during the 13th Five-year Plan period. And Hebei Province also signed a framework agreement with Tianjin to help poor counties in Chengde, build higher vocational education institutions, promote tourism integration, carry out modern agriculture and animal husbandry cooperation, and support the construction of Liugou Industrial Park and so on.

1.2.6 Comprehensively deepening reform and accelerating the construction of mechanisms for coordinated development

In order to ensure the success of coordinated development, Beijing, Tianjin and Hebei Province have speeded up the removal of restrictions and institutional barriers that restrict the development of work and the flow of productive factors, and have improved relevant institutional mechanisms in areas such as regional cooperation, industrial connectivity and ecological joint prevention, and gradually improved the system of complementary regional advantages and mutual benefit.

The regional coordination mechanism has been gradually improved. Beijing, Tianjin and Hebei Province jointly set up regular meetings and joint system among the chief executive and the functional departments of the executive deputy provincial (city) office. And the regional exchange of cadres and personnel should be further standardized. Infrastructure cross-regional cooperation mechanism has achieved a breakthrough, under which BTH inter-city railway investment company, and Bohai Tianjin-Hebei port investment company have been set up. The process of synergistic innovation has been accelerated. Some universities in the three places have set up various alliances such as the BTH Collaborative Innovation Alliance and the BTH Normal University Alliance. The sharing mechanism of industrial interests has been gradually formed, and the implementation of the tax revenue sharing method for industrial transfer and docking enterprises has been implemented, and the integrated working mechanism of regional tax risk control has been accelerated. The mechanism for ecological protection is getting better and better, jointly establishing the cooperation mechanism for the prevention and control of the atmosphere, water pollution prevention and control in the surrounding areas, and regional motor vehicles, jointly building a platform for sharing information on prevention and control of atmospheric pollution, unifying the pre-grading standards for heavy-polluted weather in the region, and takeing the lead in exploring and promoting pilot cross-regional forest carbon trading and inter-regional carbon emissions trading across the country. Public service cooperation mechanism has been gradually strengthened. And in three areas, social insurance information of regional insured persons can be checked, and coordinated with each other in areas such as emergencies and health emergency. Langfang Yanda Hospital has been identified as the fixed-point medical settlement unit for medical treatment in different places in Beijing. The cooperation in traffic integration management has been further strengthened and customs of Beijing, Tianjin and Hebei Province have been fully integrated. Substantial progress has been made in the optimization of administrative divisions, the administrative divisions of six cities of Shijiazhuang, Qinhuangdao, Zhangjiakou, Baoding, Handan and Hengshui have been adjusted, thus the space for urban development in Hebei Province has been further expanded. Coordination and control mechanisms are increasingly improved in the related fields, jointly establishing a joint conference system for vocational education in Beijing, Tianjin and Hebei Province. The regulatory regime for food and drug administration in different places has made a breakthrough. Three major operators, Telecom, Mobile and China Unicom, took the lead in canceling mobile roaming charges and long distance charges in the BTH Region .

1.3 The main problems in the coordinated development

Over the years, coordinated development has made positive progress in many fields. However, compared with the phased objectives of the plan, there are still many shortages and gaps. Thorough in-depth investigations and studies on this region, more than 10 provincial departments, eight districts and cities and nearly 30 counties (cities)in Hebei Province, the research group also found that there were still some problems in the promotion of coordinated development.

1.3.1 Underlying problems in major areas are in urgent need to be solved

The state has conducted overall planning and deployment for the three pioneering fields in transportation, ecology and industry, which has achieved some achievement. However, some deep-seated problems in the actual promotion of the three places have not been effectively resolved.

In terms of traffic integration, firstly, the progress of low-grade road connecting projects is relatively slow, while the high-level road connecting projects in the national transportation planning system develops faster. However, they are not in alignment with provincial-level or lower-level roads in the neighboring areas of Beijing and Tianjin. Problems such as unsynchronized project promotion and inconsistent road levels were prominent and the progress of the development lagged the construction of backbone routes. Secondly, the construction of transit transport infrastructure in Beijing is not progressing well. As at this stage, the improvement of the regional road transport system is mainly centered around Beijing, and the channel construction to ease the pressure of cross-boundary traffic in Beijing is relatively small. At the same time, key cities in Hebei Province are interoperable with each other, suburbs, in particular, the railway has entered into the work of Beijing Light Rail Transit and the progress of planning and construction of the cross-border transit hub in Beijing is relatively slow. As a result, Beijing is still facing great pressure of cross-boundary traffic. Thirdly, there are still some problems in the traffic conditions in some impoverished areas around Beijing and Tianjin. Through the investigation and study in Zhang Cheng area, due to the complicated traffic conditions, difficulty of self-financing, and the construction costs and benefits do not match, the capacity of the local high level road service in parts of the region remains to be strengthened. Provincial road construction is relatively lagging behind, county and township roads need to be improved and construction standards also needs to be improved, and the overall construction of roads at all levels is not progressing well. The lack of the docking mechanism, the lack of market mechanism and the lack of regional development concept are still the bottleneck of the three-way traffic integration, there is still a wide gap in terms of regional transport planning, construction synchronization and transport integration and market unification development requirements.

In terms of ecological environment protection, firstly, there is still a large gap in investment in ecological construction. In the survey, Zhang

Cheng district generally reflects that there is not enough investment in ecological projects such as Beijing-Hebei ecological water source protection forest, sandstorm source management and degraded grassland management. Public welfare forests and sections Water and other maintenance costs are not enough to meet the daily cost of expenditure. Secondly, the regional management system of ecological protection is not yet perfect. At present, the BTH Region has formed a relatively perfect cooperation mechanism in the co-construction and sharing of atmospheric environment. However, there has not yet been a mechanism for cooperation in regional coordination and governance involving water, soil and rural environment. Thirdly, the mechanism of cross-region ecological compensation is slowly advanced. Although BTH Region embarks on a pioneering exploration in the construction of ecological forests and water diversion from Luanhe to Tianjin, the value and distribution system of eco-resources products has not yet been established. The division of responsibilities and obligations of ecological and environmental protection is not yet clear. The ecological compensation mechanism which fully embodies the ecological value is not yet perfect in the marketization, normalization and standardization, and the key content of the global cross-regional ecological compensation is not yet made substantial progress. The Plan Outline puts forward higher requirements for ecological construction and environmental protection of Hebei Province. It is difficult to guarantee the long-term maintenance of high level ecological construction, governance and restoration of the BTH ecological environment solely relying on state-led ecological construction support and the weak local resources of Hebei's key eco-construction area.

In terms of industrial upgrading and transfermation, firstly, the industrial transfer-mation and convergence system needs to be improved urgently. In the survey, most of cities and aveas reflect the qualification of high-tech enterprises need to be re-certified when they are transferred to and from Hebei Province. The cross-provincial mutual recognition mechanism of corporate finance and tax payment has not been established, and the sharing of medical and construction certification information areas has not been realized. Secondly, the high-end industries transferred from Beijing and Tianjin to Hebei Province are relatively few. Up to now, most of the industries transferred from Beijing and Tianjin to Hebei are regional logistics wholesale market, general manufacturing enterprises and industrial production and processing sectors, and the transformation of high-end manufacturing sectors of scientific and technological achievements enterprises and corporate headquarters are relatively small. Thirdly, industries that can lead the development of Hebei Province are less. The industries in Beijing and Tianjin are mostly scattered, with weale radiation driving ability. Most industries are not able to generate a strong driving force for the overall development of the region, and industries which can gather industries in the same field (such as Biomedical Industrial Park, Bohai New Area, Cangzhou, Beijing), promoting leapfrog promotion of regional industries (such as Beijing Hyundai No. 4 Factory) and further driving parks or enterprises in large-scale and cluster-based industries throughout the region are few. Fourthly, the industrial transferation of the region into the mechanism still needs to be optimized, the government-led industries have transferred from Beijing-Tianjin to Hebei Province, especially large-scale ones, playing significant role in the industrial upgrading in Hebei enterprises, most of them are separated from the tax ares of Hebei Province. However, the rigid constraints on the project construction of land, environmental protection, energy consumption and other indicators have not yet cousidered the regions as a whole. The reason of above problems are mainly that Hebei Province still has a big gap with the requirements of Beijing-Tianjin transfer and transformation enterprises in terms of comprehensive development environment and supporting platform support. As a result, Beijing-Tianjin scientific and technological achievements transformation enterprises and high-end manufacturing enterprises cannot be attracted and undertaken, it is difficult to realize the conversion of the Hebei Province in the near future, and the effect of Hebei Province on the promotion of industrial upgrading has not been concentrated.

1.3.2 Coordinated development mechan-ism is not yet sound

At present, the coordinated development of the BTH Region has been transformed from top-level design to full implementation stage, and the implementation of the work organization is the basic guarantee for the successful promotion of the coordinated development. Although extensive exploration has been carried out from pilot demonstration and collaborative co-management, relative to the complexity of coordinated development and the urgency of achieving the goal, the promotion of collaborative development work organization needs to be further strengthened and perfected. Firstly, the mechanism of regional cooperation needs to be improved. High-level dialogues and work docking mechanisms between Hebei and Beijing-Tianjin have been initially established. However, institutional mechanisms and dialogue mechanisms among municipalities, counties (areas) and corresponding departments in Beijing and Tianjin are not perfect, and there is a lack of accurate and effective docking with between Beijing and Tianjin, resulting in blind, repetitive and disorderly situation in the process of regional coordination. Secondly, lack of normalization between the areas of cooperation. Although various areas have adopted a series of measures in the coordinated development, the integrated coordination and promotion mechanism across departments is still not perfect. The implementation of collaborative development in various fields is often affected and restricted by other fields, it is difficult for the single department to coordinate and make decisions in all directions; There is also lack of long-term and stable communication and cooperation in areas such as regional investment promotion, industrial connectivity cooperation, collaborative innovation and public service connection, regional special investment conferences and special talks, and inter-regional cooperation in scientific and technological innovation. The competent department of coordination and communication mechanism is not perfect. Thirdly, the division method of internal coordination needs to be optimized. At the national and provincial levels, although the top-level design has been initially completed, some special plans already issued by the state and Hebei lacks relevant supporting implementation plans. The specific work carried out by cities and relevant functional departments of the province lacks implementation basis and starting point. Hebei Province and different national ministries and commissions clearly undertook the platform to take more care of the balance among the regions, with varying degrees of a large number of different locations with overlapping functions and other issues. As the provincial level department has not made clear overall arrangements for the specific division of labor between platforms, it is difficult to form a strong gathering effect, there are vicious competitions within each region of Hebei Province and repeated constructions; Capability of non-capital lacks of coordination within Hebei Province, in the process of Beijing Dahongmen market and Dongpi market moving into Hebei Province, market competing was introduced into a number of cities, which was neither conducive to non-capital effective ease, nor conducive to undertake overall development.

1.3.3 Development policies have obvious gaps in different regions

Compared with Beijing and Tianjin, Hebei Province is in a backward situation in development status, basic develop conditions and local financial support, and there are also clear gaps in support policies in many fields compared with Beijing and Tianjin. First, in terms of the introduction of enterprises and projects, there is a big gap between the strength in policy support and industrial tax relief, land support, and financial capital protection between Hebei Province with Beijing and Tianjin, which has led some enterprises even to return to Beijing and Tianjin. For example, Tianjin will give the highest 50 million yuan for introduction of corporate headquarters, while Hebei Province lacks a clear subsidy standard at the corresponding level. Second, in terms of supporting industrial development, Hebei Province also has significant differences with Beijing and Tianjin in respect of financial support, technological innovation support, introduction of talents and subsidies for industrial development. The benefits of some Beijing and Tianjin enterprises that have been transferred to Hebei Province enjoyed have a marked drop. For example, the highest award that Hebei Province supports for listing of enterprises is two million yuan, while that is up to five million yuan in Tianjin, which is more specifically and clearly classified in reward grade, bonuses and specific implementation. Third, in terms of pilot demonstration and carrier platform building, Hebei Province has not formed a pilot carrier of Beijing's Zhongguancun Independent Innovation Demonstration Zone and service pilot expansion of the overall pilot area, and lacked of national major policy integration platform similar to Tianjin Binhai New Area and Free Trade Zone. Fourth, in the aspect of public service policies, there are obvious differences in medical insurance catalogs such as medicines, clinics and medical service facilities. The distribution of quality education and medical resources is highly differentiated in different regions. There is a huge gap between the basic education per capita and the investment in basic public services. Problems such as the transfer of social insurance connections, cross-district pension services, medical insurance reimbursement docking have not yet reached the regional co-ordination requirements, personnel management services for floating personnel standards have not yet unified, as well as local enrollment problem and return limitation of Beijing-Tianjin immigrants' children is also existed. The difference in policy gradient among regions not only leads to serious concerns about the transfer of enterprises and high-end elements in Beijing and Tianjin to Hebei Province, but also easily strengthens the "Matthew Effect", impeding the improvement of Hebei's concentration and absorption functions, and seriously affecting the successful progress of coordinated development. It may further widen the gap between regional development.

1.4 Major challenges of coordin-ated development

Hebei Province will cope with many challenges to play its role well in coordinated development, take a good role in the coordinated development, fulfill the clear objectives and tasks of the "Outline Plan".

1.4.1 Challenges in narrowing the devel-opment gap with Beijing and Tianjin

Since there is a great gap in economic development between Hebei Province with Beijing and Tianjin, the economic development level is urgently needed to be enhanced in the course of coordinated development to narrow the gap with the economic development in Beijing and Tianjin. However, due to inadequate leading and supporting capacity, Hebei Province has a huge gap in the level of public service and development environment with Beijing and Tianjin, and there is a level gap and technical dislocation between industries of Beijing and Tianjin. It is difficult not only for industries to effectively connect with Beijing and Tianjin, but also for Beijing-Tianjin scientific and technological achievements to land in Hebei Province, and high-end elements of Beijing and Tianjin flowing to Hebei. Hebei even faces the "reverse flow" of the high-end development elements, and such pressures and challenges will further widening the gap between the economic development with Beijing and Tianjin. From 2013 to 2016, the share of Hebei's GDP in the BTH Region dropped by 2.77 percentage points, while the share of GDP per capita in Beijing and Tianjin dropped by 4.25 and 2.52 percentage points respectively. The share of local general public budget revenues in per capita GDP with Beijing and Tianjin dropped respectively 1.76 and 0.27 percentage points, and the economic development gap between Beijing and Tianjin was still widen.

1.4.2 Challenges in realizing public service area balance with Beijing and Tianjin

There is a gap between the level of public services in Hebei Province and Beijing. In 2015, per capita education funding of Hebei Province was only 29.02% and 35.70% of that in Beijing and Tianjin respectively, the number of top three hospitals was respectively 19.09% and 7.75% with Beijing and Tianjin, medical insurance expenditures of urban workers per capita were 50.81% and 63.40% respectively with Beijing and Tianjin, and the expenditures of the basic pension insurance fund were 26.92% and 33.11% respectively with Beijing and Tianjin. The short board of public service needs to be filled in the coordinated development. However, in improving the overall public service performance, narrowing the gap with the Beijing-Tianjin public service, and achieving the goal of equalizing the public service with the Beijing-Tianjin region, Hebei Province not only lacks resources for quality public services, government public finance and lagging market-oriented reforms in public services, but also faces the challenges brought by many hidden barriers and obstacles in the institutional mechanisms in public services.

1.4.3 Challenges in building a world-class city cluster with Beijing and Tianjin

It is one of the important tasks for the coordinate development of the BTH Region to build a world-class city cluster with the capital as core. However, as of the end of 2015, the overall urbanization rate of the BTH

Region was 62.5%, a big gap from the urbanization rate of over 70% in world-class urban agglomerations. In particular, the urbanization rate in Hebei Province was only 51.3%, which was the main short board. Meanwhile, the structural imbalances between urban systems in Hebei Province and Beijing-Tianjin are serious. The urbanization rates in Hebei Province were lower than those of Beijing and Tianjin by 35.2% and 31.3% respectively in 2015. In the process of constructing a world-class urban agglomeration with Beijing and Tianjin, Hebei Province urgently needs to eliminate the "faultage" of cities and towns in scale and structure, function system with Beijing and Tianjin, and function system, enhancing the scale of cities and towns in Hebei Province, reconstructing the functional structure of Hebei cities and forming reasonable division of labor and distribution pattern with Beijing and Tianjin. It is not only affected by the "siphon effect" of Beijing and Tianjin and the "co-opetition relationship" among the cities, but also confronted with the challenge brought by the urban planning and construction management system with fragmented administrative areas.

1.4.4 Challenges in realizing the win-win of ecological construction and regional development

Hebei has a prominent ecological status in coordinated development and is a support zone for BTH ecological environment. However, at present, per capita water resources in Hebei Province occupy only 1/7 of the national average and more than 1/3 of the river water quality is monitored as grade V or inferior V class, air qualities of more than half of cities rank in the last 10, thus the task of ecological construction and environmental protection is arduous. At the same time, the GDP per capita in the province ranks the last but one among the coastal provinces and municipalities. By the end of 2015, the number of poor population in the rural areas was as high as 3.1 million, and the demand for quickening the pace of poverty and accelerating development was very urgent. Overloaded resources and environment, fragile ecological environment, prominent conflicts between development and environmental protection, ecological and poverty intertwined and many other challenges impede the win-win of economic and social development and ecological environment construction.

1.4.5 Challenges in establishing reformation of promoting coordinated development

There are still differences between Hebei Province with Beijing and Tianjin on specific demands and operating paths of promoting coordinated development. The major institutional reforms concerning basic public services, taxation and finance, and other core interests have not been broken yet. At present, the management system of administrative division causes the production elements to be difficult to realize free flow and efficient configuration in the region. Breaking obstacles of ideology and concepts, breaking barriers of interests, eliminating hidden market barriers, to establish institutional rules conducive to the coordinated development of the BTH Region, forming a unified and open market system in the region, face the challenges of unequal status among the three places, large gap in policies, fair game difficulty.

2. The strategic thinking of Hebei Province to promote the coordinated development of BTH Region

To promote the coordinated development of the BTH Region, Hebei Province should take the spirit of the 19th National Congress of the Chinese Communist Party as a guide, implementing the new development concept, following "BTH Collaborative Development Plan" to promote free flow of production elements and promote the layout of the regional functional optimization as the main line. Hebei Province should reduce non-capital functions, cultivate the growth pole in the region and push the industry toward the middle and high end as the sally port. The local government also should put forth efforts to promote the construction of the Xiong'an New Area, explore innovative development modes, promote the coordinated development of the region and make efforts to improve the quality of the ecological environment, expand opening-up and cooperation with the outside world, advance the sharing of synergies and play the role well in the coordinated development, so as to make greater contribution to the formation of a new pattern of coordinated development of the BTH Region and the construction of a modern economic system.

2.1 Promote the construction of Xiong'an New Area, build a new framework for coordinated development

The planning and construction of the Xiong'an New Area is conducive to accelerating the update of Hebei's ideology and promoting the centralized transfer of high-end resources from Beijing to Hebei Province, and conducive to promoting the adjustment and optimization of the spatial structure and urban layout, which is an important opportunity to speed up the short board of Hebei Province. The construction of Xiong'an New Area has brought a lot of good benefits to Hebei Province. Hebei Province must promote its name and shape in order to promote synergetic development. By leveraging its potential, the project should have a high starting point and a high standard to build Xiong'an New Area, to create a synergistic development model, and play a good lead to its coordinated development in the BTH Region.

2.1.1 Insist on the guidance of new deve-lopment concepts

In accordance with the high requirements of "making major achievements in the millennium and national affairs", the Xiong'an New Area carries the historical responsibility of "carrier" of China's reform and opening up in the 21st century and shoulders the task of "guiding" the implementation of the Five Development Principles. The construction of Xiong'an New Area is a grand strategy of coordinated development of BTH Region and a major layout for reform and opening up. The "new" of Xiong'an New Area is an innovation of the development concept of the new district. Under the guidance of the new development concept, Hebei should create green wisdom, livable habitat and open up sharing new areas. The "new" of Xiong'an New Area is an innovation of urban development concept. Xiong'an New Area is a pioneer area for China's smart city, exploring ahead in terms of its ability to manage cities and modernization of its governance system, creating a model for urban construction, providing solutions for breaking the "big city disease" and building a modern livable city. Xiong'an New Area opened an innovative paradigm for urban development in BTH Region, breaking the "twin cities" layout. The coordinated development of BTH Region may shift from the strategy of "twin cities" centered at Beijing and Tianjin to the strategy of "triangle" at Beijing, Tianjin and Xiong'an. The establishment of the Xiong'an New Area will surely provide a powerful impetus for BTH Region to further optimize the urban system, adjust the urban form and provide endogenous power for the city.

2.1.2 Insist on the guidance of great goals

The planning and construction of Xiong'an New Area will surely have a significant and far-reaching positive impact on the strategic thinking and goal of Hebei's coordinated development in the future. With the establishment of Xiong'an New Area as a sign, Beijing's non-capital function will be drastically accelerated and the level of transformation, upgrading and innovation in Hebei Province will also be substantially increased, which will speed up the magnificent goal of the planning and construction of the Xiong'an New Area. By 2020, the embryonic form of Xiong'an New Area will initially appear, the backbone transportation network will basically take shape, and infrastructure construction and industrial distribution framework in the starting areas will basically take shape. By 2030, Xiong'an New Area will be built into a modern new city with green, low-carbon, information-smart and livable industries, which has strong competitiveness and influence. To undertake Beijing's non-capital function ease, effectively attract Beijing population and non-capital function ease and transfer, the population pressure ease in the capital; build green livable new city area, innovation-driven development lead area, coordinated development demonstration area, opening up development zone; it will also make efforts to create innovative and developing demonstration area to implement the new development concept. The capability of boosting the radiation in the Bohai Rim and the hinterland of the north will be significantly enhanced, which will be conducive to supporting the economic restructuring and development of North China and promoting the balanced development of the entire country.

With more than 10 years of unremitting efforts, the long-term goal of casting the second brilliant of Hebei Province should be achieved in the process of promoting coordinated development of BTH Region. By 2030, the gap between the development of Hebei with Beijing and Tianjin will continue to narrow, and the pattern of regional development coordinated with Beijing and Tianjin will basically take shape. A town system with complementary functions to Beijing and Tianjin, and the co-construction of a world-class city cluster with Beijing and Tianjin have taken shape. A regional industrial system with a horizontal division of labor with Beijing and Tianjin has been initially established, and the industry is characterized by a high level of development toward the middle and high end. Linked collaborative innovation and technology system have been established, and the driving force of economic growth has realized innovation-driven conversion; the quality of ecological environment has been effectively improved and the overall quality has been maintained at a good level. The establishment of a public service system with a basically balanced and benign interaction with Beijing and Tianjin will bring about a balanced public service level, and the establishment of a system of policies, laws, government services and policies in harmony with Beijing and Tianjin will significantly improve the government ability.

2.1.3 Adhere to creative promotion

The Xiong'an New Area is a breakthrough point for comprehensively deepening the reform under the new economic normal. It will explore the path of technological, management and institutional innovation, establish institutional mechanisms and a new highland for policy environment, and explore new ways to comprehensively improve the efficiency of resource allocation through market means. The construction of the Xiong'an New Area is a new fulcrum for the coordinated development of BTH Region. As China's innovation capital, it has the most direct leading role for the innovation-driven development of BTH Region. Hebei Province should explore a new path consistent with the construction of the Xiong'an New Area and easing non-capital functions, establish a coordinated innovation mechanism between the New Area and Beijing, and create a synergistic and innovative situation of complement and benign interaction between the New Area and Beijing. To explore the docking mechanism of the industrial development planning of the New Area and Tianjin, especially the Binhai New Area, and create a national and even global innovation resource gathering area and a source of science and technology small and medium-sized enterprises. Xiong'an New Area will restart a new era of reform, and the spirit elements of the reform and innovation core of the new district will give Hebei Province the most profound spiritual strength. Hebei Province will speed up the reform of institutional mechanisms, create a super-superior development environment, create a platform for innovation and energy release and acceptance in the Xiong'an New Area, to achieve functional docking with the New Area, complement advantages with each other and integrate and interact with each other.

2.2 Innovate in development patterns, build new impetus of coordinated development

Innovation is the primary driving force of development, which determines the future and promotes development. BTH Region should make full use of their respective comparative advantages in collaborative innovation, simultaneously promote scientific and technological innovation and system innovation, and bring together innovative resources for integration so as to complement advantages and win benefits with each other. Hebei Province should grasp the opportunities for innovation, vigorously promote concept innovation, mechanism innovation, technological innovation and industrial innovation and form a new highland for regional innovation and development.

2.2.1 Create an innovation base in Xiong'an New Area

As the innovation capital, Xiong'an New Area should actively coordinate with Beijing and Tianjin to promote collaborative innovation, technological innovation, policy innovation and system innovation in an all-round way and foster new engine of innovation-driven development. Taking advantage of the huge innovation energy diffusion in Xiong'an New Area, and coordinated with the state-level collaborative innovation new city, Hebei Province will be established as the releasing area for innovative energy in Xiong'an New Area, the receiving area for innovative resources and the interactive area for opening and innovation. Giving full play to positive geographical advantages, capital accumulation of high-end provincial capitals, important transportation hub in North China and carrier role of high open platform, the two sides should, under the leadership of the Xiong'an New Area, together lead the innovation and development of central and south Hebei and even the entire Hebei Province.

2.2.2 Achieve breakthroughs in coor-dinated innovation focused on three areas

Traffic integration, ecological environment protection and industrial upgrading and transfer are the key areas for coordinated development of Hebei Province with Beijing and Tianjin in the first place, as well as the key links in the reform and innovation of institutional mechanisms. In accordance with the development requirements of traffic planning, building synchronization, transport integration, unified market, to perfect traffic integration and interaction mechanism. The BTH Region will establish an ecological co-establishment and sharing mechanism, improve the mechanism of environmental coordination and governance, and further explore institutional docking paths, market operation mechanisms, benefit sharing modes and loss compensation modes in key areas, so as to gradually reverse the low-end situation of Hebei Province in BTH division of labor, gradually shift to the value chain division of labor and horizontal division of labor. Besides, it will establish industries alliance for innovation in Hebei Province, and a community of synergistic innovations in the high-tech fields with industrial base advantages in Hebei Province, and establish and perfect the mechanism of industrial transfer and convergence and benefit-sharing.

2.2.3 Strengthen coordinated innovation of management system

The backwardness of the management system is the largest short board of Hebei Province. Establishing and improving a scientific management system is the main direction of collaborative innovation. In order to enhance competitiveness, cohesion and innovation, Hebei Province should take transformation of government functions as the focus and take "putting on the tube and clothing" as its direction. Benchmaring the Beijing-Tianjin government management model and service efficiency, focus on reform, optimize service innovation, actively guide and relax the market innovation, in accordance with the law, improve the rule of law on innovation, and strengthen restraint, trustworthiness and innovation on the whole, to integrally improve government management capabilities and service levels.

2.2.4 Promote coordinated innovation in regional policies

To narrow the gap with Beijing and Tianjin, the key is to promote the collaborative innovation policies. Focusing on the linkage with the Beijing-Tianjin policy, Hebei Province should comprehensively promote policy co-innovation in such aspects as elements supply, fiscal and taxation support, land allocation, social security and public service.To promote the formation of a coordinated development policy support system that is consistent with the Beijing-Tianjin standard, goal, co-ordination and integration, and to create a favorable policy environment for the coordinated development of the BTH Region.

2.3 Promote regional coordination and enhance new vitality of coordinated development

Coordination is an inherent requirement of the coordinated development of the BTH Region. To promote the coordinated development among Hebei Province, Beijing and Tianjin, the key is to properly handle the main functional regional relations among Beijing, Tianjin, the hinterland of Hebei Province, the eastern coastal areas and the central and western regions. In order to give full play to the main role of Hebei Province in the coordinated development with Beijing and Tianjin, it is imperative to highlight the coordinated linkage among Beijing, Tianjin and its neighboring regions, the coastal and inland regions, the cities of Beijing, Tianjin and Hebei Province, to create a new situation of regional development of Hebei Province and Beijing-Tianjin interdependence, complementary advantages and positive interactions.

2.3.1 Coordination of Beijing-Tianjin and surrounding areas

Beijing, Tianjin and Hebei Xiong'an New Area, Baoding, Langfang and some parts of Cangzhou are the core area for the development of the BTH Region. At present and for a period in the future, we must stand on the long-term, strategic and global perspective and promote the coordinated and interactive development of the four regions with Beijing and Tianjin, making every effort to explore the coordination and linkage of regional space development, regional functional division, regional comprehensive governance, regional industrial system and regional public services in the four regions and the Beijing-Tianjin. We will make efforts to innovate the mode of regional spatial integration and interaction development, regional function upgrading and reconstruction, comprehensive management of regional ecological environment, the upgrading of regional industries and the promotion of regional public services so as to establish a model for national inter-administration regional integration and development.

2.3.2 Coordinated development of coastal and inland areas

Hebei Province is an important coastal region in the eastern China. Promoting the coordination and cooperation between coastal areas and inland, and playing the leading role in the opening up of Beijing, Tianjin and even the central and western regions are the necessary requirements for Hebei Province to promote the coordinated development of the BTH Region, and also a matter for the whole development of the BTH Region. In order to enhance the capacity and standard of opening up the BTH Region as a whole, we must stand at the global level and move forward with the regional development center of gravity, and rationalize the relations between coastal and inland development, shifting the focus of urban development to the coastal areas, shifting the focus of heavy industrial development to the coastal areas, and putting the port as the center of the marine and land integrated transportation hub development in a prominent position.

2.3.3 Coordinated development of Beijing-Tianjin with cities in Hebei Province

Beijing and Tianjin are leaders of the BTH city cluster, and Hebei Province is the node and support. To handle the internal relations between Hebei and Beijing and Tianjin and to coordinate with Beijing and Tianjin is the key to Hebei's cooperation with Beijing and Tianjin in building a world-class city cluster. According to the geographical location, basic conditions and the status and role of Hebei Province, differently formulate linkage development strategy with Beijing and Tianjin; comprehensively consider the development requirements of open coastal cities, mountain transitional cities and the northern eco-city, to determine the development model with Beijing and Tianjin respectively; the BTH Region follows the objective laws governing the development of core cities and node cities in world-class city cluster, scientifically determines urban functions, rationally sets the size of cities, strives to create urban features, and promotes the rational division of labor and coordinated development with Beijing and Tianjin.

2.3.4 Coordinated development of trans-ferring and undertaking non-capital functions of Beijing

The orderly resolution of Beijing's non-capital functions and the resolution of the "big city disease" are the basic starting points for promoting the coordinated development of the BTH Region. As an important source of non-capital functions in Beijing, Hebei Province undertakes a major task of concentrating, resolving and dispersing. To do a good job of easing non-capital function and industrial transfer,

Hebei Province should strengthen the coordination with Beijing, on the one hand, set up the centralized load-carrying area of the province- Xiong'an New Area; on the other hand, key construction projects should focus on the strategic cooperation functional areas such as Caofeidian District, Capital Airport New Airport Economic Zone and Zhang(jialou) Cheng (de) Ecological Function Zone, taking Bohai New Area, Zhengding New Area, Baiyangdian Science and Technology City and Beidaihe, Industrial Innovation Demonstration Zone and other strategic platforms to support the functionality to undertake the platform. We should strengthen government guidance and support, improve the coordination and docking system and mechanism, give full play to the role of market mechanism, systematically defuse Beijing's non-capital functions, form a gathering effect and a leading role in demonstration, and promote Hebei's transformation, upgrading and innovation in undertaking transfer.

2.3.5 Promote regional interconnection and interaction

First, interconnection and interaction between LangBaoCang and Beijing-Tianjin. Langfang,Baoding and Cangzhou are close to Beijing and Tianjin, which are important areas for urbanization and industrial radiation transfer of Beijing and Tianjin. These three cities should play a close geographical advantage of Beijing and Tianjin, to speed up the transfer of non-capital functions, focus on the development of high-tech industries, equipment manufacturing and trade logistics industry, forming industrial transformation and upgrading demonstration base and an important business and trade logistics base. At the same time, we should actively integrate with Beijing and Tianjin and effectively attract elements and resources such as capital, technology and talent from Beijing and Tianjin, to build a high-level platform for innovation and development. Second, interconnection and interaction between TangQinCang and Beijing-Tianjin. Tangshan, Qinhuangdao and Cangzhou are important sea-going passages for the BTH Region and are the best conditions for Hebei Province to the outside world. In the future, we will focus on promoting the development of high-end manufacturing, high-end services and ports and other infrastructure projects in Beijing and Tianjin. We should strengthen industrial park to build the cooperation, attract the Beijing and Tianjin high-end resources and industry transfer, become the key area of two-way open of Hebei Province, expanding to the export-oriented economy driving force in the province. Third, interconnection and interaction between ZhangCheng and Beijing-Tianjin. Zhangjiakou and Chengde are water sources of Beijing and Tianjin and an important supporting area for

BTH ecological environment. They are also the worst areas for development in the areas around Beijing and Tianjin. In the future development, we should further strengthen the deep cooperation with Beijing and Tianjin, improve the ecological environment compensation mechanism, water resources purchase mechanism and counterpart poverty alleviation aid mechanism, improve self-development capability, increase precision poverty alleviation, develop green industries with special characteristics, strengthen the construction of cities and townships and the development of the region by leaps and bounds.

2.4 Optimize the ecological environment and build the new image of coordinated development

Hebei Province is an important ecological barrier in the BTH Region as well as of the entire Northern China region. It is a strategic water source of Beijing-Tianjin region and a major supplier of fresh food and ecological products, its status of ecological security in the BTH Region is very prominent. Hebei Province is also the most prominent area of ecological environment in the BTH Region. It is the main influence area of water and soil erosion area and pollutants of the mother river in BTH Region. The task of ecological construction and environmental management is very arduous, which is the main battlefield of the ecological construction and environmental management of the BTH Region. Therefore, advancing green development in Hebei Province is not only an urgent need for the construction of ecological civilization, but also an inevitable choice for the future development of the BTH Region. Hebei should take the construction of the Xiong'an New Area as an opportunity to promote the restoration and management of the Haihe River ecosystem, to establish the key ecological and economic development zones in Zhangjiakou and Chengde-Hebei regions as the key areas for supporting the eco-environment, adjust the layout of regional productive forces according to the environmental capacity, and accelerate the focus of industrial development shift to the coast.

2.4.1 Establish the concept of regional ecological system

Ecological security has the systematic, regional and integrated characteristics. In order to ensure the ecological security of the Xiong'an New Area and realize the strategic requirements of "making major achievements in the next millennium", we should systematically promote the comprehensive management of Baiyangdian and its related watersheds, and study the construction of flood control projects, water supply projects, wastewater treatment and ecological conservation projects in one ecological security system. Focusing on enhancing the overall protection of ecological security in the BTH Region, taking the Daqinghe River basin where Xiong'an New Area located as a breakthrough point, making overall efforts to improve the management of the ecological system in the Haihe River basin, and establish a more complete, more standard and more functional system of ecological supply and ecological safety in the Haihe River basin.

2.4.2 Expand regional green ecological space

Strengthen the construction of water conservation area in northern Hebei Province. Starting from Hebei Province, which is an important eco-conservation functional area of Beijing-Tianjin-Hebei and an important task of accelerating the development of poverty eradication, we should establish the ecological economic win-win demonstration zone of Zhangjiakou and Chengde. We will also build a system of urban development that is compatible with the capacity of resources and environment, and set up an ecological protection system for forest grassland protection, water resources development and energy utilization. Establish scientific ecological compensation policy and market-oriented water resource allocation method. We will step up investment in ecological construction in northern Hebei and establish a supportive aid mechanism for infrastructure, green industry and public services in less-developed areas in northern Hebei.

2.4.3 Adjust the regional productivity distribution according to the environmental capacity

For a long time, Hebei Province has supported the development of economy by relying on Taihang Mountain and Yan Mountain. The heavy chemical industry, such as steel and chemical industry, has become the main pillar of urban economic development. However, with the expansion of cities and industries, the contradictions between the heavy chemical industry and the sustainable development of cities have become increasingly prominent. In the critical period of industrial transformation and upgrading, Hebei Province should proceed from the long-term plan of protecting the environment and achieving sustainable development and make overall plans to solve the unreasonable industrial distribution in the central cities. We have determined to relocate the city's steel, chemical and other heavy chemical industries, So as to promote the focus of heavy chemical industry development from the piedmont "area" to the greater environmental capacity of the coastal transfer, form high-end industrial belt before piedmont and coastal heavy chemical industry with "double belt" supporting the new pattern of industrial development.

2.5 Expand opening-up and cooperation, expand new space for coordinated development

Opening up is a process of emancipating mind, reforming concept and transforming development paths. Opening up and development can tap development potentials and bring development vitality. Hebei should establish an open mind, innovate open measures, speed up opening up to the outside world, stimulate vitality and enhance competitiveness in a coordinated development.

2.5.1 Promote future opening up of Hebei Province under the guidance of "The Belt and the Road" Initiative

The government should actively connect with major national strategies such as the "The Belt and the Road" and strive to build a strategic hub for "The Belt and the Road", to foster new advantages in participating in international competition and cooperation.We should take Caofeidian Port and Huanghua Port as the hub and junction in advancing the "The Belt and the Road" strategy, take advantage of Hebei ports in energy and raw materials gathering and trade development in north China, and promote the "three routes" of waterways, railways and highways. Hebei Province should also strengthen the organic connection between ports and inland ports, and build a large logistics system with ports as the leading role, which will form an important engine for the development of manufacturing and logistics in China's eastern, central and western hinterland. The government is supposed to strengthen the in-depth cooperation with countries along the "The Belt and the Road", take the international cooperation of leading enterprises such as Hebei Iron and Steel Group and Jidong Cement as guide, promote the process of international cooperation in production of superior capacity, and speed up the pace of going out and widen the new world.

2.5.2 Promote all-round open-up of Hebei Province in the lead of Xiong'an New Area

Xiong'an New Area is a new engine and a new opportunity for Hebei Province to expand its opening up. As a first-rate international zone for opening up, Xiong'an New Area will accelerate its agglomeration through opening up and attracting the world's most advanced and innovative resources, and become a new platform for expanding the new highland and foreign cooperation. Hebei Province should take Xiong'an New Area as the core lead, with all kinds of new districts as important carriers, expand all-round opening up and gather more high-quality elements at home and abroad. We should promote institutional innovation, break the concept of ideas and institutional constraints, establish management rules and systems with international standards.

2.5.3 Expand the opening effect with new platform construction

Hebei Province should seize the opportunity of the 2022 Winter Olympics and play the role of an integrated platform such as an integrated free trade zone and an inland port, to speed up the process of opening to the outside world. The joint hosting of the 2022 Winter Olympics by Zhangjiakou and Beijing is a new platform and a new impetus for Hebei to expand its opening up to the outside world, and especially will bring about an important opportunity for Zhangjiakou to promote urban development and internationalization of cities. With Zhangjiakou and Beijing's traffic network construction speeding up as a breakthrough, Hebei should comprehensively enhance the cooperation level between Beijing and Zhangjiakou and promote the economic links between Hebei Province and the central and western provinces. The Olympic Games will be the impetus for Hebei Province to emancipate the mind and promote the innovation of government management mechanism. It is necessary to manage and approve the Olympic Winter Games construction projects and related projects in a more efficient and efficient manner, and innovate financing means such as infrastructure. As important bridgehead for Hebei's opening to the outside world, Shijiazhuang and Caofeidian Comprehensive Free Trade Zone should play an important role in undertaking international industrial transfer, connecting domestic and international markets and promoting the coordinated development of regional economy. Hebei Province should strive to establish a free trade zone in the coastal cities and counties, urban new areas and parks that have a good foundation for opening up and development, make greater efforts to transform government functions, highlight reforms and innovations, and further raise the level of full liberalization.

2.6 Insist on fairness and common benefits, share the new outcomes of coordinated development

In the coordinated development of the BTH Region, people in Hebei and Beijing and Tianjin sharing more outcomes of coordinated development is the fundamental starting point and the foothold for promoting the coordinated development of the BTH Region. In order to achieve breakthroughs in the equalization of basic public services in the BTH Region, we should work together to solve the problem to bring about common benefits and promote the realization of the shared development goals. As a result people in Beijing, Tianjin and Hebei Province will share the fruits of development.

2.6.1 Establish a coordinated solving mechanism for development problems

Hebei Province should work together with Beijing and Tianjin to solve the problems of deteriorating ecological environment, decreasing the carrying capacity of resources and the environment, poor traffic congestion and the urgent need for industrial restructuring. As the mainstay of the BTH Region and the short board for development, Hebei Province should work together with Beijing and Tianjin to solve the problems of poor environment, weak cities and poor industry. As a supporting area for ecological environment in the region, Hebei Province should work with Beijing and Tianjin to solve the problem of air and water pollution, coordinate the interests of all parties of Beijing and Tianjin, and attract more high-end resources from Beijing and Tianjin in a more excellent hardware and software environment. In view of the intertwined ecological environment and poverty in the areas around Beijing, especially in northern Hebei, the government should promote the establishment of ecological co-establishment mechanism for sharing the cost and benefits of the BTH Region. Hebei Province should establish an ecological compensation mechanism that fully reflects the cost of ecological construction and a cross-regional ecological environment protection market system to build a normalization, growth and rolling counterpart assistance mechanism, to promote environmental protection, poverty elimination and economic transformation around Beijing and Tianjin. The government should make efforts to promote ecological areas in Beijing and Tianjin to fight with poverty, and share synergy development outcomes with Beijing and Tianjin.

2.6.2 Strive to promote equalization of regional public services

Hebei Province should promote the equalization of public services in the BTH Region. In the key area of transferring non-capital functions of Beijing-Tianjin to Hebei Province, the government should firstly carry out the pilot projects of equalization of public services in the BTH Region, to provide experiences in supplementing the shortcomings of Hebei Province public service, and reaching the standard of Beijing-Tianjin public service. Hebei Province should promote the integration of social policies in the BTH Region, promote resource sharing, mutual recognition of qualifications, mutual trust in regulations and policy cooperation in public services, such as education, health care, pension services and social insurance. The government also should improve continuation of social insurance and medical treatment, and unify BTH college entrance examination system. Hebei Province should accelerate the market-oriented reform of Hebei public services and enrich the supply of high-end public services in the province, and eventually promote the integration of household registration and benefits in the BTH Region. So Hebei people can get more benefits in the coordinated development of the BTH Region. The government should speed up cooperation of system rules such as basic public services in the region, and gradually introduce policies of mutual benefit, mutual recognition of credentials, exchange of information. The government should create a social policy system in favor of the free flow of talents and other productive factors that attract talents from Beijing and Tianjin to Hebei Province. Hebei Province should optimize and coordinate the development of the institutional system, accelerate the transformation of driving force of development, and explore institutional mechanisms to maximize market vitality, enterprise vitality, capital vitality and human vitality.

3. Hebei Province's strategic measures to push forward the BTH coordinated development

3.1 Restructure Hebei's city fun-ctions and spatial layout following the lead of the Xiong'an New Area and build a world-class city cluster together with Beijing and Tianjin

The further advance of the BTH coordinated development strategy, especially with the Communist Party of China (CPC) Central Committee and the State Council's decision to set up the Hebei Xiong'an New Area, will inevitably change regional functions and spatial layout significantly; greatly affect the factor flowing direction and development motivation; effectively alleviate Beijing's "big city ills"; widen regional development new space and tackle regional development problems. During the BTH urban development, some long-time accumulated and deep problems have greatly restricted city cluster's sound and sustainable development. The most evident problems are: Beijing and Tianjin are overwhelmed with resources while their surrounding cities are in shortage; especially that Hebei Province doesn't have an undertaking city which has the equivalent comprehensive service capability and driving force of radiation, and it's difficult to form an 'anti-magnetic force' center. The result is that population and resources are centralized towards a "singular core", aggravating Beijing's "big city ills". Urban system structure is out of balance: bloated megacities, too many small cities, relatively less and under-developed big and medium cities, showing evident disruption in city scale structure. There is no close bond and cooperation between cities, and their functions are overlapped and competition among them are very chaotic; cities of different scales don't have rational division of labor. Cities are over concentrated in the frontier of Taihang Mountain and Yan Mountain, and coastal development is falling far behind; so that it's difficult to make use of coastal advantages and to effectively improve the opening up. With city cluster as the main subject, Hebei Province should make full use of Xiong'an New Area's planning and development to build an urban pattern of coordinated development of small, medium and big cities and small cities and towns, to actively optimize regional urban system, expand and enhance regional center cities, to emphasize on cultivating emerging cities with districts, and to build a coastal urban belt and speed up construction of featured satellite cities and towns surrounding Beijing. It thus can eventually build a world-class city cluster together with Beijing and Tianjin via restructuring Hebei's city functions and spatial layout.

3.1.1 Plan and construct the Xiong'an New Area, adjust and optimize the development pattern of its surrounding cities

Hebei Xiong'an New Area is another new area with the state-level significance after Shenzhen Special Economic Zone and Shanghai Pudong New Area. Its planning and construction will exert great influence on surrounding existing spatial structures and city labor division and production. Hebei Province must adapt to new trend to take initiative to change the pattern of Xiong'an New Area's surrounding cities and space, and adjust and optimize city function positioning; so that they can be complimentary to Xiong'an New Area's advantages; thus mutually promote a win-win regional development new pattern and assist Beijing and Tianjin in building a world-class city cluster.

In order to plan and construct the Xiong'an New Area from a high starting point and with high standards, to adjust and to optimize surrounding cities' development patterns, Hebei Province needs to focus on four aspects: a. With the principle of "world vision, international standards, Chinese characteristics and high goals", it should build an environment-friendly, information-intelligent, livable and workable modern city with relatively strong competitiveness and influence where human and the nature coexist harmoniously; cultivate and build a place to undertake Beijing's non-capital functions and a new regional growth pole; fully absorb high-end factors that are ready to enter Beijing but are non-capital functions; alleviate Beijing's pressure; form Beijing's new wings with its sub-centers and form Hebei's new wings with the north Hebei region. b. It should speed up the coordinated development pace of the Xiong'an New Area and Baoding city; jointly form group cities with a population over 5 million; jointly form the "Beijing-Tianjin-Xiong'an" great triangle; construct city cluster core area; push for the regional development mode to shift from "one core, two cities" to "one core, three cities"; improve BTH city cluster's comprehensive service capability, technology innovation capability and factor attraction capability in an all-around way; gain a position in the world that it deserves. c. It should overall plan city and industrial development space; focus on the New Area's surrounding cities such as Baoding, Langfang, Cangzhou to identify the development direction of relevant cities and regions; draw regional ecological red line and city development boundaries; realize reasonable separation while interactive development between surrounding cities and the New Area. Drive forward function division and coordinated linkage between surrounding cities and the New Area. According to its function positioning, the Xiong'an New Area is to be a livable and environment-friendly new city area, a leading area where development is driven by innovation, a coordinated development demonstration area and an opening-up development pilot area. Such high goals will catalyze a new round of urban and regional function restructuring. Hebei must take initiative to adapt itself to this trend, emphasize on coordinating a rational labor division and a supplementary development in innovation and opening-up between Xiong'an New Area and Beijing; guarantee the industrial unification and opening-up cooperation between the New Area and Tianjin, advance ecological so-construction and industrial interaction between the New Area and Baoding, give full play to the New Area's influence of radiation in the middle and south Hebei Province; form a landscape where the New Area and its surrounding cities have supplementary functions, effective interaction and coordinated development.

3.1.2 Expand and improve provincial center cities and enhance regional influence of radiation

Currently, it's common for world-class cities to adopt a multi-center development mode to avoid over expansion of a singular core, to better make use of regional comparative advantages, to tighten regional economic bond and to effectively drive forward regional coordinated and balanced development. But according to the development reality of the BTH city cluster, it's facing a pressing issue of urban system structural imbalance, especially which as provincial center cities of Hebei Province, Shijiazhuang and Tangshan are of small-scale and weak influence of radiation. It is the main reason resulting in BTH developmental gradient differences. As a result, in order to fix problems in urban development, Hebei must expand and improve its provincial center cities and enhance regional influence of radiation.

In order to cultivate and expand provincial center cities, five aspects should be emphasized on: (1) With the goal of building a megapolis with a population of 5 to10 million and a type I megacity with a population of 3 to 5 million, it should speed up the construction of Shijiazhuang and Tangshan; gradually improve city scale and function status; enhance high-end factor attracting capability and influence of radiation on surrounding areas; it should make these two cities provincial center cities of the middle and south Hebei Province and east Hebei Province, and wings underpinning urban development of the entire province. (2) Construct the Zhengding State-level coordinated innovation new city; accelerate preparation work including city planning, ecological planning, policy study, mechanism design; construct core starting zones with high standards; speed up improving civil infrastructure and utility facilities; actively undertake transferred industries from Beijing and Tianjin and non-capital functions from Beijing; spare no efforts in building a Beijing-Tianjin coordinated development demonstration area, a modern provincial city construction new high ground, an urban and rural overall-planned development pilot area and a province-level integrated reform pilot area, providing underpinning support for scale expansion, capability improvement, taste positioning and industrial transformation for provincial capital cities. (3) Push forward Tangshan Caofeidian sub-center area development and construction. Directed by the integration of "harbor, harbor district, harbor city", make full use of its advantages in harbor, space and environment capacity; undertake general manufacturing industries transferred from Beijing and Tianjin; overall improve city functions of the Tangshan bay ecological city and the Caofeidian harbor-front commercial area; improve service facilities of recreation, culture and education, Medicare; accelerate coastal industrial agglomeration and population concentration; build a world-class circular economic demonstration area, a shipping and logistics center of the northeast BTH Region, a trade and financial integrated development pilot area, a BTH coordinated development demonstration area, providing key support for Tangshan in building an economic cooperation window city in the Northeast Asia region. (4) Taking the opportunity of division restructuring of cities with administrative districts, emphasizing on establishing an integrated planning system, enhance traffic facility extension and connection; optimize city industrial layout, achieve integrated development; scheme a development framework for Shijiazhuang and Tangshan; realize the transformation from a single city to a city group; fundamentally transform city spatial outreaching methods; restructure and optimize city regional functions; improve and expand city functions. (5) Taking the opportunity of new-type urbanization and urban-rural overall planning demonstration area, advance innovation of city development institution and mechanism; speed up the process of rural population adapting to the urban environment; continuously optimize urban-rural spatial layout and patterns; effectively strengthen city comprehensive undertaking capability and influence of radiation; inject powerful driving force into provincial center city development.

3.1.3 Take initiative to cultivate emerging cities divided into districts and provide solutions for city scale structure disruption

Based on development experience of city clusters worldwide, it is necessary to set up a rational urban scale hierarchy in order to narrow regional development gaps and improve urban function systems. A rational city scale hierarchy appears as a pyramid, i.e. the smaller a city, the lower level it's at, the more of its kind. Compared to major city clusters worldwide, the megapolis in the BTH city cluster is too big; the city cluster consists of too many small cities while a comparatively small number of big and medium cities; the city scale hierarchy appears like a "dumb bell" and is evidently disrupted (see Table 1). Currently, Hebei Province only has three type II big cities with a population of one to three million and 6 medium cities with a population of 500,000 to one million, 10 and four less than those in the Yangtze Delta city cluster, respectively; it is difficult for them to underpin the deployment of the BTH city cluster (see Table 2). From Hebei Province's urban development path, the delayed administrative division restructuring and a small number of prefecture-level cities and county-level cities are key factors restricting urban scale expansion. Orderly advancing administrative district division restructuring, supporting qualified counties and cities in administrative upgrading, and increasing numbers of big and medium cities have become priorities in tackling the issue of city cluster disruption.

As the main battlefield of the national new-type urbanization, urban-rural overall planning demonstration area and BTH urbanization, Hebei Province has to cultivate more regional center cities. (1)Actively propel county-level cities and key counties in upgrading to prefecture-level cities. For advantageous counties and cities with competitive economic strength and development potential such as Dingzhou, Xinji, Huanghua, Laoting, and Renqiu, it should speed up integration of their surrounding counties and towns with strong economic ties, expand boundaries of administrative divisions, upgrade them into prefecture-level cities timely, enhance their industrial and factor agglomeration capability, and build them into regional new center cities, striving for adding 5 prefecture-level cities within 5 to 10 years, each with a population more than 500,000 or even over 1 million if possible.(2)Actively advance general counties upgrading to county-level cities. For counties with a large population, a reasonable distance to prefecture-level cities and certain economic strength such as Huailai, Changli, Yutian, Qingxian, and Wexian, it should make individual plans for each of them, upgrade them individually when appropriate, strive for adding10 county-level cities within 5 to 10 years and each with a population over 200,000, integrate surrounding cities and towns step by step when the time is ripe, and build medium cities with a population over 500,000.

Table 1 World-class city clusters

City clusters	Atlantic coastal city cluster of Northeast US	City cluster of Northwest Europe	City cluster of Middle and South UK	Pacific coastal city cluster of Japan
World-class center cities	New York	Paris	London	Tokyo
Regional center cities	Boston, Philadel phia,Was hington	Brussels, Amsterdam, Bonn	Birmingham, Liverpool, Manchester	Nagoya, Osaka
Other cities	Atlantic City, Baltimore, Harrisburg, Vir ginia, Portland, Richmond, Ne wark	Marseilles, Lyon,Toulouse, Bordeaux, Nantes, Rotterdam, The Hague, Antwerp, Kolner, etc.	Leeds, Sheffield, Wel wyn, Letchworth, Redditch, etc.	Kawasaki , Yokohama, Shizu oka, Hamamatsu, Kyoto, Kobe, Hiroshima, Fukuoka, etc.
Small towns and cities	200+ other towns and cities	Other small towns and cities	other small towns	300+ other towns and cities

Note: quoted from Tuxuan, *Comparison of Yangtze Delta city cluster and international city clusters and its revelation,* Shanghai Economics, Issue 4, 2015.

Table 2 Comparison of city scale hierarchy between BTH and the Yangtze Delta city clusters

<table>
<tr><th colspan="2">Scale hierarchy</th><th>criterion (annual average population of municipal districts)</th><th>Cities from the Yangtze Delta city cluster</th><th>Cities from the BTH city cluster</th></tr>
<tr><td colspan="2">Megapolis</td><td>Over 10 million</td><td>Shanghai</td><td>Beijing, Tianjin</td></tr>
<tr><td colspan="2">Megacity</td><td>5 to 10 million</td><td>Nanjing, Hangzhou</td><td></td></tr>
<tr><td rowspan="2">Big city</td><td>Type I big city</td><td>3 to 5 million</td><td>Suzhou</td><td>Shijiazhuang, Tangshan</td></tr>
<tr><td>Type II big city</td><td>1 to 3 million</td><td>Hefei, Wuxi, Changzhou, Nantong, Yancheng, Yangzhou, Zhenjiang, Taizhou, Ningbo, Huzhou, Shaoxing, Taizhou, Wuhu</td><td>Qinhuangdao, Handan, Baoding</td></tr>
<tr><td colspan="2">Medium city</td><td>500,000 to 10 million</td><td>Jiaxing, Jinhua, Zhoushan, Ma'anshan, Anqing, Chuzhou, Chizhou, Xuancheng, Yiwu, Cixi</td><td>Xingtai, Zhangjiakou, Chengde, Cangzhou, Langfang, Hengshui</td></tr>
<tr><td colspan="2">Small city</td><td>Under 500,000</td><td>Tongling, Yixing, etc.</td><td>Renqiu, Xinji, etc.</td></tr>
</table>

Note: quoted from *China City Statistical Yearbook of 2016*.

3.1.4 Lay emphasis on constructing the coastal urban belt, overall improve opening-up level of the city cluster

From international experience, constructing urban belt of vertical coastal line led by harbors, with the assembling and evacuating system as axis, coastal and inland center cities as connections is an urbanization development strategy commonly adopted by major developed economies. Although Hebei Province is a coastal region, due to long-term lack of strong support from harbors, it has gradually developed into a radial, resources-directed, inward urban system along major traffic arteries such as the Beijing-Guangzhou railway and the Beijing-Qinhuangdao railway. It is centering on Beijing and Tianjin, concentrating its resources in the piedmont plain, and regarding center cities as major connections. Against the backdrop of increasingly depleted mineral and inland resources, in order to further expedite its industrialization process and make use of advantages of its heavy chemical industry,Hebei Province has to rely on the increasingly improved coastal harbor system and its supporting assembling and evacuating systems to construct a coastal urban belt led by harbor cities.

Construction of coastal urban development belt should focus on three lines:(1) Following the lead of Huanghua harbor, Tangshan harbor and Qinhuangdao harbor, relying on coastal backbone highways such as the Bohai-rim intercity highway, the Tianjin-Qinhuangdao passenger highway, the coastal express highway, the Tianjin-Shantou express highway and the railway, improve the agglomeration ability of the Caofeidian District, the Bohai New Area and the Beidaihe life and health industry innovation demonstration area; build a coastal urban cluster. (2) Lay more emphasis on the cultivation and development of counties and cities along the Shijiazhuang-Huanghua assembling and evacuating passageways such as Huanghua, Cangzhou, Xianxian, Shenzhou, Xinji, Jinzhou and cities and towns along the Handan-Huanghua assembling and evacuating passageway; construct two urban development belts of Shijiazhuang-Huanghua and Handan-Huanghua led by the Huanghua harbor. (3)Intensify cultivation and development of cities and towns such as Xushui and Bazhou along the Baoding-Tianjin line and construct a Baoding-Tianjin urban development belt led by the Tianjin harbor. The aim is to gradually form a beaded coastal urban system led by harbors, with major assembling and evacuating passageways as axes, and to transform Hebei's inland urban layout system to a coastal one.

3.1.5 Cultivate Beijing's featured satellite cities and towns to orderly undertake Beijing's functions and alleviate its population burden

It is the starting point of the BTH coordinated development to alleviate Beijing's non-capital functions and provide solutions for Beijing's "big city ills". Currently Beijing has entered the stage of sub-urbanization, both its population and industries have showed a tendency of expanding towards surrounding areas. But as Hebei region near Beijing has no satellite cities and towns with supporting functions, it is difficult for Beijing's non-capital functions to transfer to its surroundings and for its "city ills" to be cured. Within one to two hours' distance from Beijing, Hebei boasts multiple small cities and towns with ecology-friendly environment, rich culture and humanity, full service facilities and industries with distinctive characteristics, and they have great advantages as capital satellite towns and cities and in undertaking high-end transferred functions. Cultivating a number of featured satellite towns and cities with both modern city civilization and local traits in Beijing's surrounding areas is an effective measure to undertake Beijing's non-capital functions, absorb Beijing's population in entrepreneurship, recreation and retirement, as well as an important path to improve Hebei's economic and social development level, improve its regional urban system and make use of capital function overflow.

To develop featured satellite towns and cities, it should focus on reform and innovation, accelerating factor agglomeration, industry agglomeration and humanity integration of industries and cities; making efforts to build featured satellite towns and cities a key link of the BTH world-class city cluster, a strategic platform undertaking Beijing's non-capital functions and a key carrier of Hebei's industrial upgrading. (1) Select to develop and cultivate. Overall consider the feasibility and requirements of undertaking Beijing's non-capital functions. Taking into consideration fundamental elements of their transportation, ecology, culture and industry, focusing on selecting key villages and towns in Beijing's surrounding towns and cities such as Huailai, Zhuolu and Zhangbei of Zhangjiakou, Luanping, Xinglong of Chengde, Zhuozhou, Gaobeidian, Laishui of Baoding, Xianghe, Bazhou and Dacheng of Langfang, build featured satellite towns and cities with strong appeal and capability to undertake transferred non-capital functions. (2) Identify function positioning of featured satellite towns and cities. Based on endowed resources and location features of towns and cities, focus on featured industrial clusters and modern service industries such as culture and tourism, health and retirement, differential positioning, and supplementary development; look into deeply; enhance agglomeration of featured industries; avoid homogeneous competition.(3) Innovate the development and operation mode of featured satellite towns and cities. With the principle of government as the guide, enterprises as main subjects and market-oriented operation, on the premise of basic work of planning, supporting infrastructure, guaranteed resource factors, cultural discovering and carrying forward, ecological protection, take initiative to encourage strategic investors such as CFLD, Wanda and Hengda to take part in the development and operation of featured satellite towns and cities; improve development efficiency and building quality of featured satellite towns and cities, making them key undertakers of Beijing's non-capital functions.

3.2 With the goal of improving the industrial status, reinforce undertaking platform construction, system and mechanism innovat-ion; build high-standard state-level industrial transformation and upgrading pilot areas

Generd Secretary Jinping Xi clearly states that "industrial integration is the practical content and key underpinning of the BTH coordinated development". Hebei is featured with a big economy, low-level industries, high resource consumption and severe environmental pollution; its industrial development is falling far behind Beijing and Tianjin, and it is the key weak link in the BTH coordinated development. Currently, Hebei is facing major problems in terms of industrial upgrading: it has kept the traditional industrial labor division relationship with Beijing and Tianjin, which is a divisional or vertical labor division method; it hasn't developed a visionary, clear and detailed strategic orientation that applies to world-class city cluster industrial labor division rules in terms of industrial upgrading goals; and it doesn't give due emphasis and deployment to factor conditions and environmental support necessary for industrial development; prominent structural problems at the supply side such as lagging behind in building high-level industrial undertakers, lacking of high-quality talents, difficulty in introducing quality financial and intelligent factors, underdeveloped soft and hard operation environment, make the goal of Hebei's industrial upgrading out of reach and the process slow. Against the backdrop of the BTH coordinated development, pushing forward Hebei's industrial upgrading should be based on the industrial upgrading goal of BTH rational division of labor, directed by improving industrial labor division status, focus on building an undertaking platform, center on system and mechanism innovation, emphasize on building high-level State-level industrial transformation and upgrading pilot areas, and drive forward Hebei's industrial upgrading.

3.2.1 Optimize industrial labor division with Beijing and Tianjin, and improve Hebei's industries to medium and high level

An area's role positioning and goal in regional industrial labor division determine its development orientation, which exerts in-depth influence on policies and actions of its industrial upgrading and has a decisive impact on results of its efforts to propel industrial upgrading. As a result, in order to advance Hebei's industrial upgrading, the first things is to position its role and set up its goal in the BTH industrial labor division; so as to provide a basis for identifying a more rational and effective industrial upgrading orientation and path.

At present, the existing BTH labor division is a low-level vertical one formed during the process of almost 20 years of interaction and adjustment, i.e. "Beijing provides knowledge innovation and high-end services—Tianjin provides R&D, design and high-end manufacturing—Hebei is left with general processing, manufacturing and services". Although some progress has made compared to the previous structure, and has enabled all to make use of their comparative advantages and has realized resources and advantages complementation in the region; from the perspective of value chain, it is still a quite primitive divisional vertical labor division, which is typically seen in developed areas and under-developed areas. From long run, it is quite dependent and tends to develop towards low-end industries, which is not good for industrial upgrading of the entire region.

City cluster itself is an open city regional labor division system, whose internal industrial labor division should be based on its part in the labor division of global industrial value chain, and it should make efforts in gaining more influence and competitiveness in it. In the future, if the BTH Region intends to build a world-class city cluster with international competitiveness and influence, it has to push for existing regional industrial labor division which is mainly a vertical division, to transform to a more detailed horizontal division and industrial value chain division. For this reason, Hebei's industrial upgrading should improve its level with international standards in mind, break the existing vertical labor division pattern, propel transformation to a horizontal and industrial value chain labor division, form a regional labor division pattern consisting mainly horizontal and industrial chain labor division. Only in this way can industries in Hebei improve as soon as possible and a higher-level of coordinated development in the BTH Region achieved.

According to the reality of Hebei's industrial upgrading tasks and BTH industrial labor division, two ways can be considered to realize the above goals:(1)Directed by value chain labor division, drive forward an overall integration of traditional advantageous industries with Beijing and Tianjin; connect industrial chain; fill development gap and together build a closer, fully integrated industrial chain with linked development. The concept of regional production complex can be drawn in this case: with industries with traditional advantages at the center, discipline as the unit, integrating the BTH Region and absorb relevant scientific and research institutions, institutions of higher learning, manufacturers, suppliers, distributors, and financial institutions outside the region, and creating industrial alliance of steel, chemistry, equipment, textile and costume, food and construction materials.(2)Directed by horizontal labor division, push forward a rational differential positioning with the BTH Region in high-tech industries, strategic emerging industries and modern service industries; detail industrial labor division; develop distinctive characteristics of one's own; together construct an industrial cluster with complementary advantages, orderly competition and coordinated development. For high-end and high-tech industries, with the existing industrial foundation and non-capital function undertaking feature, aggregate industrial resources home and abroad to establish three industrial features and advantages of bio-medicine, new energy and energy conservation; in the field of financial services, based on a huge manufacturing industry and relying on regional center cities, focus on developing industrial finance such as industrial investment fund, venture capital fund and financial lease; support and encourage development of all kinds of industrial fund management companies; build a BTH industrial financial service base; in the field of life and health, relying on its advantages in location, ecological environment and space, enhance advantages in outdoor sports, recreation and retirement industries.

3.2.2 Led by planning and construction of the Xiong'an New Area, build four categories of industrial upgrading platforms

Cities and development areas are key undertakers supporting and leading industrial development of a region. Over a long time, Hebei has been facing the following issues: its center cities are under-developed; its new area construction is lagging behind; the overall level of its development areas is low; its industrial upgrading lacks support and lead from high-level platforms. The setting up of the Xiong'an New Area is not only a breakthrough for Hebei's absence of state-level new area; moreover, it provides rare opportunities for Hebei to build a multilevel industrial upgrading platform led by it. Currently, Hebei should lay emphasis on building the following four categories of platforms:

(1) Construct the Xiong'an New Area with a brand new concept and build a pioneer demonstration platform for industrial upgrading. Following the principle of "world vision, international standards, Chinese characteristics and high goals", innovate regional and city planning mechanism; plan both overall and in specific for the New Area with high standards; scientifically plan and allocate all kinds of resources and function space; set up an example for green and livable cities. With the goal of building a new generation of international leading technology city, We should innovate the industrial and factor introducing mechanism; overall integrate non-capital functions, introduce quality financial and intelligent factors home and abroad with a high starting point; innovate resource and industrial capital; form industries with more incentives and a talent development mechanism; cultivate and develop high-end and high-tech new industries with purposes; set up an example of innovation-driven development; form a new engine and driving force for Hebei's industrial development. With a more international vision, We should deepen system and mechanism reform including administrative management, land development, investment and trade, capital financing, and talent flow; establish an institutional rule system

matching international standards; explore new modes for development, building and operation of the New Area; set up an example as a New Area with efficient development and operation.

(2) Build green, intelligent, livable and workable cities with complete functions, and platforms for factor agglomeration. Speed up administrative division restructuring of Cangzhou, Xingtong, Chengde, and Langfang; improve absorbing and undertaking capacity of industries and population of regional center cities; give more support for the Zhengding New Area, the Beidaihe New Area, the Bohai New Area, the Jinan New Area, the Yanghe New Area, the Xingdong New Area and the Binghu New Area; drive forward city layout optimization and improve functions; select a number of small cities with desired locations, good conditions and promising potential to advance the reform of "counties under the direct administration of the province", and to give them corresponding priorities to develop into medium cities; propel the "big county strategy"; speed up the process of expanding capacity and improving quality of counties; cultivate a number of quality small cities, with the mentality of industry-city integration and industry-education-city integration. Following the notion of building an ecological, intelligent and civilized city, carry out uplifting projects of fine city construction, management and public services; improve city's capability and level of public services; make them a center attracting high-level talents and capital.

(3) Build an industrial park with high-end positioning and efficient operation, and build an industrial undertaking platform. Carry out a project upgrading the development area, targeting a high end, focusing on existing province-level development areas, aiming at "vacating cage to change bird" and improving the level, speed up improving function facilities; innovate institutions and mechanisms such as business, capital and talents attracting, property ownership transfer investment and financing, overall improve levels of industries, and factors and services; push for several development areas to upgrade into State-level development areas. Carry out administrative innovation projects in development areas, focusing on 100 selected development areas, following the principle of "one area one institution", "one area one policy"; make new modes of operation and management such as "corporation-style operation" and "holistic hosting"; look into new mechanism in personnel identity, position management and income allocation; realize efficient operation for development areas. Combining the layout and construction of "micro center", plan and develop a number of specialized parks, making "micro center" the core of high-end factor agglomeration of relevant fields and carrier of high-end industrial development. Accelerate improving

supporting policies for bonded areas of Caofeidian and Shijiazhuang, actively facilitate the Cangzhou and Bohai New Area in declaring themselves as integrated bonded areas; build three outward leading platforms for industrial development.

(4) Build featured towns with distinctive characteristics and supporting services, and build platforms for innovation and entrepreneurship. Undertake non-capital functions; select areas surrounding the capital with convenient traffic and ecological environment to plan and construct a number of featured towns themed with innovation, entrepreneurship, bold ideas, distinctive features, complete functions and appropriate scales; create platforms of innovation and entrepreneurship supporting industrial upgrading. Making use of undertaking Beijing education resources, following the mode of "town + universities and colleges + technology parks", plan and build several towns of higher learning; catering to construction requirements of achievements transformation bases of Beijing science research institutions, following the mode of "to wn+institution+incubator+product ion base", plan and construct several innovation and entrepreneurship towns with functions of R&D, incubating, achievements transformation and science spreading; adapt to trend of population aging to alleviate Beijing's medical and rehabilitation pressure; plan and construct several rehabilitation and retirement towns that provide for the elders, with functions of recuperation, rehabilitation, health and medicine researching; catering to the development need of the cultural and creative industry, focusing on providing services for preparation work of Beijing's cultural and innovation products, plan and build several cultural and creative towns; for new needs in recreational sports and health, with the opportunity of preparing and hosting the Winter Olympic Games, plan and build several sports and health towns integrating outdoor sports, event services, sports medicare and equipment research; focusing on pushing forward the innovation development of traditional featured industries and techniques, plan and build towns characterized with featured products making, restoration of traditional techniques and innovation.

3.2.3 Carry out in institution and mechanism innovation experiments and provide environmental support for industrial upgrading

A sound development environment is the key premise for factor agglomeration and industrial development, and it has become a core competitiveness of a region and a city's development. In today's world, those with sound development environment have the future of industry, city and region. Currently, no countries or regions will neglect building such environment, and competition in developing such an environment is getting increasingly fierce. In order to fundamentally change Hebei's development environment, environment construction must be moved to a higher priority; it should speed up institution and mechanism innovation and provide sound environment for industrial upgrading.

(1) Carry out industrial policy innovation experiments, providing industrial upgrading with a policy environment with a unified goal, supporting measures and coordinated linkage. Industrial policy is an aggregate of all kinds of policies used by the government to intervene industry forming and development, in order to realize certain economic and social goals; it is a key means for a country or a region to guide industrial direction and promote industrial upgrading and coordinate industrial structure. Currently, Hebei is at the key stage of industrial transformation and upgrading, it desperately needs strong industrial policy support; however, in-depth insight reveals that Hebei's existing industrial policies are to a large extend misleading, i.e. under most circumstances, industrial orientation reflecting government intention doesn't match the reality, policies closely related to industrial development such as those in finance and taxation, land, environment protection, energy, credit and loan, do not match nor coordinated; for example, although it explicitly supports and encourages development of high-tech industries and strategic emerging industries, it still keeps previous standards of investment scale and intensity, resulting in a greatly weakened effect of industrial policies. For this reason, in order to improve the effectiveness of industrial policies, it should carry out industrial policy innovation experiments taking the opportunity of building a State-level industrial transformation and upgrading pilot area. Apart from existing industrial catalogs which are banned, restricted or outdated, based on the national industrial restructuring guidance catalogue, it should issue encouraging an industrial catalogue reflecting Hebei's requirements in industrial upgrading and scientific labor division with the *Hebei Province industrial development guidance catalogue*, and enhance its biding force with the means of local legislation, and speed up Hebei's industrial upgrading. It should actively experiment the concept of "integration of multiple policies"; with "integration of multiple rules" as reference, corresponding to industrial development oriented catalogue, develop factor supply policies in finance and taxation, land, environmental protection, energy, credit and loan at the same time, guarantee coordinated policies and improve their effectiveness.

(2) Carry out management system reform experiments, create a government environment with guidance, supervision and service in place. An efficient government environment is a key underpinning point of a successful

industrial upgrading. In recent years, with the deepening of the "streamlined administration and institute decentralization, impartial supervision and efficient service" reform, Hebei's government environment has been improved; however, issues such as industrial project approval red tapes, complicated process, weak government service awareness, low work efficiency are still prominent due to long due management system reform. As a result, it should carry out management system reform experiments, improve administrative efficiency, create quality and efficient government environment taking the opportunity of building a State-level industrial transformation and upgrading pilot area: a. Further deepen the "streamlined administration and institute decentralization, impartial supervision and efficient service" reform; further streamline administration and decentralize institutions; continue to cancel and delegate a number of approval items that restrict industrial development and dampen enterprise vitality; maximally unlcash market energy. b. Deeply restructure administrative approval procedures; carry out an overall reform of relatively concentrated administrative permission; create and improve the list management system such as list of administrative power of city and county-level government departments, list of responsibility, negative list, list of fees, agent service list of administrative licensing and supervision list; set up administrative approval bureaus at all the city and county level, sparing no effort in building a new government service platform of "one-stop approval, one-stop service". c. Improve comprehensive supervision; advance the reform of "integration of multiple certificates, one license one code"; implement a new supervision mode of "two random, one open", speed up the complete coverage of inter-divisional and inter-disciplinary integrated law enforcement in cities and counties. d. Innovate service methods; thoroughly implement an online approval system; create an "internet + government service" system with overall linkage, divisional coordination, overall planning at the provincial level and do-it-all website; form a connected and shared online service platform covering the entire province.

(3) Carry out experiments in creating a capital market, providing industrial upgrading with financial environment of diversified products, verified levels and complete services. An active capital market is a booster and lubricant of industrial transformation and upgrading. Currently, Hebei is going through a critical stage of industrial transformation and upgrading, and a stage intensively undertaking transferred industries from Beijing and Tianjin. It has active needs for company restructuring and merging, as well as frequent property ownership and equity changes; thus it is in urgent need for strong support

from the capital market. For this reason, it should carry out capital market building experiments, seek to form a diversified and multilevel capital market taking the opportunity of building a state-level industrial transformation and upgrading pilot area, providing industrial transformation and upgrading with adequate capital market support and explore paths and accumulate experience for building a state-level multilevel capital market. a. Seek to set up a trans-regional "BTH Equity Trading Center" in the Xiong'an New Area or integrating the Beijing Equity Trading Center, the Tianjin Equity Trading Center and the Shijiazhuang Equity Trading Center, providing BTH SMEs with services such as equity listing transferring, equity mortgage financing, privately raised company bonds issuing, capital increase and share enlargement. b. Seek to set up platforms for company merging, restructuring and trading, providing market-oriented passageways for traditional disciplines and companies to transform and to phase out excess capacity. c. Implement bond market pilot areas; strive for State-level support; set up a State-level bond trading center in the Xiong'an New Area; experiment and implement the company bonds registration system; open up the corporate bonds individual investor market; expand financing channels for corporate transformation and upgrading. d. Explore new modes of financing service development such as financial leasing, trust fund, investment fund, venture investment, and fund management, providing a wide range of financial products for industrial development.

3.3 Focusing on the Haihe Plain and the northeast mountain area of Hebei Province, expand ecological space, improve environmental quality and create a high-standard BTH ecological supporting area

The Program Outline for the Coordinated Development of the BTH Region points out that making Hebei Province a "BTH ecological supporting area" is the key foundation and task for undertaking Beijing's non-capital functions, realizing Hebei's leaping development and green rising, and propelling the BTH coordinated development. Setting up, planning and constructing the Xiong'an New Area provide great opportunities and strong motivation for building a BTH ecological supporting area; lay a greater burden and demand more from Hebei's ecological construction and environmental protection. For Hebei to build an ecological environment supporting area with high standards: in the plain area, it should stress on safeguarding Xiong'an New Area's ecological environment and advance a comprehensive ecological treatment in the plain area of the Haihe basin; in mountain areas, it should build an ecological barrier in northwest Hebei to improve the BTH ecological environment supporting capability.

3.3.1 Focus on safeguarding Xiong'an New Area's ecological environment, advance a comprehensive ecological treatment in the plain area of the Haihe basin

Both the CPC and the State Council explicitly put forward the goal to make the Xiong'an New Area a "clean and bright water-friendly ecological city with blue and green colors". In order to advance the Xiong'an New Area ecological city construction, its ecological environment should be safeguarded first. But areas to be developed and constructed in Xiong'an New Area and Baiyangdian on which it relies are posing prominent ecological environment issues. These issues, though appear to show in development and construction areas of new cities, can be attributed to problems from the water conservancy project and ecological deterioration of the Daqinghe Basin in the upstream of Baiyangdian, and lie in ecological system function deterioration of the plain area of the Haihe basin. As a result, in order to safeguard the ecological environment of the Xiong'an New Area's development and construction, it should firmly establish a system concept, an area concept, an overall concept and a comprehensive concept; it should protect and restore Baiyangdian's ecological functions and advance comprehensive treatment of the Daqinghe basin. At the same time, it needs to focus on the entire North China Plain, to overall advance ecological system restoration, treatment, protection and construction of the Haihe basin plain area.

(1) Protect and restore Baiyangdian's ecological functions. As the key support of Xiong'an New Area's ecological building, Baiyangdian's ecological environment quality has a direct impact on Xiong'an New Area's ecological safety and quality of ecological city building. At present, prominent ecological issues faced by the Baiyangdian area are: Baiyangdian and areas to be developed and built in the Xiong'an New Area are low-lying, which are greatly lower than the average alleviation of the Hebei plain area; Baiyangdian is short of water source with unstable water level, it mainly depends on water transferring work such as emergency water transferring from the Yellow River to Baiyangdian, and it hasn't established a perpetual and normalized water supply system; water quality of Baiyangdian hasn't yet reached standards; the issue of water pollution and ecological function deterioration are pressing. In order to protect and restore Baiyangdian ecological functions and safeguard Xiong'an New Area's ecological safety, it should expedite construction of the Baiyangdian flood control engineering system, water supply engineering system and wastewater treatment system. a. Integrate flood control facilities

including Baiyangdian thousand-mile embankment, Yongdinghe diversion floodgate, Daqinghe flood diversion and detention areas and Baiyangdian water control project; form a flood control and draining engineering system with higher standards, more complete systems and better functions; make sure that it can resist flood seen once in a thousand years. b. Construct a linkage engineering system between the Xiong'an New Area and the "five waters" of underground water, surface water, transferred water, rainwater and recycled water, to guarantee water supply of the Xiong'an New Area and Baiyangdian, to stabilize Baiyangdian's water level and amount, expand water coverage, to restore deteriorated and shrunk depressions and shallow lakes. c. Make full use of the elevation gap between the north, west, south bottom of Baiyangdian and its center bottom; add the drop control project; connect Baiyangdian with the Haihe channel; set up Baiyangdian water restoring and transferring system; speed up evacuating population of the Baiyangdian area; increase Baiyangdian water activity and natural purification ability; improve water quality and restore water ecological functions via measures such as water control project.

(2) Advance the comprehensive treatment of the Daqinghe basin. Baiyangdian is part of the Daqinghe basin whose ecological safety bears a direct impact on ecological safety of Baiyangdian and the Xiong'an New Area. At present, north branch of Daqinghe has only one large water reservoir, i.e. Angezhuang, lacking of necessary flood control engineering system, and posing certain flood and draught risks to the Xiong'an New Area. The major task of water reservoir at upstream Daqinghe is to supply water for cities like Baoding; water resources of the Daqinghe water system are mainly allocated to cities instead of Baiyangdian, resulting in unstable surface water supply to the Xiong'an New Area and Baiyangdian. The Daqinghe basin doesn't have a sewage water efflux channel and sewage water in the basin is discharged to Baiyangdian directly or indirectly; that's why it's difficult to achieve evident results in Baiyangdian pollution treatment. In order to ensure Xiong'an New Area's ecological safety, from a long-term, strategic and overall perspective, the area should initiate a comprehensive treatment project in the Daqinghe basin at the appropriate time. Treatment work should include improving flood control security engineering system, speeding up process of planning and constructing a "once in a thousand years" flood control projects such as the Jvmahe Reservoir, to build the Xiong'an New Area a super-flood-resistant city; optimizing water storing and transferring engineering system, linked by projects such as transferring water from the Yangtze River and the Yellow River via the Middle Route Project, plan and construct surface water co-transferring engineering system in the

Xiong'an New Area and Daqinghe middle and downstream towns and cities; overall plan water supply to the Xiong'an New Area and relevant cities such as Baoding; build a clean water and sewage diversion drainage system; accelerate planning of the "diversion of clean water and sewage" project in the Daqinghe basin plain area; plan and construct passageways in the Daqinghe basin especially the Xiong'an New Area and Baoding city for discharging sewage water into the sea; enhance ecological building in the upstream area, improve standards of comprehensive treatment for upstream water source conservation mountain area, ecologically-conserved forest, scenery gardens and small basins; restore upstream waterway eco-functions, improve upstream water source conservation capability, making the Daqinghe upstream mountain area the backyard of the Xiong'an New Area.

(3) Restore eco-system of the Haihe basin plain area. As one of the five river systems of the Haihe basin, Daqinghe is an independent ecological system with close relationship to other four river systems. Water transferring projects between basins such as transferring water from the Yangtze River via the Middle Route Project, transferring water from Luanping to Tianjin, transferring water from the Yellow River via the Middle Route Project, as well as new river projects including the Ziya New River and the Zhangwei New River for the purpose of channeling flood have connected Daqinghe and other four rivers into an entire system. A comprehensive treatment of the Daqinghe system will affect river systems nearby. As a result, in order to tackle ecological safety issues faced by the Xiong'an New Area, ecological system of the Haihe basin plain area should be considered as a whole and its ecological comprehensive treatment needs to be propelled. a. Drive forward a comprehensive treatment of the plain's natural riverway; adjust river turns and curved streams; reinforce river dams, add water interception and storage projects; shrink the bottomland; renovate beaded gardens; restore functions of flood diversion and detention areas; turn plain riverways into manmade or half-manmade wetland and water net with functions of flood draining, water supply, greening, beautifying and sightseeing. b. Restore deteriorated lakes and depressions. Carry out restoration and treatment of lakes and depressions; restore dozens of natural depressions in the Haihe plain area such as Dongdian, Wenanwa Depression, Ningjinpo Lake, Xianxianwa Depression, and Daluze Wetland; build a comprehensive ecological area with functions of water storing, water supply, aquaculture, greening, sightseeing and tourism. c. Expand urban ecological space of Beijing, Tianjin, Langfang, and Baoding; turn rivers, lakes, depressions, shallow lakes and flood areas between Beijing, Tianjin, Langfang and Baoding into ecological segregation areas; build an ecological transition belt between

these cities. d. Build coastal plain city ecological barriers, effectively protecting coastal wetlands, protective coastal forests, lagoons, depressions, tourist attractions and natural reserves; control coastal line development and natural disasters such as transgression; build coastal ecological function area with functions of wind prevention and sand fixation, water storage and transferring, afforestation and greening, pollution prevention and treatment.

3.3.2 Build an ecological barrier in northwest Hebei with high standards, improve BTH ecological environment supporting capability

Northwest Hebei located windward and upstream of Beijing and Tianjin, and is the ecological barrier, water resource supplier and backyard of Beijing and Tianjin, and key priority of the BTH ecological environment supporting area construction. It possesses a delicate ecological location, a special ecological status and plays a key ecological effect in the BTH Region. Due to facts such as poor natural endowment, late opening up, and being an area with ecological fragility and a concentration of impoverished population, the burden in protecting the ecology, developing economy, improving life standards for the northwest Hebei is incredibly heavy. For many years, the state has been increasing investment in its ecological building and poverty relief. Zhangjiakou and Chengde have also expedited the pace in self-development; however, their problem of "ecology for the state, revenue for the local government and income for the people" still presents. For this reason, it should construct the high-standard northwest ecological barrier from the level of the BTH coordinated development, innovate ecological construction concept, improve ecological construction system and mechanism, optimize ecological construction policy design, ensure that regional ecological functions can be better utilized and regional economy can be advanced in a fast and sustainable way; thus to achieve a win-win result for both ecology protection and economic development.

(1) Consolidate and improve northwest Hebei's function as an ecological barrier. Focusing on sand prevention and treatment in water sources, sand sources, wind inlets and windways in Zhangjiakou and Chengde, continue implementing projects such as the Three-North Shelterbelt Project, Beijing-Tianjin sand source treatment, returning the grain plots to forestry, national non-commercial forest construction, halting commercial logging of natural forests and afforestation with financial subsidy from the central government, reinforcing water conservation for forests and construction of wind prevention and sand fixation forest; make more efforts in wetland protection and restoration; build an ecological function area featured with water

and soil conservation, water source conservation, wind prevention and sand fixation, foresting and fruit growing, ecological diversity protection. It is suggested reinforce rural source pollution treatment, carry out pollution treatment from the source in the rural area in northwest Hebei, solve the problem of environmental damage caused by domestic waste, sewage and overuse of fertilizers and pesticides, and curb area non-point pollution that has great impact on water sources.

(2) Make full use of policies in pilot areas and pilot sites. Taking the opportunity of the building of the Zhangjiakou state-level "Industrial Green Transformation Pilot City", making use of state supporting policies, advance environmental treatment, restoration and improvement of Zhangjiakou industries in the Yanghe and Sangganhe basin, and reduce pollution in the Guanting Reservoir. Making use of the "green development comprehensive evaluation index system" pilot site in the Zhangjiakou region, monitor resource utilization, pollution treatment, environmental quality and ecological protection of the region, and promote a green economic transition of Zhangjiakou. Taking advantage of the building of the "ecological civilization pilot area" in the Zhangjiakou-Chengde region, seek for an innovation institution and mechanism path with which the Zhangjiakou-Chengde region can play a leading role in realizing ecology protection and economic development at the same time.

(3) Explore an ecological compensating mechanism that is market-oriented, normalized and standardized. Establish a market-oriented mechanism for water resource allocation, utilization and protection in the BTH Region; and eliminate water resource allocating methods in the form of executive order, unfair water resource supply methods, and unreasonable water environment protection methods. Establish a water rights transfer mechanism in the region and between upper and lower streams; increase the water price in downstream regions and raise sewage treatment fees. Downstream regions should pay water resource fees to upstream regions regularly according to market price to compensate water source conservation regions with costs in water conservation and losses in transferring water rights. Set up trans-administrative-regional fund of ecological compensation for the purpose of compensating losses in water resource rights transfer in the Zhangjiakou and Chengde region, limiting traditional industries' losses of development rights and interests, improving environmental quality standards, reducing local economic losses and enhancing management and protection of ecological projects and natural reserves. Seek for diversified compensating methods such as upstream regions making more room for downstream regions to develop, downstream regions in Beijing and

Tianjin conduct more investment and development in upstream regions in Zhangjiakou and Chengde, driving forward poverty relief and economic development of upstream regions.

3.4 Targeting at realizing ecology protection and economic development at the same time, advance construction of north Hebei and regional poverty relief, realize leaping development and green rising of the north Hebei region

The north Hebei region refers to cities of Zhangjiakou and Chengde located in the north of Hebei Province. This region serves as a crucial ecological barrier for the BTH Region, but is also concentrated with the largest impoverished population—ecological problems and the poverty issue intertwined. For many years, the State and the BTH Region have been enhancing policy support for its poverty relief and ecological building, resulting in evident results in poverty relief in the region with poverty incidence decreased from 21% in 2005 to 12% in 2015 and its ecological deterioration has also been curbed. Nevertheless, generally speaking, the overall development of the north Hebei region is still lagging behind, with prominent restrictions in infrastructure, talents and technology, and unstable foundation for poverty relief. It hasn't formed a pattern of which ecology protection and economic development can be achieved at the same time; its gap with surrounding regions is still widening; and it is the weakest link of BTH Regional economic development. In order to accelerate development of the north Hebei region, it is suggested continue regional poverty relief and build regional ecological barriers; meanwhile shift development pivot to speeding up narrowing development gaps with other regions, effectively easing conflicts between ecological environmental protection and sustainable development. Currently, strategic deployment such as the BTH coordinated development, hosting the Winter Olympic Games jointly by Beijing and Zhangjiakou, speeding up development of Hebei and north Hebei, precise poverty relief strategies by the State have provided new opportunities, injected new motivation and tapped into new vitality for development in the north Hebei region. The region should seize and make use of theses great strategic opportunities, themed at improving regional sustainable development ability, targeted at achieving ecology protection and economic development at the same time, advance north Hebei construction and regional poverty relief, expedite leaping development and green rising of the north Hebei region, strive for making it a new high ground for regional economic development of the BTH Region.

3.4.1 Seizing the opportunity of jointly hosting the Winter Olympic Games, construct Hebei's north wing of development

Beijing and Zhangjiakou will jointly host the 2022 Winter Olympic Games, which closely associates Zhangjiakou with the state image and interests and puts Zhangjiakou on the international arena. This will not only provide an unprecedented opportunity for Zhangjiakou to display itself to the world, and improve its international status, awareness and reputation; but also significantly benefit improvement of its investment environment, infrastructure improvement, cultivation of an opening-up undertaker, business and capital attraction, and development of industries related to Olympic Games; overall improve its competing advantages, service capability and development level. These will provide a historical opportunity for Zhangjiakou and the entire north Hebei region as a whole in fixing problems in development, improving regional image and realizing an overall leaping development. For this reason, it is suggested firmly grab this opportunity of jointly hosting the Olympic Games, spare no effort in generating and expanding Olympic economies, turn this historic opportunity into strong power for transformation and development, propel Zhangjiakou's opening up, development and green rising with this opportunity, making itself an internationally well-known "Olympic city" and the "north wing of Hebei" leading the development of the north Hebei region.

(1) Make great efforts in developing Olympic economies. According to business opportunity characteristics of the preparation, hosting and post-Olympic stage, relying on ecological advantages and development environmental advantages from hosting the Olympic Games, speed up the construction of a green industrial new system with the Winter Olympic Games as its brand, ecology as its foundation, innovation as its motivation and health as its feature; construct a new high ground of Olympic economies to lead a green transformation and high-end development of economies. Take full advantages of the Olympic Games to create a tourism industry centering on ice-snow industries and featured with Olympic charm; cultivate and expand Olympic related industries such as sports goods, recreation and retirement, cultural and sports expos; speed up Olympic extended industries such as finance and insurance, modern logistics, commercial and information service; develop urban modern agriculture, green and safe food refined processing industry that cater for the needs of Olympic Games; realize industrial replacement emphasizing on green economy and service economy. Make full use of the "Forced effect" formed from hosting the Olympic Games to expedite transformation and upgrading of traditional industries and absorbing

excessive capacity, achieving a high-end, low-carbon and intensive development. Make full use of the force generated from hosting the Olympic Games that drives forward technology and talent introduction and exchange, cultivate and introduce new participants, create innovation and entrepreneurship platforms, create a favorable innovation environment, develop high-end and high-tech industries and innovation economies.

(2) Spare no effort in creating an Olympic city. Seize the new opportunity brought by the Olympic Games of city construction and development, city brand improvement and all-around application of intelligent technology. Combine Olympic concept, requirements and standards with propelling the new-type urbanization process, integrating it into every detail of city planning, construction and management; bring out its taste; display its characteristics and livability; spare no effort in building an Olympic city that is internationally well-known and highly intelligent. Launch a new round of city construction with world vision and international standards; improve city layout step by step, improve functions of design, infrastructure, greening and beautifying to international standards; overall improve Zhangjiakou city functions and quality; create a brand new city image. Taking advantage of Beijing's open resources as a world city and an international platform such as local government united organizations; make efforts to build an international institutional environment, an international language environment and create a city atmosphere that promotes multicultural exchanges and integration; and improve international influence of the city brand. Accelerate building an "intelligent city" supporting system; actively advance the "intelligent life"; build a city intelligent management system; promote industrial intelligent development; create an intelligent city with overall awareness, ubiquitous interconnection and is highly intelligent.

(3) Make efforts in building an opening-up high ground. Making full use of the agglomeration effect and brand effect from hosting the Olympic Games, overall improve Zhangjiakou's level and capability in opening up, exchange and cooperation. Based on the great picture of BTH coordinated development, seizing the opportunity of co-hosting the Winter Olympic with Beijing, overall push forward infrastructural connectivity, industrial mutual complement and promotion, Beijing-Zhangjiakou joint eco-environmental protection and treatment, realizing "urban integration" development of Beijing and Zhangjiakou. Fully leveraging the great passageway role of inland bridgeheads, the north China hinterland east exit and the Asia-Europe continent south exit; build connectivity system for regional transportation passageways centering on Zhangjiakou; plan and construct various port groups and

opening-up undertaking groups; deepen exchanges and cooperation with Beijing, the Bohai-rim and surrounding inland areas; build an inland comprehensive doorway city facing Beijing and Tianjin, radiating Shanxi Province, Inner Mongolia Autonomous Region and Hebei Province. Meet the strategic requirements of an internationally well-known Olympic city; reinforce international regional economic cooperation undertaking development; construct a multifunctional and high-level international communicating platform; create an opening-up environment with higher standards and efficiency; improve Zhangjiakou's image as an opening-up city to the world; propel Zhangjiakou to integrate into the world economic industrial system.

(4) Strive to create a brand new image. Hosting the Winter Olympic Games has provided a great opportunity for Zhangjiakou to improve its city brand and set up a desirable international image. The city should take this opportunity to achieve "Olympic spirit, Olympic awareness, Olympic standards", change outdated notions and habitual thinking modes, and discard old inland mentality and inertness. It should aim for an innovation spirit, customs and impression of hospitality, an open and inclusive social atmosphere, and a people and business-friendly government image. It should encourage local culture to integrate and interact with regional cultures of its surroundings and imported and advanced cultures; optimize manners and improve its people's intelligence; rise up to the international standards; aim at a new-era Zhangjiakou spirit of "admiring integrity and loyalty, worshiping inclusiveness and harmony, being innovative and pioneering, opened-up and progressing". It should make use of hosting the Olympic Games to build cultural brand, county-level brand, park brand, enterprise brand and product brand, to improve the region's image to the outside world by building brands. It should deepen the "streamlining administration and delegating power, delegating and controlling at the same time, optimizing services" reform, facilitate administrative procedures, establish and guarantee rules of law, implement an administrative service system that fits market economy system operation, develop a government environment with high quality, high efficiency, openness and convenience.

3.4.2 Restructure regional development framework, achieving ecology protection and economic development at the same time

The north Hebei region is the main constituent of the BTH northwest ecological conservation area, and one of the regions with biggest developmental gap with Beijing and Tianjin. Its special regional ecological position and huge developmental gap mean that the north Hebei region has to expedite the economic-ecological transformation in a green and sustainable way while expanding ecological product supply and reinforcing regional ecological function. In recent years, in order to forward regional sustainable development, get rid of eco-environmental restrictions, all-level of governments in the north Hebei region have one by one started an economic-ecological transformation: Zhangjiakou has aimed at advancing green development and green rising with ecology as its core competitiveness; Chengde has aimed at expediting industrial transformation and upgrading with the guideline of ecological industrialization and industrial ecology, achieving green rising. But due to its spatial land use structure, industrial development system, urban development layout, and ecological development pattern, the region is far from meeting the requirements of its ecological function positioning and the needs of its economy's ecological transformation; its ecology has not fundamentally improved, and its transformation process towards an ecology-friendly economy moves slowly. Currently, the north Hebei region needs to re-develop the regional development strategic framework from a strategic height led by building a demonstration area with ecology-friendly economy, to transform its economy to an ecology-friendly one, achieving ecology protection and economic development at the same time.

(1) Construct a spatial land use system that fits ecological function positioning. For the north Hebei region to build ecological conservation areas, two preconditions are required: on the one hand, it needs sufficient ecological space; and on the other hand, it needs to achieve maximum ecological benefits in unit ecological space, with the former precondition as its basis and premise. As a result, it needs to consider the region's ecological position and land use foundation in an overall way, from the strategic height of overall improving the BTH Region's ecological safety function, restructure land use of the north Hebei region as soon as possible, and significantly reduce arable land coverage. At the same time, it should increase grassland coverage, and build a regional land structure mainly for ecological land use.

(2) Establish a green industrial system fits an ecology-friendly economy mode. Developing green industries and going down the path of transforming its economy to an ecology-friendly one is the objective requirement and inevitable choice of its development. For this reason, it needs to speed up cultivating big ecological industries such as ecological tourism, recreation, rehabilitation and retirement, economic forestry, green food; to excel in high-end equipment industries such as automobile and parts, machinery equipment manufacturing; to develop renewable energy industries such as wind power and photoelectricity; to develop a big data industry integrating storage, service, device manufacturing

and software; and to construct a green industrial system fits regional features and function requirements.

(3) Establish an urban development system that fits its resource and environmental bearing capability. The ecological environment of the north region is very fragile: less than 30% of its land is suitable for development and utilization. As a result, it should consider regional population size, migrating trend, urban foundation and ecological requirements; encourage population dispersed in ecologically fragile and sensitive regions to move to center villages with better conditions; encourage village population to move to designated towns, counties and center cities; encourage population in the region to move to towns and cities outside the region; establish a population allocating system centering on towns and cities; form an urban population distribution pattern equally consisted by center cities, towns and designated towns.

(4) Establish an ecology protection system that fits the need of ecological safety. It is the north Hebei region's core task to reinforce ecological functions of wind prevention and sand fixation, water source conservation, tourism and recreation, ecological product supply; to construct BTH ecological barrier, to provide quality ecological environment and services for the BTH Region. In order to reach this goal, it should build a sound forest protection system, grassland ecological system, wetland ecological system, water loss and soil erosion treatment system, water resources and energy exploitation and utilization system; it should build an ecological protection system integrating ecological barrier, resource exploitation and energy utilization.

3.4.3 Beef up precise policy support, contribute to the region's poverty relief

For many years, the State and Hebei Province have seen the north Hebei region as a crucial region for poverty relief, and for implementing strategies including development and poverty relief, regional poverty relief and precise poverty relief. With the poverty relief deployment effectively in place, life standard of population living in poverty in the region has been improved significantly, and situation in the poverty-stricken region has also been improved. But due to factors such as a fragile ecological environment, the north Hebei region is still most extensively and severely affected by poverty in the BTH Region, with the largest impoverished population. It is the home of some deeply impoverished counties such as Kangbao, Shangyi, Yangyuan, with prominent issues of high poverty incidence, low per-capita disposable income, weak collective economy and difficulty in increasing income for the impoverished population. It is a tough task for the region to achieve poverty relief. In order to lift population in the north Hebei region from poverty, eliminate all impoverished counties and provide solutions for poverty relief of the whole region under the State's existing standards, more intensive support should be given to the region and more effective poverty relief measures should be adopted, paying attention to both "blood transfusion and blood generation".Taking the opportunity of the BTH coordinated development and hosting the Winter Olympic Games, We should make great efforts in attracting greater support from the state and relevant parties in aspects related to the north region's development, such as infrastructure construction, industrial green transformation, ecological development investment, investment environment optimization and assistance system improvement. It needs to further improve the poverty relief system, to innovate poverty relief modes, to improve poverty relief methods, to intensify the cultivation of endogenous driving force, to tap into the region's endogenous vitality for poverty relief, and to improve impoverished populations' self-development ability.

(1) Support the north Hebei region's infrastructure construction. Taking the opportunity of hosting the Winter Olympic Games, it should accelerate function expansion and upgrading of infrastructure such as transportation, energy, water conservancy and environmental protection in Zhangjiakou and the north Hebei region as a whole, fundamentally consolidating the foundation of regional development. The same as the last round support for the region's infrastructure construction, it should continue to issue the *Zhangjiakou-Chengde region infrastructure construction planning*, and to support the infrastructure construction of the north Hebei region; it should provide subsidies and policy support for construction of "dead-end roads" between the Beijing-Tianjin region and impoverished villages in Hebei, and set up green passage for traffic approval.

(2) Support the north Hebei region's green industrial transformation. The State should mobilize relevant ministries and commissions, as well as Beijing and Tianjin to set up an industrial development fund for ecological water conservation for the development of green industries in the north Hebei region. Set up supportive funds such as green industry introducing fund, special fund; via methods such as direct subsidy for featured ecological industries, loan with discounted interest, land transfer subsidy, loan guarantee reward, labor transfer training subsidy, support high-end green industrial projects in the north Hebei region, and invest in green industries, as well as leading enterprises and cooperative organizations engaged in poverty relief and development. It should formulate more preferential supportive policies for clean energy industry and energy conservation and the environment protection industry, expand policies for the Zhangjiakou renewable energy

demonstration area to Chengde to support its intelligent and environment–friendly industrial bases.

(3) Beef up ecological construction of the northwest Hebei. Based on the special geographical environment and ecological protection needs of Bashang and the mountain area, rationally identify project planning and investment standards; improve the central government's subsidy standards in projects such as Beijing-Tianjin sand source treatment, Beijing-Hebei water source forest, water loss and soil erosion treatment, riverway treatment, afforestation, rural non-point pollution treatment, and drinking water project. Strive for more investment from the State in management and protection of forest, trees and grass; set up stable management and protection teams in the Zhangjiakou-Chengde region; so as to tackle the issue of "focusing on investment, neglecting management and protection".

(4) Support the north Hebei region in improving investment and approval efficiency. Taking the opportunity of carrying out investment approval reform pilot programs for Zhangjiakou Winter Olympic projects, it should support the north Hebei region to exam its own development reality and plan a batch of infrastructure and public service projects, projects related to Olympic venues and events, Olympic agricultural and sideline products production and deep processing projects, and clean energy guaranteeing projects, to list them into the Winter Olympic development projects for preferential policies in investment and approval. It should support the north Hebei region in deepening investment and approval system reform, draw experience from Jiangsu Province's anonymous approval (service) reform, optimize approval process, streamline approval procedures, improve approval efficiency, explore the "north Hebei" template that innovates administrative service approval and reform.

(5) Improve the partner assistance mechanism. It should improve Beijing and Tianjin's mechanism in assisting the north Hebei region, innovate work methods and means, strive for Beijing and Tianjin's assistance in capital, projects and personnel, explore partner poverty relief new modes of "co-construction and sharing" and "enclave economy". It should initiate partner assistance actions between leading enterprises and impoverished villages, create connecting and communicating platforms between them, facilitate two-way partnership and free choice between leading enterprises in Beijing, Tianjin, other regions and impoverished villages, guide leading enterprises to carry out poverty relief and development projects based on their own developmental needs and impoverished villages' industrial characteristics and development potential.

(6) Identify precise point of strength and point of force for poverty relief. The impoverished population that is featured

with "the old, the disadvantaged, the sick and the disabled" of the north Hebei region is concentrated in the mountain barrier area. It should further identify the focus and direction of precise poverty relief, and facilitate its implementation according to locations and individuals. For population living in areas with extreme natural conditions, it should intensify assistance in moving them out; for population living in no-development areas and development-restricted areas with fragile ecological environment, it should increase posts of public interests like rangers; it should intensify medical assistance, temporary assistance and charity assistance for impoverished population due to diseases; for families that are not able to get rid of poverty with industrial assistance and employment assistance, it should provide policy guarantee. Impoverished counties should lay emphasis on developing industries that can benefit impoverished population. Its transportation projects should be close to village households; its water conservancy projects should benefit impoverished villages and small-sized agricultural production; and its ecological protection project should improve impoverished population's engagement and interest.

(7) Innovate modes and methods of precise poverty relief. Targeted at improving self-development ability of impoverished population, it should promote new modes of poverty relief such as "tourism+" poverty relief, "internet+" poverty relief, "PV+ poverty relief"; explore and improve poverty relief methods such as "insurance policy for impoverished households shared by the government, the bank and the insurance company", "branch+ association + rural households", "share cooperation", "industries allocated to households", "bundled loan". It should extensively adopt poverty relief mechanism such as production reward and subsidy, labor subsidy, work-for-the-dole, supporting and encouraging impoverished population to get rid of poverty by hard work. It should facilitate dynamic integration and mutual facilitation and common progress between poverty relief, development and modern agricultural development, beautiful villages, making the rural population rich, the agriculture strong, and the village beautiful.

3.5 Emphasizing on constructing an integrated traffic hub, fast and convenient road network, optimize regional traffic network structural layout, expedite the traffic integration of the BTH Region

The Program Outline for the Coordinated Development of the BTH Region explicitly sets out the need to expedite the traffic integration of the BTH Region and build a multi-connection, net-like and all-inclusive traffic network with rail at its core.

Traffic integration is the "main skeleton" of the BTH coordinated development, the pioneer in undertaking non-capital functions and regional industrial connection and coordination; it is the solid support for building the world-class BTH city cluster. In recent years, the State and the BTH Region have achieved desirable progress in advancing breakthroughs in traffic; however, the BTH traffic integration is still confronted with pressing issues such as unsmooth traffic network connection, uncoordinated planning, construction and management. There is still a big gap for achieving goals of "planning according to the drawing", "construction with the same pace", "integrated transportation", and "coordinated management". Hebei Province should seize opportunities, lay emphasis on coordinated requirements, innovate methods and means, accelerate the BTH traffic integration, forming a modern integrated traffic network pattern underpinning the BTH coordinated development as soon as possible.

3.5.1 Centering on Xiong'an New Area in developing a rapid and efficient traffic network, create a one-hour commuting circle between regional center cities

One of the key tasks of Xiong'an New Area's planning and construction is to develop a rapid and efficient traffic network, and create a green traffic system. It is to demand new and higher standards from traffic infrastructure construction in the BTH Region and improve transportation's comprehensive capacity; it also provides unprecedented opportunities for optimizing traffic function layout in the BTH Region and improving regional traffic network. In order to meet Xiong'an's needs in integrated traffic, regional traffic, rapid traffic, commuting traffic, the State will plan and construct a new batch of key traffic infrastructure projects and speed up key traffic infrastructure work that is relevant. This will deeply change the BTH Region's transportation development pattern and exert all-around, in-depth and systematic impact on Hebei Province, especially Xiong'an's surroundings.

Hebei needs to seize this historic opportunity, to overall plan the New Area's needs in transportation security, to plan and implement a number of key traffic infrastructure projects in advance; it needs to maximally optimize regional traffic facility layout and to improve regional transportation network. At present, it should focus on four aspects: (1)Centering on intercity railway and express highway, taking the BTH Region's economic and social development, world-class city cluster construction, and regional function layout optimization into full consideration, speed up the process of building a fast and convenient traffic network that connects Xiong'an and Beijing, Tianjin, as well as other cities nearby; create a "half an hour" commenting radius between the New

Area and its surrounding cities such as Beijing, Tianjin, Shijiazhuang and Langfang, form a "0.5 to 1 hour" traffic network between neighborhood center cities of the BTH Region. (2)Targeting Xiong'an's opening up and development needs, plan and construct new express mainline roads and integrated traffic hubs throughout the province; improve express highway, trunk highway network between Xiong'an and the outside, especially backbone traffic lines from Xiong'an to the east coastal area, the south plain area and the west mountain area; study, connect and reserve existing key roads. (3) Plan to advance construction between key towns and cities such as Xushui, Baigou, Gaoyang, Bazhou, Renqiu, and Gaobeidian, as well as function areas with Xiong'an, and put in place traffic integration planning, same-standard pairing, same-pace construction, same-city development. (4) Following closely progress of Xiong'an's green traffic development, simultaneously advance green traffic system development in areas surrounding Xiong'an; establish green, advanced and intelligent traffic system together with Xiong'an, push forward it's green traffic and extend it to a wider areas.

3.5.2 Speed up construction of Beijing's surrounding traffic hubs, optimize regional traffic hub function layout

Currently, the railway, highway and airline in the BTH Region have formed a radiating traffic network layout centering on Beijing, with lack of connectivity between individual cities. This transportation pattern not only overloads Beijing as a traffic hub with huge traffic burden, but also interrupts Hebei's traffic in every direction and severely hinders transportation efficiency of the BTH Region. Although the Central government and the region have deployed thoroughly in regional road network layout and traffic hub layout, regional traffic network layout has yet fully demonstrated a desirable result in alleviating Beijing's burden as a traffic hub and easing its transit pressure. This is neither good for forming a regional traffic integrated network, nor in alleviating Beijing's traffic pressure, even worse for development of key connection cities of Hebei near Beijing and Tianjin.

The core of optimizing BTH integrated transportation hub layout and restructuring the regional traffic hub function is to alleviate Beijing's overloaded traffic function and change the pattern of Beijing as a singular center. The key is to expedite development of traffic hubs outside Beijing and to improve traffic hub function of other cities: from "singular center" to "multiple centers", from "radiating" to "network", forming a distributary integrated traffic hub system with multiple supporting points. (1)Build Shijiazhuang as the "third pole" of the BTH traffic, and form a three-region transportation center of Beijing, Tianjin and Shijiazhuang. From both traffic foundation, spatial location, time and spatial distance, and population, economy and industrial factors, Shijiazhuang is advantageous over other Hebei cities in generating passenger and goods transportation demands; and it is fully capable of serving as the third traffic hub in the BTH Region and an integrated distributary traffic hub south of Beijing and Tianjin. As a result, it is compel to improve Shijiazhuang airport's transportation function and capability, to enhance dynamic connection of facilities such as railway, highway and airline, to realize multi-means point transportation of goods, and to improve its city integrated traffic function, turning it into the "third pole" of the BTH traffic as soon as possible. (2)Strengthen regional connection towns and cities' traffic hub function. It should accelerate construction of three national integrated traffic hubs of Shijiazhuang, Tangshan and Qinhuangdao, strive for the central government-level support in making Zhangjiakou, Chengde and Cangzhou distributary traffic hubs of northwest, northeast and southeast of Beijing and Tianjin, and transfer Beijing and Tianjin's traffic hub function to a wider area. It should overall improve transit traffic distributary function of Beijing's peripheral towns and cities such as Zhuozhou, Huailai, Bazhou and Langfang, to distribute Beijing's passenger and goods transportation to a closer distance. (3)Focusing on the Xiong'an New Area's integrated traffic needs, combining Beijing's new airport construction, plan a modern integrated traffic hub with railway, highway, airport and rail transportation; improve integrated traffic capability of the big-triangular region of Beijing, Tianjin and the Xiong'an New Area. (4)Usher in a second transportation passageway inside the Shanhaiguan Pass. Strengthen construction of the great passageway of Zhangjiakou-Chengde-Shenyang and Cangzhou-Tangshan-Shenyang; transfer transit traffic trunk lines in Beijing and Tianjin city center to regions between them; alleviate Beijing and Tianjin's transit pressure from inside and outside the Shanghaiguan Pass.

3.5.3 Connect dead-end roads and further improve connectivity of regional road network

It is a key task for the traffic to connect dead-end roads for a convenient and complete highway traffic network. At present, the BTH Region has achieved concrete progress in connecting dead-end roads: connection and expansion projects of multiple roads such as the Beijing-Taiwan express highway and the Beijing-Hong Kong-Macao express highway have been completed; a number of dead-end roads such as the Cangzhou-Hebei-Shandong section of the Beijing-Shanghai express highway and the Langyashan-Pocang section of the Rongwu express highway have been serving the traffic. But in reality, although goals and planning of traffic integration have been set up, and the State and the region are devoted to facilitating traffic road network' connectivity, issues such as disconnected traffic planning and management, unsynchronized plan and practice, and disconnection still present. Traffic connectivity in the BTH Region requires not only well-connected hardware facilities, but also well-functioned systems and mechanisms. Meanwhile, dead-end roads in villages and counties and traffic disconnection caused by the"1 km barrier" also need to be tackled urgently. To connect dead-end roads in the BTH Region, both "arterial mainlines" at the State and province level, and "capillary lines" at the village and county level need to be connected.

For this purpose, three aspects need to be worked on. The first is improving the traffic integration advancing mechanism. Drawing experience from developed countries in developing urban circles and city clusters, facilitate a traffic integration mechanism with more authority and binding effect, overall coordinate crucial issues in trans-regional transportation, advance inter-provincial and inter-city traffic facility planning, construction and management; supervise and press the region to put traffic planning, deployment and construction in place. The second is unifying traffic facility planning and construction. With overall traffic infrastructure planning and layout, overall traffic routes study and development, overall implementing plans, overall technology and construction standards, it should promote an complete integration in proposals, construction arrangement and technological standards, ensuring that traffic facilities in the region are constructed under the same standard with same procedures. The third is improving regional road network connectivity. It should expedite dead-end road connectivity in counties and cities surrounding and inside Beijing and Tianjin, improving levels and standards of trunk highway at the State and province level; it should improve connecting lines between express highway and truck highway, counties, new cities and key function areas, strengthen connection between inside and outside passageways in impoverished areas, outstretch rural highway's coverage and servicing capacity, connect regional traffic capillaries, and make better use of road network's overall efficiency.

3.5.4 Complete rail traffic network as soon as possible, jointly create "BTH Region on the rail"

Building an efficient and intensive traffic network can significantly secure Beijing's non-capital function transfer, as well as industries and population transfer; it can support its participation in productivity layout and function restructuring in a wider region; and it is a key priority in the BTH modern integrated traffic system development. But from the existing rail traffic foundation in the BTH and issued traffic planning and deployment, the region still presents problems in rail traffic planning and construction. In order to build an efficient and intensive rail traffic network and "BTH on the rail", these problems need to be fixed urgently.

(1) Accelerate Beijing's inter-city suburban railway. From international experience, metropolitan suburban railway tends to extend to nearby towns and cities outside its boundary. They tend to construct thousands of kilometers of suburban railway in the radius of 50-70 km to support commuters from the metropolitan circle; for example, the New York metropolitan circle has a railway coverage of more than 3,000 km, Paris over 1,800 km, London over 3,600 km and Tokyo over 2,000 km. In terms of inter-city suburban railway in Beijing, currently only the Pinggu Line has just initiated its work; other railways are mostly still at the level of intention and concepts. In order to fix Beijing's inter-city suburban railway construction problems from the height of creating modern new-type metropolitan circle, it should accelerate rail traffic connection between Beijing and its surrounding counties and cities, coordinate and facilitate Beijing's light railway and metro lines to extend to Yanjiao, Gu'an, Langfang, Zhuozhou; construct suburban railway to Sanhe, Dachang, Xianghe, Yongqing, Baigou, Luanping, and Laishui; it should make full use of excessive capacity of existing railway and passenger transportation lines, open trans-regional suburban express lines, and form a metropolitan inter-city rail traffic network with a radius of 50-70 km.

(2) Facilitate Hebei's inter-city railway and suburban railway construction. Hebei's existing railway transportation system mainly serves long-distance passenger transportation. Its inter-city railway construction has just started and is not able to meet the need of intensive and fast short and medium-distance traveling, especially that a fast and efficient passenger passageway between northwest Hebei and middle and south Hebei, east Hebei has not yet been built. In order to fix problems in Hebei's inter-city railway construction, it should speed up main passageway and regional connecting line projects of the high-speed railway network inside Hebei, develop inter-city railway between center cities in Hebei, plan and construct a fast and efficient passenger way between northwest Hebei and middle and south Hebei, east Hebei. It should consider development needs and economic power of individual cities, advance metro lines, urban and suburban railway lines between center cities and new cities, satellite cities stage by stage; it should increase pace in building a highly-intensive, multi-level and convenient inter-city and intra-city rail traffic network; so as to meet the need of short-distance intensive and

fast traveling.

(3) Construct railway assembling and evacuating great passageway connecting harbors and inland. Currently, planning and layout of Hebei's harbor assembling and evacuating railway system is not complete. Its assembling and evacuating capability is under-developed and its transportation structure is not reasonable. It is not well connected with inland passageways, especially lacking of heavy-load railway transportation passageways directly to the west and the north. In order to fix harbor railway's problem of imbalanced assembling and evacuating functions, it should strengthen harbor assembling and evacuating capability, especially in assembling and evacuating passageways construction between coastal harbor cluster and inland center cities. It should enhance effective connection with airports and land ports in Beijing and Tianjin, strenthen communication and integration with goods source inland of the middle, west and north region. It should plan to build great inland passageways from Huanghua harbor to middle and south Shanxi, northwest Shandong and even to middle Asia and Europe; from Tangshan harbor to Shanxi, Inner Mongolia, Shaanxi and the far east region of Russia; from Qinhuangdao harbor to east Inner Mongolia; build key outlet to the sea for the "New Silk Road" and great trade passageway for BTH outward economic development.

(4) Establish a diversified and sustainable rail traffic investment and financing mode. Rail traffic construction has a huge need for capital, merely the four inter-city railways in the BTH Region costs more than 100 billion yuan. Government revenue alone is not enough; it is thus in urgent need to seek for new paths of financing from the society. It should give full play to function of main investors such as the BTH inter-city railway investment company, seek to establish a balanced-benefit and cost-sharing mechanism in BTH rail traffic construction, operation and management. It should promote the application of the "rail traffic + land comprehensive development" mode, improve land comprehensive development supporting measures along the BTH inter-city rail traffic, inject capital to rail traffic's construction and operation with land development revenue. It should support the social capital to be invested in rail traffic's construction and operation solely or jointly, promote the PPP mode, raise construction fund via methods such as franchising and equity cooperation.

3.6 Stressing on creating an innovation environment, set up an innovation ecological system that attracts innovation resource factors, and create a BTH coordinated innovation community

Innovation is the first driving force of development and the strategic support of modern economic system construction. Taking opportunity of innovation resources of Beijing and Tianjin and the Xiong'an New Area in the future, making use of the great trend of coordinated development and fixing problems in technology and innovation are strategic choices and best paths to realize economic transformation and upgrading. In recent years, centering on creating the BTH coordinated innovation community, Hebei Province has issued a series of policies and measures, built a number of undertakers and platforms, and formed a number of modes and templates of coordinated innovation; it thus has achieved preliminary results in attracting innovation factors from Beijing and Tianjin to Hebei. But overall, as Hebei doesn't have undertaking platforms corresponding to functions, facilities, services and environment of Beijing and Tianjin, and policy environment, institution design, supporting services and factor support that fits development need of Beijing and Tianjin's innovation factors, it is still facing quite a few problems and barriers in advancing the coordinated innovation with Beijing and Tianjin. Innovation talents from Beijing and Tianjin are not willing to come to Hebei and innovation results cannot be transferred. For Hebei to join Beijing and Tianjin in creating a coordinated innovation community and making use of coordinated innovation to improve its innovation development capability, it is key and fundamental to improve its innovative ecological system as soon as possible and optimize both software and hardware innovation environment, maximally improve its attraction and undertaking capacity of innovation factors from Beijing and Tianjin.

3.6.1 Spare no effort in making Xiong'an an internationally first-class high ground for innovation environment

Becoming a leading region in innovation-driven development, an innovation high ground and technology new city, China's "Silicon Valley" and an international innovation center are key historical missions of the Xiong'an New Area. From development experience of same-kind regions in other countries, the underlying reasons that Silicon Valley has become a hub of innovation factors from all-around the world and the synonym for innovation; and the reason that Shenzhen is the "city of innovation" and "capital of innovation talents" are their quality living environment, efficient innovation institution, beneficial innovation policy, and open and inclusive innovation culture, as well as an energetic and appealing innovation environment due to its integration, and innovation atmosphere that actively seeks for innovation. For Xiong'an to build a leading region where development is driven by innovation and to build an innovation high ground and technology new city, the key is to create an innovation and entrepreneurial environment with global influence and appeal and to create an internationally first-class innovation environment high ground where innovation factors highly concentrate, innovation vitality interact and innovation results effectively protected and innovation value fully show.

For this reason, emphasis should be laid on the following four aspects:(1)Create a more comfortable and livable environment. Aiming at the overall requirements of world vision, international standards, Chinese characteristics, high-point positioning, adapt to the new trend, new features of innovation-driven development of modern cities; spare no effort in building a green and intelligent new city with most-advanced notion and internationally first-class standards; provide good ecological environment, high-standard public services; develop a fast and efficient traffic network; plan and construct Xiong'an into a modern city that is green and low-carbon, intelligent and highly efficient, environment-friendly and livable, with good services. (2)Create a policy environment with more vitality and magnetic attraction. Encourage policy innovation boldly; develop special talent policy, population and housing policy that fit the need of innovation development; put in place basic public services and social security policy of the same standard of Beijing; complete innovation incentive policies such as technology R&D, transferring and trading, achievement incubating and transformation; implement more preferential innovation assistance policies of land, finance and investment; integrate high-standard innovation policies home and abroad such as Zhongguancun as a pilot pioneer, and establish appealing innovation policy system with accumulated policies. (3)Create a more relaxed and eased institutional environment. Overall deepen reform of innovation institution and mechanism; formulate a motivating and innovative market competition mechanism, and a coordinated mechanism led by enterprises; encourage interest-oriented mechanism of innovation achievements, scientific and flexible talent development mechanism, streamlined innovation resources introducing mechanism, diversified innovation investment and financing mechanism, and affordable housing security mechanism; bring the market's decisive role in allocating innovation resources into full play and maximally stimulate innovation passion and potential of all major participants. (4)Create an open environment that is more diversified and inclusive. With broader global vision, more proactive cooperation will, an all-inclusive heart, actively seek for a higher-level open innovation mode; progress a deeply integrated and open innovation mechanism;

form innovation rules and system with international standards; focus on creating an open and sharing market environment with fair competition; intensively cultivate an innovation culture of "adventurous, innovative, aspirational and failure-tolerant"; create an innovation atmosphere that is open and cooperative; develop in diversified, inclusive and harmonious way; integrate itself into global innovation network, absorb global innovation resources, drive forward innovation development nationwide and even worldwide.

3.6.2 Establish and improve an innovation ecological system that attracts innovation resources and factors from Beijing and Tianjin

Beijing and Tianjin are concentrated with talent resources, innovation factors and innovation achievements. Their innovation resources account for half of those in the scientific field, and cover every link of the innovation chain and involve an extensive innovation area. They are high ground of international influence and attract all sorts of innovation factors. For Hebei Province, making good and full use of Beijing and Tianjin's innovation resources, sharing and using their innovation factors and achievements for its own needs are core tasks of jointly building a coordinated innovation community with Beijing and Tianjin, as well as the best way to improve its own innovation development ability. Considering Hebei's existing foundation for innovation platform development, its gradient differences in innovation environment with Beijing and Tianjin, and higher requirements from Beijing and Tianjin in innovation factors transferring and transformation; in order to make good and full use of Beijing and Tianjin's innovation resources, it has to establish an more dynamic, and appealing innovation ecosystem, bring innovation main participants, innovation undertakers, innovation policies and innovation mechanism together, tap into more vitality, close the gap with Beijing and Tianjin, create both a software and a hardware environment that attract innovation talents and for innovation achievements to incubate and transform, and form a strong magnetic force that attracts innovation resources and factors from Beijing and Tianjin.

(1) Create a high-end undertaking platform for innovation resources and factors from Beijing and Tianjin. On the one hand, it needs to strive to improve existing strategic and symbolic coordinated innovation platform. Following confirmed function positioning and task requirements, matching Beijing and Tianjin for innovation eco-environment of high-end innovation undertaker, expedite construction of coordinated innovation platforms such as the Shijiazhuang-Baoding-Langfang overall innovation and reform pilot area, the Hebei-south Beijing national scientific achievements transferring and transformation

demonstration area, and the capital-rim modern agriculture and technology demonstration zone; improve innovation infrastructure and innovation service ability; optimize innovation policy and government environment; develop a quality innovation and entrepreneurship ecology; make full use of its reputation as "state-level"; maximally play out its leading, radiating and driving role in coordinated innovation. On the other hand, it needs to continue cooperating with Beijing and Tianjin in jointly creating an innovation and entrepreneurship undertaker. Draw experience from joint construction of parks; emphasize on introducing innovation notions, innovation new modes and innovation genes from Beijing and Tianjin; strengthen innovation cooperation with technological parks and technological and research institutions in Beijing and Tianjin; adopt modes such as "multiple parks in one area", "HQ-bases", "whole hosting", and "innovation chain cooperation"; jointly construct a number of high-end technology parks, science and research institutions; and jointly set up a number of high-end technology parks and bases for technology achievements transformation; make full use of linked effects, spread effect and demonstration effect of the cooperation parks.

(2) Create an industry-chain supporting environment that efficiently connects with the innovation chain of Beijing and Tianjin. It is a general rule of technology innovation for technology achievements to be incubated and transformed in surrounding area; however, those in Beijing are mostly skipping Hebei. It is mainly due to Hebei's under-developed industrial supporting ability, and weak complement and loose relationship between its industrial chain and the innovation chain in Beijing and Tianjin. As a result, Hebei needs to focus on developing industrial chain supporting ability, to improve industrial chain supporting conditions as soon as possible, to seek for effective modes for integrated development of its industrial chain and Beijing and Tianjin's innovation chain, to create an industrial-chain supporting environment that efficiently connects Beijing and Tianjin's innovation chain. It should make efforts in three aspects. a. Aim for new innovation sources in Beijing and Tianjin, target Beijing and Tianjin's innovation chain needs; plan and introduce related industrial chain projects in advance; cultivate and develop high-end industries corresponding to Beijing and Tianjin's technology achievements transformation. b. Aim for emerging industry's development, via modes such as joint development, advantage complementation, interest sharing, risk sharing; cooperate with backbone enterprises, science and research institutions, technology agents in Beijing and Tianjin; jointly form regional industrial technology and innovation strategic alliance. c.

Centering on traditional industries' transformation and upgrading needs, via methods such as jointly building, aiding and setting up branch institutions, jointly build technology platforms such as key lab, engineering and technological innovation center, enterprise technology innovation center, and industrial technology institutions.

(3) Form an innovation and entrepreneurship ecology concentrated with innovation talents and factors. In order to attract high-end innovation factors from Beijing and Tianjin to stay and develop in Hebei, it has to create a more favorable policy environment, cultivate all kinds of innovation and entrepreneurship platforms, establish institutions of innovation talent recruitment, remuneration, review, scientific research management, social security, with the same standards of Beijing and Tianjin; set up a service system integrating finance, living, technology, law, information and acceleration; form innovation and entrepreneurship ecology gathering innovation talents and factors from Beijing and Tianjin. (1) Relying on high-end parks such as high-tech areas, create a new type of technological enterprise incubator featured with "start-up nursery + incubator + accelerator" together with Beijing and Tianjin, to undertake Beijing and Tianjin's functions of technology achievements incubating, transformation and industrialization. (2) Centering on industrial needs and chain extension, cooperate with well-known makerspace in Beijing and Tianjin; build various types of makerspace with distinctive disciplinary traits and targeted needs; attract innovation talents from Beijing and Tianjin to Hebei to conduct innovation and start business in Hebei. (3) Choose qualified areas to cooperate and introduce strategic investors with big scientific research institutions and key universities and colleges in Beijing and Tianjin; cultivate and construct several featured innovative towns; and attract Beijing's innovation resources and intelligent factors.

(4) Establish policy and institutional system for trans-regional technology achievements transfer and transformation. Facilitating technology achievements in Beijing and Tianjin to be transferred to and transformed in Hebei is the task for Hebei to advance construction of coordinated innovation community and the realistic choice to realize industrial restructuring and transformation and upgrading. Hebei needs to cater for the realistic needs of technology achievements transfer, transformation, and industrialization of Beijing and Tianjin, to seek for cooperation paths for trans-regional technology achievements transfer and transformation platforms, to establish new modes undertaking Beijing and Tianjin's overflow and transferred innovation factors. It needs to integrate and transfer Hebei's industrial and innovation needs, to complete institutions and mechanisms for trans-regional technology

achievements industrialization and capitalization, to improve trans-regional technology achievements transfer and transformation service system. It needs to follow the lead of the Shijiazhuang-Baoding-Langfang all-around innovation reform pilot area, to rely on the Hebei-south Beijing national inter-regional technology achievements transfer and transformation demonstration area, to push forward early implementation and early experiment of coordinated innovation institution and mechanism's reform and policies, to come up with a number of feasible policies and measures in trans-regional technology trading, enterprise transfer, achievements transformation, resources sharing, talents importing, and in technology and finance, and to advance in formulating coordinated innovation policies and an institution system featured with "R&D in Beijing and Tianjin, transformation in Hebei".

3.6.3 Create a policy, institution and market environment integrating with Beijing and Tianjin

Building fair and unified regional innovation policies, a coordinated and unified regional innovation system and an open and unified regional innovation market are key premises for innovation factors to flow freely in the BTH Region and for their optimized allocation. But looking at the reality in the BTH Region, innovation policy for Beijing's Zhongguancun national independent innovation demonstration area enjoys the most favorable policies in the country; innovation dividends received by the Binhai New Area in Tianjin thanks to the policy of "prior to carry and try" is out of reach for Hebei. There is a quite big gap between Hebei and Beijing and Tianjin as for innovation policy and environment. At the same time, influenced by the administrative system and the mentality of preserving existing interests, Beijing, Tianjin and Hebei have formed comparatively independent regional innovation system of their own; therefore, innovation coordination in the BTH Region is insufficient and the connection is loose; an unified and open coordinated innovation institution and mechanism, and market system are not yet established. These have resulted in innovation competition in the region, which has hindered innovation efficiency and blocked innovation factors' free flow, open sharing and optimized allocation in the region.

For innovation resources to flow from Beijing and Tianjin to Hebei, technological enterprises to move to Hebei, and technology achievements to be transformed to Hebei, Hebei's gap with Beijing and Tianjin in innovation policy needs to be closed, integration with Beijing and Tianjin's innovation policies has to be achieved; barriers in institution and mechanism have to be eliminated; and its innovation institution and market need to match those of Beijing and Tianjin. (1)Facilitate innovation policy integration with Beijing and Tianjin. Establish an integrated innovation policy system; systematically look into supporting policies of Beijing and Tianjin in talents, achievements, platforms, high-tech enterprises, innovation SMEs; advance overall integration with Beijing and Tianjin's innovation policies; drive innovation policies such as the Zhongguancun national independent innovation development demonstration area, the Tianjin national independent innovation development demonstration area and the Tianjin national free trade pilot area to spread and implement in Hebei. (2) Advance a coordinated innovation institution with those in Beijing and Tianjin. Create innovation institutional environment for regional innovation factors to flow freely and technology achievements to transform efficiently; establish a BTH coordinated innovation joint conference system and form a normalized and standardized innovation communication and coordination mechanism; establish a mutual recognition mechanism for high-tech technological enterprises, technological SMEs and innovation platforms in Beijing, Tianjin and Hebei; promote an institution of unified innovation coupon system and government procurement of high-tech products; improve the open mechanism for regional innovation resources and achievements sharing, and the interest sharing mechanism of shared funds, platforms, parks, bases and transformation. (3)Push for a unified innovation market with Beijing and Tianjin. Build an innovation market that is open to and shared by Beijing, Tianjin and Hebei; push to build a technology trading market fȯr BTH connectivity; develop unified technology and information standards, trading service process, technology transfer service norms; build innovation talents service and information network of connectivity; advance trans-regional optimized allocation of BHT talent resources; build technological SMEs equity trading market of connectivity; create platforms where Beijing and Tianjin's technological achievements and Hebei's market needs can be effectively integrated and traded.

3.7 Speeding up the supply-side reform of public services, push forward joint development and sharing of public services and realize a balanced BTH public services

Equalized public services is the premise for production factors to flow freely in the region following economic rules, realizing spatial rational allocation and improving economic development quality and benefits. In terms of the BTH Region, high quality public service resources in the region are overly concentrated in Beijing and Tianjin, and the huge gap between Hebei and Beijing and Tianjin severely hinder the free flow and rational allocation of production factors such as population, capital and technology in the region. As a result, concentrating high-end public services, advancing public service joint development and sharing, and realizing inter-regional balanced public service are inevitable practices in realizing positive regional interaction in alleviating Beijing's non-capital functions, and promoting common development of the three places. From international experience, such as the liberalism public service equalization mode in Anglo-Saxon countries, the conservatism public service equalization mode represented by Germany and France, the social democracy public service equalization mode represented by Scandinavian countries, and the compulsory savings public service equalization mode represented by Singapore, these countries mainly stress government's main participant responsibility in basic public service supply to advance rational allocation of inter-regional financial power, and to realize basic public service equalization. Some countries diversify main suppliers via improving high-end public service' market engagement, to meet the public's need for high-end public services (see Table 3). From Hebei's reality, the main task at this moment is to solve the problem of insufficient public service supply. As provincial financial power, Hebei is not able to afford the huge expenses of public services and it won't be improved effectively; in order to narrow the gap with Beijing and Tianjin, it needs to make full use of international experience to speed up public service' supply side reform, to advance joint building and sharing with Beijing and Tianjin, to make breakthroughs in key regions and fields first, to set up public service pilots, to encourage and support social capital to participate in public service supply, to strive for measures such as State financial transfer and payment, to improve Hebei's public service quality as soon as possible via optimizing regional high-quality public service resources allocation.

Table 3 Supply modes of mainstream developed countries and regions

Mode	Main practice
Liberalism basic public service equalization mode in Anglo-Saxon countries	In the field of basic public services, for example, Canada achieves basic public service equalization by realizing provincial financing equalization. Meanwhile, it stresses on playing the role of market mechanism in fields such as preliminary education, public culture, and social security; with government purchasing the service, introduce competition and incentive mechanism in basic public service supply fields, and improve public service ' s supply efficiency.

continued

Mode	Main practice
Conservatism basic public service equalization mode represented by Germany and France	For basic public services, Germany sets up a relatively stable balanced transfer payment mechanism combining horizontal transfer payment and vertical transfer payment to ensure that its citizen can enjoy equal basic public services nationwide. Meanwhile, it facilitates the country, the society and the market to form a partnership in providing public services; for example, in social security management, Germany implements the management institution of high autonomy of the employer and the employee, with supervision by the government. Except for unemployment insurance, social insurance institution engages both the employer and the employee with autonomous management.
Social democracy basic public service equalization mode represented by Scandinavian countries	"Fair" as the prioritized value, the State is the main participant that bears direct responsibility and obligation providing security to all of its citizens in every aspect. Governments of these countries bear direct financial responsibility as well as responsibility of implementing, managing and supervising public service. At the same time, these countries have a large number of public service programs with high reward standards; programs cover all the welfare needs of each social member from "the cradle to the grave". Individuals usually bear no or little costs.
Compulsory savings basic public service equalization mode represented by Singapore	Stress on self-support and self-dependence. The State forces individuals or households to save to secure themselves via legislation, plus leak filling and safety net, eventually realizes public service equalization in the whole society.

Note: quoted from the Social and Cultural Teaching and Research Division of the National Administrative Institution, *International Experience in Advancing Basic Public Service Equalization*, China Economic Times, August 5, 2013.

3.7.1 Taking the opportunity of developing the Xiong'an New Area, advance allocation of quality public service resources in Beijing and Tianjin to Hebei

Uneven allocation of regional quality public service resources is the main factor contributing to the huge gap between Beijing, Tianjin and Hebei in public service; therefore, advancing quality public service resources in Beijing and Tianjin to be transferred and allocated to Hebei is a crucial means in tackling the issue. In April 2017, the CPC and the State Council have made the great strategic decision to set up the

Hebei Xiong'an New Area, building an area centralized in undertaking Beijing's non-capital functions. While focusing on undertaking some of the central administrative bodies, enterprise and public institutions, it also undertakes public service institutions such as education, medicare, and culture. This will provide rare opportunities of optimizing quality public service resources allocation between Hebei and Beijing and Tianjin, improving proportion of Hebei's quality public service resources.

Hebei Province needs to firmly grab this crucial opportunity to assist Beijing in identifying key factors to undertake, to strengthen integration, to develop supporting policy for introduced institutions, to orderly undertake Beijing's quality public service resources, and to tackle the problem of insufficient quality public service resources in the province. (1)Identify key undertaking points of quality public service resources. Overall integrate the guideline and the list of Beijing's non-capital functions; closely follow Beijing's public service institutions' moving schedules; achieve breakthroughs in undertaking universities and colleges directly under the direct administration of the Ministry of Education, key grade Ⅲ class A hospitals, science and research institutions and public communications institutions under the direct administration of the central government; improve the overall level of Hebei's higher education, high-end medical services, cutting-edge technological R&D and modern communications and media. (2) Seek for establishing an integrating institution for undertaking Beijing's non-capital functions. Establishing the Xiong'an administration committee and the Beijing government regular joint conference system; advance timely communication and coordination of both parties in public service institution's moving and construction; jointly negotiate and study targeted solutions regarding prominent issues in the moving and construction of transferred projects; provide institutional guarantee for Beijing's public service institutions to complete their undertaking task smoothly. (3) Study and develop corresponding policies for public service institution's transfer and development. Based on their needs, study and develop guidance for undertaking Beijing's non-capital functions; provide all-around support for transferred institutions in land, facility, finance, investment, taxation and HR; make sure that public service institutions from Beijing are willing to come, stay and are able to thrive.

3.7.2 Focusing on areas undertaking Beijing and Tianjin's functions and industries, advance public service equalization pilot projects

Realizing public service equalization in the BTH Region is a prolonged and complex systematic project. With limited resources and capital, Hebei is not able to improve its overall public service level; therefore, it is a more rational choice to try public service equalization pilot projects in key areas and then roll them out in the entire region. Featured towns (micro-centers) undertaking Beijing's non-capital functions in Hebei, as well as key areas undertaking Beijing and Tianjin's transferred industries such as the Caofeidian BTH coordinated development demonstration area, the Bohai New Area bio-medicine industrial park, and the Cangzhou development area automobile industrial parks, are major undertakers of Beijing and Tianjin's functions and industries and are strategic underpinning points to facilitate self-development. They are endowed with favorable conditions in BTH public service joint development and sharing; so that setting up public service equalization pilot projects in these areas will be half the work with double results.

It needs to combine regional conditions and focus on key fields and links to carry out public service equalization pilot projects in areas undertaking Beijing and Tianjin's functions and industries step by step, with an overall plan. (1)Focus on advancing public service policy integration. Encourage building platforms for social security information sharing, jointly by Beijing, Tianjin and areas undertaking functions and industries from Beijing and Tianjin. Study and develop policy integration proposals. Implement medical, pension, unemployment, work insurance and housing fund institution that follow the same policy, fee standard and security level of industrial areas undertaking functions. Innovate education policy integrating institution; emphasize tackling the issue of differential policies of collage admission in the region; gradually realize the goal of "one exam paper, one queuing line and admission according to merits" in those areas. Strengthen policy integration in the field of employment service; co-issue unified regional policies in employment information sharing, professional title mutual recognition, and professional technicians practicing in other places. Strengthen assistance in securing workers' rights and interests in the region; gradually build a unified inter-regional employment market. Talents via above efforts can be ensured to enjoy the same public service level and quality after transfer. (2)Innovate housing security mechanism in the Beijing-Tianjin function and industry transfer undertaking areas. Referring to Singapore's public group house institution, via setting up affordable housing management institutions, innovate the application qualification review and punishment mechanism of affordable housing; implement its sales placement, transfer and leasing policies; avoid malicious speculation on house price by developers; effectively reduce living costs for individuals moved-in; provide sound environment for talents' employment and business start-up. (3)Abiding by the principle of "achievements and costs sharing", set up basic public service joint construction and sharing institution in areas undertaking Beijing and Tianjin's functions; set aside a certain proportion of Beijing and Tianjin's taxation revenue to assist local finance; invest in public service facility building and public service supply in undertaking areas; meanwhile led by Beijing and Tianjin's public service resources, via innovation modes such as setting up campuses, branch collages, co-construction and mandatory administration, build inter-regional public service cooperation undertakers in education, medicare, pension and employment; facilitate undertaking areas to form a development environment matching Beijing and Tianjin's basic public service standards; so that transferred population, industries and institution are willing to leave Beijing and Tianjin, to stay in Hebei and are able to thrive, providing talents for Hebei's rapid development.

3.7.3 Advance public service market-oriented reform, enrich high-end public service supply

For a long time, governments in Hebei are responsible for investment, construction and allocation of public services. With economic and social development, aggregate demand for public service has significantly improved and its types and levels are increasingly diversified. The mode that the government is the sole public service provider is not able to keep up with the new trend of the changing public service demand with pressing conflicts in total amount and structure of public service. With insufficient financial power and the urgent need to improve its public service, Hebei Province has to be fully aware of the restriction of government as the sole provider, respect differences in public service demand and public preference, advance public service market-oriented reform experiments in key fields; so as to effectively relieve government's public financial pressure, speed up improving regional public service level and quality, narrow gradient differences in public service with Beijing and Tianjin as soon as possible, providing favorable conditions for alleviating Beijing's non-capital functions, for Beijing-Tianjin industrial transfer and for Hebei's effective undertaking.

To push forward the market-oriented reform experiment of public service, it has to alter the traditional public service supply mentality, set up a public service supply mode that "the government provides security, the market plays the main role", and improve public service supply efficiency and quality. (1)Identify service supply boundary between the government and the market. Via formulating and improving laws and regulations, identify the government's leading role in basic public service fields such as education, medicare and health, social security, and identify the market's role in resource basic allocation in differential, high-quality public service fields; so that residents in the region are able to enjoy basic public service with unified standards and "fair safety net"; at the same time, various groups all have channels to get high-quality differential services. (2)Lower threshold for various social investors to enter the public service sector. Exploring and formulating access list of the public service sector; identify qualification of public service providers; expand scope and limit for social capital to enter the public service sector; guide private enterprises, non-profit organizations and public organizations to participate in public service providing and operation; increase flexibility and diversity of public service supply. (3) Innovate capital partnership modes between the government and the society. Propel market-oriented reform of public service via tendering, franchising, contracting and loosen up access for enterprises to provide public services. (4)Improve incentive and supervision mechanism for social capital to provide public service. Explore preferential policies such as tax reduction, finance discount, small-amount loan, and land assignment, to encourage enterprises and social organization to enter the public service sector; meanwhile intensify supervision and binding in qualification, facility and services of supply institutions, guaranteeing public service supply quality.

3.7.4 Strive for more State-level financial support, strengthen Hebei's public service supply capability

Due to various economic development levels in the BTH Region, there is a huge gap between Hebei and Beijing-Tianjin in public service financial expenditure. According to statistics, in 2015, public service expenditure in general public budget expenditure of Beijing, Tianjin and Hebei was 30.012 billion yuan, 17.83 billion yuan and 50.332 billion yuan, respectively; per-capita public service expenditure was 1,382 yuan, 1,153 yuan and 678 yuan, respectively. Per-capita public service expenditure in Beijing and Tianjin is twice and 1.7 folds of that of Hebei. With huge financial gap within the region, it is hard for Hebei to supply the same public service with that of Beijing and Tianjin merely by increasing public service supply with its local finance; it is compel for the central finance to take more responsibility, to increase transfer payment to Hebei's finance, and to advance basic equalization of local finance, in order to achieve the goal of equal public service in the BTH Region.

Catering for the endogenous needs of BTH public service equalization, drawing experience from financial transfer payment from other countries, under the principle of people-oriented, improve the BTH public finance system and effectively enhance Hebei's public service supply capability. (1) Proposing the State to set up a fund of the BTH public service equalization finance, used for filling the gap of basic public service supply in the BTH Region, increase finance transfer payment to under-developed areas of Hebei. (2) According to the medium and long-term goals of BTH basic public service equalization, identify scope, type and standard of the BTH public service equalization; adjust dynamically according to trend development and changes, which should be the main indicator for the State to decide transfer payment amount to Hebei's finance and its support for Hebei in narrowing gaps with Beijing and Tianjin in public service. (3)List Hebei public service key projects or projects with significant development differences in Beijing, Tianjin and Hebei as national key projects; identify advancing targets and methods; improve Hebei's public service supply capability. (4)Establish a sound assessment and supervision mechanism for the use of financial transfer payment. It is suggested make Hebei's use of State financial transfer capital for the public service sector a constituent of assessment system of local governments and officials, track and monitor the entire process, comprehensively evaluate transfer payment capital's effect, comprehensively exam its social and economic benefits; so as to guarantee transfer payment capital's efficiency.

4. Suggestion for advancing forming a new pattern for the BTH coordinated development

4.1 Suggestions to Hebei Province

4.1.1 Actively strive for the State's support in setting up the Hebei Zhengding State-level coordinated innovation new city

Setting up Zhengding as the State-level coordinated innovation new city has great significance for Hebei's innovation development, especially accelerating development in the middle south region. (1)It contributes to gathering high-end innovation resources from Beijing and Tianjin, creating a Beijing-Baoding-Shijiazhuang development axle, creating a key advanced manufacturing development zone and urban gathering axle in the BTH Region. As a capital city, Shijiazhuang is equipped with the advantages and development foundation to be the key growth pole of the BTH

Region. Inside the Zhengding county, the airline, railway, express highway converge together; airport bonded-areas, inland logistics ports cluster; therefore, it bears a key function in building a modern commercial and trading hub in the North China Region, and it is a symbolic area of key trading ports in the North China Region and a high ground for opening up to the outside world. (2)It is beneficial to undertake the huge energy unleashed from the Xiong'an New Area's innovation development, which has a significant impact on influencing and to lead development of the southeast Hebei region. Taking Xiong'an as an example of innovation, speed up attracting high-end factors with institution and mechanism innovation; the Zhengding coordinated innovation new city can thus facilitate the Xiong'an New Area's development experience to be applied in Zhengding. It is meanwhile beneficial to interact with the Xiong'an New Area, to rely on Shijiazhuang's bio-industry base, electronic information industry base and high-end equipment manufacturing industry foundation, to combine innovation resources of the Xiong'an New Area, and to push forward Hebei's strategic emerging industrial growth pole. (3)It is beneficial to drive forward Hebei center cities' integrated supporting reform experiments, to advance a series of system and mechanism reforms such as city management system, function area management system, administrative area management system, and industrial park management system, providing pilot demonstration for province-wide in-depth reform.

Zhengding's reform priority should follow the Xiong'an New Area's construction; overall facilitate streamlining administration and power delegation with institution and mechanism reform and innovation; make breakthroughs in delegating power and strengthening regulation at the same time; explore new modes of innovation-driven development; build free trade zones and the BTH international logistics center; expedite interaction between airports, inland ports and the Huanghua harbor; create a new BTH high ground of opening up; speed up Hebei's pace in opening up to the outside world.

Setting up of the Zhengding New City is crucial in promoting the BTH coordinated development in an in-depth way. It is suggested that the provincial Party committee and the provincial government of Hebei put declaring the Zhengding New City to the agenda and push it forward.

4.1.2 Explore and roll out rural collective land use rights transfer and reform pilot projects throughout the province

The Program Outline for the Coordinated Development of the BTH Region confirms to set up a state-level demonstration area for new-type urbanization and urban-rural overall planning. Hebei needs to push for breakthroughs in demonstration area development emphasizing on tackling crucial issues faced by new-type urbanization and urban-rural overall planning. Currently, pressing issues in new-type urbanization and urban-rural overall planning are as follows: on the one hand, when rural residents move to the urban area, house stead left home cannot be traded due to restrictions of state institutions; on the other hand, as a large number of farmers pouring into urban areas, they have to be provided with construction land, attributing to problems e.g. farmers having lands in both places, land demand in the urban area increasing, large amount of rural construction land vacant, and rural cultivated land reducing each year. These problems present throughout Hebei Province with different degrees. As a result, effectively tackling the "land predicament" should be a priority in Hebei's new-type urbanization and urban-rural overall planning.

Domestically, some provinces and cities have made beneficial exploration in tackling this issue and have gained useful experience. Early in 2008, Chongqing made trials in conducting deepened rural land institution reform, pushing for urban-rural integrated development, advancing a coordinated development of land and population urbanization. In 2008, as a state-level urban-rural overall planning comprehensive pilot area, Chongqing initiated the land ticket trading system reform. Under the principle of "increase and decrease connection of urban and rural construction land, acquisition-compensation balance of arable land", it increased amount of arable lands by restoring rural vacant collective construction lands to arable lands, and then replaced them with urban construction land index. Chongqing's land ticket system has driven forward its fast economic growth, which has benefited the construction of its Liangjiang New Area. Against the backdrop of a depressed economic growth rate in many areas, Chongqing has been growing its economy in two digits for many years— the top of all provinces and cities. It is the direct beneficiary of effectively tackling land issues. At the same time, Chengdu of Sichuan Province and Henan Province have also made attempts in this matter with positive results. In recent years, provinces like Guangdong take a bigger step in rural collective land use entitlement reform, rolling out pilot projects for rural collective lands to enter first-level market, and made beneficial exploration in fully reuse and utilization of collective construction land.

In order to effectively tackle the problem of development restricted by land, it is suggested that in the process of new-type urbanization and urban-rural overall planning, Hebei choose some regions to explore, study and draw experience from Chongqing, Chengdu, Henan in implementing the "land ticket institution"; learn from places like Guangdong in listing rural collective lands in the market; appropriately handle multiparty relationship between land use、urbanization, food security and protecting farmers' interests; rely on institutional innovation; seek for new path with Hebei characteristics to tackle land problems.

4.1.3 Lay emphasis on playing out the role of fiscal and taxation policies in pushing forward coordinated development

(1) Making a bigger "fiscal support cake" with the method of reform and an open thinking method. a. Seek for central and Beijing-Tianjin fiscal support. Make full use of the Xiong'an New Area's same policy status with Shenzhen Special Economic Zone and Shanghai Pudong New Area; strive for central policy support. Actively fight for State development banks to fully play their roles as policy banks, forcing them to actively conduct work with methods of "planning before financing, reforming and innovating financing system, market operating financing"; support the Xiong'an New Area's initiative construction with high starting point and high standards; actively strive for the central government's fiscal support in the Xiong'an New Area's infrastructure work and public service facilities; negotiate with Beijing-Tianjin fiscal departments or applying from the central finance to ask for Beijing-Tianjin horizontal transfer payment capital being used in public service facilities. Increase provincial fiscal support for the New Area construction. Other regions of Hebei should also actively tap into other policy advantages and speed up local economic construction. Taking advantages of hosting the 2022 Winter Olympic Games, apply from the central government for supporting fund for public facilities via rational planning, making use of policies regarding the BTH coordinated development; apply from the central government for vertical transfer payment capital which can be used as special funds in traffic integration, medical and education service equalization, eco-forest building, as well as general fund for integration development. b. Seek for social capital support other than the government finance. In terms of capital supply, it should encourage capital cooperation between the government and the private sector, making full use of government capital leverage. According to fields involved in PPP, it should mainly involve fields providing public goods, follow requirements of coordinated development, and mainly guarantee funds for traffic integration and ecological environment protection. Project capital is mainly from loans from banks and financial institution and insurance payments from insurance institutions. Among them, it is suggested re-insure insurance payment invested by insurance institution to improve its safety. For fund used for

industrial transformation and upgrading and industrial bases, it is suggested adopt the form of construction and service outsourcing; via public tendering, choose competent companies to carry out construction of industrial bases and infrastructure and promise to give all the proceeds generated from venue facilities during soft opening to contractors to compensate their construction fund and fully absorb social capital.

(2)Actively integrate Beijing and Tianjin's financial and taxation policies. For a long time, the Beijing-Tianjin region have been enjoying quite a lot of preferential policies due to distinctive political advantages and thus have attracted large numbers of companies. On the contrary, Hebei is a politically forgotten land that enjoys much less preferential policies. In order to undertake Beijing-Tianjin's industries successfully, Hebei has to set up financial and taxation policies that are the same of or better than those of the Beijing-Tianjin region. In formulating preferential policies, Hebei needs to take good advantages of policy position advantages brought by setting up the Xiong'an New Area, and make it a pilot area of industrial transformation and upgrading; it needs to drive forward industrial transformation and upgrading in the entire region via making a series of preferential policies encouraging its high-tech enterprises' development. In terms of reducing taxes for enterprises, Xiong'an can reduce 2–3 percentage points based on the current corporate tax rate of 15% for high-tech enterprises; it can allow a higher tax deduction percentage based on existing preferential tax policy for R&D costs; based on preferential fixed assets accelerated depreciation policy, it can raise the unit value standard of allowed one-off deduction of enterprises purchasing fixed assets from 1 million yuan to 1.5 million yuan, for the purpose of attracting relevant enterprises to register in the Xiong'an New Area. In terms of reducing risks for enterprises, it can formulate loss compensation policies to reduce risks for new and existing enterprises in setting up and transformation. For innovation enterprises and venture capital enterprises, it can allow later repayment of their losses in the early stage; so as to reduce their operating risks and reduce their tax burden in the beginning stage. For enterprises undergoing transformation and upgrading, it can allow them to use annual revenue to make up for their losses due to upgrading; so as to encourage local enterprises to transform and upgrade and to adapt to the New Area's industrial function positioning. For enterprises with trans-regional business, it should also offer preferential policies to attract quality enterprises to set up branches in the area and encourage its local quality enterprises to develop their business outside, strengthening their capability. For enterprises setting up their HQ and branches in different taxation administrative areas, if the HQ is in the Xiong'an New Area, then annual losses of the branch is allowed to be deducted from the HQ's taxable revenue; if the branch is set up in the Xiong'an New Area, then it is allowed to pay taxes with local preferential tax rate, and its taxable revenue doesn't need to be calculated based on certain percentage of the enterprise's aggregate taxable revenue.

(3) Speed up the pace of improving tax levying and management capability. Currently, tax bureaus in Beijing, Tianjin and Hebei all have their own tax returns filling systems and differential procedures in tax services and service implementing. This will inevitably incur the situation that enterprises moved out from Beijing and Tianjin and registered in Hebei are not able to adapt to its local taxation rules and will bring problems for trans-regional enterprises in paying taxes and for tax bureaus in levying taxes. As a result, Hebei should assist Beijing and Tianjin in jointly building a BTH information-sharing platform for tax source information, policy information and auditing information. On top of this, it should make full use of levying and management information provided by the information platform to come up with short-term, transitional levying and management measures targeting enterprises moved from Beijing-Tianjin and to improve Hebei's tax levying and management ability.

4.2 Suggestions to the State, Beijing and Tianjin

4.2.1 Research on and establish a BTH Regional technology and innovation coordinating mechanism

The Program Outline explicitly requires to "establish a sound regional innovation system, integrate regional innovation resources, and forming a BTH coordinated innovation community". Currently, innovation resources and capabilities in the region vary significantly, and a unified technology market is not yet formed; so that Beijing and Tianjin's rich technology and innovation resources are not able to flow freely. As a result, it is suggested accelerate establishing a technology and innovation integrating and coordinating mechanism in the BTH Region, for the purpose of facilitating technology resources to flow freely and to be shared in the region, forming a firm foundation for the BTH coordinated innovation community. (1)Build a unified and efficient technology market in the region to facilitate technology achievements, talents and capital to flow freely. Discuss technology and innovation coordinating development mode in the region; explore how to build an innovation platform, a coordinated innovation community featured with industry-university-research cooperation and a technology transfer service system.

(2)Set up the Hebei industrial transformation technology and assistance coordinated development mode. Based on regional industrial development foundation and requirements of transformation and development, integrate innovation resources and mobilize BTH technology forces to tackle issues together. Focusing on restrictions, such as key upgrading technologies and key devices of traditional advantageous industries such as steel, concrete and chemistry, play out Beijing and Tianjin's technological resources advantages and set up problem-tackling teams. Build technology and innovation community such as environmental protection industry, marine industry, high-end equipment manufacturing industry, agriculture and sideline product processing industry with Hebei features; support industrial research of technologies. Hebei should set up bases for technology and innovation achievements application, demonstration and promotion, key industrial technology R&D bases, and pilot areas for industrial restructuring, transformation and upgrading underpinned by technologies. (3) Jointly plan and construct regional technology corridors; set up brand new reform pilot areas, technology achievements transformation demonstration areas, innovation towns, technology satellite cities, and master mobile studio. (4) Make full play of the leading role of the Zhongguancun State independent demonstration area and the Binhai New Area industrial innovation core area; support high-end innovation team and institution building; set up innovation institutions and participate development and management of development areas; give full play to enterprises such as CFLD with competitive innovation resources; drive forward BTH especially Hebei's innovation capability; advance cultivation of new motivation for growth. (5) Support Beijing and Tianjin in jointly building a future technology city in Hebei. Build talent special areas, high-end industrial cluster areas; set up innovation enterprises; introduce innovation talents, high-quality technology, innovation and entrepreneur teams, overseas high-level talents innovation and entrepreneurship platforms.

4.2.2 Support Hebei to become a "policy high ground"

In the BTH Region, Hebei is a depression in terms of economic and social development and both policy. Beijing and Tianjin enjoy regional development policy for their State-level new areas, opening-up policies for their free trade zones, technology and innovation policies with the Zhongguancun State independent innovation demonstration area. Many supporting policies that advance regional development are exclusive to Beijing and Tianjin, which is a key reason widening the gap in the region. It is suggested lay emphasis of the BTH coordinated development on policy coordination, offering Hebei more preferential reform and opening-up policies. (1)Support Hebei in building the Zhengding state-level coordinated innovation new city; assist Hebei in creating a strategic growth pole of developing new development driving force.(2) Support Hebei in rolling out financial reform experiments with Xiong'an as the pivot; look at BTH as one financial unit to calculate and eliminate trans-regional limits; build a unified financial platform for information sharing, inventory overall planning and uniform settlement; jointly build a fund and equity market, realizing financial market co-building, financial resources sharing, financial service co-creating and financial reform co-discussing; allow private banks to be set up in Hebei, providing financing services for SMEs and micro enterprises and technology SMEs; support more economic and development zones and high-tech zones in Hebei to upgrade to state-level ones. (3)Approve to set up free trade zones and agree to extend Tianjin's free trade zone policy to the Caofeidian area and the Bohai New Area. (4)Set up social undertakings development pilot projects in Hebei, with BTH public service equalization as the breakthrough point. (5)It is suggested set up a "national chemical industrial base" in Cangzhou. Cangzhou currently has already had more than 30 million tons of chemical and industrial production, the chemical industry intensive Bohai New Area has been approved as a state-level economic and technological development area. In fact, Cangzhou has already become a national key chemical base, and both its chemical and industrial foundation and its advantages as a coastal harbor have laid a foundation for great development for the chemical industry. The state chemical and industrial policies are suggested benefit the high-level and rapid development of the chemical industry.

4.2.3 Establish a complete institution and mechanism in key BTH fields

(1) Improve the ecological compensating mechanism. As the ecological barrier and water source located windward and upstream Beijing and Tianjin, Hebei has made outstanding contribution to the environment building and water resources protection of the Beijing-Tianjin region. At the same time, Hebei has been forced to shut down a large number of manufacturing companies, which has slowed down Hebei's economic development pace and many development opportunities have been lost. As beneficiaries of Hebei's environmental building and water resources, Beijing and Tianjin should compensate Hebei. As a result, it is compel to formulate an unified BTH ecological compensating standard, to improve ecological compensating mechanism, to improve horizontal

ecological compensating mechanism in the BTH Region with the principle of "those benefit pay", and to deepen cooperation in the BTH ecological environment. a. The BTH Region should start to establish ecological compensating policies and rules, and ecological compensating coordinating institutions: on the one hand, setting up an ecological compensating policy emphasizing on drinking water source, water conservation and soil erosion, ecological public-welfare forests, wetland protection and mineral resources compensation, providing ecological compensating ground for the region; on the other hand, it should start to establish special institutions coordinating interests of Beijing, Tianjin and Hebei, specialized in measuring the ecological compensating value and carrying out relevant actions. Via expert evaluation, it should rationally demonstrate benefits and losses of each place in ecological building; so that ecological compensating value is scientific and reasonable. b. It should establish a horizontal and a vertical transfer payment system for regional ecological compensation. Horizontal transfer payment is generally applied to trans-basin and trans-regional environmental standard reaching practices; transferring routes and the amount of the fund are decided by institutions especially responsible for the transfer under the principle of "those benefit compensate, those damage pay" and they also supervise responsible region's government to perform timely. While vertical transfer payment is generally applied to the waste discharging practice of industrial enterprises. The central government sets up a discharging quota. If they discharge more than their quota, the excessive part is to be levied by various governments in the form of environmental tax and submitted to the central government; it is then issued to each place in the form of vertical payment.

(2) Establish a public service cost sharing mechanism. As there is a huge gap between Hebei and the Beijing-Tianjin region in economic development, and due to Hebei government's weak financial power, Beijing and Tianjin should start to research on and set up a public service sharing mechanism, assisting Hebei in improving its public service level; so as to realize equalized public service in the BTH Region. In terms of Medicare and health, Beijing and Tianjin should establish a medical cooperation mechanism with Hebei: the government designates some hospitals to establish long-term cooperation agreement with designated hospitals in Hebei; the government funds to encourage Hebei's medical departments to update medical equipment and provide regular exchanges and training for medical practitioners; so as to facilitate medical service standard equalization in the BTH Region. In science and education, it should encourage well-known universities and colleges to

establish campuses or subsidiary institutions of scientific research, invite reputable scholars to universities and colleges in Hebei for regular academic seminars, improving the region's science, research and education level. In traffic integration construction, the BTH Region should set up a special rail and express highway construction decision institution for its management, and invite experts from the traffic department in the BTH Region and other experts to make decisions together and to provide proposals for the decision-making institutions; fiscal capital will be allocated rationally to each region according to the proposals. Local fund will be invested in local construction under the principle of "those benefit pay". Fund from the central government will not be allocated to specific places, but will be used to compensate for local finance due to large amount of finance construction projects; thus avoid "dead-end road" and improve the overall importance of traffic integration. In terms of public service facility costs sharing, the Beijing-Tianjin region should focus on the overall picture of a coordinated development, enhance overall awareness, sign long-term agreement of facilitating public service level in Hebei region with Hebei, and confirm scope and proportion of cost sharing.

(3) Improve industrial transformation coordinating mechanism. Due to gaps in economic development level, policy environment, market environment and infrastructure, Beijing and Tianjin enjoy significant advantages in attracting factor resources. It needs targeted policy guidance to rationally allocate factor resources between Beijing, Tianjin and Hebei. The BTH Region should further identify industrial function positioning based on requirements set out in the Program Outline, and reasonably identify focus and directions of industrial development; on top of this, via thorough discussion and top-level design strengthening, it should come up with differential preferential policies that benefit industries in Beijing, Tianjin and Hebei, and direct various industrial enterprises to transfer and flow rationally in the region. Taking preferential tax policies as an example, as for the function positioning of commercial and trade logistics bases, Hebei should formulate preferential tax policies for commerce and trade logistics enterprises; for enterprises newly moved from Beijing and Tianjin to Hebei commercial and trade logistics bases, it should draw experience from Inner Mongolia for it's encouraging policy for logistics business development: local share of corporate income tax is exempted for the first two years, corporate income tax will be halved for the next three years; for start-up enterprises, corporate income tax from years prior to profits is exempted, and corporate income tax is halved for the first three years starting from the first year profits are generated. Corporate income tax is levied normally from

commerce and trade logistics enterprises in Beijing and Tianjin to direct commerce and trade logistics enterprises to transfer to Hebei.

(4) Optimize talent cultivation and flow mechanism. Based on requirements of building BTH coordinated innovation community, attaching importance to Hebei's shortage of talents, it should speed up its pace in improving a BTH innovation talents cultivation and flow mechanism, break institutional and policy bottlenecks in innovation talents cultivation, recruitment, flow and assessment. It should build BTH Regional human resources development incubation bases, and jointly build a HR market, a talents service center, a talents innovation driving center (workstation). It should strengthen co-cultivation of BTH technological talents and technology management talents, advance unification cooperation of BTH key talent cultivation projects, focusing on cultivating technological agent talents such as professional technology brokers and patent agents. It should build flexible and varied flow and recruitment mode for BTH innovation talents, encourage higher-learning institutions and research institutions in the region to recruit talents from each other; it should allow them to set up a certain percentage of mobile posts to attract talents from other places for part-time jobs, and allow teachers and technology personnel to get engaged part-time in technology transfer; as for talents conducting teaching and research in more than one regions, their workload will be taken into their company assessment. It should improve institutional integration in human resources archiving, social security and professional technician titles, look into social security relationship transfer and continuity of innovation talents flowing between Beijing, Tianjin and Hebei, identify social security's continuity method and subsidy standard. It should improve the BTH talent supporting service system, providing convenience and guarantee services for high-level talents trans-regional flow, in housing conditions, children education, spouse employment, medical service.

4.2.4 Research on and launch a compreh-ensive treatment of the entire Haihe basin

Water resource shortage and worsened water pollution are severe ecological problems commonly faced by the BTH Region. Although this issue has drawn great attention from the State and the government from the three regions, an effective coordinated solution mechanism has yet formed, let alone a holistic, systematic and unified project treatment measure. The construction of Xiong'an New Area has given great importance to the water ecological governance of the Baiyangdian, and has provided great opportunities for tackling water ecological problems of Baiyangdian and the Daqinghe system. As the Daqinghe river system is independent from but closely related to other four river systems of the Haihe basin, the water ecology problem of the Daqinghe river system cannot be tackled without affecting other river systems. As a result, State ministries and commissions in charge and the government of the three regions are suggested, from a long-term, strategic and overall perspective of safeguarding ecological security of the BTH Region, especially the Xiong'an New Area, center on the theme of restoring the ecological system of the Haihe basin and the Yellow River, follow the mainline of preventing severe water disaster, control regional water shortage, provide a radical treatment for urban-rural pollution, and improve the living environment centering on the Daqinghe, Yongdinghe and Chaobaihe basin; improve key links of treatment engineering system and project construction standard; restore riverway ecological functions; expand basin ecological space; establish modern controlling system; with a comprehensive treatment in the Daiqnghe basin where Xiong'an is located as the breakthrough point, plan, study and advance the Haihe basin's comprehensive treatment as soon as possible; plan to carry out a basin-wide, systematic and all-around Haihe comprehensive treatment project; build a BTH ecology supply and ecological security system with a complete system, higher standard and better functions; solve ecological environmental issues faced by the entire BTH Region; safeguard BTH ecological security; set up a new example and provide new experience for building ecological security capability.

4.2.5 Set up an ecological north Hebei region

Zhangjiakou region and Chengde region provide ecological barrier and water source for the BTH Region. They possess delicate locations with prominent ecological status, huge gap in development with Beijing and Tianjin, as well as pressing poverty issues. As Zhangjiakou region and Chengde region have special and significant impact on the BTH coordinated development, it is suggested that the central government provide preferential policies to the regions, set up an ecology-friendly economy demonstration area, innovate institutions and mechanisms, optimize policy design, advance an accelerated ecological transformation in these regions, give full play to ecological functions in the regions, continue narrowing regional development gap, realize a win-win result for both the ecology and the economy, seek for new paths for regional development and ecological treatment throughout the country.

Emphasis should be attached to conducting exploring experiments and pilot demonstration in six aspects. (1)With investment approval and reform of the Winter Olympic Games as the breakthrough point, beef up power delegation of underdeveloped regions and intensify reform of combined monitoring and control; advance government function transfer; speed up the Zhangjiakou-Chengde region's opening up, attracting investors home and abroad. (2)Roll out the application comprehensive innovation demonstration of renewable energy. With building the Zhangjiakou renewable energy application comprehensive innovation demonstration area as its core, relying on Zhangjiakou-Chengde region's rich resource portfolio of wind, light, heat and biomass and renewable energy industrial foundation, centering on overcoming the restrictions of renewable energy development, advance the three innovations of mechanism, policy and technology; expedite building a renewable energy development and application system integrating generating, storage, transmission, utilization, equipment manufacturing, technology R&D, and integrated services; seek to form a renewable energy development and application mode that can be duplicated and promoted. (3)Roll out trans-regional ecological space purchasing pilot projects. On top of setting out regional ecological red line, arable land red line and city development boundaries, seek to establish a linkage mechanism between adding new construction lands and trans-regional ecological land purchasing, encourage urban regions that have expanded construction land to purchase ecological land quota from ecological regions without crossing the local ecological red line and city development boundaries; so that ecological regions can receive ecological construction fund and development benefits compensation continuously, and city region lands can also be used intensively and efficiently, forming a long-term mechanism benefiting ecological construction of the entire region. (4)Conduct experiments on water right allocation and transfer in the basin. Seek to set up a water market and water rights trading mechanism, reasonably compensate water source conservation areas for their water protection costs and losses in transferring water rights—it is an incentive for the government and people of the water protection regions and it improves water use cost at the same time, forming a long-term mechanism of water source's efficient allocation and use. (5)Roll out the BTH ecological industrial park demonstration. The co-construction mode of innovation park adopts multiple forms such as "hosting, joint-stock cooperation, production bases and enclave". Adopting the method of co-construction and co-management with Beijing and Tianjin, with Beijing and Tianjin playing the main role, expedite building and improving several featured industrial parks; facilitate development of featured industries that are friendly to the ecological environment; seek to form a feasible mode for trans-regional industry assistance. (6)Launch ecological migration and new-type urbanization demonstration; direct population in the region to gather in key towns and cities with good development conditions; establish regional population layout system led mainly by towns and cities; seek for population layout new mode in regions with fragile ecology; effectively relieve ecological pressure of population layout.

4.2.6 Seek to conduct assets accounting of ecological resources in the BTH Region

The point of conducting assets accounting of ecological resources such as water, land, mineral and forest: (1) initiate assets accounting for BTH ecological resources; research and formulate an assets accounting system of ecological resources suitable for the BTH Region based on ecology system's features and social economic development level and is beneficial for gaining a scientific understanding and evaluation of the BTH ecological resources. (2) formulate a BTH ecological product production performance table; conduct quantity accounting on tangible ecological products' value and intangible ecological services provided by the Eco-system; objectively reflect output performance of ecological assets production; evaluate and analyze the relationship between economic development and ecological benefits. (3) by including resource environment accounting into ecological value of the national economic accounting system, precisely learn to know status quo of resource utilization; evaluate development cost; scientifically formulate resource exploitation and utilization policy; establish scientific assessment mechanism of local government heads; pay more attention to issues such as resource waste, environment damage during economic development, ensuring a successful ecological civilization construction. (4) accounting can reveal everything of ecological resources assets in the north Hebei region, estimate development opportunity cost, and calculate the cost to restore ecological protection, lay a foundation for market trading, and advance ecological environment supporting area construction.

As a result, it is suggested: (1) conduct the BTH ecological resources assets accounting; establish a supporting system; set up a BTH ecological resources coordinated development pilot zone; and include ecological protection production into System of National Accounts. (2) set up a BTH ecological compensating fund; change the status quo that the existing ecological compensation is arbitrary with unreasonable standards and improve efficiency of ecological compensating fund. (3) establish a mechanism of government purchasing ecological products; adjust ecological production relationship; based on ecological resources assets, formulate compensating proposals linked to ecological products quality. (4) implement an institution of ecological civilization performance assessment and accountability, making ecological resources assets a key part of outgoing auditing of government heads. (5) establish an ecological poverty relief mode; facilitate underdeveloped regions to eliminate poverty with ecological resources assets protection; and speed up development gap with other regions.

References

[1] 魏丽华 . 建国以来京津冀协同发展的历史脉络与阶段性特征 [J]. 深圳大学学报 (人文社会科学版),2016(11).

[2] 杨开忠 . 京津冀协同发展的探索历程与战略选择 [J]. 北京联合大学学报 (人文社会科学版),2015(10).

[3] 蔡如鹏 . 京津冀规划纠结 30 年 : 各地利益博弈无法平衡 [J]. 中国新闻周刊 ,2015,(6).

[4] 新华网数据新闻部 . 协同发展三周年 , 京津冀交出怎样的"成绩单". 新华网 ,2017-2-15.

[5] 特别关注·京津冀协同发展调研行 . 新华网 ,2017-2-20.

[6] 冯红英 , 赵金涛 . 北京非首都功能疏解与河北产业承接问题研究 [J]. 区域经济 ,2016(1).

[7] 阎庆民 , 张晓朴等 , 京津冀区域协同发展研究 [M]. 北京 : 中国金融出版社 ,2017:34-37,49-51.

[8] 高智 , 努力把雄安新区建成开放发展先行区 [N]. 河北日报 .2017-4-28(7).

[9] 方创琳 . 京津冀城市群一体化发展的战略选择 [J]. 改革 ,2017(5).

[10] 张军扩 . 促进京津冀协同发展 , 打造世界级城市群 [J]. 改革 ,2017(5). 中国发展观察 ,2015(9).

[11] 薛晴 , 陈会谦 , 彭文民 . 京津冀协同发展视角下新型城镇化空间布局优化研究 [J]. 城市管理与科技 ,2016(12).

[12] 高智 , 孔慧珍 . 京津冀协同发展与河北省产业转型升级 [J]. 河北大学学报 (哲学社会科学版),2016(2).

[13] 边继云 , 薛维君 . 京津冀协同发展产业突破的"三要点"[N]. 光明日报 ,2016-3-2.

[14] 杨洁 , 辛灵 . 京津冀产业协同发展策略探究 [J]. 人民论坛 ,2016(4).

[15] 金福子 , 崔松虎 . 基于京津冀协同发展加速河北省产业转型升级对策 [J]. 开发研究 ,2016(2).

[16] 李惠茹 , 杨丽慧 . 京津冀生态环境协同保护 : 进展、效果与对策 [J]. 河北大学学报 (哲学社会科学版),2016(1).

[17] 罗振洲 , 赵英博 . 河北省建设京津冀生态环境支撑区研究——基于京津冀协同发展视角 [J]. 经济论坛 ,2016(2).

[18] 路森 . 京津冀生态环境支撑区建设的机制与路径研究 [J]. 河北企业 ,2016(7).

[19] 胡俊达 . 全面推进京津冀协同发展战略 着力打造京津冀生态环境支撑区 [J]. 河北林业 ,2016(5).

[20] 李岚、高智等 , 京津冀北区域经济发展和资源环境保护研究 [M]. 石家庄 : 河北人民出版社 ,2006:84-90,113-116.

[21] 马玉芳 , 沙景华 . 环京津贫困带问题研究 [J]. 首都经济贸易大学学报 (双月刊)2016(7).

[22] 兰传海 . 环京津贫困带扶贫开发研究 . 经济研究参考 .2015(2).

[23] 马明 , 马衍军 , 关昌余 . 交通领跑京津冀——京津冀协同发展下的交通一体化 [J]. 中国公路 ,2015(9).

[24] 鞠明明 , 黄晓雪 , 张锁祥 . 京津冀协同发展下津冀港口群协调机制创新研究 [J].

合作经济与科技，2016(1).

[25] 冯蕾．京津冀交通一体化如何实现[N]. 光明日报，2015-9-10(7).

[26]孙明正，余柳，郭继孚，李先，周凌．京津冀交通一体化发展问题与对策研究[J]. 城市交通，2016(5).

[27] 孙丽文，李跃．京津冀一体化下协同创新研究[J]. 河北工业大学学报(社会科学版)，2016(3).

[28] 颜廷标．以协同创新推动京津冀协同发展[N]. 河北日报，2016-3-16.

[29] 王岳森．加快构建京津冀协同创新共同体[N]. 河北日报，2016-9-2.

[30] 苏炜，彭晓静，杨珊．河北省推进京津冀协同创新的路径分析[J]. 河北金融，2016(10).

[31] 陈丽莎，孙伊凡．构建京津冀协同发展中有效衔接的公共服务供求关系[J]. 河北大学学报(哲学社会科学版)，2016(7).

[32] 高树兰．京津冀基本公共服务协同发展与财税政策支持探讨[J]. 经济与管理，2016(10).

[33] 曾红颖等，基本公共服务均等化标准与阶段性目标研究[M]. 北京：中国计划出版社，2013:76-78; 136-138.

[34] 陈志国等，京津冀基本公共服务发展比较研究[M]. 北京：人民出版社，2015:10-12、34、51、68、115、167.

Industrial Upgrading of Hebei Province

Principal Investigator: Gao Zhi
Investigators: Yang Huan, Wu Xuan

In the context of the coordinated development strategy in the BTH Region, the industrial upgrading of Hebei should be guided by an international perspective and be targeted at enhancing the overall competitiveness and development sustainability of BTH. In accordance with the requirements of The Program Outline for the Coordinated Development of the BTH Region (the program outline), the most fundamental and core aim of coordinated development in BTH Region is to develop the world-class city cluster with international competitiveness and significant influence, foster a new engine of innovative development in Pan-Bohai Area, and lead to the economic development nationwide. The industrial integration of BTH plays the most important role in achieving this target, integrating industrial development of BTH at a higher level, optimizing the industrial division, and promoting the overall upgrading of BTH industry. This is good for its neighboring regions to develop industry and reach a higher level.

The paper starts from the analysis of current situation and position of Hebei Industries in the BTH Region. Based on the coordinated development in BTH Region and international vision, the paper discusses the role that Hebei plays in the coordinated development in BTH Region, analyzes the industrial upgrading obstacles that Hebei would face, puts forward the direction, path and strategy of Hebei industrial upgrading and makes suggestions to the government on the basis of policy reform of Hebei, policy coordination in BTH Region and national supporting policy.

1. The Industry position of Hebei Province in BTH Region

1.1 Scale and characteristics of Hebei industries

In 2015, the GDP of Hebei Province reached 2,980.61 billion yuan, accounting for 43% of the BTH Region, and Hebei is obviously prominent in economic scale across the BTH Region. As to three industries, the value-added of the primary, secondary and tertiary industry was 343.94 billion yuan, 1,438.80 billion yuan and 1,197.87 billion yuan, accounting for 90.75%, 54.01% and 30.81% of the BTH Region respectively (see Table 1). Hebei was dominant in primary and secondary industries. Although Hebei's tertiary industry was less prominent compared with other two industries, it still achieved roughly the same size as that of Beijing and Tianjin.

Table 1 Scale and proportion of three strata of industry of the BTH Region

	Total of BTH	Beijing		Tianjin		Hebei Province	
	Absolute value	Absolute value	Proportion	Absolute value	Proportion	Absolute value	Proportion
	(100 Million yuan)	(100 Million yuan)	(%)	(100 Million yuan)	(%)	(100 Million yuan)	(%)
Total	69,312.89	22,968.6	33.14	16,538.19	23.86	29,806.1	43.00
Primary Industry	3,790.11	140.2	3.70	210.51	5.55	3,439.4	90.75
Secondary Industry	26,638	4,526.4	16.99	7,723.6	28.99	14,388	54.01
Tertiary Industry	38,884.78	18,302	47.07	8,604.08	22.13	11,978.7	30.81

Source: *Statistics Bulletin of the National Economic and Social Development of Beijing, Tianjin and Hebei in 2015.*

1.2 Structure and development level of Hebei's Industries

As to three industrial structures, the value-added of the first industry accounted for 11.5% of the GDP in Hebei Province, the proportion of secondary industry was 48.3%, and the proportion of the tertiary industry was 40.2%. At the same time, the ratio of three strata of industry of Beijing and Tianjin were 0.6 : 19.6 : 79.8 and 1.3 : 46.7 : 52.0 respectively (see Table 2). Obviously, Beijing and Tianjin have already formed the industry structure of "Tertiary-Secondary-Primary", which marks that they have overall completed their industrialization and begun entering the post-industrialization period. However, Hebei is at a transition period from mid-industrialization to late-industrialization. The industry and agriculture occupy the greater proportion and there is a big gap of the industry level among Hebei, Beijing and Tianjin.

As to internal structure of the industry, in 2005, the revenue from principle business (RPB) of the industrial enterprises above the designated size in Hebei Province reached 4,564.81 billion yuan. Therein, the PRB of resource-based industries reached 2,295.62 billion yuan, accounting for 49.54% of the industrial enterprises above the designated size, and the ferrous metal smelting and pressing industry, the largest one in Hebei,

Table 2 Industrial structure of the BTH Region in 2015

	Total of BTH		Beijing		Tianjin		Hebei Province	
	Absolute value	Proportion	Absolute value	Proportion	Absolute value	Proportion	Absolute value	Proportion
	(100 million yuan)	(%)	(100 million yuan)	(%)	(100 million yuan)	(%)	(100 million yuan)	(%)
Total	69,312.89	100	22,968.6	100	16,538.19	100	29,806.1	100
Primary Industry	3,790.11	5.47	140.2	0.6	210.51	1.3	3,439.4	11.5
Secondary Industry	26,638	38.43	4,526.4	19.6	7,723.6	46.7	14,388	48.3
Tertiary Industry	38,884.78	56.10	18,302	79.8	8,604.08	52.0	11,978.7	40.2

Source: *Statistics Bulletin of the National Economic and Social Development of Beijing, Tianjin and Hebei in 2015.*

occupied the highest proportion, accounting for 21.7% of the industrial enterprises above the designated size (see Figure 1). The revenue from principle business of the high-tech manufacturing industry was only 138.10 billion yuan, accounting for less than 0.3% of the industrial enterprises above the designated size, and both the RPBs of aviation and space equipment industry as well as computer and office equipment manufacturing industry were less than 0.1% of that of the industrial enterprises above the designated size (see Figure 2). In the meantime, the resource-based industry in Beijing accounted for only 11.57% of the industrial enterprises above the designated size, while the proportion of high-tech manufacturing industry accounted for 20.47% of the industry. It was 6.9 times of the proportion of high-tech manufacturing industry in Hebei Province. Computer and office equipment manufacturing industry accounted for 3.74% of the industrial enterprises above the designated size, which was well above that in Hebei. Though resource-based industries were in a higher proportion in Tianjin, the high-tech manufacturing industry was also well developed, accounting for 15.67% of the industrial enterprises above the designated size. It was 5.3 times of the proportion of high-tech manufacturing industry in Hebei (see Table 3). Based on the analysis above, Hebei is still in the process of industrialization. Industrial development is lagging behind, mainly driven by natural resources and labor factors, while Beijing has entered the post-industrialization stage, mainly driven by knowledge and technical factors.

In terms of the industrial status among the BTH Region, in 2015, the PRB of the industrial enterprises above the designed size in Hebei accounted for 49.56% of BTH, of which the PRB of resource-based industries accounted for 61.98% of resource-based industries in BTH, while the high-tech manufacturing industry's prime operating revenue accounted for only 14.61% of that in BTH; at the same period, the resource-based industries in Beijing and Tianjin only accounted for 5.89% and 32.19% of that in BTH, high-tech manufacturing accounted for 40.49% and 44.90% of BTH, far higher than the proportion of high-tech manufacturing in Hebei Province. It is obvious that Hebei is the provider of natural resources and raw materials in BTH while Beijing and Tianjin are the suppliers of high-tech factors, which turn out huge gaps between Hebei and Beijing-Tianjin in industrial development.

For the service industry structure, Hebei's commerce and trade industry is highly developed while high-end services are comparatively backward. The service industry can be divided into three categories which are commerce and trade industry, high-end services and common production and consumer services according to different development level. In 2015, the value-added of the service industry in Hebei was up to 1,182.079 billion yuan, among which the value-added of commerce and trade industry was 514.475 billion yuan, made up of a 43.52% of Hebei's tertiary industries while the added value of high-end production services was in a small scale and only accounted for 8.83%. The same period in Beijing, in turn, the value-added of the service industry in 2015 was up to 1,819.93 billion yuan, which was 1.5 times the total added value in Hebei. As to the service industry structure of Beijing, the high-end services occupied the greater proportion, which accounted for 32.81% of the total service industry, especially the value-added of the information transmission, software and information technology services reached 238.39 billion yuan, accounting for 10 % of the service industry which was much higher than the proportion of that in Hebei. In 2005, the value-added of service industry in Tianjin was 860.471 billion yuan. Though the gross scale was less than that in Hebei, the proportion of its high-end production services added value reached 19.97%, which was higher than Hebei of 11.14 percentage points. It was obvious that the structure level was better than that in Hebei (see Table 4, Table 5). By contrast, the internal structure of the service industry in Hebei is unreasonable. High-end services are seriously lack of development and the service industry still has a big gap with Beijing and Tianjin.

Table 3 Comparison of resource-based and high-tech manufacturing industries among the BTH Region

	Total of BTH		Beijing		Tianjin		Hebei Province	
	Absolute value	Proportion	Absolute value	Proportion	Absolute value	Proportion	Absolute value	Proportion
	(100 million yuan)	(%)	(100 million yuan)	(%)	(100 million yuan)	(%)	(100 million yuan)	(%)
Resource-based industry	37,040.5	40.21	2,162.6	11.57	11,921.6	44.03	22,956.2	49.54
High-tech manufacturing industry	9,450.6	10.26	3,826.2	20.47	4,243.4	15.67	1,381.0	2.98

Source: *Statistic Yearbook of the National Economic and Social Development of Beijing, Tianjin and Hebei in 2016.*

Figure 1 The prime operating revenue structure of resource-based industry in BTH (%)

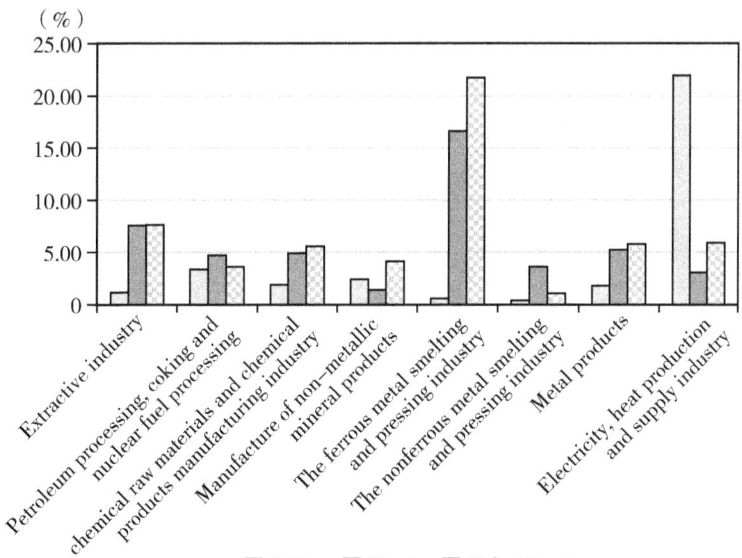

Source: Data above are calculated on the basis of *Beijing Statistical Yearbook 2016, Tianjin Statistical Yearbook 2016* and *Hebei Economic Yearbook 2016.*

Figure 2 The prime operating revenue structure of high-tech manufacturing industry in BTH (%)

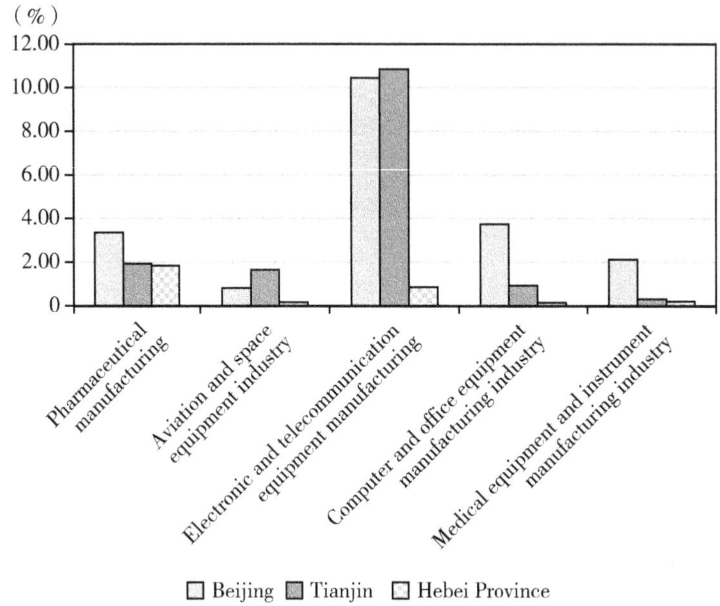

Source: Data above are calculated on the basis of *Beijing Statistical Yearbook 2016, Tianjin Statistical Yearbook 2016* and *Hebei Economic Yearbook 2016.*

Table 4 The service industry structure of the BTH Region in 2015

	Beijing		Tianjin		Hebei Province	
	Value-Added (100 million yuan)	Proportion (%)	Value-Added (100 million yuan)	Proportion (%)	Value-Added (100 million yuan)	Proportion (%)
Commerce and Trade	3,733.80	20.52	3,047.14	35.41	5,144.75	43.52
High-end Services	5,971.30	32.81	1,718.74	19.97	1,043.21	8.83
Common Production and Consumer Services	8,494.20	46.67	3,838.83	44.61	5,632.83	47.65

Source: Data above are calculated on the basis of *Beijing Statistical Yearbook 2016, Tianjin Statistical Yearbook 2016* and *Hebei Economic Yearbook 2016.*

Table 5 The internal structure of the service industry of the BTH Region in 2015 (%)

	Beijing	Tianjin	Hebei Province	Total of BTH
Wholesale and retail	12.93	24.06	20.14	17.61
Transportation, warehousing and post service	5.41	8.47	19.96	10.54
Accommodation and restaurants	2.18	2.88	3.42	2.72
Information transmission, software and information technology services	13.10	3.12	3.73	8.01
Finance	21.57	18.63	12.53	18.15
Real estate	7.90	7.19	11.11	8.73
Leasing and business services	9.71	8.55	2.06	7.11
Scientific research and technical services	10.00	8.30	3.03	7.49
Water conservancy, environment and public facilities management	0.99	2.03	1.20	1.29
Resident service, repair and other services	0.78	5.15	5.27	3.13
Education	5.31	3.98	4.45	4.75
Health and social work	3.17	2.14	4.59	3.38
Culture, sports and entertainment	2.90	1.14	0.90	1.90
Public administration, social security and social organization	4.04	4.36	7.60	5.20

Source: *Statistics Bulletin of the National Economic and Social Development of Beijing and Tianjin in 2016* and statistics feed of Hebei in 2015.

From the perspective of regional status of service industry among the BTH Region, Hebei is the national commercial and trade base, having prominent advantages in the field of commerce and trade industry. In 2015, the value-added of commerce and trade industry made up of a 43.14% of BTH tertiary industries, among which the value-added of transportation, warehousing and post service was 235.909 billion yuan and accounted for about a half of the total value added of the BTH Region. While the high-end services and common production and consumer services occupied the lower proportion in BTH Region, especially the high-end services that served the people's production and living, such as information transmission, software and information technology services, leasing and business services, scientific research and technical services and culture, sports and entertainment, the proportion of which were less than one-sixth in BTH Region. The same period in Beijing, in turn, the tertiary industries at all levels accounted for a relatively high proportion in BTH Region, especially high-end production service industry had an absolute advantage in BTH Region, accounting for 68.37%, among which, the value-added of information transmission, software and information technology service accounted for 77.06% of the industry in BTH Region. Tianjin took an advantage in high-end services and the proportion of the BTH Region was 7.73 percentage points higher than that of Hebei Province (see Table 6 and Figure 3). By contrast, the service industry of Beijing and Tianjin is comparatively developed and the two municipalities are the main suppliers of high-end services in the BTH Region.

Table 6 The position of service industry of the BTH Region in 2015 (%)

	Beijing	Tianjin	Hebei Province
Commerce and Trade	31.31%	25.55%	43.14%
High-end Services	68.37%	19.68%	11.95%
Common Production and Consumer Services	47.28%	21.37%	31.35%

Source: Data above are calculated on the basis of *Beijing Statistical Yearbook 2016, Tianjin Statistical Yearbook 2016* and *Hebei Economic Yearbook 2016.*

Figure 3 Value-added structure of service industry in BTH (%)

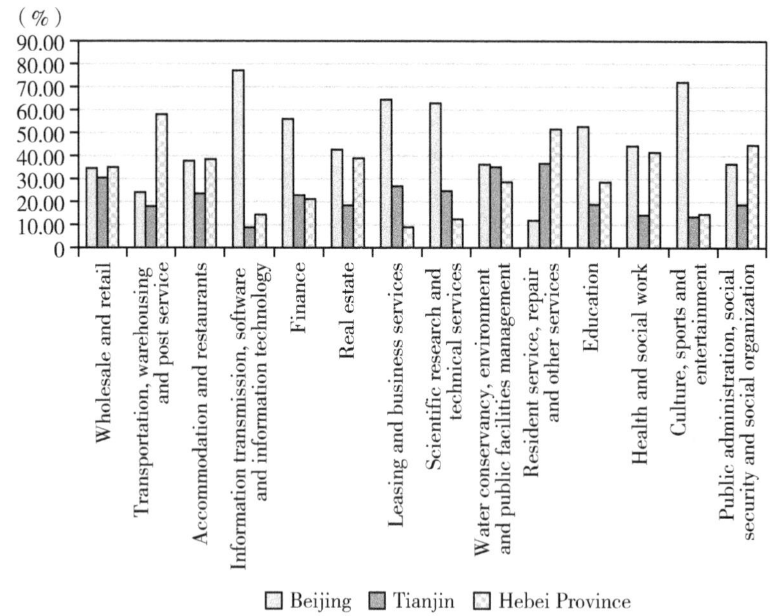

1.3 Characteristics of industrial division across the BTH Region

This part is divided into four sections which are business headquarter, R&D, manufacture and marketing service. This part analyzes the different production links among the BTH Region and then summarizes the characteristics of industrial division across the BTH Region and the function of Hebei.

Business headquarter. As the highest policy-making body of the enterprise, headquarter is in charge of the development strategy of enterprise including research, organization and implementation, transaction coordination and resource allocation. The enterprise headquarters are usually located in the areas of well-developed high-end services, excellent transportation and communication conditions, rich scientific and technological resources and high-quality talent. According to the analysis on business headquarters' distribution of enterprises in lists of global top 500, China top 500, China private top 500 and China financial top 500, by the end of 2015, there were 18 headquarters of private top 500 in Hebei, accounting for 43.9% of the headquarters of the privately top 500 enterprises in BTH Region. However, relatively few headquarters of the other top 500 enterprises settled in Hebei Province. Obviously, Hebei takes an advantage in private enterprise headquarters, but shows no advantage in other kind of headquarters. Over the same period, the business headquarters of global top 500, China top 500, China financial top 500, settled in Beijing, reached 134, 99 and 83 respectively, accounting for 96.40%, 70.71% and 76.15% of the total corporate headquarters in BTH Respectively. Beijing, with its position as a political, cultural, economic and foreign exchange center in the country, had an unparalleled advantage in the business headquarters (see Figure 4).

R&D occupies the high-end of industry chain, requiring the highest technology. R & D is always located in areas of intensive resources, convenient infrastructures and perfect living services. By analyzing the distribution of R&D institution, college and key laboratories in BTH Region, it can be seen that Hebei is in a weak position in R&D. The R&D institution is in a small number and at a low level. There is no "985 Project" college, while the only "211 Project" college is located in Tianjin. In addition, there are only nine national key laboratories with small numbers and few resources about basic and cutting-edge technologies.

Figure 4 The distribution of top 500 business headquarters of BTH Region (%)

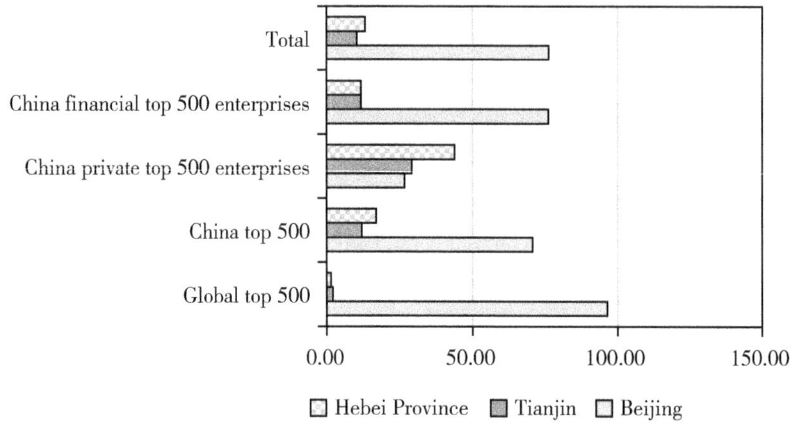

Source: The data of Global top 500, China top 500, China private top 500 and China financial top 500 was gathered and calculated by the Fortune Global 500 list, China Enterprise Union and China Entrepreneur Association, ACFIC (All China Federation of Industry and Commerce) and NetEase Finance respectively.

Beijing, as the center of capital, information and talent, has a unique advantage in R&D link in the BTH Region. In 2014, all kinds of scientific research institutions, colleges and key laboratories in Beijing reached 405, 76 and 192 respectively, accounting for 66.27%, 30.52% and 41.56% of the innovative resources of BTH respectively. Though the colleges in Beijing is less than that in Hebei, the colleges in Beijing generally have high level and strong sci-tech strength, among which the "985 Project" and "211 Project" colleges accounted for 80% and 85.71% of BTH respectively(see Table 7). Beijing is also home to a large number of state-level key laboratories in China, playing a high-end leading role. It has core technical advantages in areas such as basic medicine and bio-medicine, aerospace, energy saving and environmental protection, new generation of information technology, new energy, new materials and intelligent manufacturing. Tianjin, as the largest open city along the coastline in northern China, has certain advantages in terms of economic strength and scientific research. With a good foundation of education, science and technology, Tianjin is at the forefront of the whole country and is obviously better than Hebei in the BTH Region but second in Beijing (see Table 7).

Table 7 The distribution of sci-tech resources of the BTH Region (%)

	R&D institutions	College				Key Laboratories		
		985 College	211 College	Other college	Sum	National Level	Provincial Level	Sum
Beijing	61.27	80.00	85.71	20.85	30.52	65.85	22.18	41.56
Tianjin	22.39	20.00	10.71	23.70	22.09	29.76	41.63	36.36
Hebei Province	16.34	0.00	3.57	55.45	47.39	4.39	36.19	22.08

Source: Data is gathered and calculated from the date of the Study on Coordinated Innovation Community of the BTH Region by MRI, HBDRC, Shijiazhuang, 2016.

Manufacture. By analyzing the enterprise number and the revenue of general manufacturing industries and high-tech manufacturing industries, it can be seen that general manufacturing industries are relatively concentrated in Hebei. The enterprise number and RPB of these industries in Hebei Province occupy more than fifty percentage of the total number in the BTH Region. Tianjin is in the second place where the enterprise number and the PRB of general manufacturing industries respectively reach 22.96% and 30.93% respectively of BTH Region (see Figure 5). From the perspective of high-tech manufacturing industry, Hebei is at a disadvantage, especially the revenue level, regardless of the enterprise number, revenue or profitability of the high-tech manufacturing industry. In 2015, the PRB of Hebei high-tech manufacturing industry accounted for only 15.17% of the BTH Region. At the same period, the development level of high-tech manufacturing industry in Beijing and Tianjin is apparently higher than that in Hebei (see Figure 6). The manufacturing sector is in the low-end of the distribution of value in the industry chain, having relatively low demand for technology and high demand for resources such as land, minerals, water and labor in the industry chain. High-tech manufacturing sector is in the high-end of the industrial chain, which has comparatively high demand for talents, technology and capital. For a long time, Hebei Province, relying on advantage of plentiful resource and low elements cost, gained great development in general manufacturing industry and lived in the low end of the manufacturing value chain. However, with good talent, technology and transportation location and industrial foundation, Beijing and Tianjin occupied the high end of the manufacturing value chain.

Marketing and service. At the end of the industry chain, the marketing and service include numerous industries and have great difference in technology. The marketing and service can be divided into two categories, one of which is sales and general service, the other is knowledge-intensive or technology-intensive high-end service. From the aspect of sales and general service, there are more employees in Hebei, reaching 5.6239 million, accounting for 61.32% of the sales and service personnel in BTH. It is the provider of sales and service industry in BTH. The proportion of sales and general service workers is relatively low in Beijing and Tianjin (see Figure 7). From the perspective of high-end service, the number of high-end service workers in Hebei Province

Figure 5 The enterprise number and PRB structure of general manufacturing industry in BTH Region (%)

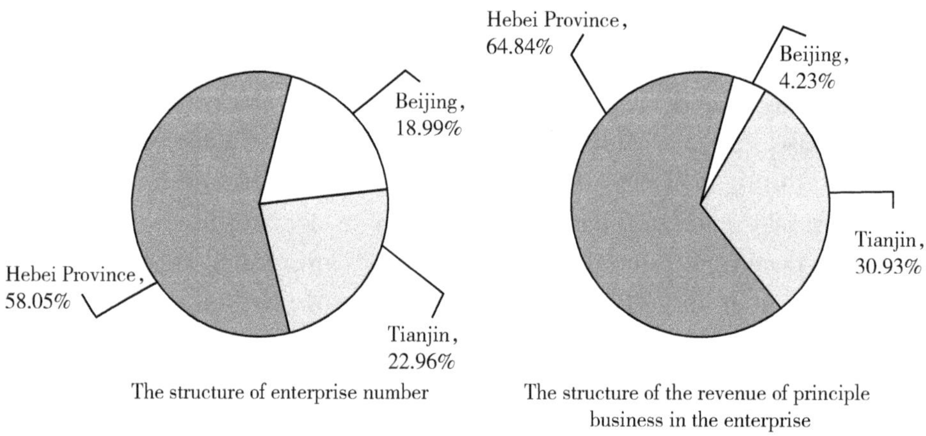

Source: Data is calculated from the date of the Economic General Investigation of BTH.

Figure 6 The proportion of high-tech manufacturing industry among the BTH Region (%)

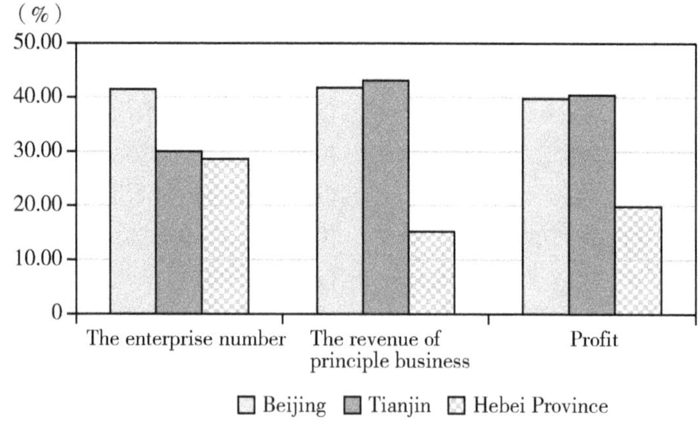

Source: Data is calculated from *China Yearbook for the Statistic of Science and Technology* (2015).

Figure 7 The number of sales and general service workers in BTH (%).

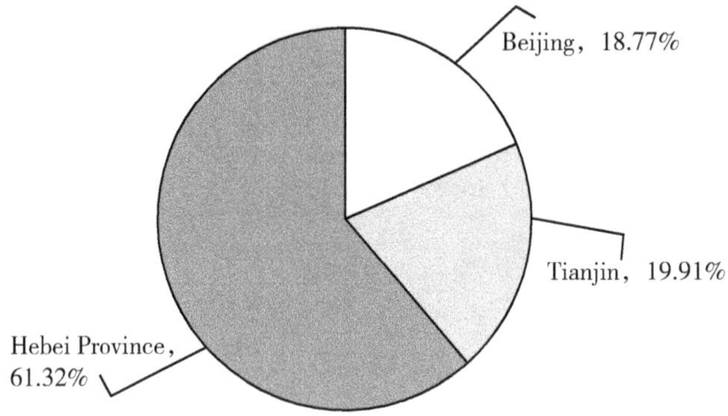

Source: Data is calculated from the date of *Economic Yearbook of Beijing, Tianjin and Hebei.*

was 1.3 million, accounting for 21.11% of the total high-end service workers in BTH Region, while Beijing's high-end service workers were nearly as three times as that in Hebei Province, accounting for 60.47% of BTH(see Figure 8). It is obvious that Tianjin and Hebei are quite different in the link of marketing and services. On one hand, Beijing has advantages in funding, information and sci-tech service, and occupies the high-end of industry chain; on the other hand, Hebei is at a disadvantage.

In summary, the characteristics of the industrial division in the BTH Region can be concluded as follows:

(1) There exists an obviously vertical labor division among the BTH Region. On account of respective developing stage, requirement and the factor endowment, it has formed a vertical industrial division in BTH. With advantageous science-technology resources and abundant industry foundation, Beijing and Tianjin are at the top of vertical industry chain by developing an industrial structure dominated by high-tech industries. By contrast, though the total scale of the industry is big, Hebei is relatively backward with low-leveled industries. Dominated by resource deep-processing industry and agriculture, Hebei is inevitably at the bottom of regional industrial chain (see Figure 9).

(2) Beijing is the core of industrial division among the BTH Region. Beijing is the heart of our country in polities, economy, education, science technology, culture and finance, gathering a good deal of production factors. Beijing is the core region of corporate headquarters and R&D institutes, having more than 90 universities such as Tsinghua University and Peking University, more than 230 independent research institutes including Chinese Academy of Science and 29 world famous multinational R&D institutes. Beijing

Figure 8 Proportions of workers in high-end services among the BTH Region (%)

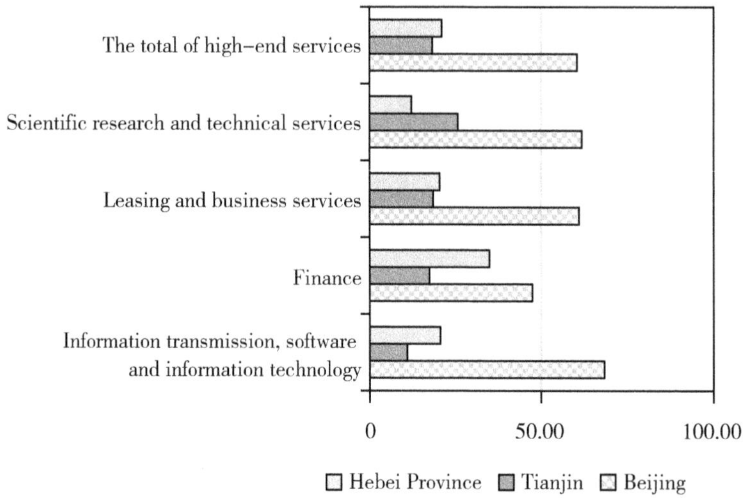

Source: Data is calculated from the date of *Economic Yearbook of Beijing, Tianjin and Hebei.*

Figure 9 The diagram of industrial division system in BTH Region

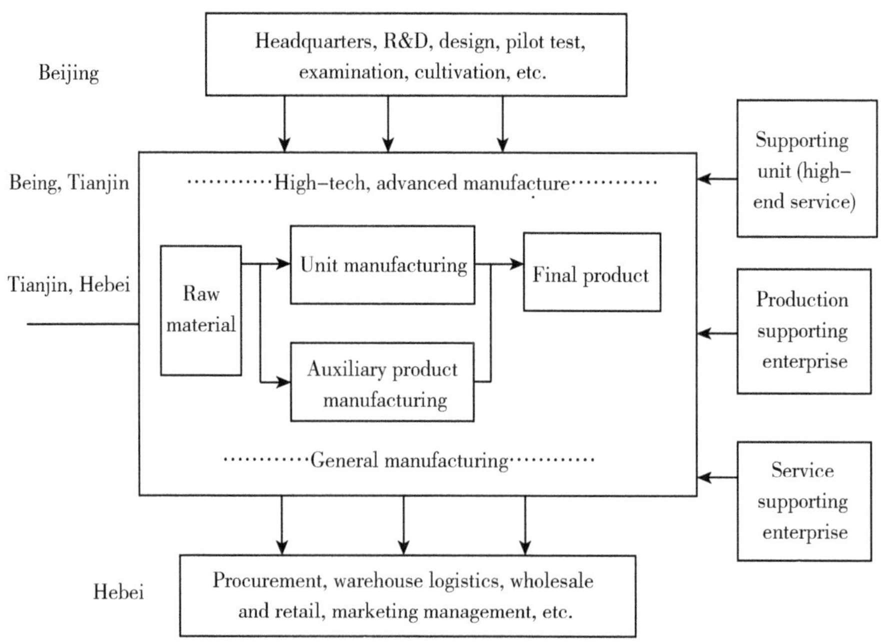

becomes a new highland in the R&D of industry chain with the superiority of abundant innovation resources, obvious talent aggregation and high-tech industry advantages and definitely plays a leading role in the process of the BTH coordinated development.

(3) The industrial division in Hebei and Tianjin is different but a little overlapping. Tianjin, as a secondary city in BTH Region, is in the second level overall in BTH industrial division. With abundant manufacturing industry foundation and excellent port shipping conditions, Tianjin has made great progress in manufacturing industry, especially in advanced manufacturing industry. However, due to the relatively weak facilities and industrial base in Hebei, there is a big gap of the manufacturing industry between Hebei and Tianjin. In the meantime, there exists identical industrial structure and homogeneous competitions in the industry such as the ferrous metal smelting and pressing, chemical raw materials and chemical products, metal products and so on between Hebei and Tianjin. The well-bedded industrial division and effective regional competition force haven't been formed between Beijing and Tianjin.

(4) Hebei is at the bottom of the industrial division in BTH. In BTH Region, Hebei has always been the strategic hinterland of Beijing, located in the periphery of the core area. Hebei has great advantages in agriculture, resource-based industry and general service industry. However, most of these sectors are in the low-end link of the value distribution of the industry chain and have low added value. Therefore, Hebei is in a subordinate position in the industrial division of BTH.

(5) Hebei has not established an efficient industry chain coordinated with Beijing and Tianjin. On the one hand, Hebei is mainly dominated by resource-based industries such as coal, metallurgy, petrochemicals and building materials. These industries have little industrial correlation and are not easy to form a long-term industry chain. On the other hand, Hebei has not established an effective joint of industrial chain coordinated with Beijing and Tianjin in equipment manufacturing, electronic information, biological medicine and other industries that may establish a longer industry chain. All industries in BTH are developed in their own way without much connection. The function division is not clear and the parts supporting system is not established. The surrounding area of the industry is less prominent compared with the Yangtze River Delta and the Pearl River Delta. Therefore, many enterprises would rather take the long progress to pursue cooperation beyond BTH Region. For example, most of the IT manufacturing enterprises in Beijing choose to procure parts or directly seek for OEM from Guangdong Province, Jiangsu Province and so on.

(6) It is quite difficult to integrate the industry chain and innovation

chain in the BTH Region. Gathering many high-end and diversified innovation resources such as national key laboratories, engineering and technology centers, research institutes and so on, and having a large number of advanced technologies and cutting-edge achievements, Beijing is in an urgently demand to transform the scientific research into application. At the same time, having a good foundation of manufacturing industry, Hebei has a strong demand for industrial transformation and upgrading through the application of technological achievements. On the surface, the integration of innovation chain and industry chain between Hebei and Beijing will not only meet the needs of both sides, but also be of practical significance. However, it is quite difficult to integrate the industry chain and innovation chain between Hebei and Beijing. It is mainly because of the different actual need of the both sides. Most of the research achievements in Beijing are high-end and cutting-edge, while the level of Hebei's manufacturing industry is relatively low, which is difficult to meet the need of Beijing's transformation. In addition, it is hard to break the invisible barriers of the innovation elements communication in Beijing and Hebei. In 2015, the proportion of undertaking Beijing's technology transfer in Hebei was only accounted for 2.81% of its total output. Most of scientific and technological achievements in Beijing were transferred outside the BTH Region.

2. Macro-background of industrial upgrading in Hebei Province

Experience indicates that under the current system and development environment in China, the direction and aim of industrial development in a region is the result of the interaction among various internal and external environmental which is strongly influenced by the strategic orientation of national industrial development in a certain period of time and restrained by the resources and the supply of factors at the specific stage of development. Apart from that, it also depends on the definition of the industry functions in this region by the state and the layout of major productive forces. In terms of current Hebei, there are three major backgrounds of industry upgrading, including the basic direction of Chinese industry transformation and upgrading, the requirements for industry transformation and upgrading of Hebei in the coordinated development in BTH and the requirements of ecological environment protection for the sustainable development of Hebei industries, etc.

2.1 Basic direction of China's industry transformation and upgrading

At present, the world is facing a time of great changes and huge adjustments. New breakthroughs are in the making in the new round of scientific revolution and industrial transformation. In order to seize the commanding heights of industrial development, the process including re-industrialization and the industrialization of emerging economies has been obviously sped up in developed countries. China is facing a "double squeeze", with the high-end backflow of developed countries and the low-end backflow of emerging economies. The government has put forward a few strategic moves including implementing a strategy of innovation-driven development, Made in China 2025, the Internet+ action plan and so on on the basis of the new change of international industrial division and trade environment, the new situation of international scientific revolution and industrial transformation and the new demands for a better quality life and environment of people. The 19th CPC National Congress put forward a clear aim: we should focus on the scientific concepts and orientations, set up modern economic system, work hard to shift the model of economic development, and give impetus to industrial transformation and upgrading so as to advance to a medium to high level in industrial development.

So far, from the policy documents and planning of the industrial development issued by the Chinese government, the directions of China's industrial transformation and upgrading can be interpreted as six goals, namely high-end oriented development, intellectualization, industry integration, ecologicalization, industrial clustering development and industrial internationalization. High-end oriented development refers to the process to strengthen the key links including R&D, design, core technology, software, key parts, key equipment, supply chain management, sales and brand, so as to promote the industry chain and value chain to transform from the low-end links to high-end products, high-end elements, high-end services and high-end platforms and seize the high-end value chain. This will help to realize the high-end oriented development. Intellectualization is to establish the "Internet +" eco-industrial system which is networked, intelligent, service-oriented and collaborative by utilizing the modern technology such as Internet, big data, artificial intelligence and so on, so as to promote the transformation of production, management and sales pattern and realize the intelligence of the full chain from users' demand to production supply. Industry integration is a new pattern which is diversified, multi-level, multi-form and multi-channel, realized by accelerating the infiltration and integration of the new generation of information technology in various fields, and promoting the "cross-border integration" of diversified industries based on the network and intelligence. Ecologicalization, that is, integrates the concept of "ecology" into the whole process and steps of industrial transformation and upgrading, accelerates the development of green and low-carbon recycling economy, actively promotes the ecological innovation of technologies such as ecological engineering, ecological design and process design, vigorously enhances agricultural greening , low-carbon circulation in industries, environmental protection in service industries, and constructs an industrial structure with low resource consumption and little environmental pollution, so as to realize a coordinated complexion between industrial development and resources. Industrial clustering development means utilizing the institutional innovation to optimize the enterprise layout and specialized cooperation of the overall industrial clusters, promote the complementation of the internal enterprises rather than competition, so as to form the agglomerate effect, enhance innovative strength, develop core industries, and create a regional industrial cluster which has advantage in innovation, connection, driving force, radiation and intensification. Industrial internationalization is to seek the best combination of elements and optimal utilization of resources worldwide and integrate international innovative resources by means of utilizing global resource, reengineering business process, integrating industry chain and operating capital market. This will promote international cooperation which is dominated by manufacturing to turn to the high-end links such as cooperative R&D, joint design, marketing and brand cultivation, and enhance the self-development capability and core competitiveness of industries in cooperation.

According to the current situation and future needs of industry development, Chinese government raises these six goals which are high-end oriented development, intellectualization, industry integration, ecologicalization, industrial clustering development and industrial internationalization for the purpose to adapting new situation of international economy. These six goals are in line with the main trend of international industry development. They will serve as forward-looking instructions and guidance on the national industry development as well as the industry policy and strategy formation standards for local governments. Therefore, Hebei should follow these industry development directions.

2.2 Hebei's orientation of industrial function and requirements of industrial transformation and upgrading decided by the program outline

In the context of the coordinated development in BTH Region, the direction of the industrial upgrading in Hebei is constrained and influenced by the program outline. Overall, based on the location characteristics and comparative advantages, the Program Outline for the Coordinated Development of the BTH Region, which was deliberated and adopted by the Politburo of the CPC Central Committee on April 30, 2015, focuses on optimizing and enhancing the overall functions of the BTH Region, takes the long-term development needs into consideration and utilizes the strategic position and unique role in the development process. It clearly puts forward the overall functional orientation of the BTH Region: the world-class city group with the capital as its core, the leading area of regional co-development and reform, the new engine of national innovation-driven economic growth, and the demonstration area of ecological restoration and environmental improvement. Under this circumstance, the functional orientation of Beijing, Tianjin and Hebei is as follow: Beijing will focus on building a national center of polities, culture, international communication and technical innovation; Tianjin will focus on building a national advanced manufacturing research and development base, northern international shipping zone, financial innovation operation demonstration zone, and the reform and opening pilot region; Hebei will emphatically build the national commercial and trade base, industrial transformation and upgrading demonstration zone, new-type urbanization demonstration zone as well as eco-conserving division of the BTH Region.

From the perspective of industrial development and deployment, the Program Outline explicitly requires that Beijing should optimize three industrial structures, give full play to the role of science and technology innovation center, highlight the orientation of high-end, service, congregate, confluent and low carbon, vigorously develop service economy, knowledge economy and green economy, and speed up the construction of highly sophisticated economic structure on the basis of dispersing the four types of functions which are general industries, especially high-consumption industries; tertiary industries such as regional logistics bases and specialized markets; social public service such as institutions of education, medical and training and some administrative and institutional service agencies and corporate headquarters. Tianjin should optimize the development of advanced manufacturing industry such as high-end equipment, electronic information and so on, vigorously develop the strategic emerging industry such as aerospace, biological medicine, energy saving and environmental protection and modern service industry including finance, aviation logistics, service outsourcing and so on, so as to build a national R&D base of advanced manufacturing and a agglomeration zone of productive service industry.

And the Program Outline also requires Hebei not only to actively undertakes the non-capital function transferred from Beijing, but also takes full use of R&D achievements transformation from Beijing and Tianjin to upgrade its traditional industries and promote emerging industries. Based on that, Hebei should also focus on advanced manufacturing industries, modern services and emerging industries and strive for new-type industrialization base as well as the test zone of industrial transformation and upgrading. The aim of Hebei's industry upgrading is to create a better industry pattern with clear regional industrial function orientation, favorable industrial distribution and division, free mobility of factors as well as interactive development of upstream and downstream industries.

It can be seen clearly from the orientation above: a. both central government and local governments of Beijing and Tianjin expect that Hebei can fully play a fundamental role in industrial upgrading, urban construction and ecological protection. b. The functional orientation of Beijing and Tianjin is more clarify while apart from the national commercial and trade base and eco-conserving division of the BTH Region, the orientation of Hebei is relatively vague, which offers Hebei huge imaginable space as well as development freedom to promote its industry upgrading. c. The orientations' intention is obvious that there should be a vertical division across the BTH Region, which can be described as "Beijing puts priority on innovation, Tianjin focuses on R&D, and Hebei relies on manufacturing industries". Under such a vertical division of labor system, Hebei will face challenges in setting its industrial upgrading goals as well as in realizing its orientations by central government. For example, with the construction of new airport, there is no doubt that Beijing will be a gateway towards northern China's airports. Tianjin will become the northern harbor port with the construction of "Northern international shipping core zone". What should Hebei do to build "the national commercial and trade base" under this circumstance.

2.3 The requirements of ecological environment protection for the sustainable development of Hebei industries

Ecological environment is another important macro-background for industrial upgrading in Hebei, which is also one of the important factors causing the coordinated development in BTH Region. At present, BTH Region has become one of the areas with the most serious environmental pollution in China (see Table 8). In 2015, a total of 1,710 days of heavy pollution occurred in 70 cities covering BTH and surrounding areas (including Shanxi, Shandong, Inner Mongolia and Henan), accounting for 44.1% of China. Among them, Hebei has discharged most in BTH Region. Since 2011, the emissions of sulfur dioxide and chemical oxygen demand accounted for 76% and 80% of the BTH Region (see Table 9) which was 32.5 and 36.2 percentage points higher than its GDP in BTH (2014). Undoubtedly its traditional industries such as thermal power generation, steel, chemical engineering and building materials discharged the most. In response, the central government issues the most stringent environmental management policies in history including Action Plan for Air Pollution Prevention (Guofa, 2013, No.37) which is known as "Ten Terms of Air" and Action Plan for Water Pollution Prevention (Guofa, 2015, No.17) which is known as "Ten Terms of Water", and explicitly requires Hebei Province to cut the overcapacity of steel, cement and glass as well as coal consumption, and eliminate the backward production facilities of industries polluting waters. Thus, since 2013, according to the deployment of central government, Hebei has implemented a series of strict environment policies, such as the "6, 643 Project" which refers to cut 60 million tons of steel, 61 million tons of cement, 40 million tons of coal and 36 million boxes of glass by 2017, "the air pollution emission limit" as well as regulations on both quality and intensity of pollution. Under this background, it is impossible for Hebei to expand its traditional industries along the original path and the industrial upgrading in future must be conducive to pollution emission control and regional environment quality improvement. In fact, the economy in Hebei, especially industrial growth, has clearly felt strong constraints from environmental policies since 2013.

Table 8 The air condition in BTH Region

Year	PM2.5 concentration in BTH Average concentration (μg/m^3)	The proportion of BTH in China %	The proportion of Hebei Province in BTH %	The last ten cities of Hebei Province in China
2013	106	147	145	Xingtai, Shijiazhuang, Handan, Tangshan, Baoding, Hengshui Langfang
2014	93	145	110	Baoding, Xingtai, Shijiazhuang, Tangshan, Handan, Hengshui Langfang
2015	77	154		Baoding, Xingtai, Hengshui, Tangshan, Handan, Shijiazhuang Langfang

Source: *China Environmental Status Bulletin 2013–2015.*

Note: BTH and surrounding areas including Shanxi, Shandong, Inner Mongolia and Henan; National ranking refers to composite index ranking for city air quality monitored and implemented by 74 new standards in the first phase.

Table 9 The discharge amount of main pollutant in BTH and the influence of Hebei Province

Year	Chemical oxygen demand		Sulfur dioxide	
	Total of BTH (10 thousand tons)	The proportion of Hebei Province in BTH (%)	Total of BTH (10 thousand tons)	The proportion of Hebei Province in BTH (%)
2011	181.8	76.4	174.1	81.1
2012	176.5	76.4	165.9	80.8
2013	171.0	76.4	158.9	80.9
2014	165.2	76.8	147.8	80.5
2015	157.9	76.5	136.5	81.2

Source: *Economic Yearbook of Hebei 2016.*

3. Restrictions of industrial upgrading in Hebei Province

At present, the restriction of industrial upgrading in Hebei mainly comes from the following four aspects:

3.1 The lack of high-level industry development platform

Experience shows that cities and development zones are important carriers to support and lead the economic development of a region. From the perspective of the basic conditions of Hebei industrial development, the central cities is underdeveloped, the new urban district lags behind, the overall level of development zones is low, and there is a lack of high-level platform to support and guide industrial upgrading.

In the era of urbanization, cities are not only the platforms for the gathering of factors and industries, but also the carriers of regional industry competition. Without the development of cities, there will be no industrial development and regional competitiveness. However, in Hebei, there are only 4 cities having over 1 million people including Shijiazhuang, Tangshan, Baoding and Handan. Even Shijiazhuang, the capital of the province, counts only 4.65 million people, with the addition of Luquan, Gaocheng and Luancheng which are new districts after the adjustment of administrative divisions (2014). The lack of city scale has seriously hampered the development of factor agglomeration, industrial facilities and comprehensive service capabilities. According to the Blue Book of Urban Competitiveness 2015, released by the Chinese Academy of Social Sciences (CASS), the comprehensive competitiveness of Shijiazhuang ranked only 42nd in the country, and the city's sustainable competitiveness did not reach the country's top 50.

From the perspective of the future development, the national central city is the core city of the national urban system, playing a pivotal role in finance, management, culture and transportation and giving impetus to international economy and cultural communication. The speed of approving national central cities was accelerated in 2016. By the end of 2016, there were already 8 national central cities formally approved by the State Council, namely Beijing, Tianjin, Shanghai, Guangzhou, Chongqing, Chengdu, Wuhan and Zhengzhou. Entering the ranks of the central cities of the country means greater allocation of resources and greater driving force to the surrounding areas. Therefore, it has become the competitive focus among the domestic cities. At present, Xi'an, Shenyang, Nanjing, Hangzhou, Changsha, Shenzhen, Xiamen, Tsingdao and other cities are competing for the national central city. Shijiazhuang is likely to miss this national orientation considering the area conditions, city scale, industrial foundation and regional influence.

As for the national golden brands, the national level new zone, free trade test zone, comprehensive reform pilot zone and independent innovation demonstration zone are comprehensive functional zones approved by the State Council to undertake the strategic tasks of major national development and reform and opening up, having the advantages of policies Innovation and institutional reform. They have been a new engine of giving impetus to reform, innovation and open of related provinces and cities. By the end of 2016, there have been 18 national level new districts, 11 free trade test zones, 12 national comprehensive reform pilot zones and 17 national independent innovation demonstration zones nationwide, but Hebei only had Xiong'an New Area which was just established with no scale and no driving force. In terms of national industrial agglomeration platforms, Hebei has 5 national level high-tech zones, 6 national level economic and technological development zones and 2 comprehensive bonded zones respectively (as shown in Table 10). Although the quantity is not lagging behind in the country, there is a huge gap with the advanced provinces and municipalities on the scale and development level. In 2014, the enterprises number and total industrial output of five national level high-tech zones in Hebei only accounted for 7.7% and 28.8% of Zhongguancun in Beijing and 35% and 73% of Tianjin Binhai New Area respectively (as shown in Table 11) .The total income is less than 1/4 of that in Hubei, 1/2 of Sichuan and Hunan, and only half of Henan, and the overall level of development is not as good as that of the four central and western provinces (as shown in Table 12). In terms of national economic and technological development zones, in 2015, the regional GDP of six national economic development zones in Hebei achieved 134.84 billion yuan, accounting for only 3.5% of the GDP of Hebei, which is less than half what it is in one of the Tianjin economic development zones.

Table 10 The situation of national important functional areas in Hebei Province

The name of functional area	The numbers in China	The numbers in Hebei Province
National Level new district	18	1
Free trade test zone in China	11	0
National comprehensive reform pilot zone	12	0
National independent innovation demonstration zone	17	0
Comprehensive bonded zones	46	2
National-level high-tech industry development zone	145	5
National-level economic and technological development zone	215	6

Table 11 The comparison of national level high-tech zones in BTH (2014)

The name of high-tech zone	Enterprise number (number)	The high-tech enterprise number	Total industrial output value (100 million yuan)	Net profit (100 million yuan)	Tax and fee (100 million yuan)
Zhongguancun in Beijing	15,645	7,292	9,289	2,582	1,857.6
Tianjin Binhai New Area	3,437	479	3,665.9	603.5	208.4
Total of Hebei Province	1,204	310	2,674.9	212.5	194.22
Shijiazhuang High-Tech Zone	626	162	970	97.1	81.9
Baoding High-Tech Zone	192	65	960.2	80.2	68.4
Tangshan High-Tech Zone	152	48	133.4	9.1	8.03
Yanjiao High-Tech Zone	200	27	465.8	19.6	27.57
Chengde High-Tech Zone	34	8	145.5	6.5	8.32

Source: *China Torch Statistic Yearbook (2015)*.

Table 12 The comparison of national level high-tech zones in Hebei, Henan, Sichuan, Hubei and Hunan (2014)

Province	The number of national level high-tech zones	Total income (100 million yuan)	The proportion of Hebei's total income in other provinces (%)
Hebei	5	3,515	—
Henan	5	6,936	50.68
Sichuan	4	7,381	47.62
Hubei	5	14,900	23.59
Hunan	5	7,843	44.82

Source: *China Yearbook of High-tech Industrial Development Zone (2015)*.

Problems do exist in the construction of development zone, which is having carrier without content, having policy without implement and having project without efficiency. Up to now, there are 184 development zones above the provincial level in Hebei, of which 150 are economic development zones, 30 are high-tech industrial development zones and 4 are special customs supervision zones. However, there is a general lack of large projects with support and promotion among these zones. Even if there are projects, the efficiency is relatively low. For example, as the first comprehensive bonded zone, Caofeidian comprehensive bonded zone should have been the signal of opening up the coastal areas of Hebei, the "golden brand" of reaching out to the world and an important window for international visits in BTH. However, during the five years' development and construction, it doesn't reach the desired result: the number of strategic support projects is too small, and the leading role of the platform remains to be further developed. Large projects in Caofeidian don't go well such as the millions of tons oil refining signed with Sinopec. The implementation is difficult and the supportive industry is not confirmed.

3.2 Insufficient high-end talents in Hebei

For a long time, there are insufficient high-end talents in Hebei. In terms of the education level, according to the 1% sample survey of population of the National Bureau of Statistics in China in 2015, only 1,021 people per million people in Hebei had college degrees or above, less than the national average, and only slightly higher than Yunnan, Guangxi, Henan, Guizhou, Tibet (see Table 13), accounting for 91.1%, 43.8%, and 24.1% of national average, Tianjin and Beijing respectively. Moreover, with the promotion of talents category, the talents shortage in Hebei was more obvious (see Figure 10). Among them, there were 371 undergraduate students per 10,000 people, only slightly higher than that of Henan and Tibet, accounting for only 62.6 of national average, 31.7% of Tianjin and 16.8% of Beijing. The number of postgraduate students per 10,000 people is 29, slightly higher than those in Jiangxi, Henan, Guangxi, Hainan, Sichuan, Guizhou and Tibet, accounting for only 49.2% of the national average, 24% of Tianjin, and 4.3% of Beijing. Higher-level talents, such as specialists (including high-skilled talents) receiving special government allowance from the State Council, millions of talent specialists and academicians are even scarcer. The number of these three kinds of high-level talents per 10,000 people in Hebei was only 25%, 14% and 6.8% of the national average up to 2015 (see Figure 11).

Table 13 The number of people per 10,000 with college degrees or above

Region	The number of people	Region	Number of people	Region	Number of people	Region	Number of people
China	1,333	Heilongjiang Province	1,328	Henan Province	874	Guizhou	845
Beijing	4,234	Shanghai	2,870	Hubei Province	1,499	Yunnan	948
Tianjin	2,333	Jiangsu Province	1,642	Hunan Province	1,189	Tibet	711
Hebei Province	1,021	Zhejiang Province	1,466	Guangdong Province	1,199	Shaanxi	1,774
Shanxi Province	1,374	Anhui Province	1,173	Guangxi Autonomous District	921	Gansu	1,252
Inner Mongolia Autonomous District	1,614	Fujian Province	1,300	Hainan Province	1,085	Qinghai Province	1,045
Liaoning Province	1,693	Jiangxi Province	1,057	Chongqing	1,256	Ningxia Autonomous District	1,524
Jilin Province	1,317	Shandong Province	1,263	Sichuan Province	1,099	Xinjiang Autonomous District	1,455

Source: *China Statistical Yearbook (2015).*

Figure 10 The comparison of education level among population in different areas of China

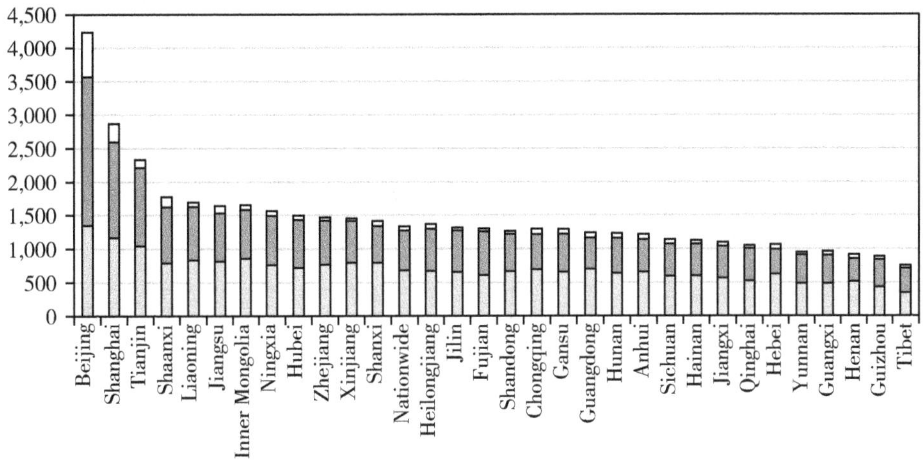

Figure 11 The proportion of talents per 10,000 at all levels of Hebei in China

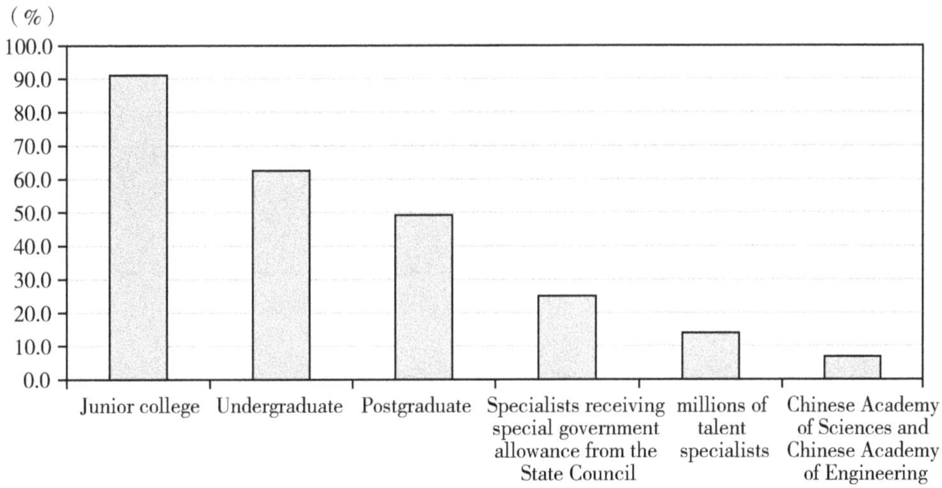

At the same time, there is a clear mismatch among the talents. According to the China Yearbook of Science and Technology, among the 1.175 million professionals in Hebei in 2014, the engineering talents only accounted for 11%, which was half of the national average and ranked 21st in China; the scientific researchers only accounted for 0.35%, which was less than 1/4 of the national average and ranked the last place in China (see Figure 12 and Figure 13). Not only that, though Hebei has dealt with the requirement of the industrial development and the cultivation of talents' team the over the last decade, the total number of talents was up to 4.3 million, of which high-tech talents accounted for 26.7% by the end of 2013. However, there exists serious brain drain. Since 2004, at least one quarter of the more than 40 "Gold Medal Blue-collars" in Hebei that won awards in the National Numerical Control Skills Competition have already moved out of Hebei.

Figure 12 The proportion of engineering staffs among the professionals in all regions in China

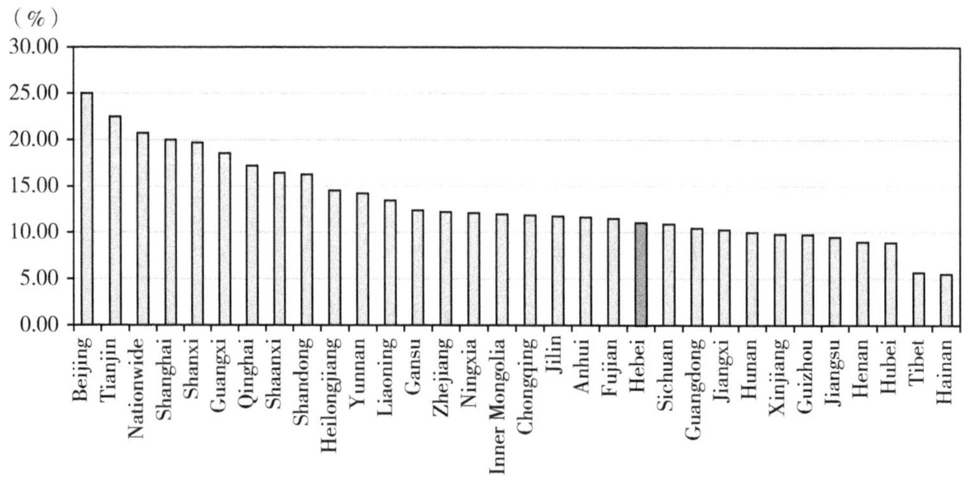

Figure 13 The proportion of engineering staffs among the professionals in all regions in China

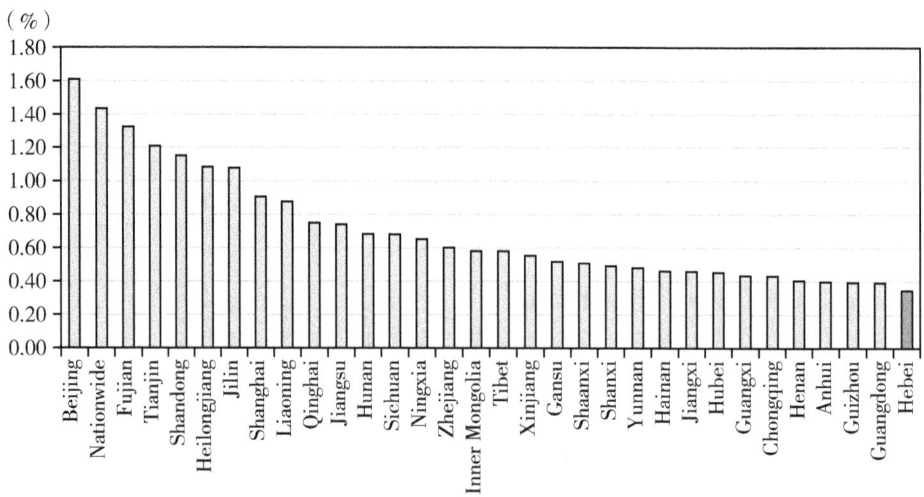

3.3 The leading-in of factors is confronted with institutional obstacles

Experience at home and abroad shows that the industrial upgrading in a region depends largely on the introduction of advanced production factors, as well as the speed and scale of the introduction. Hebei has been confronted with many institutional obstacles in the introduction of advanced production factors over the years. For the three years of the coordinated development in BTH, Beijing has evacuated more than 370 wholesale markets outside Beijing such as Zoo, Dahongmen and Tianyi markets. Hebei imported 4,100 projects and 382.5 billion yuan from Beijing and Tianjin only in 2016, accounting for 42% and 51% respectively in Hebei. However, the industrial relocation did not simultaneously bring the population and enterprises to Hebei.

From the perspective of population, the increment of permanent population and migrant people in Beijing has been continuously declined over five years (see Figure 14). In 2016, the number of migrant people was up to 8.075 million, decreased by 15,100 over 2015. It became the second largest city in the world after Shanghai that had the negative growth of migrant people. The same situation occurred in Tianjin too (see Figure 15). There were 5.08 million of migrant people in Tianjin in 2016. Although reaching an increase of 71,900 than the previous year, it was significantly lower than the increase of 241,700 in 2015, the increase of 352,700 in 2014 and an increase of 479,500 in 2013. However, the reduced permanent resident population in Beijing and Tianjin did not flow to Hebei. The same year, the total permanent population of Hebei was 74.7 million, achieving an increase of 451,300 over the previous year, of which the population of birth and deaths was respectively 925,000 and 473,700. The population growth in Hebei mainly depends on the population of birth.

As to enterprises, according to what we have learned during the symposium with some enterprises in Zhongguancun, about 30% of SMEs (small and medium-sized enterprises) in Beijing, especially technology enterprises, prefer to move to other cities for development considering the operating costs such as house rent and staff salaries. However, when it comes to select of a new city, most enterprises prefer to choose southern cities which has better ecological environment. Only less than 10% enterprises are willing to move to Hebei.

Though there are various factors contributing this situation, it is undeniable that the "tax-sharing" financial and tax system, the different public service policy and the smog which also occured in Beijing and Tianjin, are main factors.

Figure 14 The incremental changes of permanent population and migrant people in Beijing over the past five years

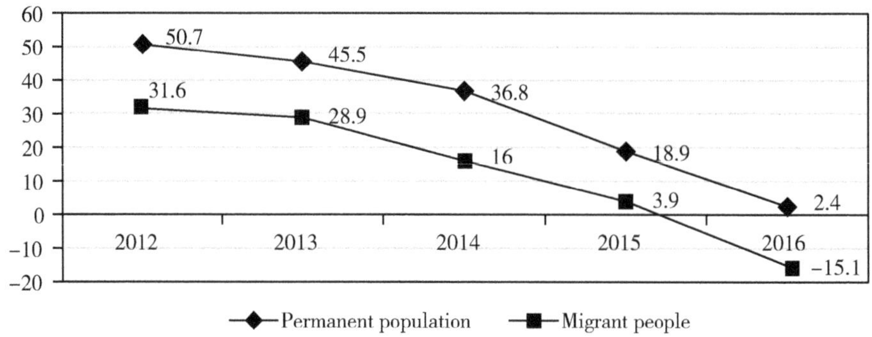

Source: *Beijing Statistical Yearbook 2016.*

Figure 15 The incremental changes of permanent population and migrant people in Tianjin over the past five years

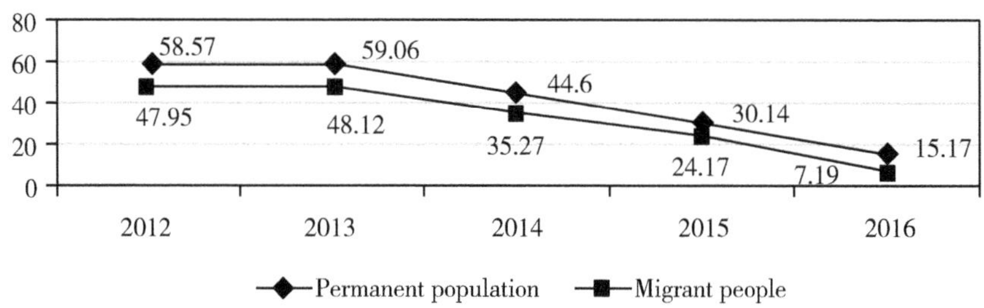

Source: *Tianjin Statistical Yearbook 2016.*

As to the financial and tax system, the "tax-sharing" fiscal system leads to the local conflict of interest, which influences the free distribution of enterprise according to market logic. Since China now implements the financial and tax system of "tax-sharing", all local governments are willing to keep as many enterprises as possible so as to ensure that they have sufficient sources of tax revenue. They set up various administrative obstacles for the transfer of enterprises in different regions, which have caused the administrative separation between regions. It has been one of the important obstacles for the coordinated development in BTH Region for a long time. Although after the strategy of the coordinated development in BTH Region was put forward, the governments of Beijing, Tianjin and Hebei have formulated the financial and tax sharing measures for industrial transfer projects and building parks (irrespective of the rationality of such sharing measures) under the guidance of central government, transferring enterprises still faces many invisible obstacles in practice. For example, some enterprises in Beijing and Tianjin implement the industrial transfer projects in forms of establishing branch office. Since the branch office is not an independent corporate juridical person, its revenue should be merged into head office and then be paid to the place of registration. From the perspective of Hebei, it provides resources including land, energy and environmental capacity and public service without obtaining any revenue, so enterprises must be registered in the local as an independent legal subsidiary, which also brings another problem that all the original qualification such as the identity of high-tech enterprise will be lost. The enterprises need to be registered or approved again, not only adding the time and operating costs, but also affecting the business development. It is impossible for these kinds of enterprises to enjoy preferential policies related to the two governments. These problems greatly affect the transfer inclination of enterprises in Beijing and Tianjin to Hebei.

In public policy, the huge public service gap caused mainly by the public policies which are segmented in the region has hindered the free flow of factors in the region such as population, especially high-quality people. Per capita high education resource, per capita public education investment, per capita public health resource and social security level of BTH are shown in Table 14, Table 15 and Table 16.

Table 14 The comparison of public expenditure on education in BTH

	The number of higher education institutions per million people	Per capita public financial expenditure on education (yuan)	public financial budget on education of all levels of students				
			common Primary school	common Junior middle school	common High school	Secondary vocational schools	General colleges and universities
China	1.86	1,781	8,838	12,105	10,821	10,961	18,144
Beijing	4.19	3,904	23,757	40,444	42,193	34,433	61,344
Tianjin	3.56	3,001	18,128	28,209	32,848	26,481	20,415
Hebei	1.59	1,348	6,753	9,558	9,992	12,008	13,829

Source: *Treasury Department Statistical Table on the Implementation of National Education Funds, 2015*

Table 15 The comparison of public health resource in BTH

	Per million people havingThe number of hospitals	Per 10,000 people having The number of beds in hospital	Per 10,000 people having The number of health workers
Nationwide	20	39	58
Beijing	29	48	104
Tianjin	26	36	59
Hebei	21	34	50

Source: calculated from the data of *China Statistical Yearbook (2016).*

Table 16 The comparison of the per capita wage and social security in BTH (2015)

Unit: yuan

	Average annual wage of employed persons in urban units	Per capita pension monthly of urban retirees	Per capita social pensions monthly for the urban and rural residents	Unemployment insurance amount monthly for unemployed person
Nationwide	62,029	2,354	119	2,706
Beijing	111,390	3,398	559	10,579
Tianjin	80,090	2,577	299	3,715
Hebei	50,921	2,572	89	2,900

Source: *calculated from the data of China Statistical Yearbook (2016).*

3.4 The business environment has not been fundamentally improved

Good business environment is an important prerequisite for factor aggregation and industrial development. For a place, a good business environment is just like air and sunshine which can't be ignored. It can be said that a good business environment has become the core competitiveness of the development of a region or a city. The city with good business environment will own the future of the industry, the city and the region. At present, all countries and regions worldwide attach great importance to the construction of business environment. In order to improve the business environment and create a favorable atmosphere for industrial development, Hebei has taken a series of measures and introduced some policies such as Several Opinions on Vigorously Improving Business Environment. The business environment has been improved unprecedentedly. But in general, compared with Beijing, Tianjin and the developed provinces, Hebei's business environment is not loose enough, affecting the investment environment and restricting the industrial transformation and upgrading. Mainly in the following four aspects:

First, the capital market is less developed. Theoretically speaking, the adjustment and upgrading of industrial structure can't be separated from the effective support and coordinated development of the capital market. According to the international experience, the more active the areas are, the more active the capital market is. The capital market of Hebei is less developed and active which is directly related to the stage and status of its own development. At the same time, Hebei's capital market is directly relevant to the level of development of the entire country. China's capital market is not well developed, which only has floor market. Apart from that, the OTC market is less developed and the market transaction scale is very limited. At present, the total market value of A share market is only about 70% of GDP, not only less than the corresponding relationship of 1:1 to 1:2 between the capital market and the real economy which was said by the famous investor Buffett, but also less than the mature market level of 150%.

In terms of Hebei, a multi-level capital market system with rational construction, perfect function, transparent standard, stable and efficient operation is far from being formed, and its ability to support industrial upgrading is seriously inadequate. Taking the funds raised by listed companies in A-share market as an example, Beijing is the highest with 14 times the per-capita in Hebei Province. Tianjin, though not as good as Beijing's per capita, is also 1.48 times the per capita in Hebei (see Figure 16). Up to December 31, 2015, there were 53 listed companies in Hebei, accounting for 1.87% of the total number of listed companies in China and ranking the 14th in the country. The total market capitalization of listed companies was 803.834 billion yuan, accounting for 1.51% of the national total capitalization and ranking the 14th in the country; 239 managers who took part in Privately Offered Fund have been registered in Hebei, ranking 16th in China. The scale and quality of the capital market can't match the degree of economic development (economic scale ranked 7th in the country), and the supportive role of capital markets in economic development has not yet been brought into full play. Shijiazhuang Equity Exchange, the only regional equity exchange in Hebei Province, has a big gap compared with Beijing Equity Exchange and Tianjin Equity Exchange, no matter from the number of listed companies or capital service functions.

Figure 16 The comparison of per capita funds raised by stocks in Beijing, Tianjin and Hebei Province from 1990 to 2015(Ⅰ) (Unit: yuan)

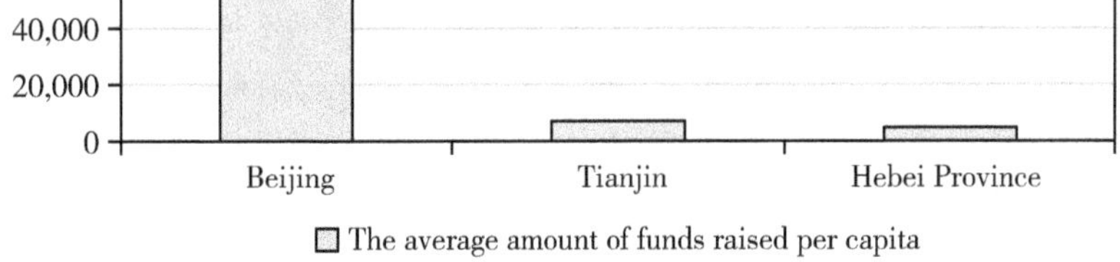

Source: http://blog.sina.com.cn/s/blog_51bfd7ca0102w57m.html

Figure 17 The comparison of per capita funds raised by stocks in Beijing, Tianjin and Hebei Province from 1990 to 2015(Ⅱ) (Unit: thousand yuan)

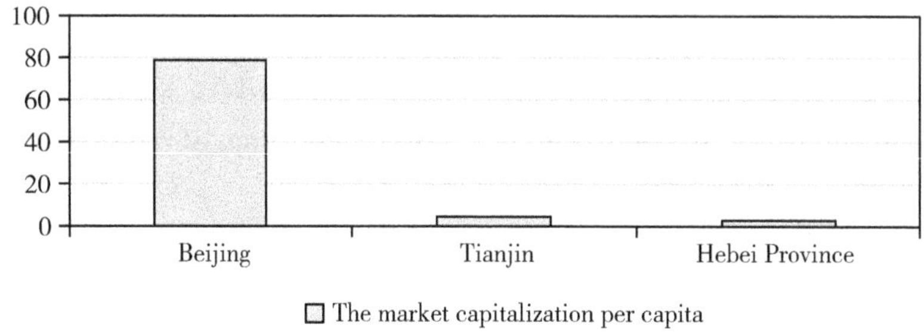

Source: The same as that in Figure 16.

Second, the credibility system is not perfect. As a concept of economy, culture and society, integrity has been one of the core ideas in the society of market economy. A good social credit system is an important guarantee for establishing and regulating the order of the market economy, as well as a significant prerequisite for building an economically strong and beautiful province of Hebei. At present, Hebei is in a critical period of industrial upgrading when it is necessary to accelerate the construction of a market credibility system. Since the 18th CPC National Congress has put forward the target of "strengthening the construction of government affairs integrity, business integrity, social integrity and judicial public trust", Hebei has made some progress in promoting the development of social credit system. However, the conflict which is unmatched, uncoordinated and incommensurate is still prominent between the social credit system and the economy and society developing level. The main problems are as follows: First, the underdevelopment of the construction and sharing of the credit information platform. Up to the end of May, 2016, the construction of credit information platform failed the assessment and the information system failed to realize information interconnection and resource sharing among units and departments, citing the assessment of construction and sharing of the credit information platform in provinces from the State Information Center. Second, the credit reporting system covering the whole society has not been formed yet. The credit record of business is lacking and the mechanism which includes encouraging the integrity and punishing the dishonesty is unsound. Third, the credit service market is underdeveloped, the service system is not perfect, the service behavior is not normative, and the rights' protection mechanism of the credit information subject is deficient. Fourth, the social credit consciousness and the credit level are low. The social atmosphere of keeping one's promise and being credit has not been formed yet.

Third, the lacking of fair market environment. A fair competitive market environment is an essential condition for a stable and long-term regional economic development. Building an orderly market with fair competition will effectively reduce the market access threshold and the operating costs of enterprises, stimulate the vitality of market bodies as well as fully release the momentum of economic growth. For a long time, Chinese government has made tremendous efforts in building a fair, transparent and predictable market environment, constantly reducing barriers to entry for non-government investment and creating conditions for fair competition. Apart from that, it has introduced market regulatory plans to promote fair, law-based and convenient market conditions. The market condition has improved dramatically. There are also many advanced domestic and international experiences in building a fair market condition. For example, Hong Kong conducts a pilot program of low-cost taxation and formulates a policy of nurturing and supporting professional service agencies. The United States has established a unified public database of corporate and personal credit information. In terms of Hebei Province, the fair market environment has lagged behind with relatively limited market access. The dominant or recessive market barriers that exist in many industries have not been broken yet so it is hard for the innovative private-owned enterprises and small and medium-sized enterprises to enter. The public sphere is not totally open to private capital, the operating costs are keeping high in competitive areas and the investment and operating costs are high for enterprises. Apart from that, there are still some unfair problems in the access of resources between enterprises and individuals and the financial market condition is unfavorable which only gets 394 point and ranks 12th of the country in the evaluation of the national financial and ecological environment, accounting for 74.1% of that in the eastern coastal areas and 35 points lower than the national average (429). Hebei still has a long way to go in creating a fair, transparent and predictable market environment.

Fourth, the lacking of efficient government environment. Government environment is one of the most important environments for the development of regional economy and society. A good government service environment and efficient administrative efficiency can maximize the attraction of various resources such as capital, technology and talents, thereby promoting the transformation and development of local economy and society. In recent years, Hebei has carried forward implementation of the decisions and arrangements of the country, accelerated the reform of "combining the management with devolution and optimizing service", and promoted streamlining administration and delegating power, so that the government environment has been greatly improved. However, on the whole, the reform of "combining the management with devolution and optimizing service" has not been deepened yet and the government environment has not been fundamentally optimized. For example, in some areas, the delegated items requiring administrative approval are with low quality, so that the devolution is inadequate, unsynchronized and unconnected; the government approval is inefficient and the cycle is long, resulting in that enterprise would take irregular actions to avoid approval and management; the mechanism that "the approval and management belongs to one subject" is not suitable for the reform demands of separating the approval from management and centralizing the examination and approval, above all, the responsibility boundary of the examination and approval department and supervision department is not clear, which is lacking legal protection; the lack of strict law enforcement by the government leads to illegal production and management in some enterprises(such as Anfeng Steel event).

4. The goal and route of the industrial upgrading in Hebei Province

4.1 Hebei's goals of industrial division based on coordinated development

The role and goal of an area in the regional industrial division determine the direction of its industrial development and further influence its industrial upgrading policies and actions, which have a decisive influence on the promotion of industrial upgrading. To establish the industrial upgrading goal of Hebei, we must first establish the role orientation of Hebei in the industrial division in BTH, so as to provide the basis for establishing a more reasonable and effective industrial upgrading direction and route in Hebei.

4.1.1 The historical evolution and tendency of the industrial division in BTH

Since the reform and opening up, the evolution of industrial division in BTH can be divided into two stages. Before the middle of 1990s, the industrial division of BTH was horizontal and at a low level, so the industries were more isomorphic with intense competition among regions. In 1994, seven of the top ten industrial sectors in BTH were the same, with the top ranked ones being ferrous metal smelting and processing industries; among the top five service sectors, three industries were the same, which included wholesale and retail, finance and insurance industry and transportation, accounting for more than 60% of their respective service industries (see Figures 18 to Figure 23).

Figures 18 The proportion of total industrial output value of the top ten industries in Beijing in 1994

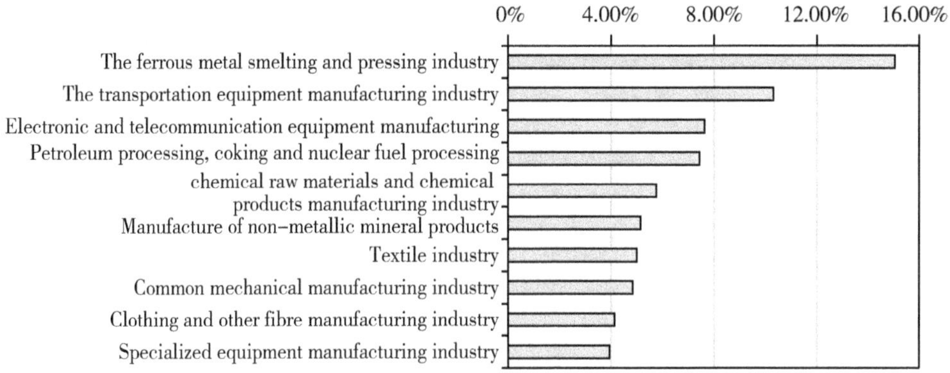

Figures 19 The proportion of total industrial output value of the top ten industries in Tianjin in 2004

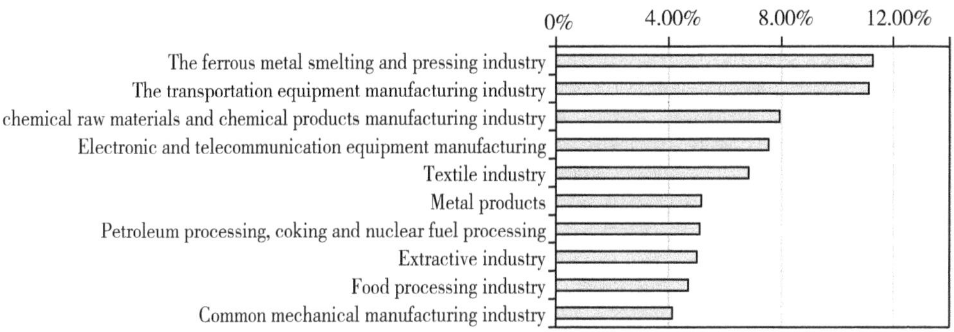

Figures 20 The proportion of total industrial output value of the top ten industries in Hebei Province in 1994

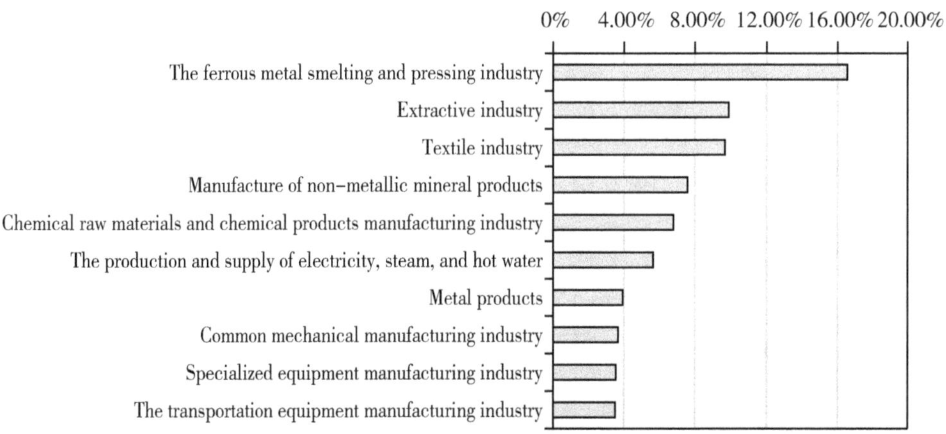

Figure 21 The proportion ranking of the value-added of tertiary industry in Beijing in 1994

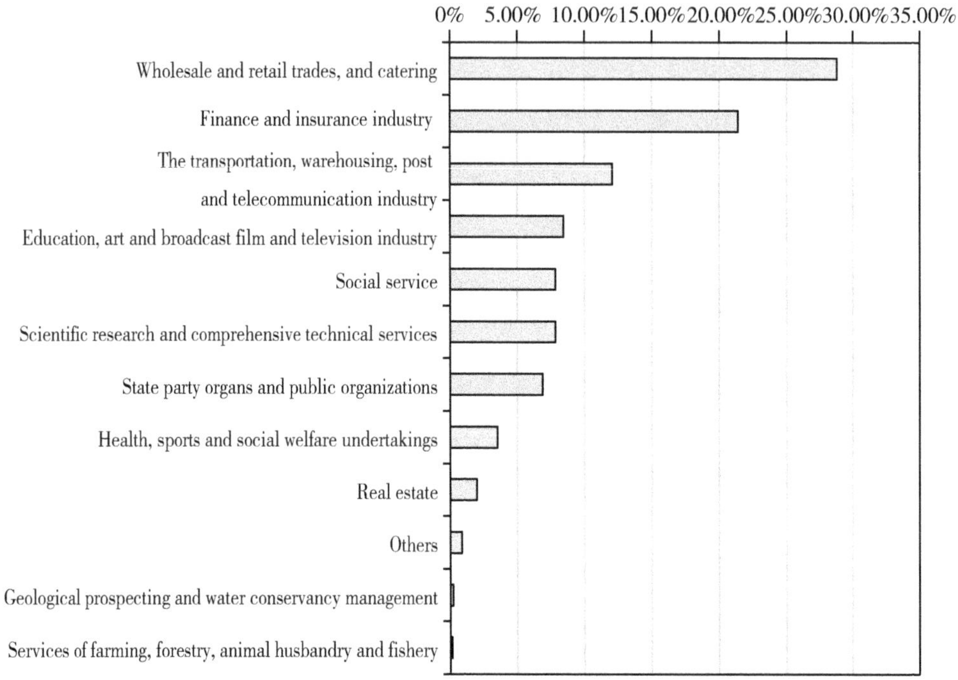

Figure 22 The proportion ranking of the value-added of tertiary industry in Tianjin in 1994

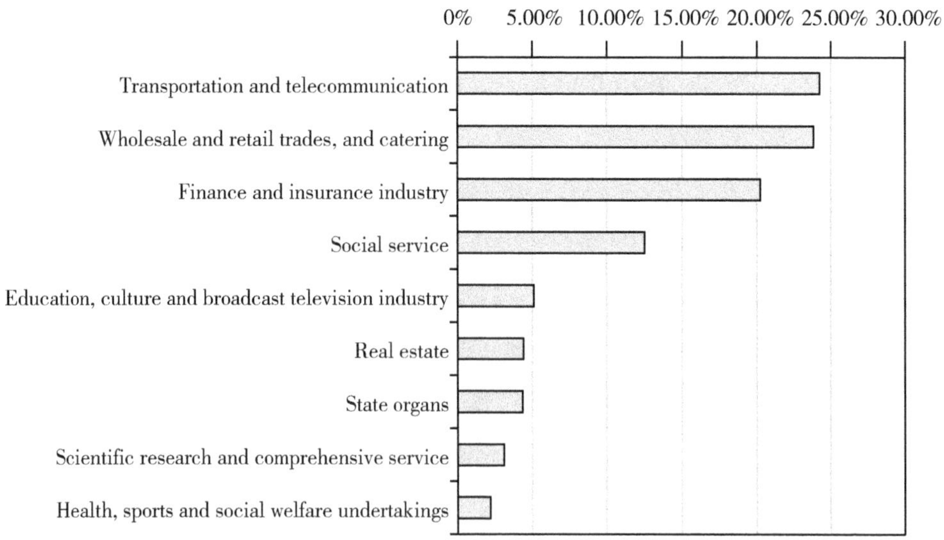

Figure 23 The proportion ranking of the value-added of tertiary industry in Hebei Province in 1994

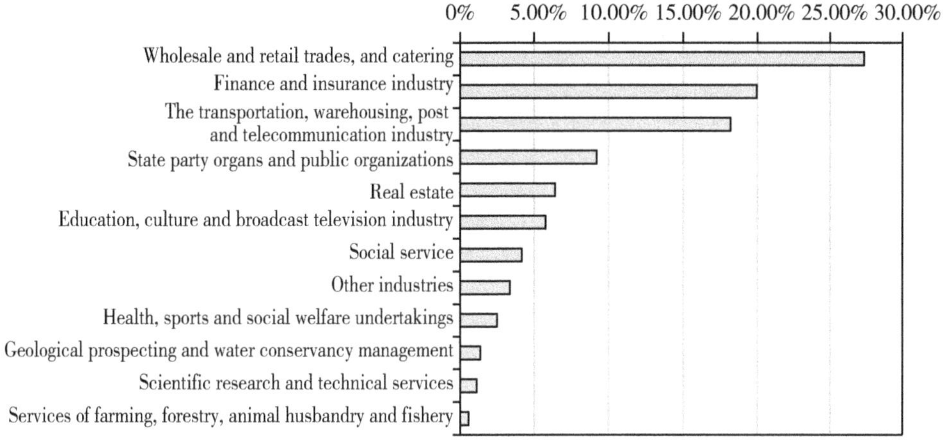

Source: The data of Figure 18 to Figure 23 are from *Economic Yearbook of BTH in 1995.*

After that, the governments of Beijing, Tianjin and Hebei all realized the drawbacks of the homogeneous competition under such a low-level industrial division and started to readjust their industrial structure one after another. At the 8th party congress in 1997, Beijing put forward the development of the capital economy for the first time including the knowledge economy as the essence, the high-tech as the forerunner, the developed tertiary industry, the rational industrial structure, the high benefit and high quality which was suitable for the capital, and began the process of "de-industrialization". When it came to 21 century, at the "10th Five-Year Plan" in 2001, Beijing put forward the development of capital economy with the orientation of scientific, service, cultural and open, speeding up the transition from manufacturing economy to service economy. At the "11th Five-Year Plan" in 2006, Beijing further put forward the idea to fully explore and utilize the high-quality resources of the capital, and develop tertiary industry dominated by productive service and creative industry, taking road of industrial development which was high-end, efficient and radiating. After nearly 20 years of adjustment, by 2015, the added value of the tertiary industry in Beijing accounted for 79.8% of the GDP, accounting for nearly 50% of the added value of the tertiary industry in BTH. This was no doubt that Beijing reached the top end of the industrial value chain in this region.

In the same period, in 1994, Tianjin proposed to basically complete the Binhai New Area in about 10 years. In 1997, the state positioned Tianjin as the economic center of the Pan-Bohai Area. The industry in Tianjin developed rapidly and the economy developed in a high-speed mode. In 2005, the Central Government incorporated the development and opening up of Tianjin Binhai New Area into the national strategy which became the new pole of economic growth after Shenzhen Special Economic Zone and Pudong New Area. In 2006, Tianjin was positioned as an international port city, an economic center in the north and an eco-city. During the "12th Five-Year Plan", Tianjin further proposed to vigorously develop a modern industrial system with structural optimization, advanced technology, clean and safe environment, high added value and strong employability, form a high-end, high-quality, high-tech industrial structure and build a high-end industrial highland . In 2014, the state set up a free trade test zone in Tianjin and proposed that the free trade zone should be built into a high-level open platform for the coordinated development in BTH Region, a pilot area of reform and opening up and institution innovation, and a high-end free trade zone to the world. During this period, an important breakthrough was made in the development of Tianjin's tertiary industry. In 2014, the added value of the tertiary industry exceeded 50%, achieving transition change of the industrial structure.

At this period, Hebei also gradually realized the prominent problems of unreasonable economic structure, extensive growth mode and poor capacity of science and technology. In the "10th Five-Year Plan", they proposed to speed up the strategic readjustment of the economic structure and take advantageous industries as dominant one, develop the industries such as metallurgy, energy, medicine, chemical engineering, machinery, building materials, construction, food, and so on, and build a number of production base for product with characteristics. In the "11th Five-Year Plan" period, Hebei further proposed to readjust the economic structure strategically, especially the optimization and upgrading of the industrial structure should be the top priority of economic development. The priority should be given to the development of top ten leading industries, including iron and steel, equipment manufacturing, petrochemicals, food, medicine, building materials, textiles and clothing, electronics information, modern logistics, and tourism. In the "12th Five-Year Plan" period, Hebei put forward to speeding up the transformation of economic development mode, accelerating industrial restructuring and upgrading, promoting the coordinated development of the three industries, emphasizing the promotion of traditional industries, speeding up the development of strategic emerging industries and expanding three industry. However, by 2015, the industrial development situation, which was dominated by industry, supported on resources, with prominent structure and high proportion of raw materials industry has not changed fundamentally.

Vertically, compared with ten years ago, only 2 industries in the top 10 industries in the three provinces were the same in 2015. In the top 5 tertiary industries, only 2 industries were the same, and the industrial low level isomorphism had been significantly improved (see Figure 24 to Figure 29).

Figures 24 The proportion of total industrial output value of the top ten industries in Beijing in 2015

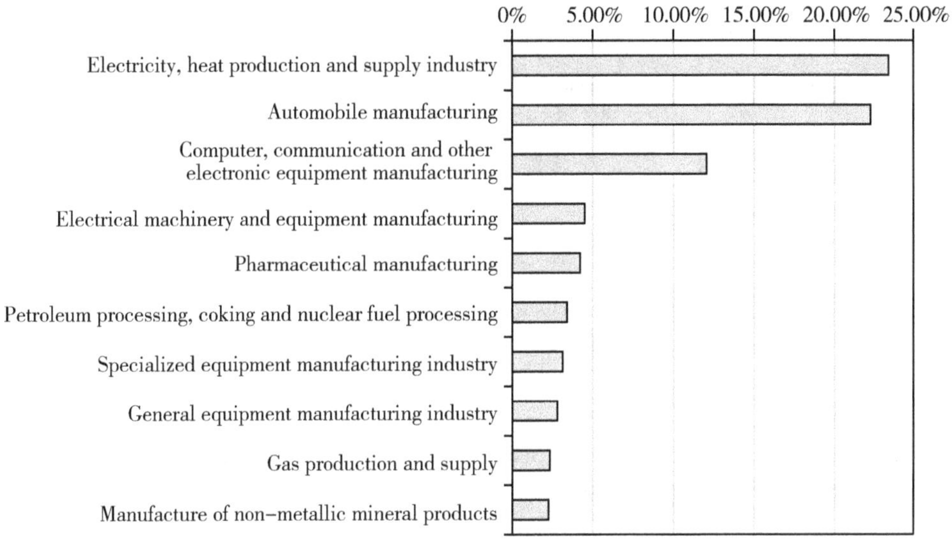

Figures 25 The proportion of total industrial output value of the top ten industries in Tianjin in 2015

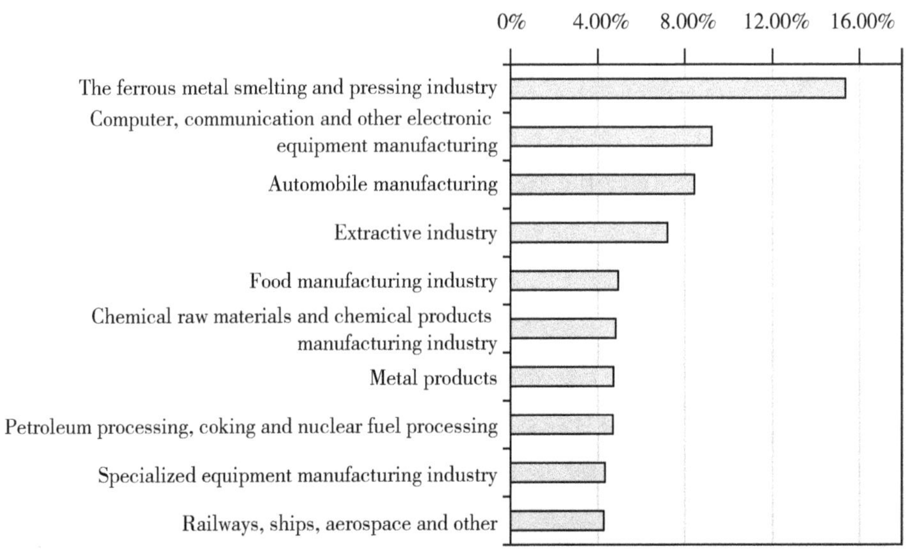

Figures 26 The proportion of total industrial sales value of the top ten industries in Hebei Province in 2015

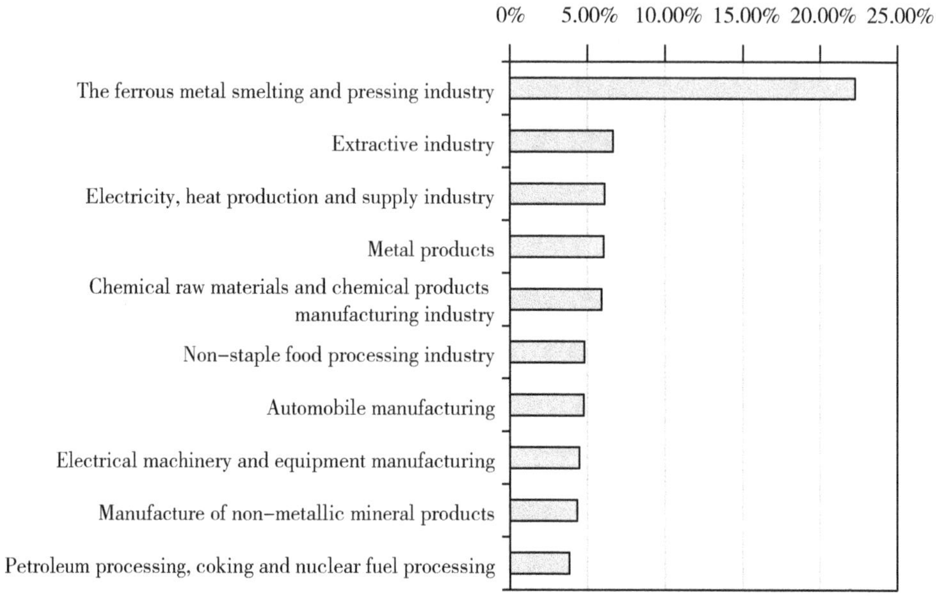

Figure 27 The proportion ranking of the value-added of tertiary industry in Beijing in 2015

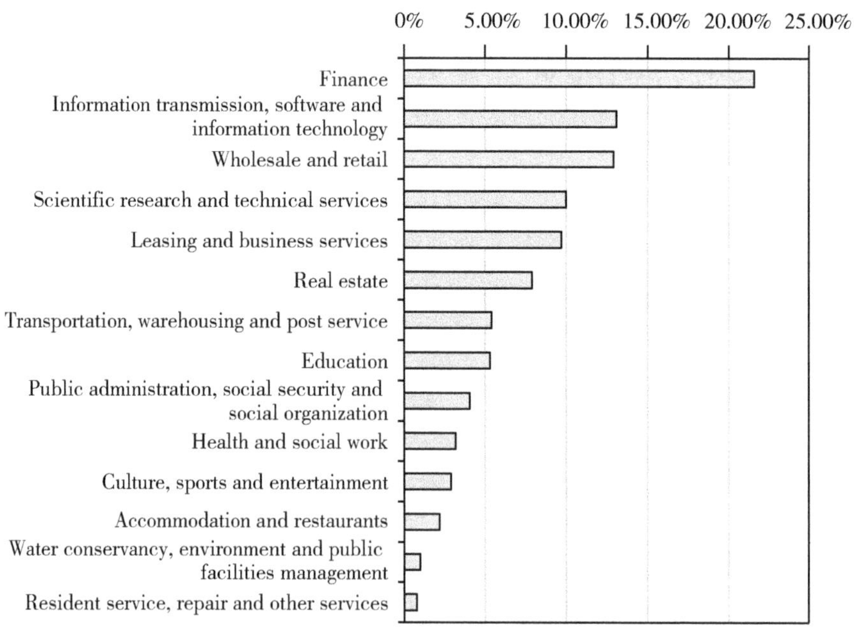

Figure 28 The proportion ranking of the value-added of tertiary industry in Tianjin in 2015

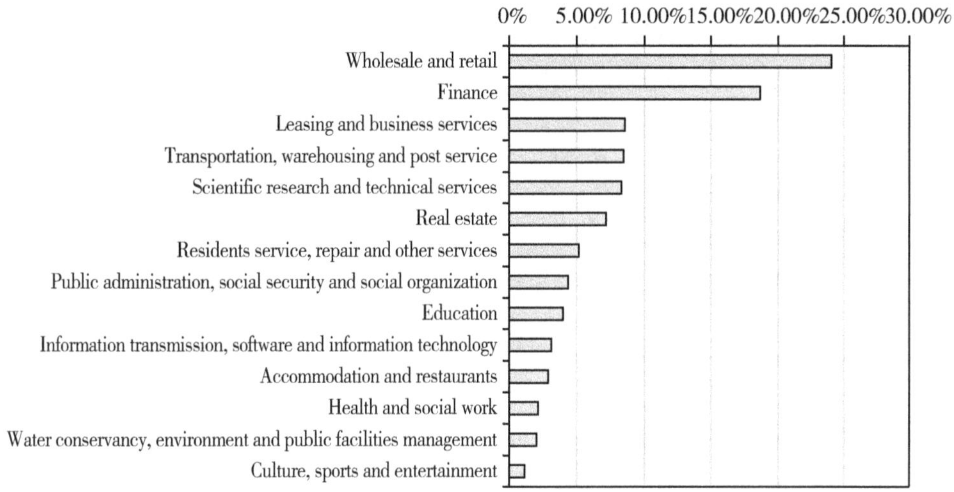

Figure 29 The proportion ranking of the value-added of tertiary industry in Hebei Province in 2015

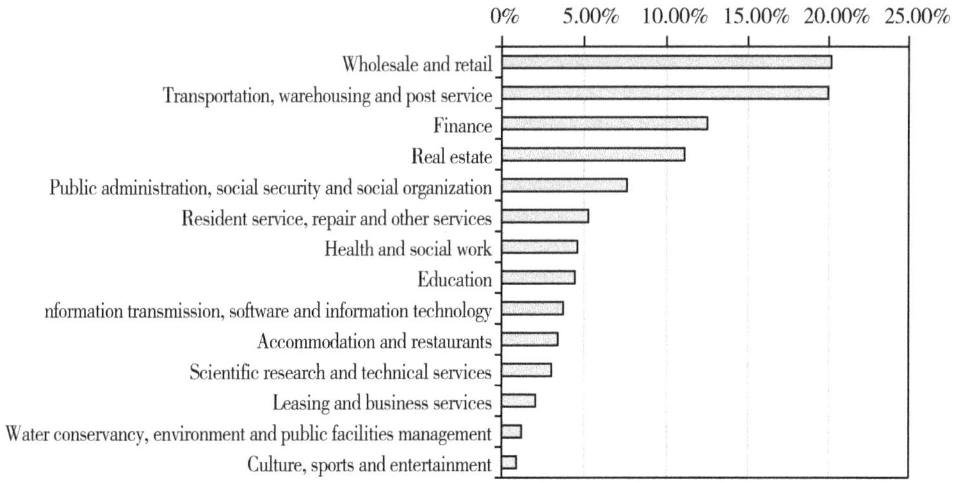

Source: The data of Figure 24 to Figure 29 are from *Economic Yearbook of BTH in 2016.*

At the macro level, after nearly 20 years of interactive adjustment, there is a vertically low-level industrial division system among the BTH Region, which can be described as "Beijing putting priority on innovation, Tianjin focusing on R&D, and Hebei developing a manufacture-based economy". Compared with the previous low-level isomorphism, this pattern of industrial division has made some progress, giving comparative advantages to various places in a short period of time and giving play to the complementarity of regional resources and advantages.

From the perspective of the law of industrial division in the value chain, at present the industrial division between Beijing, Tianjin and Hebei still stays in a more primitive status which is the typical division mode between developed and underdeveloped regions and is still the primary form of regional division. In the long term, there is strong dependence. If it is settled for some reason, the industries in the less developed regions will be at the bottom of the industrial chain for a long time and will always be suppressed by the developed regions at the high end of the industrial chain. This will easily lead to the industrial low-end locking tendency which is not conducive to the upgrading of industries in the entire region.

4.1.2 Hebei's Role in the division of industries in BTH

According to the Program Outline, the goal of coordinated development of BTH is mainly in five aspects: First, to solve the prominent problems the development of the capital faced, to optimize and enhance the core functions of the capital, to explore the optimized development mode in the dense population and economic areas, finding a way to solve the "urban disease"; second, to get rid of the invisible barriers and break the administrative division, so as to promote the complementary and integrated development of BTH and to explore new mechanisms for the coordinated regional development; third, to improve the pattern of urban agglomerations, optimize the layout of productive forces and the spatial structure; fourth, to strengthen the ecological construction and environmental protection, promoting the coordinated development of economic society and population resources, and exploring the sustainable development of the region; fifth, to enhance the comprehensive strength and overall competitiveness of BTH Region, to improve the radiation capability of the Pan-Bohai Area and the hinterland of the North China so as to make greater contributions to the transformation and development of the entire country and the all-round opening up. According to the above goals, the most fundamental and core aim of coordinated development in BTH Region is to develop the world-class city cluster with international competitiveness and significant influence, foster a new engine of innovative development in Pan-Bohai Area, and lead to the economic development nationwide. That is the starting point why the central government takes the coordinated development in BTH Region as the major national strategy. However, in order to achieve the above objectives, it is necessary to integrate the industrial development of BTH at a higher level and optimize the coordination of industrial division. Only in this way can we achieve the overall improvement of the industrial development level of BTH Region.

From the experience of the development of the world urban agglomeration, first of all, although all urban agglomerations pay attention to the functional division within each city in the development, there is no obvious gradient difference in the categories and levels of industrial development, which is an important foundation for the urban agglomeration to give play to the overall effects and keep its competitiveness. Second, although the secondary cities pay attention to the misplace development with the core cities, the misplacement is about the level or the industrial value chain rather than the branch of industry, so that secondary cities gain huge upgrading space during the complementation of advantages and integrated development and play important role in the division of industrial value worldwide. For example, in the northeast U.S. Atlantic coast city group, although New York is a global financial center in financial development, Boston's financial industry is equally developed which has well-known asset management companies such as Fidelity Management & Research Corp, State Street Corporation and so on. Its mutual funds and risks investment funds play important role in the United States; Philadelphia not only has the stock exchange, but also has insurance company CIGNA, Lincoln Financial Group, the largest US fund company Vanguard Group and other financial service providers; As for Washington, the headquarter of NASDAQ stock market is located here. There are also the international financial institutions headquarters including World Bank, the International Monetary Fund and so on, as well as financial-related Fortune 500 companies such as Booz Allen Hamilton, Freddie Mac, Fannie Mae, Pepco, etc. Another example is port development. New York Port focuses on the development of container transport, the Philadelphia Port is mainly engaged in offshore freight, and Baltimore is the transshipment port of the ore, coal and grain, while Boston is a commercial port given priority to the transshipment of local products as well as a fishing port. Therefore, they are integrated together and form a "1+1>2" overall functional effect. Third, although each city in an urban agglomeration has its own special functions and dominant industries, they are not separated from each other. Instead, on the basis of a common market, various kinds of factors of production flow in urban agglomerations, prompting the larger gathering of population and economic activities so as to form a huge overall effect of urban agglomerations.

The law of industrial development at home and abroad shows that with the continuous development of economy and society, the similar coefficient of industrial structure between different regions will increase day by day, that is, the phenomenon of industrial convergence appears. However, the convergence of industrial structure does not mean the weakening of the industrial division and specialization in complete sense. On the contrary, the convergence of industries and the deepening of division of labor in the area can coexist. Recent research shows that in the background of industrial convergence in recent years, new features have emerged in the industrial division, that is, develop the intra-industry labor division and industry chain division. This is a more detailed and developed form of industrial division. For example, in recent years, the specialization of the departments in American cities has been continuously weakened, but their functional specialization has been gradually increased. The division of labor among cities has been further deepened, that is, the management and functions of large cities have been continuously strengthened while that of small and medium-sized cities have been gradually intensified (Duranton & Puga, 2002). Another example is the Yangtze River Delta of China, many multinational corporations and enterprises in Jiangsu and Zhejiang have built their corporate headquarters, regional headquarters and research and development institutions in the downtown area of Shanghai, and have built their manufacturing bases in the suburbs of Shanghai and Jiangsu and Zhejiang. This forms an industrial division pattern based on different stages of the industry chain. Another example is cities in Zhejiang including Shaoxing, Ningbo, Hangzhou, Wenzhou and Huzhou. All of them are developing the clothing industry, but its products are quite different and the specialized division of labor within the product is clear, that is, menswear in Ningbo, casual clothes in Wenzhou, dress in Hangzhou, children's wear in Huzhou, tie in Shengzhou, and the fabric in Shaoxing. The deepening of regional division of labor makes Zhejiang one of the most important clothing production and sales base in the world.

On the other hand, in BTH Region, (1) The most fundamental problem of the poor overall effect in BTH urban agglomeration is that Hebei has a huge gap in development with Beijing and Tianjin on industry level. The low-end industries in Hebei have become a huge barrier for BTH urban agglomerations to exert their influence. (2) The biggest problem for BTH is that a primitive vertical division of labor has been formed with Beijing and Tianjin during the industrial development in Hebei. Industrial sectors with higher added value are in Beijing and Tianjin, especially in Beijing, which lead to the fact that the upgrading of many industries in Hebei is under severe pressure in the region. (3) The biggest barrier for exerting overall function of BTH urban agglomerations lies in the fact that the administrative division, institutional barriers and policy differences cause the artificial market segmentation, which has made it difficult for the factors of production to realize effective flow and efficient allocation in the area.

The urban agglomeration is not a closed system but an open system of urban regional division of labor. Its internal division of labor should be based on its participation in the division of labor in the global industrial value chain, striving for more prominent influence and competition in the division of the global industrial value chain. In the future, BTH must transform the industrial division of labor which mainly focuses on the vertical division of labor in different departments into a more sophisticated division of labor of level and industrial value chain, so as to create a world-class urban agglomeration with international competitiveness and significant influence. From the perspective of the role in BTH, it is essential that Hebei must break the vertical industry division and promote the transition from a vertical division of labor to a horizontal style for creating a new industrial division system among the BTH Region. Only in this way, the industry in Hebei can move forward to a higher level as soon as possible, and BTH can achieve a higher level of coordinated development.

4.2 Hebei's goals of industrial upgrading based on coordinated development

4.2.1 Direction of industrial upgrading based on coordinated development

Since the beginning of 2016, Hebei has successively released the 13th Five-Year Plan for Economic and Social Development in Hebei, Hebei's Plans for Promoting the Coordinate Development in BTH and the "Plan of National Industry Transformation and Upgrading Pilot Area in Hebei, which clearly put forward the goal of industrial upgrading, that is, speeding up the advanced manufacturing industries and modern services, boosting both traditional industries and emerging industries, and elevating Hebei's industries to the high-end of industrial chain.

In the manufacturing sector, resolutely resolving excess capacity, we will speed up transformation and upgrading of traditional industries such as equipment manufacturing, steel, petrochemical, textile and clothing, food and building materials, vigorously develop emerging industry such as high-end equipment, electronic information, biomedicine, new energy, new materials, energy saving and environmental protection, new energy vehicles and so on, and continuously improve manufacturing which should be digital, networked, intelligent, service-oriented and green.

In terms of service industry, we give priority to the development of productive service industries such as modern business logistics, financial services, information services, science and technology services and business services, vigorously develop life service industries such as culture, tourism and health care, encourage transboundary competition and integration, and promote productive service industry to extend to the specialization and high-end of the value chain. Apart from that, life service industries are transformed into facilitation, refinement and high quality. Correspondingly, the development directions and key products (services) of key industries are presented in Table 17.

Table 17 The direction and focus of classified development of the industry in Hebei Province

Classification	Industry	Direction	The focus of development
Traditional advantage industry	Equipment	High-end, intelligent and service	Transport equipment, energy equipment, engineering and specialized equipment and basic parts
	Steel	Large-scale equipment, intelligent production, high-end products, and informationalized services	High-end products including steels for high-speed railway, automobile, shipbuilding, mould, high-speed tool, electric, high grade line pipeline and so on. Vigorously develop new varieties of steel and steel materials which are high intensitive, attrition resistant, weather-resistant and long-lived.
	Petrochemical	Fine, green, and circulating base	Scale up the oil refining in a fine and high-end mode and promote the development of coalification, salinization, chemical new materials and high-end fine chemicals
	Textile and clothing	High-end, brand-oriented, different and intensive	High-performance fiber and composite materials, high-end textiles, self-brand clothing and so on
	Food	Prominent features, intensive gathering, deep processing, brand building, and quality safety.	Grain and oil processing, convenience foods, meat products, dairy products, liquor and beverages and so on.
	Building materials	Optimized layout, new product, green and low carbon equipment.	Cement-based products, deep processing glass, and new building materials

continued

Classification	Industry	Direction	The focus of development
Strategy new emerging Industry	High-end equipment	Integration of design, development, manufacturing and service.	High-speed rail EMU, CNC (Computerized Numerical Control) machine tools, industrial robots, marine engineering equipment, aviation equipment, new energy vehicles, etc.
	Electronic information	Extend the chain, strengthen the foundation, and apply the driving force	Big data, cloud computing, integrated circuits, satellite navigation and location services
	Biological medicine	Green, preparative and high-end raw material and normative traditional Chinese medicine	Biological pharmacy, modern traditional Chinese medicine, high-end medical equipment and so on.
	New energy	Enhance technology level and market competitiveness of the products	Photovoltaic, wind power, nuclear power, geothermal, energy storage batteries, intelligrid and so on.
	New materials	High-end industrial chain	Liquid crystal display, vanadium titanium products, carbon fiber, high quality special steel, graphene and so on
	Energy saving and environmental protection	Serial and large-scale technical equipment for energy saving and environmental production	Equipment for environmental monitoring, smoke gas treatment and sewage treatment, and solid waste utilization

Source: Based on the relevant economic and social development plans of Hebei.

Classification	Industry	Direction	The focus of development
Productive Service industry	Business logistics	Specialized and high-end	Bulk raw materials such as coal, iron ore, steel, building materials, fine chemical engineering and agricultural products; manufactured products such as automobiles, pipeline equipment, metal products, food; product with characteristics such as leather bags, apparel, household products and Chinese herbal medicines.
	Financial service		Banking, financial leasing, consumer finance, fund notes, Internet finance, inclusive finance, venture capital, etc.

continued

Classification	Industry	Direction	The focus of development
Productive Service industry	Information service	Specialized and high-end	Value-added services such as software services, Internet access services, Internet content services, web applications and so on; New mobile Internet information services such as mobile game, mobile commerce, mobile payment and location services and so on; value-added network communications services such as video telephony, mobile video, digital home, mobile office, mobile phone, etc.
	Science and technology service		Research and development, technology transfer, innovative entrepreneurship, science and technology finance, intellectual property and inspection and testing certification
	Business services		Commodity e-commerce trading platform, e-commerce platform with county features, cross-border e-commerce, business exhibition, legal advice, accounting audit, engineering consulting, credit evaluation, leasing, etc.
Life Service industry	Culture	Convenient, specific and high-quality	Support the traditional culture industry to grow bigger and stronger, vigorously develop the new format, accelerate the integration of new media development, implement cultural brand strategy, and promote the development of creative design services.
	Tourism		Special tourism such as Red Army Tour, Royal Tour, Coastal Tour, Grassland Tour, Snow Tour, Village Tour and so on; tourism format including leisure, vacation, health, research, shopping, etc.
	Health care		The medical industry with medical service agencies as the mainstay, the pharmaceutical industry with pharmaceuticals, medical devices and other medical consumables as its mainstay, the health care industry with health food and health products as the mainstay, health management service industry with personalized health testing and evaluation, consulting services, rehabilitation and protection as the mainstay.

4.2.2 Rational evaluation about the direction of the industrial upgrading in Hebei Province

From the above deployment, it can be seen that although Hebei has no clear definition of what role it should play in industrial competition in BTH and even the whole world in the future. Hebei has been trying to establish its advantages in the industrial development of BTH Region, that is, to further enhance the manufacturing level of traditional industries such as equipment manufacturing, steel, petrochemicals, textile and clothing, food and building materials, and rapidly increase the scale of emerging manufacturing such as high-end equipment, electronic information, biomedicine, new energy, new materials, energy saving and environmental protection. While further promoting traditional manufacturing industries, Hebei also develops trade, R&D service, financial services and information service on the demand in market of the BTH Region even the nation, and strives to become the base of advanced manufacturing and producer services of the BTH Region even the whole country.

In theory, there are three basic directions for industrial upgrading: First, relying on the traditional industries with advantages, give play to comparative advantages and seek for more value-added along the industrial chain; Second, according to comparative advantages and market demand, develop new substitution industries based on the shaping of new regional advantages. Third, combine the above two items, that is, the combination of upgrading traditional industries and developing new industries. In practice, most of the countries and regions that have succeeded in industrial upgrading in the world have taken the third approach. Comparatively speaking, such an approach not only has small impact on infrastructure related to economic society, employment structure and industry, which is relatively steady, but also thinks highly of the need of following the technical progress and industrial transformation worldwide. From macroscopical side, the direction and path of industrial development proposed by Hebei is in line with the basic laws of industrial upgrading, and it also responds to the needs of environmental improvement in BTH.

Experience shows that industrial upgrading in one area is not a new process of creation that subverts the history and foundation of its industrial development. Instead, it continues to adapt to the requirements of new industry development and create new resources based on the existing resource and capability. For Hebei, the biggest advantage of the coordinated development of BTH lies in its huge base of manufacturing. Although such a foundation is more of raw material industry with lower value-added, there is no doubt that to abandon this foundation completely and develop new industries will face enormous challenges and risks. Service industry, especially productive service industry, is relatively lagging behind, which also means great potential for development. In fact, in recent years, the development potential of service industry in Hebei, especially that of productive service industry, is being released. In 2014-2016, the service industry in Hebei Province has been growing at about twice its industry (see Table 18). Therefore, the proportion of the whole economy and the contribution rate of the overall economic growth are rapidly increasing, so as to promote the improvement of the overall economic structure. On this basis, Hebei sets the industrial upgrading direction of "regarding advanced manufacturing and modern service industry as the mainstay", which is a relatively pragmatic and feasible option at present stage.

Table 18 The comparison of the growth rate of three industries in Hebei Province

	2014		2015		2016	
	Growth rate (%)	Contribution rate (%)	Growth rate (%)	Contribution rate (%)	Growth rate (%)	Contribution rate (%)
Total	6.5	100	6.8	100	6.8	100
Primary Industry	3.7	5.8	2.5	3.7	3.5	6.0
Secondary Industry	5.0	42.1	4.7	37.3	4.9	34.9
Tertiary Industry	9.7	52.1	11.2	59.0	9.9	59.1

Source: Statistics *Bulletin of the National Economic and Social Development of Hebei in 2014.*

At the manufacturing level, from the perspective of both degree of specialization (location entropy) and the factor efficiency (the output rate of total asset and the labor productivity), the preponderant industry in Hebei is the relatively low-end resource-processed raw materials industry. However, at the same time, the equipment manufacturing industry in Hebei and the high-tech industries including bio-industry, electronic information, new materials, high-end technology equipment, aerospace, new energy and environmental protection industries have shown great growth potential in recent years (see Table 19). Therefore, it is reasonable for Hebei to propose the industrial upgrading direction of "two driving force of traditional industries and emerging industries" in the development of manufacturing industry. What is missing is that the path of achieving digital, networked, intelligent, service and green manufacturing industry is not clear. At the same time, we need to pay more attention to the necessary elements and environmental conditions for industrial upgrading while focusing on improving the production technology, process equipment and product quality.

Table 19 The growth rate and structure change of high-tech and equipment manufacturing industry in Hebei in 2014-2016 (%)

	2014		2015		2016	
	Growth rate (%)	The industrial enterprises above the designated size	Growth rate (%)	The industrial enterprises above the designated size	Growth rate (%)	The industrial enterprises above the designated size
High-tech industry	13.2	13.1	11.6	16.0	13.0	18.4
Equipment manufacturing industry	8.8	20.6	7.0	23.7	10.2	26.0
Industry above the scale	5.1	—	4.4	—	4.8	—

Source: *Economic Yearbook of Hebei 2014–2016.*

4.3 Formulate industrial upgrading path with detailed classification

The analysis of Hebei industrial upgrading path can't be generalized because of different development foundation, development stage, and regional status of different industries. Because of different industrial upgrading goals in Hebei, this section is classified in accordance with manufacturing industry and serviced industry. This section explores the possibility and necessary path of industrial upgrading by analyzing manufacturing industry such as steel, building materials, chemical engineering and so on which have huge potentials for developing and have urgent demand for transformation and upgrading, and service industry including health care and finance.

4.3.1 The upgrading path of manufacturing industry

Traditional manufacturing industry. For Hebei, the goal of traditional manufacturing upgrading in the future is to make the industrial development digital, networked, intelligent, service-oriented and green, and achieve the industrial chain joint of Beijing and Tianjin. Basically speaking, Hebei's huge traditional manufacturing base and the industrial characteristics with the raw material industry as its mainstay determines that its industrial upgrading must be based on the upgrading of traditional industries. In terms of the path, we should give full play to the advantages of processing and manufacturing industries in Hebei, strengthen cooperation with industrial chain of Beijing and Tianjin, actively undertake and transform the advanced manufacturing technology in Beijing and Tianjin, and become the industrial supporting for the related high-tech research and development in Beijing and Tianjin; as to raw materials industries such as steel, chemicals, building materials and so on, relying on key cities including Tangshan and Handan and learning from the transformation and upgrading experience of steel industry in Pittsburgh and other cities in the U.S. , we should further reduce production capacity in the manufacturing sector, promote the gathering and circulation of the production capacity chain, so as to meet the increasing environmental constraints. At the meantime, we should make full use of the new generation of information technology, promote intelligent manufacturing with intelligent workshop, intelligent factory construction as its focus, and accelerate production efficiency. We need to adapt to the demand for new materials in modern industry and construction, and promote the expansion of new materials such as high-grade metal materials, metal-based composite materials, fine chemical materials and new building materials in the industries of steel, chemical industry and building materials; in addition, we ought to accelerate the development of downstream industry including machinery equipment, automobiles and parts, extend the industrial chain, and transform the material suppliers into finished product providers; what's more, we should cultivate the R&D institutions and marketing and service network related to industries including steel, chemical engineering, building materials and so on, striking for a more important role in the industrial division in the region and the value chain worldwide (see Figure 30).

At enterprise level, focusing on the top 10 enterprises in the industry, Hebei should spread the experiences of Hebei Iron and Steel Group and impel competitive enterprises transforming from manufacturer of steel, chemical engineering and building materials to service providers of whole industrial chain.

For textile and clothing industries, we can draw on the experience of urban transformation in New York City of the United States and Milan of Italy to change the concept of industrial development and promote the clothing industry to extend from the intermediate links in the value chain to the upstream and downstream including R&D, marketing, logistics and services. In addition, encourage clothing enterprises to develop lifestyle brand which is multi-brand, multi-category, and product + service, and actively develop shopping mall integrated with shopping and leisure, as well as big store mode combined with products and service, so as to promote clothing manufacturing to transform into fashion service industry.

Figure 30 The diagram of the upgrading path of manufacturing industry in Hebei Province

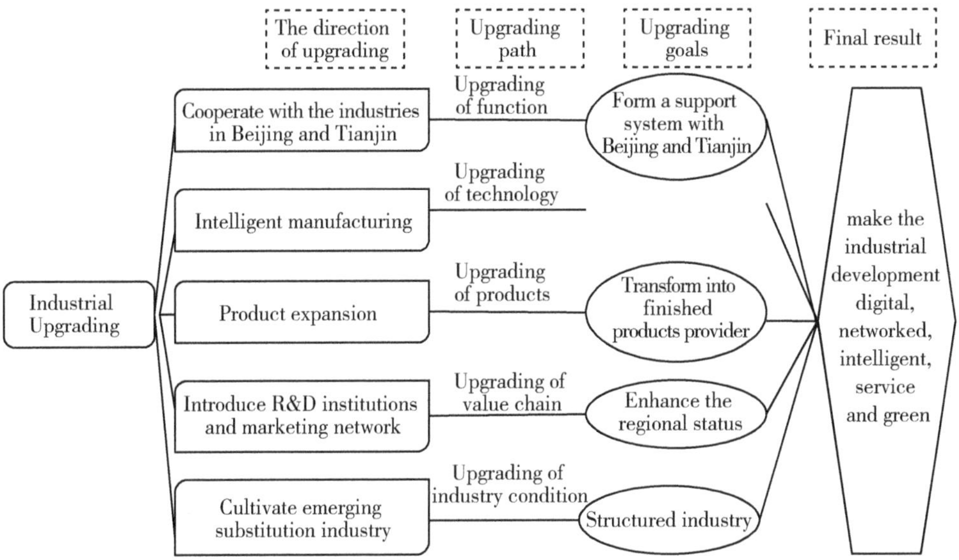

Case: Evolution of Hebei Iron and Steel Group from Steel Manufacturer to Integrated Service Provider

Hebei Iron and Steel Group Co., Ltd. (Hebei Iron and Steel Group) is a super-sized iron and steel enterprise jointly established by the former Tangshan Iron and Steel Group and Handan Iron and Steel Group on June 30, 2008 and now owns more than 20 first-level subsidiaries and 120,000 employers. Dominated by steel industry, the company includes four aspects, namely, steel, equipment manufacturing, financial services and modern logistics. In 2015, operating income was 284.5 billion yuan, with a total asset of 348.8 billion yuan at the end of the year.

Since its formation, Hebei Iron and Steel Group, while strengthening and optimizing its steel industry, has been pursuing the strategic transformation of " deeper and wider " with the global and full industrial perspective and implementing the vertical extension of the whole industrial chain and wider utilization of the full resource chain. a. Introducing the " key customer manager system " to set up the group customer service center, placing customer needs first, providing one-on-one and point-to-point service to key clients, selling steel like selling electrical appliances, and establishing a customer-oriented steel marketing model. This will completely subvert the traditional steel marketing model. b. Carrying out the delayering reform of organization structure which refers to the change of regarding production line as independent market unit. Every production line should be a management unit directly facing end-user, through which the best R&D, marketing and technician in the enterprise can be linked with high-end customer. Then develop demand-oriented productive operating mode which is managed by big company and operated by smaller company, so as to form an operation mechanism where the industry line can rapidly respond to the demand of end-user and a shortest process from supply side to demand side. c. Holding Haier Special Steel and signing a strategic cooperation framework agreement with Siemens China, which are efficient method for us to be embedded in the world' s largest supply channel for home appliance enterprises, integrated into the downstream manufacturing links of the steel industry, and opened a new mode of cooperation with downstream industry marketing, so as to achieve an effective extension of the industrial chain. d. Purchasing the biggest copper smelting enterprises in South Africa including PMC and Serbia Smederevo Steel Mill and developing the biggest steel manufacturing platform worldwide. e. Holding and purchasing DITH in Switzerland which is the biggest steel trader in the world, extending the industrial chain to high-end user at home or abroad and embedding the supply chain of end-user, so as to develop a new mode of "integration of steel enterprise and steel trade ". f. Integrating the upstream and downstream resources in the industrial chain, actively developing non-steel sectors such as equipment manufacturing, new materials, new energy, financial securities, modern logistics, comprehensive utilization of resources, engineering technology, healthcare and social services, and expanding the space for enterprise development. g. Creating "China electric business alliance of steel " with Baosteel Group and promoting operation efficiency by utilizing " Internet+ ".

In 2016, the proportion of high-grade steel in Hebei Iron and Steel Group reached 54%. The annual sales volume of high-end products such as automobile sheets, household electrical appliances sheets, pipeline steel and marine steel reached 12 million tons. The comprehensive competitiveness and international influence of the enterprises continued to increase and ranked the world' s top 500 enterprises for five years. It was selected as "World Top 500 Brands " and "the most admired company globally. "

New strategic industry since the reform and opening up, relying on the strong support of the traditional advantageous industries, the economy of our province has achieved rapid growth for more than 30 years. The industries of steel, chemical engineering and building materials have become the real strategic industries in our province. However, the development space of traditional industries is reduced and the growth momentum is rapidly dropped in recent years with the profound adjustment of the world economy, the rapid upgrading of the consumption structure and the intense impact of the new round of scientific and technological revolution. At the same time, though cultivated for many years, emerging industries, which are regarded as the new growth momentum, are still in smaller dimensions and fail to be the stabilizing force for supporting economic development.

Since 2010, relative to the traditional industries, high-tech industries in Hebei grew rapidly with an average annual growth rate of 15.7%. It is far less than that in Hubei and Hunan, which is respectively 21.9% and 23.3%. Coupled with weak base and small scale, the added value of high-tech industries in Hebei accounted for only 18.4% of the industrial enterprises above the designated size by 2016, much less than 33.8% in Shandong, 41.5% in Jiangsu, 43% in Hubei and 66% in Hunan. The reasons for this situation are mainly the lack of understanding of the law of industrial growth, the long-term development of emerging industries adopting the same method, and the deficiency of precise choice and key support for potential strategic industries.

Therefore, in the development of new industries, we must take the creation of new strategic industries, horizontal division of labor with Beijing and Tianjin, the establishment of partial advantages of industrial development as the goal, take the initiative to adapt to the law of industrial development, precisely select major strategic products with a number of long industrial chain, high correlation, comparison advantages, market potential and the ability to achieve exponential growth. We should aim at key links in industrial development, concentrate limited strategic and policy resources, and implement precise matching and key support. On the one hand, we can choose 3 to 5 industries which may form the advantage in the country and even in the world and can interact effectively with Beijing and Tianjin from the key fields including "Big data, intelligence, mobile Internet and cloud computing", bioengineering, intelligent equipment, new energy and new materials which are competed by global industries. We should introduce major products and strategic projects, cultivate precisely, and strive to build it into an emerging strategic industry leading the development of Hebei. On the other hand, it is necessary to advance the layout of the future industry and closely follow the developments in global technology revolution breakthroughs, industrial mode innovation and integration of industry fields. Standing at the height of Hebei's long-term development, we should develop strategic industries proactively such as terahertz, metastable materials, artificial intelligence, and artificial proteins and so on which have great potentials for promoting the development of industry.

4.3.2 The upgrading path of service industry

At present, one of the most important symbols of the high-end industrial structure is that the service industry contributes more than the industry for economy, and as an important component of the service industry, the modern service industry has become the main growth point of local economic development and a symbol of the comprehensive development of local economy and society. For a long time, the modern service industry in Hebei has a relatively low level of development and lags behind Beijing and Tianjin, especially Beijing. In recent years, with the further development of the coordinated development in BTH, the development of Hebei's service industry has developed rapidly, and the proportion of service industry in the local economy has been increasing year by year. In 2014, the contribution rate of service industry exceeded 50% for economic growth in Hebei for the first time. There is a big gradient difference between Hebei and Beijing in many areas of service industry and it is hard to be evenly matched. However, due to the advantages of good traffic location, excellent ecological environment and vast market, it is possible for Hebei to form a more reasonable division of labor with Beijing and Tianjin in service industry including health care, financial service and so on.

a. Health care services.The health care service is not only a people's livelihood cause that concerns the well-being of hundreds of millions of people, but also a sunrise industry with great potential for development. As the trend of aging is accelerated and the status of sub-health is increasingly common, health care services become a kind of new support for economic development gradually, and promote the development of manufacturing, services, tourism, medical service, health protection and other related industries. Actively promoting the development of the health care services is of great significance to give impetus to the sustained and healthy development of economy and society in Hebei. Hebei has a vast market for the development of health care industries. At present, the population aging in the BTH is becoming increasingly serious. According to the data of 1% national population sample survey, the proportion of elderly people aged 65 and over in Beijing, Tianjin and Hebei reached 10.65%, 9.91% and 10.23% respectively by 2015 (see Table 20), and the old who were aging, empty-nested, and disabled were increasing. The huge elderly population led to an "explosive" demand for the health care services in BTH, providing strong support to the consumption of health care services.

Table 20 The scale and proportion of the old aged 65 and over in BTH Region (thousands of people, %)

	2010		2015	
	Population over 65 years old	The proportion of the total population	Population over 65 years old	The proportion of the total population
Beijing	170.90	8.70	231.26	10.65
Tianjin	110.70	8.52	153.25	9.91
Hebei Province	592.79	8.24	755.42	10.17
Total of BTH Region	874.39	8.36	1,139.93	10.23

Source: The data of 1% national population sample survey, 2015, and *Statistic Yearbook of BTH in 2011.*

At the meantime, the suburbanization of the population of Beijing and Tianjin becomes obvious. In particular, the trend of decentralization of Beijing's population from downtown to suburbs and outer suburbs becomes increasingly obvious. According to the sample survey of population in 2014, there are 12,284,000 permanent residents among Third Ring Road and Sixth Ring Road in Beijing, accounting for 57.1% of the city's total population. Among them, there are 9,410,000 permanent residents among Fourth Ring Road and Sixth Ring Road, accounting for 43.8% of the city and there are 10,980,000 permanent residents outside the Fifth Ring Road, accounting for 51.1% of the city's total. The distribution of the population in the Ring Road expands outward in a circle, that is, it is evacuated from the inner ring of the second ring and the third ring to the outer ring of the fourth ring. From the change of population distribution in Beijing in the past 30 years, we can see that the population in the suburbs and outer suburbs is increasing year by year, and the population growth rate in the outer suburbs is more obvious (see Figure 31).

Figure 31 Structure of population distribution in three circles of Beijing

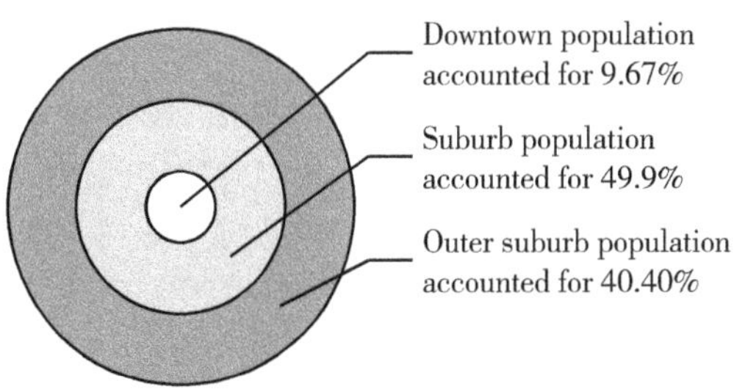

Note: In the study of population distribution, Beijing is usually divided into three circles: the downtown area, the suburbs and the outer suburbs. The downtown area includes Dongcheng District and Xicheng District. The suburbs include Shijingshan District, Haidian District, Chaoyang District and Fengtai District, while the remaining ten districts such as Tongzhou District and Changping District belong to outer suburbs.

The aging and suburbanization in both Beijing and Tianjin have brought tremendous opportunities to the development of health care industry in Hebei. Globally, the Tokyo metropolitan area, one of the few world-class metropolitan areas, has a spatial distribution according to the age of population which shows that the older tend to be far from the downtown area, that is, the distribution of aging population is in suburbanization and the development of health care industry is at a higher level outer metropolitan area. The development pattern of metropolitan area formed over many years has strong reference for the construction of metropolitan area in BTH. Although high-end medical resources are still concentrated in the downtown area of Beijing at this stage, the elderly population has not yet spread to the peripheral area. However, according to international practice and the development experience of Tokyo metropolitan area, as the non-capital function of Beijing is evaluated to peripheral area and high-end medical resources are radiated to Hebei, the elderly population will gradually move to the surrounding area suitable for leisure in the future. Cities of Zhangjiakou, Chengde, Qinhuangdao, Baoding and Langfang in Hebei, which are encircling Beijing and Tianjin, have superior transportation, beautiful nature environment and abundant tourism resources. They are good cities for developing nursing home, sanatorium, and resort for the old and other health care services relying on the tourism. In particular, Beidaihe area of Qinhuangdao has unique advantage for developing health care industry because it is excellent in ecological environment, obvious in position advantage and abundant in health resources.

At present, the greatest difficulty in the development of health care industry in Hebei is the lack of medical service resources, and the lag of the construction of high-end medical institutions. In the future, Hebei should strengthen the construction of health care service resources such as Grade Ⅲ A hospital, rehabilitation institutions, health care centers and health industrial parks, and strive to build a green ecological health care and elderly care base, focusing on building a gathering area of a number of health industries including International Health City in Qinhuangdao, Yanda International Health City in Langfang and Zhuozhou Wharf International Health Industry Park in Baoding. At the same time, we should actively strive for the radiation and transfer of medical service resources in the downtown area of Beijing, take a variety of ways to introduce Beijing's high-quality medical service resources, and speed up the construction of the demonstration base for supporting elderly people around Beijing and Tianjin, trying to be the supporting destination for people in Beijing and the gathering area of health care services for BTH.

b. Financial services. The Program

Outline explicitly claims that the function of financial management in Beijing, creative operation in Tianjin and the financial backstage service in Hebei should be strengthened. This is the division of labor based on the basic situation of the financial industry in Beijing, Tianjin and Hebei. However, as far as Hebei is concerned, it is not enough to serve as a financial backstage service base for the BTH urban agglomeration. With the powerful support of financial system, Hebei can develop the industrial transformation and upgrading demonstration zone, achieving the coordinated development with Beijing and Tianjin and promote overall competitiveness. If Hebei only serves as a financial backstage service base, it will be difficult to achieve the coupled development of the financial system and the real economy, and it will not be able to meet the demands of the industrial transformation and upgrading.

Experience shows that cities in a world-class urban agglomeration are often not divided vertically in terms of their financial development. On the contrary, they develop different forms of financial operations according to their own advantages and industrial demands in order to achieve balanced development of financial integration in the entire region. For example, in the northeastern urban agglomeration in the U.S., New York is the core city mainly developing finance and commercial service industry. It is nerve centre of world economy and international finance. The advantage of Boston lies in the high-tech industry, which forms a high-tech gathering area, along with Silicon Valley. The finance industry in Boston focuses on the financial formats that are associated with high-tech industries such as asset management, mutual funds and venture capital funds. Philadelphia is an important manufacturing base in the United States with developed securities trading, insurance and funds. As a political center in the United States, Washington has a large number of headquarters of international financial institutions.

The financial system in Hebei must conform to the transformation and upgrading of traditional manufacturing and the concentrated development of emerging manufacturing. In other words, we should promote the integration of manufacturing and finance industry. Taking into consideration the need of Hebei's industrial transformation and upgrading for the development of the financial industry and the role that Hebei should play in the development of the financial industry in BTH, the development of Hebei's financial industry should focus on industrial funds, insurance, Internet finance and logistics finance. First, vigorously develop equity investment institutions such as industrial investment funds, equity investment funds, venture capital funds and fund management companies, attract more social capital to invest in manufacturing enterprises and broaden the financing channels for enterprises. To carry out the test in Xiong'an New Area for the construction of industrial investment funds, cultivating fund manager and fund management company, integrating finance and the industrial development, and giving full play to the financial support for the real economy. Second, create the new operation mode of insurance funds, support industrial transformation and upgrading, and encourage insurance funds to set up private equity investment funds such as growth funds, mergers and acquisitions funds, strategic emerging industry funds, and industrial investment funds and so on. The third is to encourage financial innovation and develop Internet finance taking full advantage of the large amount of loans and the fast speed of the network platform. Fourth, according to the position of the national commercial and trade base, we should make full use of the convenient transportation, give priority to developing logistics finance, and strive to become a national demonstration base of logistics financial (see Figure 32).

Figure 32 Diagram of the development of finance and supporting industry in Hebei Province

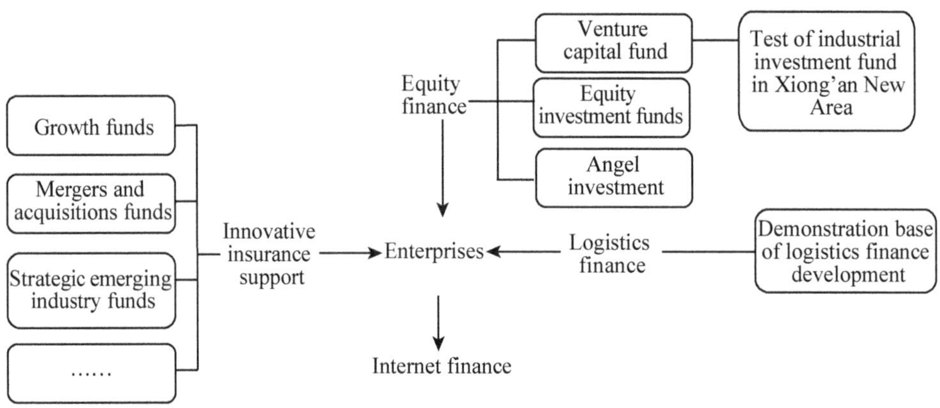

5. The construction of supporting conditions for industrial upgrading in Hebei Province

5.1 Strive to build high-level industry upgrading platforms

As mentioned above, one of the major obstacles for industrial upgrading in Hebei is the lack of a carrier platform for high-level industrial development. Although Xiong'an New Area is the first nation-grade new district in Hebei, there still exists prominent problems including insufficient carrier platform and low level of the industrial development in the whole region. More broadly, Hebei's industry upgrading needs to construct supporting platforms at four different level, in terms of new area, cities, development zones and specialized town.

5.1.1 Build high-end and world-class Xiong'an New Area and create a leading demonstration platform

Adhering to the concept of "world vision, international standards, to build green and ecological livable new city region, develop the leading zone with innovation-driven force, and promote the coordinated development of demonstration zone and the opening of pilot zone with high standards and high starting points. In addition, Xiong'an New Area should be constructed as a world-class innovation demonstration platform implementing the new development concept. From the international experiences, we should organize domestic first-class planning talents to carry out urban design, make master plans for New Area with high standards, improve special plans for economic and social development, transportation system, new urbanization and land utilization, and carry out the action of "the integration of multiple rules". Formulate industrial policies according to local conditions, promote the integration and upgrading of existing traditional industries, make the negative list of undertaking the development of industry, and develop high-end high-tech industries specifically, so as to create new engine and new incentive sources to give impetus to industrial development in Hebei Enhance ecological construction, promote the ecological restoration of Baiyangdian Lake, and construct green forest barrier and ecological corridor to create an ecological city which has beautiful scenery of blue sky, leafy trees and clear water. Promote concerted development with Beijing and Tianjin, strengthen coordination and dislocation development with the sub-center of Beijing, improve infrastructure and public service facilities in the New Area, and launch pilot project of public services equalization, so as to create a good environment for the construction and development of the New Area. We will speed up reform and innovation of mechanisms, explore new modes of management for New Area, deepen the reform of the administrative system, integrate administrative resources and establish a streamlined, efficient and unified management mechanism for New Area. Apart from that, we should explore the reform of the investment and financing system and establish long-term and stable funding mechanisms, and attract central enterprises and social capital to participate in the construction of the New Area.

5.1.2 Build a fully functional, livable modern city and create a platform for gathering elements

We should promote the cluster

development of seven cities which have finished the adjustment of administrative divisions including Shijiazhuang, Tangshan, Baoding, Qinhuangdao, Zhangjiakou, Handan and Hengshui. At the same time, we need to speed up the adjustment of administrative divisions in four cities including Cangzhou, Xingtai, Chengde and Langfang, so as to enhance the receiving and supporting capability of industries and population for central cities; To firmly support the construction of Zhengding New Area of Shijiazhuang, Beidaihe New Area of Qinhuangdao, Bohai New Area of Cangzhou, Jinan New Area of Handan, Yanghe New Area of Zhangjiakou, Xingdong New Area of Xingtai and Binhu New Area of Hengshui. Through the development and construction of the new district, the overall urban layout will be optimized and the function will be enhanced. In addition, and the city's ability to agglomerate industries and elements will be improved; to select a number of counties (cities) with appropriate location, large scale, good foundation and real potential to build medium-sized cities, continue to push forward the reform of "counties directly administrate under the province", give corresponding development chance and accelerate the development of medium-sized cities; to continue to promote the "big county strategy", improve the expansion and quality of the county, cultivate and create a number of boutique cities in accordance with purpose of the amalgamation of industry and city, and the integration of industry, education and city. According to the concept of building an ecological, intelligent and civilized city, we will carry out the projects about fine construction of city, and the improvement of management and public service, comprehensively enhance the capacity and level of urban public services so that the city will become a gathering point for outstanding talents and high-quality capital.

5.1.3 Construct high-end and efficient industrial parks and create industrial support-platform

Construct numerous high-end industrial development platform with big influence on the basis of advancing the comprehensive innovation and reform pilot area of Shijiazhuang, Baoding and Langfang, the demonstration area of scientific and technological achievements transformation in the south of Beijing, the collaborative development demonstration area of Beijing and Caofeidian in Hebei, the coordinated development demonstration area of Hebei and Hangu and Lutai in Tianjin and the construction of healthy city in Beidaihe, Qinhuangdao. This will help to form a number of high-end significant carriers for coordinated development. In combination with the layout and construction of "micro-centers", we plan to construct a group of specialized parks and strive to make "micro-centers" become the core of high-end factor agglomeration and the carrier of high-end industries development. To implement the project of transformation and upgrading of the development zone with the policy known as "emptying the cage, removing the bird" and the aim of improving the level. We should focus on the existing high-tech zones and the economic development zones in the province, promote the high-end and ecological development, and speed up the improvement of incubators and accelerators. In addition, we should improve mechanisms such as investment and intelligence promotion, intellectual property protection, transfer of property rights, investing and financing and so on, comprehensively upgrade the levels of industry, element and service in the development area, so as to develop the numerous development areas into national development areas. To implement the creative management project in the development area with the focus of 100 development areas which are excellent enough to be selected and cultivated by the government. According to principles of "one area, one system" and "one area, one policy", we should adopt new mode of operation and management including "cooperation operation" and "overall trusteeship", develop new mechanisms of personnel identity, position management and income distribution, so as to realize efficient operation of development area. Speed up to formulate supporting policies for the comprehensive bonded zone in Caofeidian and Shijiazhuang, and encourage Bohai New Area in Cangzhou to declare the comprehensive bonded zone, thus creating a leading platform for the development of three foreign-oriented industries.

5.1.4 Construct distinctive town with supporting services town and create a platform for innovative entrepreneurship

Hebei should make full use of the opportunity of non-capital functions removal, conform to the new situation of rapid suburbanization in Beijing and Tianjin, especially in Beijing, combine the construction and layout of "micro-centers", choose areas around Beijing which have convenient transportation and good ecological environment and build a series of moderately-sized distinctive towns with the theme of innovation, entrepreneurship and originality and the advantage of perfect functions and convenient conditions for work and life, so as to build innovative and entrepreneurial platform supporting industrial upgrading. Specific suggestions: a. combined with the experience of evacuating education resources in Beijing, construct a number of towns with high education degree in accordance with the mode of "integration of small town, university and science and technology park"; b. responding to the demand of achievements transformation base for research institutes in Beijing, we should construct a number of innovative entrepreneurship towns with the function of R&D, incubation, achievement transformation and science popularization in accordance with the mode of "integration of small town, science institutes, incubator and production base", such as space town in Donghuayuan, Huailai, robot town in Xianghe and so on; c. following the tendency of aging acceleration in BTH, Hebei should plan and construct numerous pension town with the function of endowment, recuperation, recovery and health-research in combination with the resources removal of medical rehabilitation in Beijing, such as medical rehabilitation town in Beidaihe New Area, health valley town in Laishui and so on; d. meeting the needs of the development of cultural and creative industries, we should plan to build a number of cultural and creative towns, such as film and television creative town in Dachang with a view to serving the pre-production of cultural and creative products in Beijing; e. adapting to the new trend of upgrading the health demands of leisure sports, Hebei should plan to construct a number of sports health towns integrating outdoor sports and event services, sports medicine and equipment research, such as the frozen town in Taizicheng, Chongli in combination with the preparation of Olympic Winter Games; f. focusing on promoting innovation and development of traditional industries and techniques, Hebei should plan and construct a number of small town featuring specialty products and traditional craft restoration and innovation, such as the Ganhong small town in Changli, the ceramic town in Lubei District, Tangshan, classical Jing style furniture town in Laishui and so on.

5.2 Effectively undertake the high-end factors transfer from Beijing and Tianjin

Both theory and experience show that in the backward areas, the basic path of implementing catch-up development especially in the areas where there is a large gap with the industries in developed areas or core cities is the introduction of industries, talents, technologies and capital, which gradually accumulate and form the endogenous motivation and advantage of its industrial development. In terms of Hebei, it is far from enough to promote its position in BTH only by the upgrading of traditional industries at present or in the future. Hebei should actively undertake non-capital functions, industries and factors spillover from Beijing, and embrace an even more open approach to seek new stimulus for economic growth by attracting industries and talents.

To do this, Hebei must attach great importance to and make good use of the suburbanization trend around Beijing and Tianjin, especially around Beijing. According to the basic law of urbanization, when the urban population exceeds 70%, it will enter the suburbanization stage. It becomes a general trend that population migrates from the downtown areas into the suburbs of metropolitan cities. At the same time, the industry and commerce are encouraged to shift to the suburbs and surrounding small and medium cities, thus bringing the development of suburbs and small and medium cities. At present, the overall urbanization rate of BTH Region has exceeded 60%, of which Beijing and Tianjin have respectively exceeded 85% and 80%, and have entered the suburbanization stage as a whole. In fact, up to the end of 2016, the permanent population in Beijing was 21,729,000, an increase of 24,000 over the same period of last year, a reduced increment of 165,000 less than the same period of last year, and a slowed speed up of 0.8% point from the same period of last year. Among them, permanent population realized the inflection point from rising to falling in six areas in Beijing, down 3% from 2015, and rising costs of living and transportation would accelerate this process. It can be expected that the suburbanization of Beijing and Tianjin which are megacities will certainly speed up in the next few years.

Facing this situation, with geographic advantages, attractive and transparent talent policy, high-level industry & innovation platforms, satisfactory public services, convenient transportation and ideal ecological and commercial environment, Hebei should strive to attract overflowing talents, technologies and capital from Beijing and Tianjin, especially from Beijing.

5.3 Create a favorable business environment for industry upgrading

Industry development can't be separate from a good business environment. All countries in the world are paying great attention to the improvement of the business environment. The Business Environment Report 2017: Equal Opportunities for All stated that 137 economies in the world implemented key business reforms in 2015. At present, the deep integration and development of industries in BTH has entered an extremely important era and the industrial upgrading in Hebei has also entered a "deepwater zone" where it is difficult to overcome difficulties. A business environment conducive to industrial upgrading is not only a significant content for economic reform in Hebei at the present stage but also the realistic requirement of the coordinated development of industries in Beijing, Tianjin and Hebei. In the future, Hebei must proceed from four aspects: capital market environment, social credit environment, market environment and government environment, strive to create a good business environment and provide strong support for industrial upgrading.

5.3.1 Cultivate active capital market

An active capital market can provide powerful supporting and impetus for the sustained and rapid development of economy. Hebei should make full use of the opportunity of building an industrial transformation and upgrading demonstration zone to carry out cultivation experiments in capital market. Explore the creation of over-the-counter share market, trans-regional property rights transaction market, and multi-level and diversified capital markets such as agency share transfer market, create direct financing channels for high-growth SMEs, especially private enterprises and try to carry out over-the-counter trading pilot in Xiong'an New Area. Strengthen financial services capability, speed up the construction and improvement of financial service center in Shijiazhuang, enhance the resource allocation and radiation capabilities of the capital market, cultivate the financial market such as commodity exchanges and so on, and actively promote offshore financial experimental zone to be first conducted in Zhengding, Shijiazhuang.

In addition, different from the path of self-evolution of capital markets in western countries, the development of China's capital market can't be separated from the promotion of the government. Therefore, all departments at all levels in the province should give full play to their initiative and financial departments should intensify training of financial knowledge and the introduction of financial professionals, and strive to build a cadre's team who know the capital market and are good at using the capital market.

5.3.2 Build a perfect credibility system

Integrity is the foundation of a civilized society and an important part of the business environment. A perfect social credit system is a symbol of the soft power of regional economic and social development. Hebei has a relatively backward development of the construction of system and trustworthiness culture. Hebei only ranked 20th in the ranking of provincial capital city system and trustworthiness culture in 2013, which did not match its rank of economic scale strength and hurt the business environment very much. In the future, Hebei should strengthen the construction of social integrity including government affairs integrity, business integrity, social integrity and so on, which should be regarded as the breakthrough point of improving the business environment in Hebei. Accelerate the construction of credit information platform, promote public credit information recording, collection, and establish various information platforms including provincial project construction supervision and credit management platform, enterprise quality credit platform, public platform of dishonesty business information, the provincial enterprise credit information publicity system and so on, so as to improve the sharing level of credit information among administrative departments. Promote the pilot demonstration of credit with Shijiazhuang, Xiong'an New Area and other eligible cities (districts) as the focus, and actively apply for the demonstration city of national social credit system construction and carry out the pilot demonstration of credit system construction in the industries and key areas. Cultivate the credit service market, set up credit service agencies, speed up the establishment of Hebei Credit Collection Co. Ltd., promote the development and innovation of credit products and the utilization of the big data of credit information, and guide to promote the development of the credit service market.

5.3.3 Build fair market environment

Fair, transparent and predictable market environment is a necessary requirement for sustained and healthy economic development. From the perspective of the open development of a city, we can't treat investors just according to whether it is domestic or foreign, state owned or private enterprises. Instead, it depends on whether they are conducive to industrial transformation and upgrading and the sustained and healthy development of the city. In dealing with the attitude towards investors, Hebei can't be inflexible to choose only one investor or attach undue attention to one of the investor. Instead, Hebei should promote the mutual development of the domestic and foreign enterprises and private enterprises by creating an open, fair and predictable market. This will further promote the industrial upgrading and bring about steady, rapid and healthy economic development in Hebei. Therefore, market access system needs to be further improved. We should clean up various "thresholds" that affect the development of market bodies, promote the management of "negative lists", allow various market bodies to enter fairly and rationally induct the direction of industrial development and the anticipation of market bodies' investment, except for prohibited items pointed out in Industry Catalogue of Prohibited Investment in Hebei and Catalogue of Investment Projects Approved By the Hebei Government. Eliminate market barriers in the infrastructure and public utilities sectors, and introduce more effective measures in the fields of livelihood such as healthcare, endowment and education so that private investment can participate in fairly. Deepen the cooperation. Foreign and domestic-funded enterprises should be treated equally in the policy links such as land using approval, environmental assessment, industrial support and market control policies so as to create a fair and open competitive environment.

5.3.4 Create efficient government environment

Government environment is an important part and a strong guarantee of economic and social development. Practice has proved that a high-quality and efficient government environment will create immeasurable "policy wealth" for the economic development in the region. For Hebei, the government environment is criticized for its cumbersome examination and approval procedures, complex processes, weak awareness of government service and poor efficiency. In the future, it is necessary to further promote the reform of "combining the management with devolution and optimizing service", try to be efficient on delegating powers, innovate the supervision mode, promote the service and improve administrative efficiency, so as to create a high-quality and efficient government environment. First, we should intensify streamlining administration and delegating power, continue the abolition of a number of items on administrative approval which restrict economic development, bind the energy of enterprises, and lead to corruption and rent-seeking, so as to release market vitality furthest. Second, deepen the re-creation of the administrative examination and approval process, and establish an overall administrative approval bureau at the city and county levels so as to create a new government service platform of "one station and one package service". Establish and improve the list management system including administrative power list, responsibility list, negative list, charges list, administrative licensing intermediary services list, regulatory list and so on in the government departments of cities and counties. Third, strengthen comprehensive supervision, speed up the reform of "integrating the license and simplifying the registration process", fully implement the new regulatory model of "randomly select test object and inspectors and disclose the results in time", and speed up the comprehensive enforcement of cross-department and multi-industry situation in cities and counties. Fourth, create the service pattern, fully implement online approval, and establish a system of "integrating internet and government service" that achieve the overall interaction, department coordination, provincial overall planning and only one network to management, so as to form an online enjoyment service platform that covers the entire province.

6. Policy suggestions on accelerating Hebei's industry upgrading

The obstacles and problems faced by Hebei industrial upgrading are the result of many internal and external factors for a long time. Although not all problems are caused by policy reasons, it is still imperative to explore the success and failure of past policies and make recommendations for improvement under the industrial development environment led by the government. Therefore, standing at the height of coordinated development in BTH Region, we should regard the promotion of regional scientific division as the overall goal and systematically put forward policy suggestions from three aspects: optimizing industrial policy of Hebei, promoting the coordination of the industrial policies of BTH and improving the top-level design of the national industrial policy.

The core appeal of the industrial policy reform in Hebei should be to achieve horizontal division of labor in BTH and help Hebei to avoid the trap of "low-end locking". We should intensify policy, enrich policy instruments and improve the decision-making mechanism; what's more, on the basis of helping Hebei to strengthen itself, great efforts should be made to promote the coordinate of industrial policy between Hebei and Beijing & Tianjin and the institutional barriers which influence the horizontal division of labor among Hebei, Beijing and Tianjin should be broken, so as to accelerate the industrial layout reconstruction, free flow of elements, and the connection between the regulatory standard and policy in BTH; finally, the government should strive to moderately delegate powers to Hebei in the fields of territorial development, land supply, financed and taxation policies and monetary credit, encourage Hebei to conduct pilot demonstration of industrial policy reform and further improve the top-level design of national industrial policies.

6.1 Recommendations on improvement of Hebei's industry policy

6.1.1 Confirm policy goals- low-end disposal, chain extension and regional coordination

In the past, Hebei's industrial policies were closely following the direction of the national industrial policy and generally met the stage characteristics and development needs. However, it was unclear what sustainable industrial division should be established in BTH. Apart from that, Hebei was not clear what path should choose to carry out industrial cooperation with Beijing and Tianjin so as to realize industrial upgrading together and was lack of judgment on the risk of industrial "low-end locking" that it would face. So we suggest that in Hebei's industrial policy, the general goal of industrial upgrading should be the high-quality industry cooperation between Hebei and Beijing & Tianjin and the achievement of overall horizontal division of labor. The goal should be the primary focus of industrial policy adjustment in Hebei and the cornerstone of realizing the industrial coordination in BTH. It is suggested that Hebei should take this goal as a guide in its planning, guidance, implementation plan, support and control measures concerning industrial development in the future. This goal includes the following policy implications:

(1) Avoiding the "low-end locking" is the fundamental starting point for policy improvement in Hebei. Long-term accumulation of policies, markets and industrial base and other factors make Beijing and Tianjin significantly superior to Hebei in industrial level, technological level and benefit structure. Hebei should face and recognize this reality, but Hebei's own industrial policy should not endorse this division of labor to develop for a long time. Therefore, the industrial policy should guide Hebei to get rid of the dilemma of low-end resource-based industries, avoid being at the low end of the industrial chain in BTH for a long time and speed up the overall horizontal division of labor with Beijing and Tianjin so as to truly realize industrial upgrading in Hebei and the coordinated development of BTH.

(2) The chain extension and the promotion of integrating industrial chain with value chain should be regarded as the realization form of the industrial upgrading. With the basic direction of industrial upgrading which is high-end, intelligent, integrated, ecological, clustered and international, Hebei should conduct the traditional industry to extend to the high-end of the industrial chain, promote the intelligence of technological equipment, utilize new technology to accelerate the integration of multi-industry development, reduce the negative ecological externalities of industrial development, build a number of advantageous industrial clusters, and facilitate enterprises transforming from pure product manufacturers to the solution providers for the industrial chain. While extending the industrial chain, more attention should be paid to making use of the advantages of innovation and market in Beijing and Tianjin to make up for the shortcomings of the original R&D, integrated innovation and marketing, and vigorously developing strategic emerging industries and modern service industries. In addition, occupy the high-end of the value chain in the region by cultivating new industries with high value-added and achieve the industrial upgrading by improving the value-added of the links.

(3) Achieve the coordinated development and establish competitive-cooperative relationship with Beijing and Tianjin which has a fair division of labor. Instead of eliminating the market competition in the region, the horizontal division of labor between Hebei and Beijing&Tianjin leads the three regions to further clarify their positions and exert their respective advantages to eliminate market distortions and inadequate competition

caused by the relatively constant roles of the three cities in regional division. In coordination with Beijing's industry, Hebei should clearly define specific policy goals in the areas of traditional industries evacuation and undertaking, high-end element mobility and new industry development. Utilizing the advantage of innovation center in Beijing, Hebei should gradually cultivate some industries with core technologies and competitive edges through industrial evacuation and high-end element spillover, so as to occupy higher links of the industrial chain and value chain together with Beijing, and achieve the horizontal intra-industry division of labor with Beijing; In terms of the industrial coordination with Tianjin, given that Tianjin's manufacturing base and upgrade direction are relatively close to those of Hebei, Hebei should strengthen its collaboration with Tianjin in areas of restraining excess capacity, breaking market barriers and promoting element mobility, cultivate some industries with good foundations and potential or product segments and start the dislocation competition with Tianjin, in order to achieve the industrial coordination with Tianjin under the situation that the level of industrial division in Hebei is relatively close to that in Tianjin.

6.1.2 Intensify policy- complete policy, same direction, and coordination

Although precious policies in Hebei are relatively comprehensive and systematic, the policy intensity is not satisfactory: the policy documents which are mainly directed planning and guidance are often lacking restriction, guidance and supporting measures; supporting policies and measures are inconsistent with the regulation direction of the policy goals and the policy direction and supporting measures are often misplaced; the policy-oriented documents are carried out first while the supporting policies and measures are "left behind", resulting in the fact that the policy implementation can't be corresponding to the specific time that policy goals determine, so that the policy is not effective in time. To this end, we suggest that:

(1) Achieve "complete policy". Industrial policy should supply a series of complete policies and measures. On the basis of defining policy orientation, industrial policy documents must introduce complete supporting policies and measures. It is suggested that we should introduce policies such as the five-year plan for national economic and social development, the special plan for industrial development and the guidance for industrial development in the future. At the same time, supporting measures that may materially affect the effect of policy should be clarified including fiscal and taxation, land supply, human resources, technical standards and market supervision, so as to ensure that the industrial policies are fully executed without fail.

(2) Achieve the "same direction". The supporting measures need to be fully consistent with the policy orientation. Under the guidance of industrial policies that promote industrial upgrading in Hebei and promote horizontal division of labor in the BTH, we should give priority to policies support in strategic emerging industries, modern service industries and transformation and upgrading of traditional industries, which are regarded as the key fields. In the area of administrative permit including major project applications, element supply , market regulation and so on, we should avoid setting evaluation criteria contrary to policy goals (such as setting excessive investment requirements for emerging industries with small investment), resulting in "mismatch" between supporting measures and policy goals.

(3) Achieve the "coordination". Supporting measures should be implemented simultaneously with the policy goals. On the basis of solving the "absence" and "mismatch" of supporting measures, the industrial policy should pay more attention to the problem of "backwardness" that the supporting policies and measures lag behind the policy goals. In the process of supporting the strategic emerging industries, modern service industries and traditional industries, the supporting policies and measures should be in full consistent with industrial policy orientation and development goals. In addition, the policy resources should be provided simultaneously by the police design, avoiding the policy is not effective in time because the supporting measures are out-of-step with policy goals.

6.1.3 Enrich policy measures-improving legislation, highlighting markets and optimizing administration

Legislation, market and administrative measures are the industrial policies as well as policy instruments for country macro-control of market economy. For a long time, influenced by the policy inertia that the industry development is led by government, industrial control measures in Hebei are obviously administrative order, resulting in the phenomena of no focus and universal application in the process of policy implementation, which have negative impact on the effect of industrial policy and the cultivation of market mechanism. Based on this, we believe that the optimization and improvement of policy measures in Hebei should adhere to the legal means as the foundation, market means as the core, administrative means for protection, take multi-pronged approach to create measures of industrial policies which can stimulate the vitality of the market, conform to the law of industrial development and provide powerful protection for coordination development:

(1) Based on the legislative measures, clarify the regulation boundary of

industrial policy. It is proposed to introduce local laws and regulations such as Industrial Upgrading Promotion Regulations in Hebei, Traditional Industries Revitalization Regulations in Hebei, Promotion Regulations for Strategic Emerging Industries and Modern Services in Hebei and so on, and stipulate the control range, form, formulation, modify mechanism and supporting measures of the industrial policy in the form of laws, clarify the power boundary of the industrial regulation for the government, give full play to the market mechanism and protect the legitimate interest of market bodies.

(2) Enrich market control measures and promote industrial upgrading from the demand side. Hebei should make related industrial policies in the demand side to conduct industrial upgrading in accordance with the purpose of synchronously regulation of the supply side and demand side. For example, formulating policies for cultivating advantageous industrial markets, expanding the demand for advantageous products such as biomedicine, rail transportation equipment, automobiles, high-end steel, green building materials and photovoltaic products through measures including livelihood construction and consumption subsidies, and guiding the traditional industries to develop toward high-end, green and low-carbon industries by utilizing the market forces so as to effectively promote the upgrading of supply side through the market demand.

(3) Optimize the realization form of administrative means which should be dominated by the differentiation and orientative measures. The administrative measures should avoid the set pattern including direct subsidy of finance and taxation, elements regulation and compulsive shut down. The government is suggested to adopt more differentiated and flexible measures. In administrative law enforcement to resolve excess capacity, the simple and crude universal measures should be avoided, such as compulsive treatment and power rationing and so on and different measures should be taken according to the prospect of the enterprise upgrade and actual progress. At the same time, more administrative policy resources should be used to foster market demand or provide public goods, guide the direction of industrial upgrading and generally reduce the cost of market bodies. For example, utilize fiscal and tax measures to provide subsidy for dominant products of Hebei on the consumer side and promote the reform of supply side by demand side; Conduct social capitals to invest innovative infrastructure including office space, research and development equipment, test sites and trial workshop in the mode of direct award and subsidy of finance and taxation, PPP and so on, and supplement public products required by the development of emerging industry by using market-based measures.

6.1.4 Strengthen the implementation of policies- establish coordinates and intensify evaluation

Another major goal of industrial policy reform in Hebei is to strengthen the implementation of policies and intensify supervision and examination. Hebei should set up an evaluation system for the implementation of industrial policies, and scientifically set evaluation indicators so as to conduct a quantitative evaluation of the implementation of industrial policies. The implementation of industrial policies should be included into the assessment system of cadres which should be regarded as an important part of cadre capabilities assessment.

(1) Further improve evaluation index system of the industrial policy implementation. "Comprehensive evaluation mechanism for industrial policy effects in Hebei" should be established. When setting policy goals of the policy papers such as Programme, Guidance and so on, clarify the implementation of policies and evaluation points and set the assessment indicators from multiple dimensions including the scientific and feasible policy objectives, the progress of investment in supporting policies, the policy of land supply, construction progress, marketing, business efficiency, industrial chain construction, cluster effect, employment promotion and fiscal contribution and so on. In addition, conduct quantitative evaluation for the effect of policy relying on scientific assessment "coordinate system", with a view to enhancing the policy implementation effect.

(2) The formulation and implementation of industrial policies should be included in the cadre assessment system. Based on the "Comprehensive evaluation mechanism for industrial policy effects in Hebei" mentioned above, we suggest that the effect of industrial policies should be taken as an important part of the assessment of the capabilities of the target people when organizing personnel departments to examine cadres. In particular, it should be regarded as important reference of assessing local leaders of the party and cadre candidates of the economic management, with a view to further enhancing scientific decision consciousness of the policy makers.

6.2 Recommendations on policy coordinated between Hebei and Beijing and Tianjin

6.2.1 Cooperate with the policies of industrial development in BTH-planning coordination, project coordination and investment coordination

At the height of coordinate development, the horizontal division of labor in the regional industry will be the overall goal of industrial coordinate development in BTH. To this end, Hebei should promote the implementation of the Industrial Development Plan of BTH by three parties in Beijing, Tianjin and Hebei and clarify the supporting measures; Hebei also needs to carry out project cooperation about industrial easement, jointly establish a "key project library of industrial development in BTH" and focus on industrial easement and practice to promote project coordination; In addition, it is important to coordinate investment policies to avoid vicious competition within the region which will damage the overall investment environment.

(1) Implement industrial development plan and promote plan and coordination in BTH. It is proposed that BTH should clearly define the horizontal division of labor at the regional level as a common goal of industrial upgrading, step up implementation of the jointly prepared Industrial Development Plan of BTH, discuss the key areas, development direction, upgrade path and layout and reconstruction in detail and clarify supporting policies and measures for promoting the industrial upgrading of BTH together. In particular, it is one of the key tasks to serve the functional evacuation of industries in Beijing and to continue the industry to develop in Xiong'an New Area. It is important to reconstruct the regional industrial layout and to formulate and perfect a comprehensive set of scientific and detailed policies, with a view to realizing regional industrial horizontal division of labor and coordinated development.

(2) Build key project library together and press ahead with project coordination. On the basis of joint preparation of industrial upgrading plan, "BTH key project library of industrial development" is established which includes the upgrade projects of strategic emerging industry, modern services and traditional industry with the aim of serving the industrial horizontal division of labor in BTH and promoting the industrial transformation and upgrading of the region. Establish scientific evaluation index system for warehousing projects, restore key projects which has rational gradient, clarify favorable measures that are reasonable, effective and all-round, and pay more attention to serving industry evacuation in Beijing and significant industrial development projects in Xiong'an New Area. In addition, BTH should apply for policy resources together such as "special construction land index of the coordinated development in BTH" and "special financial funds of the industrial development in BTH" on the basis of the construction of project library.

(3) Coordinate industrial investment policies to promote cooperation of investment. Hebei should actively connect with Beijing and Tianjin for the investment promotion policy, divide industries which belong to strategy emerging industry, modern services and traditional industry into two categories including "coordinated investment" and "free investment" in accordance with the general requirements for restructuring

and layout of regional industries in the "Industrial Development Plan of BTH" and discuss the priority order for the practice of the "coordinated investment" projects avoiding vicious competition; "free investment" will not be limited by the order of practice, so BTH should decide uniform preferential measures for various industries and projects of different scales, minimize the differences in investment policies, avoid vicious competition in the region and protect the overall investment environment in BTH Region.

6.2.2 Promote interconnection-mutual recognition of qualifications, joint supervision and benefit sharing

A major obstacle to industrial collaboration in BTH is the lacking of technical standards recognition, the separation of market supervision and the imperfect benefit-shared mechanism. Therefore, BTH should immediately recognize each other's specific standards and qualifications and break the hidden technical barriers between regions; Carry out cross-regional joint supervision in BTH focusing on undertaking industrial evacuation in Beijing and Tianjin; In view of the obstacles that finance and taxation system which is the system of dividing revenue and expenditure between the central and local governments and holding each responsible for balancing their budgets and local protectionism bring to the cross-regional migration of the enterprises, further improve the finance and taxation sharing mechanism of industrial transfer, so as to break the mechanism obstacles for the free flow of the elements in BTH.

(1) Promote mutual recognition of qualifications and break technical barriers. Establish a mechanism for mutual recognition of regional qualifications in BTH. Hebei should actively negotiate with Beijing and Tianjin on the "Mutual Recognition List of Qualifications" and promote the mutual recognition of qualification in BTH which is most related to industrial upgrading including high-tech enterprises qualifications, engineering qualifications, taxation qualifications, talents qualifications, practitioner qualification and credit qualifications, so as to ensure that people who have qualification don't need to certify again when they transfer to another place in BTH and continue to enjoy the treatment as before. This will break the hidden technique barrier in BTH.

(2) Promote joint law enforcement and break regulatory barriers. Hebei should take the initiative to discuss with Beijing and Tianjin on the establishment of the "Joint Supervision Mechanism on the Market of Beijing, Tianjin and Hebei", unify the standard of supervision and enforcement according to related laws and regulations, and establish mechanisms for real-time monitoring, emergency response and inter-regional dispute mediation. Focus on carrying out joint law enforcement in areas such as intellectual property

protection, commercial registration, credit status, Internet transactions, consumer protection, the quality of food and drug, so as to create a fair, transparent and clear industrial regulatory environment in BTH.

(3) Improve the sharing mechanism of the taxation and break the local protection. It is suggested that on the basis of the BTH Tax Receipts Sharing Method for Aimed Enterprises In the Industrial Transfer of the Coordinated Development which is jointly introduced by Ministry of Finance and state taxation administration, BTH should define the existence quantity limit that is the average total amount of the payment for the three types of taxes in first three years that the enterprise transfers into, with the principle of "constant total amount and incremental share". The amount that is lower or equal to the limit should belong to the place that the enterprise transfers from; It should be discussed by the origin area and resettled area about the amount that is higher than the existence quantity, with a view to promoting origin area especially Beijing and Tianjin to take part in the enterprise evacuation and business remove actively so as to serve the industrial reconstruction in BTH.

6.2.3 Promote free flow of regional elements-talent spillover, financial cooperation and technology sharing

In addition to policy coordination, Hebei and Beijing & Tianjin should strive to break the institutional barriers of elements flow and promote high-end talents resources to flow from Beijing and Tianjin to Hebei via functional evacuation, so as to create the balanced distribution of high-end human resources in the region; Establish a policy-oriented finance platform for regional industries as soon as possible to supply financial support for industrial evacuation and transform; Improve the trading platform for regional technology and enhance the supporting role that the transformation of scientific and technological achievements plays in industrial upgrading.

(1) Build common market for human resources in BTH. Utilize the existing provincial talent market platform of the Bureau of Human Resource and Social Security in BTH to set up the "BTH talent service center" and improve the human resources basic services including job services, settling (residence permit) services, file storage, professional-title evaluation, professional qualifications, floating population services and so on, so as to create one-top comprehensive service platform serving the industrial evacuation and the inter-regional flow of talents. Create "BTH industrial high-end talents service green path" for innovative talents in strategic emerging industry, high-end management talents in modern services and practical skilled talents in traditional industry and issue recruitment information of high-end talents through "BTH talent service

center", with a view to breaking the information barriers for the free flow of talents. We also need to improve and implement the incentive mechanism for talent innovation and entrepreneurship "within the system" in BTH, provide greater efforts to support high-end talents from colleges, research institutes, state-owned enterprises and government to carry out independent innovation and entrepreneurial activities. For high-end talents, we can extend their years for status and basic treatment and provide various innovation and entrepreneurship preferential policy and relevant human resources service to break the mechanism barrier for the free flow of talents.

(2) Improve the industrial financial cooperation mechanism in BTH. "BTH industrial development bank consortium" should be established by city commercial banks and agriculture communication systems in BTH together, emphatically serving warehousing projects of "BTH industrial key project library" and relevant infrastructure and ecological protection projects. This will help to build a regional industrial financial services infrastructure. The initial capital is undertook by the governments in BTH together and the various industrial financial innovation activities which should be market-oriented and specialized are conducted by financial institutions with good reputation such as institutions of insurance, trust, security, financial leasing and venture capital. This will promote the free flow of financial elements in BTH and fully satisfy the financial service demand of the industrial upgrading in the region.

(3) Improve the technology exchange market in BTH. Based on the China Technology Exchange "Hebei Platform of BTH Technology Exchange", China Technology Exchanges and Hebei should take the initiative to collaborate with Beijing and Tianjin to jointly establish Beijing platform and Tianjin platform of BTH Technology Exchange, making use of the existing exchange mechanism of the China Technology Exchange to build a more complete "BTH technology exchange market", so as to promote the integration of the exchange platforms in BTH and create cross-regional technology exchange service platform with the function of information publishing, technology exchange, achievement transformation, talent training and start-up incubator. This will promote the technology elements to better serve the industrial transformation and upgrading in BTH.

6.2.4 Promote the equalization of public services in BTH-direct clearing, pension evacuation and education, and educational balance

Although social public service is not the core content of industrial upgrading research, it has close relationship with residents' health and daily life, which is an important part of the soft environment for regional development and is also a "hidden factor" that can't be ignored by industrial transfer. It is of great significance for the cross-regional flow of talent, technology and capital. At present, BTH should aim at equalizing the social public services in the region and focus on the needs of public services for the floating population involved in the industry evacuation. We should do best in transferring and renewing across regions and further eliminate the "hidden" obstacles of the cross-regional flow of elements.

(1) Further improve the cross-regional relevant settlement mechanism of medical insurance. Gradually integrate the medical insurance funds of BTH into a unified "BTH medical insurance fund" and unify reimbursement catalogs, standards and policies, so as to create a remote settlement mechanism with "integrated funds, unifies standard and mutual recognition". In view of the most urgent problem of direct settlement for medical treatment in different places, it is proposed to increase the number of hospitals for direct medical settlement in different places based on the fact that 47 hospitals have realized direct settlement of medical insurance in BTH, extending from the top three hospitals to community health institutions and pension service institutions, to achieve the overall direct settlement of medical institutions for remote medical treatment in BTH as soon as possible. Further simplify the procedures for direct settlement of medical treatment in different places and change from "advance filing and registration system" to "barrier-free settlement system", which can better meet the medical needs arising from the trans-provincial flow of residents in BTH.

(2) Improve relevant mechanism of trans-provincial pension service. On the basis of the different enforcement regulation of the cross-regional pensions insurance's transferring and renewing introduced by Beijing, Tianjin and Hebei, it is proposed that BTH jointly invest and establish "BTH transitional funds for pensions insurance's transferring and renewing" in light of the different standards for getting pensions among regions. This will make up for the reduction of pensions due to the transfer of the pension relationship from Beijing and Tianjin to Hebei. In view of the differences in the supportive policies for nursing home in Hebei and Beijing & Tianjin, it is suggested that Beijing and Tianjin extend the relevant preferential policies moderately so that pension service agencies in Hebei that accept the old from Beijing and Tianjin or the branches of pension service agencies in Beijing and Tianjin enjoy equal preferential policies. At the same time, Hebei also provides local preferential treatment for the above-mentioned agencies in order to attract high-quality aged care services in Beijing and Tianjin to settle in Hebei. BTH

should realize the mutual recognition for medical institutions of pension service institutions from different places as soon as possible and enjoy the direct settlement service of medical insurance in different places.

(3) Improve relevant mechanisms of education integration. During the phase of basic education, in view of the differences input levels in BTH, we propose that the governments of Beijing, Tianjin and Hebei jointly invest and establish the "BTH basic education construction fund", focusing on supporting primary and secondary schools from Beijing and Tianjin to run schools in Hebei and improving basic education conditions in poor areas of Hebei; the education administrative departments in BTH should formulate the textbook catalogs, teaching plan and teaching evaluation criteria together for basic education in the region. During the phase of higher education, it is suggested that the governments of the three places should encourage colleges and universities in Beijing and Tianjin to set up branch schools or make complete relocation to Hebei, increase the scale of high-quality higher education resources in Hebei and optimize the regional distribution of higher education resources; In addition, the governments should promote the centralized examination and admission to realize the "one test paper, one entry line" in the stage of higher education in BTH.

6.3 Recommendations on national supporting policy

6.3.1 Give policy support in the field of land and space development and construction- increasing supply, pilot policy and fine development

Although Hebei is located in the North China Plain, it has wide mountain land, complex geology condition and sensitive ecology, so the basic space for construction and development is relatively tense. However, it is imperative to expand its supply of construction land because Hebei is facing the challenging task of its transformation and development. Therefore, it is suggested that the government moderately increase the construction land index for Hebei under the existing system and direct support the industrial upgrading in Hebei; allow Hebei to carry out land policy pilot reform, activate the land for rural construction and increase the supply of industrial construction land; allow Hebei to moderately adjust the planning of the main functional area and promote the fine development of the national land based on regional functional layout and land use status.

(1)Moderately provide preferential support to the construction land supply. It is suggested that the government should allow Hebei to moderately increase the annual scale of construction land and the proportion of industrial land under the current land supply policy, in order to better meet the land demand for industrial transformation and upgrading. In view of the "BTH industrial key project library" proposed above, we will explore and establish "BTH industry collaborative special construction land index" which is independent of the construction land indexes in three areas and assign the construction land index to the key storage projects which serve the key projects of industrial evacuation, the construction of Xiong'an New Area, major transportation infrastructure projects and ecological control projects.

(2)Hebei is allowed to carry out pilot trials of new land management mechanism. We suggest that our government should approve the cultivated land balance policy to be adopted across the whole province and simplify the approval process for land use. Simplify approval process for land using and improve the approval efficiency of construction land. As to dominant engineering with the infrastructure projects approved by the state, it can use the land first after the approval of the Ministry of Land and Resources; key construction projects which lies in a separate site should be permitted to occupy cultivated land while supplementing. Hebei should be allowed to carry out the pilot trial of "rural construction land entering the land market directly" to let the rural idle construction land directly enter into the primary market transactions without changing its nature, alleviating the tense supply and demand of industrial land.

(3)Allow Hebei to moderately enhance the strength of territorial development and improve the fine level of land development. In view of the significant changes of climate and surface runoff in BTH, it is suggested that the government should allow Hebei to adjust the planning of the main functional areas reasonably, especially to conduct a comprehensive survey and functional repair of the original flood discharge area. Hebei should moderately enhance the development intensity for the areas that have lost their flood control functions, raise the land utilization efficiency and increase construction land supply.

6.3.2 Enhance the pertinence and flexibility of fiscal and monetary policy- credit policy, policy-based finance and fiscal policy

Industrial upgrading in Hebei is inseparable from the support of the state fiscal and monetary policy. Hebei should strive to apply for credit support policy from central bank and implement the "customized" credit policy in line with the demands of industrial upgrading in Hebei; Hebei should seek for politically financial support for industrial upgrading from CDB (China Development Bank) and four major asset management companies; In addition, Hebei can seek for special financial support for industrial upgrading from the Ministry of Finance.

(1)Appropriately increase the flexibility of local credit policy in Hebei. Efforts will be made to let PBC Head Office regard Hebei and Xiong'an New Area as the key supporting areas. PBC Head Office should also make specialized credit plan for industrial upgrading of Hebei, industrial cooperation of BTH and construction of Xiong'an New Area, offer financing support for key projects of industrial development, and guide commercial banks in Hebei to increase credit support for upgrading projects of strategic emerging industries and traditional industries. What's more, banking financial institutions should avoid broad-brush credit reluctance, credit reduction and credit withdrawals and the government should enhance synergies between credit and industrial policies.

(2)Strive for financing support from national policy-oriented financial institutions for industrial upgrading in Hebei. Efforts will be made to let China Development Bank, Agricultural Development Bank of China and Export-Import Bank of China give overall credit extension for industrial upgrading, agricultural improvement and global cooperation on production capacity and offer preferential policies loans for key industry projects. Take the initiative to communicate with the Asset Management Corporation of Dongfang, Cinda, Huarong, Great Wall to establish "cooperation mechanism for disposition of real economy bad assets in Hebei", so as to properly deal with the bad assets caused by market changes, capacity reduction and technological transformation and improve the market-based bad asset management and disposal mechanism.

(3)Provide favorable fiscal policies. The Ministry of Finance is suggested to compile "special finance for BTH industrial development" to support major industrial new projects and upgrading projects in BTH. Especially, the Ministry of Finance should provide key support for significant projects including resolving overcapacity of traditional industry in Hebei and transforming high-tech achievements which are from Beijing and Tianjin in Hebei. Based on the goal of industrial cooperation in BTH, we should expand application scope of the existing preferential policies, in particular, allow the preferential policies of Zhongguancun and Tianjin Binhai New Area to be extended to Hebei, so as to further remove the institutional barriers of industrial transfer and functional dispersal in BTH.

6.3.3 Hebei is supported to establish open platform and participate in the "Belt and Road" development.

The industrial development in Hebei always has the obvious characteristic of endogeneity, which is neither in line with the laws of industrial development, nor meets the requirements of the industrial coordinated development in BTH. As a coastal province, Hebei lags behind in its foreign economic cooperation and the industrial internationalization. Therefore, the government is suggested to establish a state-level free trade zone in Hebei and promote Hebei to further utilize both domestic and international markets and resources so as to build a highland for industrial upgrading and international development. At the same time, enterprises in Hebei should be encouraged to "go out" and take full advantage of their own advantages to participate in the "Belt and Road" development. Therefore, competitive industrial capacity can be exported by global cooperation on production capacity, which can promote the industrial transformation and upgrading.

(1)Hebei is supported to build a national platform for opening up. The Ministry of Commerce is suggested to support the construction of national industrial development platform in Hebei. Under the background of the coordinated development of BTH, Caofeidian comprehensive bonded zone, Bohai New District and Beidaihe New District should be integrated into "China (Hebei) free trade zone". In addition, according to relevant policies for Tianjin free trade zone and Shanghai free trade zone, we should further lower the market access threshold, carry out profound reform and pilot trial in the fields of international trade, finance and shipping, and establish external cooperation window that reflects the industrial characteristics and development demand of Hebei.

(2)Hebei is supported to participate in the "Belt and Road" development. The ministries such as the National Development and Reform Commission and the Ministry of Commerce are suggested to support Hebei to play its own advantages and participate deeply in the "Belt and Road" construction and moderately give benefits to Hebei in the areas of national investment promotion, construction project undertaking, global cooperation on production capacity and so on along the Belt and Road. The aim is to promote the output overseas of competitive industrial capacity involving steel, building materials, textile and garment and rail transit equipment and promote the internationalization and export-oriented development of enterprises, in particular, promote the transformation of traditional industries from a single product manufacturer to a solution provider of large multinational full industrial chain production service.

References

[1] 李靖 . 新型产业分工 : 重塑区域发展格局 [M]. 北京 : 社会科学文献出版社 ,2012.

[2] 伍长南 , 林昌华 . 福建省产业转型升级研究 [M]. 北京 : 中国经济出版社 ,2012.

[3] 马晓河 . 结构转型与经济可持续发展 [M]. 北京 : 中国计划出版社 ,2014.

[4] 陈政 . 泛珠三角区域产业分工与协作机制研究 [M]. 成都 : 西南财经大学出版社 ,2013.

[5] 杜传忠 , 刘英基 . 区际产业分工与产业转移研究 [M]. 北京 : 经济科学出版社 ,2013.

[6] 许继琴 . 产业集群与区域创新系统 [M]. 北京 : 经济科学出版社 ,2006.

[7] 魏然 , 李国梁 . 京津冀区域一体化可行性分析 [J]. 经济问题探索 ,2006(12).

[8] 朱云飞 . 新型工业化过程中河北主导产业的选择、转型与升级研究 [J]. 经济研究参考 ,2014(44).

[9] 谢恒 , 周雯珺 , 王斌 . 京津冀一体化背景下的河北产业升级 [J]. 宏观经济管理 ,2015(9).

[10] 刘友金 , 王玮 . 世界典型城市群发展经验及对我国的启示 [J]. 湖南科技大学学报 (社会科学版),2009(1).

[11] 杜曙光 . 横向产业分工研究 [J]. 中国经济问题 ,2008(6).

[12] 陈永国 . 技术转移与京津冀产业分工协作 [J]. 经济与管理 ,2007(10).

[13] 陈耀 . 京津冀一体化背景下的产业格局重塑 [J]. 天津师范大学学报 (社会科学版),2014(6).

[14] 王爱兰 . 借鉴国际经验加快京津冀都市圈发展 [J]. 天津行政学院学报 ,2006(2).

[15] 石林 . 京津冀地区产业转移与协同发展研究 [J]. 当代经济管理 ,2015(5).

[16] 邢子政 . 京津冀区域产业结构趋同倾向与协同调整之策 [J]. 现代财经 ,2009(9).

[17] 徐永利 . 京津冀协同发展 : 河北省产业逆梯度推移策略 [J]. 河北学刊 ,2014(7).

[18] 孙久文 . 京津冀一体化中的产业协同发展研究 [J]. 河北工业大学学报 (社会科学版),2014(9).

[19] 秦尊文 . 美国城市群考察及对中国的启示 [J]. 湖北社会科学 ,2008(12).

[20] 高相铎 . 美国五大湖工业区产业结构演变的城市化响应机理辨析 [J]. 世界地理研究 ,2006(3).

[21] 张明艳 , 孙晓飞 , 贾巳梦 . 京津冀经济圈产业结构与分工测度研究 [J]. 经济研究参考 ,2015(8).

[22] 郑健壮 , 徐寅杰 . 产业转型升级及其路径研究 [J]. 浙江树人大学学报 ,2012(7).

[23] 张腾扬 . 京津冀这三年不寻常 [N]. 人民日报 .

Study on the Strategy of Enhancing Hebei Provincial Innovative Level Utilizing Innovation Resources from Beijing

Principal Investigator: Luo Jing
Investigators: Wang Fuhua, Qi Chang'an

Innovation-driven development is strategic choice and fundamental driving force for promoting coordinated development of Beijing-Tianjin-Hebei. Integration of regional innovation resources and establishment of innovation community are major tasks for the innovation-driven development in the BTH Region. On the basis of implementation of *Hebei Province Innovation-driven Development Plan,* integration of regional innovation resources in the BTH Region is a great opportunity for Hebei to effectively enhance innovative level utilizing innovation resources from Beijing-Tianjin and the most convenient way to realize economic transformation and upgrading.Compared with Tianjin, there are more abundant innovation resources in Beijing and stronger motivation for innovation resources to cross-regionally transfer and transform, due to the adjustment of city functions and rising developmental cost in Beijing. Therefore, this report focuses on how to effectively utilize Beijing's innovation resources. It conducts the in-depth analysis on conditions and foundations of collaborative innovation, summarizes the progress of collaborative innovation between Beijing and Hebei,proposes basic strategies and key measures of utilizing innovation resources from Beijing, and provides policy reference for Hebei Provincial Party Committee and provincial government. It should be noted that, collaborative innovation of Beijing-Tianjin-Hebei is the ultimate objective, so some chapters also concern collaborative innovation among the three regions.

1. Conditions of collaborative innovation between Beijing and Hebei Province

Cross-regional agglomeration, integration and allocation of innovation resources instill new impetus and vitality to regional development, hence have become focuses of regional cooperation and development at home and abroad. United States established the "American Innovation Community", Japan established the "National Strategic Special Zone", French established "Competitive cluster", EU implemented a series of innovation cooperation programs, and in "Yangtze River Delta" region, *Yangtze River Delta Science and Technology Cooperation Plan* has been working. From the perspective of the BTH Region, collaborative innovation between Beijing and Hebei focuses on "Innovation" and "Cooperation" which is also the key to coordinated development. Therefore, the collaborative innovation between Beijing and Hebei caters to the trend toward innovation development both at home and abroad, and is in line with the focuses of the coordinated development of Beijing-Tianjin-Hebei, hence with and hence has excellent external conditions.

On the basis of analysis on Hebei's innovation demands, characteristics of Beijing's innovation resources and trend of cross-regional cooperation, this report concludes that there are so many consistent and matched fields of innovation development and unique conditions and foundations for collaborative innovation between Beijing and Hebei.

1.1 Demands of Hebei's innovation development

Influenced by the domestic and international innovation development, Hebei has urgent demands on innovation to meet the developmental requirements in the new historical period, and has unique features in the path and major fields of innovation development.

1.1.1 Hebei Province has urgent demands for innovation-driven development

In the Post Financial Crisis Era, science and technology has become the major driving force of economic and social development, improving the innovation capacity and promoting the development of emerging industries have become important means to cultivate new growth drivers and competitive advantages in the world. China's economy has entered a period of new normal, the economic growth mode is transforming from traditional investment-drivento innovation-driven, the economic driving force is changing from demographic dividend and investment to total factor productivity elevatedby technology and mechanisms reform, science and technology and innovation accordinly become the major economic driving forces in the new normal period. Over 30 years after reform and opening up in Hebei, resource-based industrial investment has always been the major economic driving force, which is consistent with Hebei's resource endowment and development stage, and it also contributed more to rapid economic growth and big economic aggregate. With the decrease of demographic dividend and enhancement of resources and environment constraints, the economic development mode of "high investment, high consumption, high pollution, low quality, and low efficiency" has been difficult to sustain, it will be impossible to strengthen Hebei's economy, even worse become "drag" of sustained and stable economic growth. Therefore, in the view of new situation of international scientific and technological revolution and industrial transformation, new requirements of China's economic new normal and prominent contradictions, Hebei has more urgent demands for innovation-driven development than ever.

1.1.2 Enhancing innovative level utilizing external forcesis inevitable choice for Hebei Province

The functional orientation of the BTH Region defined in *Outline of Coordinated Development of Beijing-Tianjin-Hebei* is new economic engine of national innovation-driven development, which put forward undoubtedly higher requirements to Hebei due to its huge innovative gaps with Beijing and Tianjin.

Hebei's Innovation Conference was held in July 2016, at the same time when the issued *Hebei Province Science and Technology Innovation 13th Five-year Plan* proposed a series targets: by 2020, ratio of expenditure on R&D to GDP should reach about 2.5%, R&D investment of industrial enterprises above designated size should account for 1.2% of their revenue from principal business, contribution rate of scientific and technological progress reach more than 55%, scientific and technological small and medium-sized enterprises(SMEs) reach 80,000, high-tech enterprises reach 3,500, provincial comprehensive scientific and technological progress reach average level of the country. Compared with the magnificent targets, innovation foundations and conditions in Hebei are insuflicient, and regional innovation capacity lags behind more than 20 provinces in China. There is a considerable gap with the provinces having similar economic power, and a "cliff-type" gap with Beijing in terms of science and technology investment, quantity and quality of scientific and technological personnel, construction of technological platform, comprehensive service facilities etc.. It is difficult to achieve those targets in *Hebei Province Science and Technology Innovation 13th Five-year Plan,* and quickly narrow innovative gaps with Beijing and Tianjin by Hebei's own innovative power. It is also difficult to promote construction of new economic engine of national innovation-driven development jointly with Beijing and Tianjin.Therefor enhancing innovative level utilizing external forces is inevitable choice for Hebei.

1.1.3 The major demands of Hebei's innovation development utilizing external force

Promoting Hebei's innovation development utilizing external force needs to focus on the following fields:

Enhancing industrial innovation capacity utilizing external force. Transformation and upgrading is the main tone in the 13th Five-Year period with the focus of elevating industrial innovation capacity. According to the requirements of *Hebei Province Science and Technology Innovation 13th Five-year Plan*, Hebei must enhance industrial technological innovation capacity, cultivate industrial new technology, new products, new format and new mode utilizing external force by implementation of ten major technical innovation programs including advanced equipment manufacturing, big data and new generation of information technology, big health care, new energy, energy saving and environmental protection, high performance new materials, upgrading of steel industry, chemical technology, modern agriculture, modern services industry, science and technology to benefit the public etc.

Establishing backbone innovation carriers utilizing external force. Backbone innovation carriers are platforms gathering regional innovation resources and leading regional innovation development. In Hebei, backbone innovation carriers are less, low-level and lack of regional influence. The lack of innovation resources and innovation experience makes Hebei must fully utilize external force to construct strategic and innovative platforms, establish specialized and characteristic innovation carriers, promote the development of new innovation carriers, and then improve the quantity and level of innovation carriers;

Promoting mass entrepreneurship and innovation utilizing external force. Hebei should focus on decentralized-type social innovation, so mass entrepreneurship and innovation is the key of stimulating innovation vitality and improving innovation-driven development. Due to lack of innovation resources, Hebei should make efforts to establish innovation and entrepreneurship platforms, improve innovation and entrepreneurship functions, perfect soft and hard environment to attract external innovation resources.

1.2 Characteristics of Beijing's innovation resources and trend of cross-regional cooperation

Beijing is national innovation center withhigh density of innovation resources agglomeration. Influenced by strategies of *National Innovation Driven Development* and *Coordinated Development of Beijing-Tianjin-Hebei*, cross-regional cooperation of Beijing's innovation resources has entered a new phase. For further analysis on conditions and matched fields of collaborative innovation between Beijing and Hebei, we should recognize the characteristics of Beijing's innovation resources and embrace new trend of cross-regional cooperation.

1.2.1 Characteristics of Beijing's innovation resources

There are the most concentrated innovation resources in Beijing with distinct characteristics in terms of quantity, structure, fields and links.

Abundant quantity. Beijing is the concentrated area of innovation talents. In 2016, R&D personnel in Beijing is 362 thousand, ranking 5th in the country, R&D personnel per 10 thousand persons is 166.6, ranking 1st. Beijing is also such area with most concentrated universities, innovation institutions and innovation platforms, there are 95 universitiesat all levels accounting for 23.2% in the country,405 scientific research institutions, 173 key laboratories, 102 engineering technical centers which are all ranking the forefront of the country. Beijing has perfect innovation and entrepreneurship service facilities, Zhongguancun Venture Street, as a symbol,consists of 73 innovative incubators, 29 state-level science and technology incubators, 30 university science and technology parks, 37 overseas talent pioneer parks, 13 characteristic industry incubators and other innovative service platforms. Beijing has most abundant innovative achievements in the country relying on numerous high-level innovative talents and platforms, in 2016, number of patent applications granted reached 100,578, of which invention patents granted reached 40,602, number of invented per 10,000 population reached 18.7, correspondingly ranked fourth, second and first in the country. See Figure 1 to 4

Higher level. Beijing has the most concentrated high-level innovation resources, there are 389 Chinese Academy of Sciences(CAS), 352 Chinese Academy of Engineering(CAE), accounting for 52.4% and 43.9% in the country; 111 national key laboratories, 65 engineering technological centers, accounting for 30.9% and 40%; 32 "985&211" colleges and universities, of which universities like Tsinghua University and Peking University are influential in the world; scientific and technological achievements which achieved national awards each year account for one third in the country. Beijing has the most abundant and highest quality of innovative talents, innovative institutions, innovative platforms and scientific and technological achievements.

Obvious industrial characteristics. Beijing's innovation resources are widely distributed in more than 30 industries involving the primary, secondary and tertiary industry. We conduct comparative analysis on scientific research institutions, key laboratories, engineering technology centers and technological enterprise incubators and found that Beijing's innovation resources are mainly concentrated in the following six industries. (See Figure 1,2,3,4) (i) Electronic information and communications. Industrial key laboratories, engineering technology centers, technological enterprises incubators, scientific research institutions in this industry rank second among entire industries. Number of national key laboratories and engineering technology centers rankfirst. LG Electronics (China) Research and Development Center, Beijing Samsung Communication Technology Research Co., Ltd., Rosenberg Asia Pacific Electronics Co., Ltd. Beijing Science and Technology R&D Center are all world's top innovation institutions in the field of electronics information and communications. (ii) Bio-medicine. Number of industrial key laboratories, scientific research institutions and professional incubator in this industry rank first among entire industries, number of bio-engineering national key laboratories is only less than electronic information. Biotech Pharma Co., Ltd, Beijing Mediking Biopharm Co., Ltd, Beijing Sciecure Pharmaceutical Co., Ltd technology R&D Center, Beijing Fogangren Bio-Pharm Limited are all representative biomedical innovation organizations. (iii) Equipment manufacturing. Number of industrial engineering technology centers, scientific research institutions and professional incubator rank third among entire industries, national key laboratories in this industry including Tsinghua University, China Railway Research Institute, Mechanical Science Research Institute and so on, have strong original innovation power. In addition, new energy, new materials and modern agriculture are sectors with concentrated innovation resources and outstanding innovation power.

Figure 1 Fields of national key laboratories in Beijing, 2014

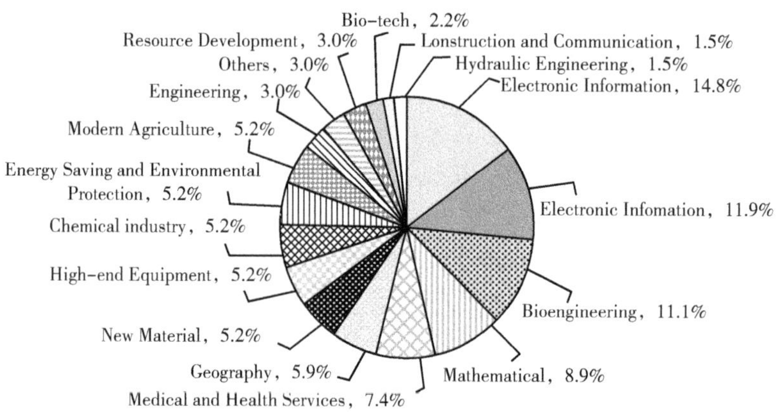

Figure 2 Fields of engineering technological centers in Beijing, 2014

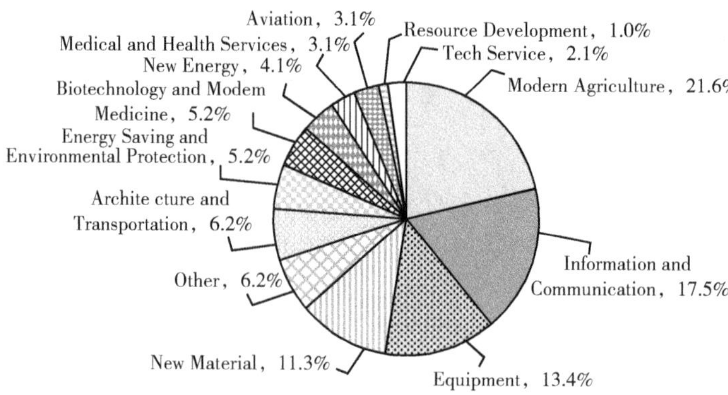

Figure 3 Fields of professional incubators in Beijing, 2014

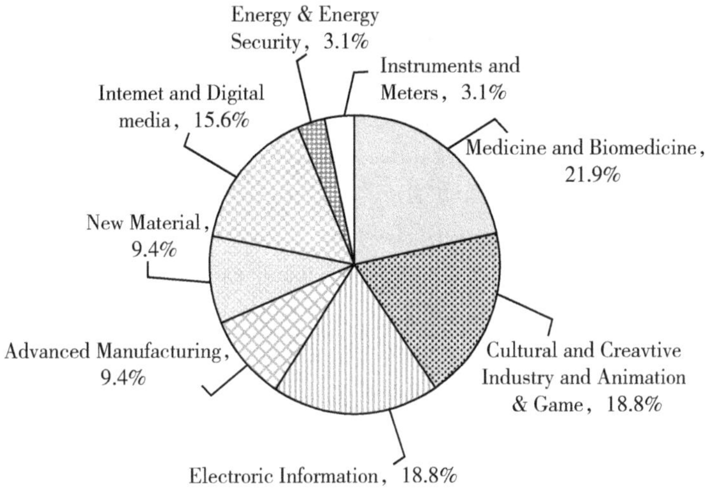

Figure 4 Fields of Scientific Research Institutions in Beijing, 2014

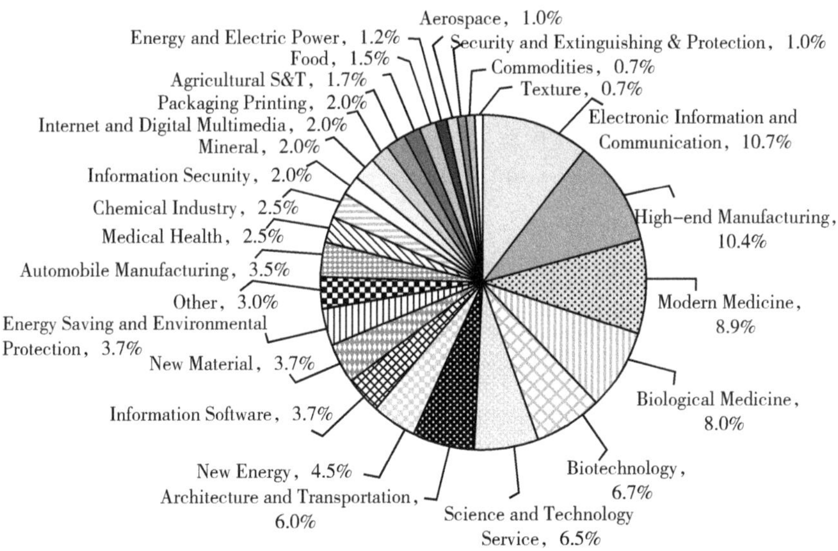

Relatively concentrated innovation chain. Innovation chain involves the upstream segments of basic and applied research, mid- and down-stream segments of pilot, industrial application and others. In general, on the basis of the massive high-level universities and research institutes and the strong original innovation capacity, Beijing has large quantity and high quality of input and output in segments of basic and applied research, but relatively weak in innovation achievements transformation and technological application.In 2015, the total R&D expenditure of Beijing reached 138.4 billion yuan, of which expenditure on the basic and applied research accounted for 36.8%, respectively 14.9 and 23.3 percentage points higher than Shanghai and Shenzhen. Research institutes and universities are the main R&D entitieswith a high R&D expenditure proportion 62.6% among all types entities, which 25 and 58.7 percentage points higher than Shanghai and Shenzhen, on the contrary, the major entities of R&D expenditure in Shanghai and Shenzhen are industrial enterprises. Scientific and technological achievements in Beijing are more abundant than Shanghai and Shenzhen, which can be easily verified by the comparison on the number of patent applications accepted and granted, scientific papers issued, scientific and technological publication. But in the segments of innovation achievements transformation and technological application, especially new industrial products development, Beijing lags behind those two cities; in 2015, internal R&D expenditure of industrial enterprises in Beijing reached 24.41 billion yuan, and gross annual revenue of new products of industrial enterprises above designated size reached 364.78 billion yuan, which are all lower than Shanghai and Shenzhen. (See Tables 1, 2, 3)

Table 1 Statistics on R&D expenditure of Beijing, Shanghai, Shenzhen 2015

	Beijing	Shanghai	Shenzhen
Total R&D Expenditure(100 million yuan)	1,384.0	936.1	732.4
Percentage of Total R&D Expenditure on GDP(%)	6.01	3.73	4.18

Soure: Data from Statistical Yearbook in related year, unless otherwise specified, the same below.

Table 2 Expenditure on R&D of Beijing, Shanghai, Shenzhen by expenditure and institution type, 2015

		Beijing		Shanghai		Shenzhen	
	Type	Total (100 million Yuan)	As Percentage of Total R&D Expenditure (%)	Total (100 million Yuan)	As Percentage of Total R&D Expenditure (%)	Total (100 million Yuan)	As Percentage of Total R&D Expenditure (%)
By expenditure type	Fundamental research	191.0	13.8	76.9	8.2	6.7	0.9
	Applied research	318.3	23.0	127.8	13.7	92.5	12.6
	Experimental development	874.7	63.2	731.4	78.1	633.2	86.5

continued

	Type	Beijing		Shanghai		Shenzhen	
		Total (100 million Yuan)	As Percentage of Total R&D Expenditure (%)	Total (100 million Yuan)	As Percentage of Total R&D Expenditure (%)	Total (100 million Yuan)	As Percentage of Total R&D Expenditure (%)
By institution type	Scientific research institutes	702.7	50.8	264.6	28.3	20.4	2.8
	Universities	162.7	11.8	86.7	9.3	8.2	1.1
	Industrial enterprises	244.1	17.6	474.2	50.7	672.6	91.8
	Non-Industrial enterprises	252.4	18.2	95.1	10.2	29.8	4.1
	Other	22.1	1.6	15.5	1.7	1.4	0.2

Table 3 Statistics on scientific and technological achievements and new products in Beijing, Shanghai, Shenzhen 2015

	Beijing	Shanghai	Shenzhen
Industrial added value (100 million yuan)	3,710.9	7,162.3	6,743.0
R&D internal expenditure of industrial enterprises above designated size (100 million yuan)	244.1	474.2	404.7
Revenue of new products of industrial enterprises above designated size (billion yuan)	3,647.8	7,312.2	8,872.0
Number of patent applications accepted (piece)	156,312	38,266	105,481
Number of patents applications granted (piece)	94,031	8,756	72,120
Number of scientific papers issued (piece)	167,719	98,035	—
Number of publications on scientific and technological (piece)	7,486	3 208	—

1.2.2 Cross-regional innovative cooperation

Influenced by regional cooperation trend in the whole worldand implementation of *National Innovation-driven Development Strategy*, Beijing's innovation resources have entered new cross-region cooperation phase to respond proactively to the changing conditions.

The *National Innovation-driven Development Strategy* has been implemented rapidly, and the cross-regional cooperation of Beijing's innovation resources will enter into the expressway.

China's economy has entered into new normal, and the traditional development pattern with characteristics of technological imitation and investment-driven becomes unsustainable. *National Innovation-driven Development Strategy* and "Mass Entrepreneurship and Innovation" have become state-level strategies, there has strong demands for innovation everywhere in terms of engines conversion, transformation and upgrading, and has clear intention to cooperate with Beijing National Innovation Center. With implementation of *National Innovation-driven Development Strategy*, China has made breakthroughs in the reform of key areasof scientific and technological innovation and mechanisms, also gradually connected technology and economic&social development. The policy of scientific and technological achievements transformation has been relaxed and the enthusiasm of scientific and technological talents has been lighted up. Under this policy environment, Beijing's innovation resources will be more actively integrated with the downstream industrial chain, and will expand their innovative and industrial chain layout in the country and even the world to give full play to their advantages of scientific research and technical reserves.

With the implementation of the Outline of Coordinated Development of Beijing–Tianjin–Hebei, scientific and technological cooperation between Beijing and Tianjin–Hebei will continue to deepen.

The Ministry of Science and Technology and the National Development and Reform Commission jointly formulated the *Science and Technology Innovation Subject Plan of Coordinated Development in the BTH Region*, which proposed a series key tasks of collaborative innovation, such as construction of Innovation Community, and establishment of innovation chain of Beijing-Tianjin-Hebei. These tasks will deepen and widen collaborative innovation between Beijing and Tianjin-Hebei. The implementation of *Outline of Coordinated Development of Beijing-Tianjin-Hebei* will gradually break the institutional barriers caused by administrative divisions among the three regions, so that the talents flow, capital docking and technology transfer will become increasingly active. Hebei and Tianjin will be preferred cooperative areas for Beijing's innovation resources. After three-years implementation of the *Coordinated Development Outline*, the depth and breadth of the scientific and technological innovation cooperation among Beijing-Tianjin-Hebei are gradually expanding. In 2016, Beijing's output of technical contracts with Tianjin and Hebei is 15.47 billion yuan, up 38.7% over the same period of last year. Enterprises from Zhongguancun newly established more than 850 all kinds of branches in Tianjin and Hebei, up 17.4% over the same period of last year. Mode of scientific and technological cooperation in terms of co-building parks, university(academy)-enterprise cooperation became rich. Zhongguancun-Haidian- Qinhuangdao Park has become the important platform between Beijing and Qinhuangdao with functions of industrial transfer, policy docking, and innovation cooperation. The Beijing-Tianjin-Hebei iron and steel industry energy-saving and emission-reducing industrial technology innovation alliance has been jointly established by more than 70 institutions from Beijing-Tianjin-Hebei, which promoted six energy-saving and emission-reducing demonstration projects implement in Tianjin and Hebei, and established the first domestic iron and steel industry energy-saving and emission-reducing fund.

Scientific and technological achievements will continue to be hatched outside due to adjustment of city function in Beijing.

A major target of the *Coordinated Development Outline* is to cure "big city disease" of Beijing by controlling population in the central city, and easing the non-capital functions. Capital functions mainly include three aspects followed by (1)the core functions of the capital, that are the national political center, cultural center, international communication center and science and technology innovation center; (2)the administrative functions closely related to and serve for the above four core functions; (3)the general city functions to meet other resident demands and serve for the above two aspects. Non-capital functions, which is beyond demands of the first two aspects, and has a bigger demand scale for the general city functions. Therefore, the manufacturing industry in Beijing is the function needed to be eased and adjusted, which means that many of Beijing's scientific and technological achievements will be transferred and commercialized out of Beijing. The focuses of Beijing's cross-regional cooperation will be establishment of innovative chain and "R&D in Beijing and commercialized outside".

Innovation backbone resources will ceaselessly expand their space outward due to limited development space in Beijing.

Limited urban development space and shortage of construction land are the main constraints of urban development. As a world-class metropolis, Beijing is facing a more serious similar problem. In the *Beijing General Urban Planning (2016-2030)*, by 2020, the scale of urban and rural construction land in Beijing should be reduced to 2,860 square kilometers, and by 2,030, 2,760 square kilometers. Therefore, in future Beijing's urban size will at least not be further expanded. Adjustment of city functions will also change the use of a small quantity of inventory land, which will be used to expand the urban greening and public service space for control and prevention of "big city disease" of Beijing. So the land used for construction of scientific and technological innovation center especially the backbone innovation carriers will be very limited, so that the backbone innovation carriers will have no choice but to expand their development space out of Beijing. In recent years, Zhongguancun and Aerospace City have set up many branches outside through joint coustruction, equity, and export brand. Basically forming a situation of "independent innovation in Beijing, and national industrial upgrading".

S&T SMEs will transfer outward faster due to the increasing costs of living in Beijing.

Cost of living in Beijing rise continually, Global Urban Living Cost Survey issued by the US human resources consulting firm Mercer shows that the total cost of living in Beijing in 2016 has ranked 10th in the world, especially, high housing cost have made some talent feeling pressure, which also push S&T SMEs outward. Beijing, for the purpose of enhancing the livability of city, strictly controls the scale of population and urban built-up area. According to the planning targets, by 2020, the scale of the resident population in Beijing will be controlled within 23 million, comparing the population of 21.729 million by the end of 2016, so the population growth is limited. It means more difficult for the immigrant to obtain household registration in Beijing and thus difficult to acquire the public services attached to household registration, which ineluctably result in quite a few talents leaving from Beijing in the future.

1.2.3 Analysis on conditions of collaborative innovation between Beijing and Hebei Province

Beijing and Hebei Province are geographically connected within an appropriate interactive radius, and have close human relationship and consistent cultural origins in along historical period. Beijing and Hebei have complementary innovative function orientation, matched demands, characteristic innovation foundations. Socollaborative innovation between Beijing and Hebei driven by the *Outline of Coordinated Development of Beijing-Tianjin-Hebei* is of inherent advantages.

Complementary demands in innovation development between Beijing and Hebei.

Conforming to the trends of innovation development and regional cooperation both at home and abroad, Beijing International Innovation Center needs to become more open and allocate innovation resources in broader fields. With the implementation of *National Innovation-driven Development Strategy*, there is a huge technological demands market around Beijing for Beijing's innovation resources to expand the development space outward; at the same time, adjustment of Beijing's urban function, limited development space, rising living costs and other issues in Beijing push innovation resources transfer outward, therefore, the depth and breadth of cross-regional collaborative cooperation of Beijing will continue to improve. On the Hebei's front, *Coordinated Development Outline* requests Hebei enhancing regional innovation capacity, narrowing the innovation gaps with Beijing and Tianjin as soon as possible. And change of development mode, cultivation of new economic engines, transformation and upgrading also lead to extremely urgent demands of innovation development in Hebei. But due to the weak innovative foundations, low innovative level, Hebei's innovation development must utilize external force. We conclude that Beijing's innovation development needs to "expand territory", meanwhile Hebei provincial innovation development needs to gather resources inward. So both regions are complementary in demands of innovation development.

Matched supply-demand fields in innovation development between Beijing and Hebei.

Hebei, as the demand side of science and technology, focuses on innovation development in terms of enhancing industrial innovation capacity, establishing backbone innovation carriers and promoting innovation and entrepreneurship. Firstly, in order to promote industrial innovation capacity, Hebei must search for technologies supporting high-end equipment manufacturing, bio-medicine, new energy, new materials, energy saving, environmental protection and other emerging industries, and seek technological cooperation for promoting traditional industries such as steel, building materials, chemicals, equipment manufacturing, agriculture and others to intelligence, servitization and high-end, which is highly matched with Beijing's innovation fields. Secondly, Beijing's backbone innovation carriers need to expand the development space and meanwhile Hebei need to use external force to establish representative backbone carriers. Thirdly, Beijing's S&T SMEs and innovative talents urgently transfer outward and Hebei need to utilize external forces to promote mass innovation and entrepreneurship.

Complementary innovation chain between Beijing and Hebei.

Beijing's innovation resources are concentrated in the segments of basic and applied research, and due to the urban function adjustment and limited development space, the weak segments of industrial incubation and transformation may be more transferred outward. In contrast, Hebei's innovation capacity is not strong, the basic research ability is weaker, but there are good foundations and conditions in the fields of technological application and transformation in some traditional industries, and strong technology commercialization demands in terms of traditional industrial transformation and upgrading, emerging industries development. Therefore, Beijing and Hebei are complementary in innovation chain, and it is feasible to establish a complete innovative chain between Beijing and Hebei.

2. Requirements of Beijing's innovation resources and foundations of Hebei Province for collaborative innovation

Collaborative innovation between Beijing and Hebei has superior internal and external conditions, with boosting of national strategy and fitness of regional demands.We conduct comparative analysis on Hebei provincial foundations and cooperative requirements of Beijing's innovation resources. We expect the analysis could be conducive for Hebei Province to enhance innovation level by utilizing fully innovation resources from Beijing.

2.1 Analysis on requirements of collaborative innovation of Beijing's innovation resources

The regions need to creategood conditions in fields of market space, educational resources, policy environment and supporting scientific research facilities to undertake the spillover effect of innovation resource. In Beijing, there are distinctive requirements of cross-regional cooperation of innovation resource. Comparing the common conditions of innovation resources spillover with distinctive requirements of cross-regional cooperation of Beijing's innovation resource, we identify the necessary and preferred conditions for collaborative innovation.

2.1.1 Market space

Market space is the primary condition of cross-regional cooperation of innovation resources from Beijing. Innovation resources need to expand market space to pursuit maximum value, which requires the destination regions have strong willingness to enhancing innovation level and urgent demands for technology. There is an typical case, in April 2015, Baoding Zhongguancun Innovation Center was established. The reasons of Zhongguancun to establish the first cooperation project in Baoding are: (1)Baoding has urgent demands to rapidly enhance regional innovative level and establish Comprehensive Innovation and Demonstration Area with Shijiazhuang and Langfang; (2)Baoding has strong industrial technological demands for equipment manufacturing industry dominated by vehicle and new energy industry dominated by photoelectric and wind power. The vast market space of innovation and technology in Baoding attracts Zhongguancun.

2.1.2 Scientific research facilities and service

High specialization of innovation means that perfect scientific research facilities and service system are necessary for transfer of scientific research personnel and institutions, and transformation of scientific and technological achievements. Specifically, the scientific research facilities mainly refer to specialized large equipment, supporting test equipment, incubation and pilot facilities, information technology facilities, supporting service system and so on, service system mainly includes entrepreneurial services, intermediary services, international cooperation, technological innovation, venture financing, human resources, policies and regulations and innovative culture and others, and its main entities include various professional service agencies or scientific and technological intermediary associations providing technology transfer, management consulting, intellectual property agents, asset evaluation, science and technology credit guarantee and marketing services etc. and a number ofprofessional services companies providing science and technology, finance, personnel, management, law and other services. Professional research facilities are prerequisite of transfer and transformation of innovation resources. Beijing has most concentrated innovation resources in the country with perfect innovative facilities and service system. Meanwhile, Beijing's innovation resources pursue development space and opportunities by cross-regional cooperation. Therefore, the specific attributes and basic intention of Beijing's innovation resources cross-regional cooperation determines that perfect scientific research facilities and service system are necessary conditions for transfer and transformation.

2.1.3 Policy environment and innovative atmosphere

The characteristics of scientific and technological activities determines that relaxed policy environment, flexible institutional mechanisms and pronounced innovation atmosphere are preferred conditions which has been verified by the development of domestic science and technology innovation and some typical innovative areas. Since the Reform and Opening up, any scientific and technological advancescan trace back to policy innovation and mechanism reform in major fields. In 2014, the Ministry of Finance, Ministry of Science and Technology and the State Intellectual Property Office issued policies to manage the use and commercialization of and the distribution of profit from scientific and technological achievements;in April 2015, *Several Opinions of the Central Committee of the CPC and the State Council on Deepening the Reform of Systems and Mechanisms and Accelerating the Implementation of the Innovation-driven Development Strategy* was issued; and in Oct 2015, *Law of the People's Republic of China on Promoting the Transformation of Scientific and Technological Achievements (2015 Amendment)* was issued by the National People's Congress.Those policies and laws greatly improved domestic environment of commercialization of scientific and technological achievements, effectively promoted the scientific and technological achievements to better serve the economic and social development. Regional innovation development also rely on policy environment and innovative atmosphere, for example, Beijing Zhongguancun, Shanghai Zhangjiang, Wuhan East Lake get breakthrough resulting from flexible system and preferential policies issued by National Independent Innovation Demonstration Areas, and Shenzhen, a young city, is developing rapidly beyond some regions with solid innovation foundation which can also result from its open and inclusive innovation atmosphere. Beijing plays a leading role in fields of innovation policy environment optimization, innovation system reform, innovation and social atmosphere shaping, creates a relatively perfect environment for innovation and entrepreneurship.Therefore, relaxed policy environment and pronounced innovation atmosphere are the preferred conditions for cross-regional cooperation of Beijing's innovation resources.

2.1.4 Public service and ecological environment

Perfect public service and superior ecological environment are the ideal conditions for Beijing's innovation resources to cooperate with other regions. Innovation resources, with prominent features of specialization and high-end, need some special requirements on regional public services and environment. In addition of basic public service facilities,innovation resources prefer business, education, health care, leisure, entertainment and other high-level services. S&T activities are intellectual-intensive and creative, with highly requirement on beautiful, quiet ecological environment. As a large metropolis,Beijing is of high quality on medical, education, sports, business, entertainment and other public services, but excluding excellent ecological environment. Therefore, comparable public services level with and better ecological environment than Beijing will strongly attract innovation resource from Beijing.

2.2 Foundations of Hebei for utilizing Beijing's innovation resources

Comparing conditions of transfer of Beijing's innovation resources, Hebei has enough foundations undertaking innovation resources, but need to do better.

2.2.1 Vast market space

With the implementation

of *National Innovation-driven Development Strategy*, Hebei has a more urgent intention to seek technology and innovation engines than any previous period and other regions to narrow development gaps with Beijing and Tianjin and meet the endogenous demands of transformation and upgrading and cultivating new driving force, so that the market space of technological innovation is very broad. At the same time, Hebei, facing prominent economic and social contradictions and issues, will have no choice but technical innovation. First, the extensive development pattern and resource-oriented industrial system have not any longer supported the sustainable development of Hebei, innovation, intensive & green development and high-end industry will be the key of economic transformation; Second, there are urgent expect on optimization of ecological environment from the public, central government and Hebei, so that Hebei must solve the regional resource and environmental problems by means of technological innovation; Third, there are also massive technology and innovation demands in terms of enhancing urban comprehensive power and improving infrastructure. Altogether, Hebei has a broader market space than Beijing.

2.2.2 Unimproved scientific research facilities

Scientific research facilities are important component of innovative environment and play a vital role in promoting company hatching, industrial technology upgrading, building a bridge between government and enterprises. Hebei's scientific research facilities increase rapidly, by the end of 2015, numbers of key laboratories, engineering and technology research centers and industrial technology research institutes higher than provincial level corresponding reached 105,231 and 28 respectively, state-level and provincial science and technology business incubators reached 16 and 45 respectively, hatching area more than 3 million square meters, hatching enterprises reached 2,936, productivity promotion centers reached 38, technology transfer demonstration agencies 24, mainly involving Chinese herbal medicine, electronic information, equipment manufacturing, new energy, new materials, energy saving and environmental protection, animation industry and other high-tech fields, among which Chinese herbal medicine and animation industry are advantageous. But compared with Henan, Hubei, Hunan, which have the approximate GDP with Hebei, scientific research facilities are still insufficient. In 2016, the number of Henan's national R&D platform reached 141, including14national key laboratories, 10 national engineering technology research centers, 3 state engineering laboratories, 80 national enterprise technology centers, and 7 national high-tech zones, all higher than Hebei Province. Quantity and quality of research universities, high-tech zones in Hubei and Hunan are all better than Hebei, number of national key laboratories several times more than Hebei Province. Therefore, Hebei's scientific research facilities need to be improvedto meet the requirements of transfer of Beijing'sinnovation resources. See Table 4.

Table 4 Quantity of S&T innovation platforms in Hebei,Henan,Hunan,Hubei, 2016

	Hebei	Henan	Hunan	Hubei
State Key Laboratory	9	14	15	27
China National High-Tech Industrial Development Zone	5	7	7	7

Note: National S&T innovation platform includes State Key Laboratory, State Engineering Laboratory, National Engineering Technology Research Center, Enterprise Technology Center, Supervision and inspection center, business incubator and other innovation and entrepreneurship platform.

Source: *Provincial Statistical Yearbook, 2016.*

2.2.3 Ossified policy

In recent years, Hebei Province issued *Decision on Accelerating Scientific and Technological Innovation and Building Pro-innovation Hebei* and a number of effective new policies to actively encourage enterprises and funds into technology R&D.But compared with other provinces, Hebei's policy environment of innovation development is still poor. In 2015, percentage of R&D expenditure to GDP is only 1.18%, only half of the national average.The enthusiasm of enterprises R&D activities is particularly low, the proportion of enterprises above designated size having R&D institutions is only half of the national average.Expenditure on R&D of all kind of enterprises is 29.51 billion yuan, increasing 9.5% over the previous year,10 percentage points lower than the ratios of government and universities. Cities in the whole country are taking more efforts to attract high-end talents by high direct financial subsidies and other policies, in contrary, ossifiedtalent system, inflexible talent policy,inadequate policy implementation lead to lack and loss of high-end talents in most cities of Hebei. Hebei's reform in scientific and technological system and institution has always been promoted by the national deployment, and it is hard to achieve breakthrough in innovation mechanism reform especially in fields of higher education, protection, use andmanagement of intellectual property, and financial innovation. So the reform dividends did not work in aspects of reducing innovation cost, stimulating innovation vitality, improving efficient allocation of innovative elements and so on.

2.2.4 Worse public service

Public service is an important factor affecting the agglomeration of scientific and technological talents and innovation institutions, which is a major short board and main obstacle for Hebei to undertake the innovation resources from Beijing and Tianjin. In the satisfaction evaluation of basic public service issued by *Blue Book of Public Service*, Chinese Academy of Social Sciences(CASS), Shijiazhuang, among 38 major cities in the country, achieved a low score in the items of resident recognition & satisfaction, and did not enter the top tenin the nine fields of public transport, environmental protection, culture, sports and public service and so on, which is far from enough attractiveness to high-end innovation resource from Beijing.

2.2.5 Weak innovation and entrepreneurship atmosphere

A good innovation and entrepreneurship atmosphere is conducive to scientific and technological activities, and directly influences innovation and entrepreneurship activities and economic vitality. The innovation and entrepreneurship atmosphere in Hebei is worse than the eastern coastal provinces. From the micro-based perspective, lesser and weaker market entities reflect, to a certain extent, the weak innovation atmosphere and lack of innovation enthusiasm. In 2015, varied market entities reached 327.7 million, ranking 8th in the country (Data from Hebei Provincial industrial and commercial departments), lesser than Henan, Sichuan, Hunan, and Hubei, which have similar economic scale with Hebei. Those entities mainly concentrated in the small and scattered traditional service sectors such as wholesale and retail and others, also in the low-end value chain such as metal products, steel and building materials, other than the modern services full of innovative activities and high-tech industries. Hebei's listed companies in Shenzhen Stock Exchange and Shanghai Stock Exchange are only 55, of which only 10 Growth Enterprise Market(GEM) listed companies, a approximately number with Xinjiang, Shaanxi and other western regions.

2.2.6 Excellent ecological environment in some areas

Hebei has a terrible ecological image with frequenthaze, lacking water resources, seriousriver and coastal pollution and low forest coverage rate, but around Beijing there are many medium-sized cities and small towns which have relatively good ecological environment, such as Zhangjiakou built-up area and Huaihua County, Chengde built-up area and Luanping County, Zhuozhou and Laishui in Baoding and others.For example, Huailai County is upwind and upstream of Beijing with excellent air quality ranking top ten among Hebei's counties for a long period. Since 2010, ecological projects such as Beijing-Tianjin Sandstorm Source Control, Beijing-Hebei Ecological Water Source Protection Forest, Guanting Reservoir National Wetland Park and others have been actively implemented, and the forest coverage rate has increased to 50.8%. This county was awarded title of National Garden County by Ministry of Housing and Construction, and won the 2013-2014 Hebei Province Habitat Environment Award. Small cities have abundant land, extensive urban framework, excellent ecological environment,livability and other comparative advantages, and hence more suitable for transfer and transformation of innovation resource than Beijing which are experiencing "big city disease".

3. Comprehensive evaluation on the progress of Hebei Province utilizing innovation resources from Beijing

3.1 Progress of innovation cooperation between Beijing and Hebei Province

Since the implementation of the Outline of *Coordinated Development of Beijing-Tianjin-Hebei*, under joint efforts of Beijing and Hebei, Hebei has achieved great progress in utilizing innovation resources from Beijing to establish strategic cooperative platforms,construct innovation development interaction mechanism, explore new innovation cooperation pattern.Transaction value in technical market between Beijing and Hebei has been doubled in recent years.

3.1.1 Construct collaborative innovation carrier of Xiong'an New Area

On 1st April 2017, a national new area, Xiong'an New Area, was established after Shenzhen Special Economic Zone and Pudong New Area. According to the intentions of CPC Central Committee, Xiong'an New Area, as the major destination of Beijing's non-capital functions dispersal, will focus on establishinga green ecological livable new city, an innovation-driven leading area, a coordinated development demonstration area and an open development pilot area, and will promote complementary development with Beijing central city and Beijing Tongzhou sub-center to become one of the new twin wings of Beijing. In the *Outline of Coordinated Development of the BTH Region,* destination of non-capital functions dispersal will also receive some of the central administration and public institutions and state-own enterprises, supplementary education, health care, culture and other public service institutions. Xiong'an New Area is the leading area of innovation development inthe BTH Region, with a high functional status in the field of scientific and technological innovation. It is also an area gathering high-end innovation elements and high-tech industries.Since the establishment, the whole province has reached consensus of ensuring Xiong'an New Area's construction. The government has established a new high-level committee responsible for construction and management of the new area, preliminarily planed the functions, transportation, environmental protection, industry, and resources introduction.Many large enterprises and institutions, research and development institutions are willing to participate actively the construction of the new area. With the start of the planning, the construction of new areas will gradually landing.

3.1.2. Construct four strategic symbolic platforms

Since the *Outline of Coordinated Developmentof Beijing-Tianjin-Hebei*, Hebei redoubled efforts to establish four symbolic functional platformsto attract innovation resources from Beijing.

Hebei Jingnan National Science and Technology Achievement Transformation Demonstration Area. Established on the basis of 10 provincial high-tech zones and S&T parks south of Beijing, Hebei gives expression to the role of this demonstration area as "bridgehead connecting Hebei and Beijing-Tianjin, new landmark conducing to innovation and entrepreneurship", and support this area in cooperating, developing different but complementary industries with Beijing Zhongguancun, Tianjin Non-trade zone and Tianjin free trade zone. At present, the Jingnan demonstration area has been approved by the Ministry of Science and Technology as one of the first batch of national scientific and technological achievements demonstration area, and included into the national list of *Action of Promoting Scientific and Technological Achievements Transfer and Transformation*. Venture capital fund for scientific and technological achievements transformation in BTH Region with one billion yuan size was registered in Gu'an County, where is the core area of the demonstration area.

Modern Agricultural Science and Technology Demonstration Zone around Beijing. On the basis of 14 counties (cities, districts) circling Beijing, this demonstration zone was approved as national modern agricultural science and technology demonstration zone. The *Overall Plan of Modern Agricultural Science and Technology Demonstration Zone* was issued and the related monitoring system was established. La total of five parks in Fengning, Luanping, Dachang, Gu'an and Zhuozhou were approved as the national agricultural science and technology park. The government also launched modern agricultural collaborative innovation institute of Beijing-Tianjin-Hebei in the demonstration zone to promote agricultural S&T achievements effective transformation and incubation. Hebei will establish this demonstration zone as Chinese agricultural Silicon Valley to leading modern agricultural science and technology innovation and development in China.

Comprehensive Independent Innovation Demonstration Zone in Shijiazhuang-Baoding-Langfang. On the basis of innovation and industrial resources, transportation, talents and other comparative advantages in Shijiazhuang, Baoding and Langfang, the State Council approved comprehensive innovation and reform in the three regions to promote rational allocation, open, sharing and efficient use of regional innovation resources in the BTH Region. Hebei has formulated pilot program of comprehensive innovation and reform in Shijiazhuang-Baoding-Langfang to promote innovation resources inthis region connecting with that from Beijing-Tianjin.

Big-data Comprehensive Exploration Zone in the BTH Region. Relying on big-data innovation and industrial resources and a reasonable functional orientation in Beijing-Tianjin-Hebei, Hebei shall make efforts to establish a Big-data Comprehensive Exploration Zone in the BTH Region, which will focus on establishing a national big-data industry innovation center, application pilot area, comprehensive reform exploration zone and industry innovation heights in the BTH Region.

3.1.3 Build jointly carriers for innovation and entrepreneurship

Co-build S&T parks. Hebei has co-build 55 parks of various types with Beijing and Tianjin. Zhongguancun Haidian Qinhuangdao sub-park has introduced 108 high-tech enterprises from Zhongguancun; Aerospace Shenzhou solar thermal industrial park, international robot R&D and production and other projects have been put into production in Cangzhou High-tech Zone; Langfang Development Zone cloud storage industrial Park has undertaken a number of e-government cloud platforms, energy enterprises information exchange platforms, and IDC center of Baidu, Alibaba and other internet companies.

Co-establish innovation bases. The innovation bases co-established with Beijing and Tianjin have reached 62; Zhongguancun has signed a cooperation framework agreement of establishing integrated circuit industry base in Zhengding high-tech zones; Caofeidian Zhongguancun high-tech industrial base has introduced five Zhongguancun enterprises;Gu'an test base of Tsinghua University major science and technology projects has started to build; the first phase of the project of Cangzhou-Beijing Hyundai automobile industry base has been started; 10 Beijing pharmaceutical companies have been officially started to construct in Zhongjie biological industrial park.

Co-establish innovation alliances. At present, Hebei has established 65 industrial technology alliances in the fields of steel, antibiotics, satellite navigation, semiconductor lighting, fruit and other industries. Tangshan high-tech zones co-established graphene industry development alliance of BTH jointly with Zhongguancun Huaqing graphene industry technology innovation alliance and other institutes; Peking University, the North technology market, Hebei Province scientific and technological achievements transformation service centers and other institutes jointly established technology transfer collaborative innovation alliance of BTH; Baoding co-established municipal industrial innovation alliances jointly with enterprises from Beijing and Tianjin on the basis of photovoltaic, rigging, paint and other local industries.

Co-establish innovation and entrepreneurship platforms. Hebei co-established Baoding Zhongguancun Venture Street, Beijing University Zhongdian Science and Technology Park, Shijiazhuang Golden Seed Valley and a number of innovative business platforms jointly with Zhongguancun and Beijing-Tianjin scientific research institutions.

3.1.4 Explore a certain number of new cooperative models

Multi-stakeholder sharing benefit. Haidian District of Beijing and Qinhuangdao co-established Zhongguancun Haidian Qinhuangdao Park, and set up a "forty forty twenty" benefit distribution mechanism, which means that Zhongguancun and Qinhuangdao will respectively achieve 40% share of the financial revenue of the park, and the rest 20% share will be used for establishment of industrial funds to support the development of enterprises in the park.

Cross-regional industry-university-institute cooperative platform. Hebei Tingshua Development Research Institute, Gu'an County Government, China Fortune Land Development Co., Ltd (CFLD) implemented jointly Gu'an test base of Tsinghua University major science and technology projects to form an industry-university-institute platform integrating four elements of "R&D, project incubation, technology transfer, supportive services".Hebei would actively popularize PPP mode of CFLD in this platform using market-oriented mechanism, introduce social capital into infrastructure construction, public service, scientific and technological innovation and other fields, explore diversified operating mode of development zone(innovative small town) .

Science and technology innovation enclave. Baoding High-tech Zone and Zhongguancun should perfect the cooperation mechanism, introducing Zhongguancun Information Valley Asset Management Company into high-tech zone responsible for operation and management of Baoding Zhongguancun Science and Technology Innovation Center, and learning the philosophy and experience of Zhongguancun in terms of business incubation, science and technology financial services, transfer and transformation of achievements and others, so as to forma cross-regional innovation and entrepreneurial ecosystem which can be popularized.

Promoting industrial development. Langfang Yongqing and Beijing Yizhuang co-construct Beijing Yizhuang-Yongqing Hi-tech Industrial Development Zone to carry out cross-regional cooperation in the whole industry chain, tax and operating income should be shared according to investment proportion.It will form an industrial cluster development model.

Cultivating scientific and technological services. Shijiazhuang technology market have comprehensively cooperated with Beijing-Tianjin innovation platforms in all levels, in terms of establishing Beijing-Tianjin-Hebei technology market service window to speed up the transformation of scientific and technological achievements from Beijing and Tianjin and the development of emerging industries.

3.1.5 Improve service facilities and environment for innovation and entrepreneurship

Co-establish transformation funds. Hebei established scientific and technological achievements transformation guiding fund with the first phasescale of one billion yuan jointly with Ministry of Science and Technology and China Merchants Group; collaborative innovation S&T achievements venture capital fund of Beijing-Tianjin-Hebei was successful registered; Hebei branch of China Construction Bank offered loans of 39 billion for supporting SMEs; Jvlu County and Beijing Silk Road Fortune Investment Fund Management Co. jointly established Julu emerging industry investment fund. 13 science and technology transformation guiding funds were encouraged to be established in several cities.

Co-build technology market. Hebei has co-established comprehensive service platforms for entrepreneurship and innovation with China Science and Technology Exchange, Beijing International Technology Transfer Center to promote the scientific and technological achievements of Beijing and Tianjin transformation in Hebei.

Improve entrepreneurial environment. On the basis of the development zone, universities, backbone enterprises, Hebei has established various public space more than 300, of which 80 at the provincial level, 72enter in the records of the state. More than 5,000 entrepreneurial teams and SMEs have settled in those public space, gathering more than 2,000 entrepreneurs andmore than 20,000 makers. Hebei has 89 incubators above the provincial level, hatching enterprises more than 6,000. Hebei made public the first "entrepreneurship and innovation map" containing information of provincial maker spaces, start-up companies, investment institutions, which can reflect the distribution of business resources and the overall developmental situation. Hebei promoted persistently "streamlining administration, improving regulation and optimizing services", cutting down pre-approval events of business registration from 226 to 34, reducing approval time from 20 days to less than 3 working days. Hebei also actively carried out special actions of typical demonstration case interpretation, policy interpretation, personnel training, taking targeted measures in poverty alleviation and others, solidly promoted special actions including entrepreneurial mentor entering into Hebei, innovation and entrepreneurship contest, "Mass entrepreneurship and innovation to promote Hebei's transformation", "Mass entrepreneurship and innovation", those actions are helpful to create a good atmosphere.

3.2 Comprehensive evaluation on Hebei Province utilizing Beijing's innovation resources

Since implementation of *Outline of Coordinated Development of Beijing-Tianjin-Hebei*, Hebei achieved great progress in utilizing Beijing's innovation resources and faced many problems.On the basis of the collaborative innovation objectives and characteristics of Beijing's innovation resources, we conduct comprehensive effect evaluation on Hebei utilizing Beijing's innovation resources.

3.2.1 Preliminary effect started to appear, but need to be enhanced

In the past three years, Hebei has fully understood the importance of Beijing's innovation resources on the sustainable development of Hebei. For transformation of geographical advantages into innovation advantages, Hebei effectively introduced Beijing's innovation resources transferring and transformation in Hebei, through a series of measures such as platform construction, policy docking, institutional innovation, environmental improvement and so on. By the end of 2016, Zhongguancun enterprises have set up 1822 branch offices and 1708 subsidiaries in Hebei. In 2016, transaction value of technical contract between Beijing and Hebei reached 9.87 billion yuan, an rapid increase of 83%. But we must clearly take cognizance of that relative to the accelerated spillover effect of Beijing's innovation resources, Hebei still have a larger space for improvement. In 2016, transaction value of technical contract between Beijing and Hebeistill only accounted for 2.5% of all technical contract of Beijing; compared with the accelerated spillover of Beijing's innovation resource, Hebei still has much space for improvement. Take Zhongguancun enterprises cross-regional mergers and acquisitions as a example, in 2015, mergers and acquisitions cases initiated by Zhongguancun enterprises out of Beijing reached 252, about 2.4 times than last year, of which 66 cases occurred in Guangdong, 88 cases occurred in the Yangtze River Delta region (Shanghai, Jiangsu, Zhejiang). Guangdong, Yangtze River Delta region and other areas where full of business startups and innovation activities are preferred regions for Zhongguancun enterprises carrying out mergers and acquisitions.

3.2.2 Top-design was basically perfect, but need to further give expression to autonomy

As the important content of *Coordinated Development Outline*, the collaborative innovation top-design was basically perfect in the past three years. Ministry of Science and Technology, and National Development and Reform Commission jointly introduced the *Guideline on Innovation-driven Development of the BTH Region*, *Special Planning of Collaborative Innovation of the BTH Region*; Hebei provincial government issued *Implementation Views on Special Planning of Collaborative Innovation of the BTH Region,* included collaborative innovation of Beijing-Tianjin-Hebei as a major task in the *Hebei Provincial Scientific and Technological Innovation 13th Five-years Plan*. There are different status, different innovation requirements and different foundations between Beijing and Hebei, Hebei will have to judge the hour and size up the situation to seek the best matched fields of collaborative innovation between Beijing and Hebei. For fully utilizing Beijing's highly agglomerated innovation resources and their spillover effect, strategic and work plan which can give more expression to initiative, enthusiasm and autonomy should be formulated to meet the innovation demands of Hebei.

3.2.3 Carriers construction was gratifying, but need to be further promoted

In the past three years, Hebei achieved the most remarkable success in construction of transfer and transformation carriers attracting Beijing's innovation resource, especial the Xiong'an New Area, Hebei •Jingnan National Science and Technology Achievement Transformation Demonstration Area and Modern Agricultural Science and Technology Demonstration Zone around Beijing. Those three carriers has been approved as national golden signboard. Hebei also established diverse carriers jointly with backbone innovation institutes such as Zhongguancun, Tsinghua University, Peking University, Chinese Academy of Sciences and others, which played an important role in collaboration innovation between Beijing and Hebei. Although carriers framework has been completed and space of collaborative innovation have been basically improved, Hebei needs to make full use of national golden signboard and further promote the carriers construction, especially establishment of efficient construction and operation mechanism, improvement of cross-regional innovation cooperation pattern, formulation of special policies and measures supporting transfer and transformation of external innovation resources, optimization of supporting environment for gathering innovation resources.

3.2.4 Small progress was achieved in model innovation and environmental construction, but need to make breakthroughs in mechanism reform

Influenced by the division of administrative regions and government departments, the traditional model of innovation development is basically constrained within administrative areas, and divided with the economic and social development. As different independent administrative regions, innovation chain in Beijing and Hebei has different characteristics.Therefore mechanism and model innovation are prerequisite of collaborative innovation between Beijing-Hebei. In addition, collaborative innovation is always driven by the national strategy, but the transfer and transformation of innovation resources are mostly dominated by market entities, so it is particularly important for the improvement of innovation soft and hard environment. In the past three years, Hebei has explored some cross-regional cooperation models and optimized the innovation and entrepreneurship environment to solve key issues of transfer and transformation. Overall, collaborative innovation in such a wide range is rare in China even the world, on the basis of the distinct collaborative cooperation traits, as well as a lagged innovation development reform, Hebei must have a breakthrough in mechanism reform, model innovation and environmental construction to fully utilizing Beijing's innovation resource.

4. Basic strategies of Hebei Province utilizing innovation resources from Beijing

Hebei should make full use of Beijing's innovation resources in the background of innovation resources integration in BTH Region. Hebei should also insist the principle of "Taking the initiative to do things well to meet demands of other regions", focus on the construction of S&T incubation center, key industrial technology R&D base, S&T pilot area supporting industrial structure adjustment and transformation and upgrading, make efforts to introduce, utilize, transfer and commercialize Beijing's innovation resource such as carriers, institutes, talents and results. Four strategical projects of creating regional innovation advantages, docking innovative chain and industrial chain, introducing and cultivating core innovation platforms, prospering S&T SMEs should be firstly carried out to optimize rational allocation, promote opening up & sharing and efficiently utilize innovation resource and then enhance Hebei's innovation level.

4.1 Create regional innovation advantages

4.1.1 Necessity and feasibility

From the perspective of the whole BTH Region,*Coordinated Development Outline* confirms this region as new engine of national innovation-driven development objectively regarding Beijing, Tianjin, and Hebei at the same level. Therefore, Beijing, Tianjin and Hebei should all clarify the developmental ideas, jointly creating innovation advantageous fields with regional characteristics. From the perspective of experience of cross-regional collaborative innovation, both EU and the domestic Yangtze River Delta region regard innovation resources integration in key fields, key technical cooperation research as major measures of regional collaborative innovation. We comprehensively analyze the distribution of innovation resources and demands, and conclude that the BTH Region has formed obvious innovation advantages, for example, electronic and information communication is sector of most obvious innovation advantage, high-end equipment manufacturing is sector of most complete innovation chain, bio-medicine is sector of most prominent innovation resource characteristics, modern agriculture is sector of best conditions of innovation resources cooperation, energy saving and environmental protection are sectors with most urgent demands of innovation cooperation and sharing. Based on theabove analysis, creating regional innovation advantages should be the important content of collaborative innovation of Beijing-Tianjin-Hebei. Hebei, with weak innovation capacity, should grasp the opportunities of collaborative innovation and spillover of Beijing's innovation resources to enhance creativity in key fields utilizing Beijing's innovation resource. Therefore, it is necessary and feasible to focus on creating regional innovation advantages in the progress of Hebei utilizing Beijing's innovative resources.

4.1.2 Thinking and priorities

Overall Thinking:

On the basis of regional innovative advantages and demands, Hebei shall establish national innovation development center radiating the surrounding jointly with Beijing and Tianjin. Following the thinking of "realizing the integration, occupying the frontier, docking the chain", the government should implement a number of joint research programs of key cutting-edge technologies, establish a number of regional key common technology platforms and establish a number of regional key innovation alliances in the industries of electronic information and communication, high-end equipment manufacturing, bio-medicine, modern agriculture, energy conservation and environmental protection. Hebei should expand the cooperative fields, deepen the cooperative level, and innovate the cooperative model with Beijing in a variety of flexible and effective ways, to enhance the innovation level in key fields in Hebei.

Priorities:

(i)Hebei shall enhance the innovation level in key fields with the implementation of Beijing-Tianjin-Hebei key technology joint research programs in the industries of electronic information and communication, high-end equipment manufacturing, bio-medicine, modern agriculture, energy conservation and environmental protection in the BTH Region. These programs focus on regional, public, complementary cutting-edge key technology research. Hebei should encourage local backbone R&D institutions to participate in joint research programs to enhance innovation capacity.

(ii)Hebei shall enhance the innovation capacity of backbone R&D institutions leveraging the construction of key technology R&D base. Hebei should keep pace with construction of regional key technology R&D bases in the BTH Region, select local key innovation institutions to participate in the construction of key technology R&D base by the means of co-construction and cooperation, to enhance innovation level of Hebei's R&D institutions. At the same time Hebei should make efforts to introduce more national key laboratories, engineering and technology centers and other major S&T infrastructure and regional key technology research and development base into Hebei, leveraging the construction of Beijing's non-capital functions destinations and micro-centers, to enhance level of R&D institutions in Hebei.

(iii)Hebei shall all-roundly strengthen cooperation with Beijing's innovation resources leveraging establishment of regional technological innovation alliances. Hebei should actively apply for construction pilot of national industrial technology innovation alliances, select ideal local innovation institutions, intermediary service organizations, industrial parks and others to dock with innovation resources from Beijing and Tianjin in the industries of renewable energy, big data, high-end equipment manufacturing, energy saving and environmental protection, modern agriculture, steel and others. Hebei should establish industry technology innovation alliances in the mode of government leading, capital co-investment, risk-sharing, benefit-sharing to enhance innovation level.

4.2 Dock innovation chain with industrial chain

4.2.1 Necessity and Feasibility

Over the past two years, the central government paid high attention to S&T achievements transformation and connecting innovation chain with industrial chain. In 2014, the Ministry of Finance, Ministry of Science and Technology, the State Intellectual Property Office issued policies involving in use, disposal and benefit distribution management of S&T achievements. In March 2015, *Opinions on Deepening the Reform of Institutional Mechanisms to Accelerate the Implementation of Innovation-driven Development Strategy* was issued by the CPC Central Committee and State Council, in Oct, *Law of the People's Republic of China on Promoting the Transformation of Scientific and Technological Achievements (2015 Amendment)* was formally implemented. It is obvious that the external environment is more conducive to connecting innovation chain with industrial chain.

In Beijing, there are 79 central transformed institutes and 59 universities, the annual S&T research results winning national awards accounted for one third of the country, the national key laboratories also accounted for one-third, number of academician of the Chinese Academy of Sciences and Academy of Engineering reached more than half of the country. Adjustment of Beijing's city functions means the manufacturing function will be weakened gradually, which will inevitably promote a large number of S&T achievements transformation and commercialization out of Beijing. Hebei is a province dominated by traditional resource-based industrial, economic transformation and industrial upgrading will bring quite a lot of demands for forefront industrial technology, some sectors with a certain technical reserves have foundations to utilize Beijing's cutting-edge industrial technology.

Due to the weak foundations of original innovation and huge gaps of scale and level of innovation resource with Beijing and Tianjin, it will be a long time for Hebei to enhance the regional innovation level, jointly research and develop, widely integrate all segments of innovation chain step by step with Beijing and Tianjin. In context of division of labor of coordinated development of Beijing-Tianjin-Hebei, the most realistic and feasible way currently is promote Hebei's industries to actively cooperate with Beijing's innovation chain on the basis of regional industrial development foundations and demands.

4.2.2 Thinking and Priorities

Overall thinking:

Following the laws and characteristics of traditional industrial transformation and emerging industries development, Hebei should focus on establishing a sound industrial innovation network, establishing carriers connecting industrial chain with innovation chain, promoting the industrial chain and innovation chain connectivity service system to complete innovative industrial chain, serve industrial transformation and upgrading. Hebei should give full play to the guiding role of government and leading role of market to attract Beijing's S&T achievements commercializing in Hebei, promote diversified cooperation between Hebei's industrial clusters and Beijing's backbone R&D institutions, promote common development and sharing of key technological innovation platforms, promote the extensive integration of Beijing's innovation chain and Hebei's industrial chain, promote transformation of Hebei's traditional industrial clusters and development of emerging industries.

Priorities:

(i) Implement Hebei traditional industrial cluster upgrading action. Aiming at enhancing R&D level and establishing complete innovation system, Hebei should integrate existing technological innovation platforms in traditional industries such as steel, chemical industry, building materials, foodstuffs, textiles and so on; while make full use of Beijing's innovation institutes to establish new innovation platforms or its branches. Hebei should encourage a close and stable industry-university-research cooperative relationship between Hebei's key enterprises and Beijing's R&D institutes, carry out a number of collaborative innovation programs, then the obstacles faced by enterprises shall be solved by a collaborative way with the help of governments, technical and innovation demands can also be settled by varied ways such as joint R&D with, commissioned R&D to and R&D outsourcing from Beijing's innovation institutes. Relying on scale advantage of Hebei's characteristics industrial clusters such as textile and garment, metal casting, agricultural and sideline food processing and others, Hebei should gather talents, capital, and enterprises to promote key technologies research and development, advance the development of new forms and new organizations of business, and promote high-end development of industrial clusters.

(ii) Comprehensively promote Beijing's scientific and technical achievements commercialization in

Hebei. On basis of analysis on Beijing's key innovation institutes and scientific and technical achievements and Hebei's innovation foundations and demands, we defined the major fields, tasks, methods and schedule of undertaking Beijing's innovation achievements transfer and commercialization. Hebei should speed up establishment of scientific and technical achievements transformation carriers such as Hebei · Jingnan national scientific and technological achievements transformation and demonstration area, define targets, focuses and cooperation objectives of each park, promote park institutional reform, encourage exploration of transfer and transformation model of scientific and technical achievements with prominent characteristic. Hebei should comprehensively deepen reform of scientific and technological transfer and transformation system, further intensify the efforts of fiscal and taxation support for transfer and transformation of scientific and technological achievements, further liberalize the right of disposal and benefit distribution of scientific and technological achievements, further reform the equity, options and dividend incentives mechanisms, further innovate financial & technical integration mechanism. Hebei should actively establish demand-oriented cross-regional technology transfer service system, establish Beijing-Tianjin-Hebei scientific and technological market and the Beijing-Tianjin-Hebei technology trading network, establish Zhongguancun Technology Trading Center branches in major cities to promote all kinds of innovative entities fully integrated and real-time communication; promote interconnectivity of Beijing-Tianjin-Hebei scientific and technological achievements databases; cultivate and develop technology transfer demonstration enterprises, agencies and bases; improve the technical broker system to promote the construction of contracted technology brokers.

4.3 Introduce and cultivate core innovation platform

4.3.1 Necessity and Feasibility

At current, Beijing has formed a backbone innovation carrier system with a strong radiation including Zhongguancun National Independent Innovation Demonstration Zone, Aerospace Science and Technology City, which have urgent willing to widen development space due to the limited urban space. Beijing's backbone innovation carriers had relatively successful experience of cross-regional cooperation, for example, Zhongguancun successfully founded the "one zone and sixteen parks" model, Aerospace city established a number of branches out of Beijing. In contrast, weak innovation capacity, backward development of backbone innovation carriers and especially lack of innovation resources and experience, mean it is hard for Hebei to support the construction of backbone innovation carriers, so Hebei has urgent demands for introducing external innovation resources and learning innovation experience. Compared with Beijing, Hebei has a wider development space for the backbone innovation carriers, Shijiazhuang, Baoding, Langfang and other cities have good conditions of talents and innovation infrastructure, Zhangjiakou, Chengde, Baoding, Langfang, which close to Beijing, have convenient transportation and excellent ecological environment. Therefore, it is necessary and feasible for Hebei introducing and cultivating backbone innovative platforms utilizing Beijing's innovation resources.

4.3.2 Thinking and Priorities

Overall thinking:

Taking building preferred destination undertaking spillover ofBeijing's backbone innovation resources as the target, focusing on Zhongguancun, Aerospace City, Yizhuang Development Zone and other innovation agglomeration areas, Chinese Academy of Sciences, Peking University, Tsinghua University and other key innovation institutes, Hebei should understand their cross-regional cooperation demands and requirements, establish a number of sharing platforms and cooperative destinations jointly with Beijing's backbone innovation resources to gather elements, sharing resources, connect industrial up- and down-stream, achieve mutual benefit by the modes of overall commission, joint investment and construction, mergers and acquisitions, authorization, brand output and others. At last, those platforms and destinations will support Hebei forming a S&T innovation center which can lead the innovation-driven development of emerging industries.

Priorities:

(i) Construction of a new national S&T city in Xiong'an New Area. Construction of the new national S&T city should honor the functional orientation of the innovation development leading area, make full use of opportunity of Beijing's non-capital functions dispersal, and actively undertake high-end S&T and education resources from Beijing. The government should construct the city as technological innovation concentrated area with high standards, and make efforts to apply for national major scientific research infrastructures extension to the city, cooperate with Beijing to establish new backbone innovation carriers. The government should also actively make efforts to apply for carrying out scientific and technological innovation system reform and establishing national independent innovation demonstration area, so as to form China's "Silicon Valley" to lead national innovation-driven development.

(ii) Construction of cooperation

and sharing platforms. The government should support development of Shijiazhuang (Zhengding) Zhongguancun integrated circuit industry base, Zhongguancun Haidian Qinhuangdao sub-park, Tsinghua University Gu'an pilot base, the Chinese Academy of Agricultural Sciences Langfang pilot base; encourage other parks, on the basis of their own developmental and regional conditions, comprehensively innovating cooperation mechanism and development model and establishing cooperation development platforms in varied forms to meet requirements of Beijing's backbone innovation resources.

(iii) Develop innovative small town. Among Langfang, Baoding, Zhangjiakou and other places, the government could select 2-3 small towns with convenient transportation, excellent ecological environment and solid development foundations. By learning the domestic and international development experience, the government could actively introduce strategic investors into, and explore new cooperative development model in those innovative small towns.

4.4 Prosper S&T SMEs

4.4.1 Necessity and Feasibility

Firstly, due to the rising costs of living in Beijing, talents and S&T SMEs actively seek development space outward, which is favorable external condition for Hebei to prosper S&T SME.

Secondly, the prosperous S&T SMEs in Hebei is prerequisite of innovation development and transformation and upgrading. S&T SMEs are the cradle of innovation. In the United States, innovation capacity of SMEs are twice than large enterprises, more than 70% of patents are created by SMEs. In the EU, innovation results per capita of small enterprises are twice than large enterprises, number of new results produced by unit R&D investment is 3-5 times than large enterprises. In China, the current 65% of invention patents, 80% of new products are from private S&T enterprises. Therefore, the upgrading of innovation capacity in Hebei depends on the S&T SMEs. The major tasks of transformation and upgrading in Hebei are to accelerate the development of emerging industries, cultivate new economic engine. S&T SMEs is the basis of emerging industries, so it is necessary for Hebei to elevate the quantity and quality of S&T SMEs.

Thirdly, Hebei has introduced a series of policies and measures to support the development of S&T SMEs. A group of "entrepreneurship and innovation bases", "technology incubation centers" have been built up, the soft and hard development environment of S&T SMEs are initially improved. Therefore, in the context of coordinated development of Beijing-Tianjin-Hebei, it is necessary and feasible for Hebei to prosper S&T SMEs utilizing Beijing's innovation resources.

4.4.2 Thinking and Priorities

Overall thinking:

In order to realize the target of *Hebei Province Science and Technology Small and Medium-sized Enterprises Growth Plan*, Hebei Province should understand demands of transfer of talents, S&T SMEs and enterprises in the initial-, growth- and development-stage and flexibly use the governmental, market and financial instrumentality to strengthen the construction of developmental carriers of S&T SMEs. The government should improve the service and policy system for S&T SMEs, create good soft and hard environment to attract Beijing's S&T SMEs transfer into Hebei and Beijing's innovative talents starting business in Hebei. Hebei should innovate the practicable and refine policies and measures, support a number of high-growth sci-tech enterprises, form a number of S&T SMEs clusters, develop a number of major technology and products with independent intellectual property rights, bring up sci-tech entrepreneurs with innovative spirit and competitiveness, and make S&T SMEs stronger.

Hebei should strengthen construction of S&T SMEs carriers such as incubator, accelerator, entrepreneurship and innovation base, venture capital alliance and others and optimize hardware environment to attract Beijing's innovation resources. Hebei should honor the principles of "diversified investment, market-oriented operation, professional services, management in network, industrialization, resource internationalization", implement scale-expansion and upgrading projects of innovative and entrepreneurial carriers to further expand the scale, comprehensively enhance the overall service level, and innovate incubator construction management system. Integrating provincial targets of industrial transformation and upgrading and innovation-driven development strategy, Hebei should make efforts to establish a progressive incubation service system of "S&T pioneering nursery - S&T enterprise incubator - S&T enterprises accelerator - S&T industrial park".

Hebei should comprehensively improve investment and financing services for S&T SMEs. Hebei should expand scale of capital and funds supporting S&T SMEs development to meet demands of varied enterprises in the initial-, growth- and development-stage. By learning mature experience of other developed provinces, Hebei should establish new investment and financing platforms for, explore new investment and financing mode of, optimize provincial financial services for, improve the financing ability of, and fully support the healthy development of S&T SMEs.

Hebei should further optimize the policy environment for S&T SMEs, and optimize the soft environment to attract Beijing's innovation resources. Hebei should enhance the financial support, and further improve and implement the preferential tax policies, strengthen the construction of integrated service platform, and establish the supervision and evaluation system for the development of S&T SMEs.

5. Major measures of Hebei' s utilization of innovation resources from Beijing

Hebei should give overall consideration on and select a few major tasks as breakthrough from the above four systematic projects. We carefully analyzed the progress of collaborative innovation of Beijing-Tianjin-Hebei, integrated the four major projects and current focuses of Hebei's innovation development, and then chose six measures in fields of carries construction, system innovation, targeted policy. The six measures will focus on connecting demands between Beijing and Hebei, giving full play to advantages and strengthening weak areas of Hebei. Hebei should adopt targeted steps and focus on breakthroughs in order to promote effectively Hebei's innovation development utilizing Beijing's innovation resources.

5.1 Speed up the construction of national S&T new city of Xiong'an New Area

Construction of non-capital function dispersal destination is the key content in the *Outline of Coordinated Development of Beijing-Tianjin-Hebei*.Xiong'an New Area will play a significant role in terms of undertaking non-capital function dispersal, regional innovation development, at least, it will be a national S&T, health care and culture base where serve the whole country and undertake annual increment of Beijing's public services, moreover it will be a innovation leading area having international influence. Xiong'an New Area is a national new area with high specification and outstanding innovation development functions. Due to the close and special relationship with Beijing, Xiong'an New Area will play a key role for Hebei in terms of establishing backbone innovation carriers, enhancing innovation development level and utilizing Beijing's innovation resource.

5.1.1 Actively undertake S&T and education resources from Beijing

Undertaking Beijing's S&T and education resources is a basic function of Xiong'an New Area as the non-capital functions dispersal destination, and a key measure of construction of innovation development leading area utilizing Beijing's innovation resources. For undertaking Beijing's S&T and education resources, Hebei should take a variety of ways to ensure that Beijing's innovation resources can smoothly transfer into Hebei, successfully develop in Hebei, and maintain creativity in Hebei.

Hebei should establish non-capital functions dispersal and undertaking mechanism. According to Beijing's non-capital function dispersal guideline and list, Hebei should study and formulate guidelines of the new area on undertaking Beijing's non-capital functions dispersal,take targeted steps to improve undertaking and supporting policies in the new area to meet demands of transfer of various innovation institutions. Hebei should establish special working mechanisms for transfer of key innovation institutions, select a special person to serve those institutions, coordinate various departments and solve problems in the progress of transfer and relocation of key innovation institutions.

Hebei should improve public service facilities in the new area. By fully learning lessons of the construction of Tsukuba S&T city, Hebei should improve innovation service facilities and comprehensive supporting facilities with international standard, construct simultaneously various comprehensive service facilities and hardware environment for transfer of Beijing's S&T and education resources.

Hebei should explore diversified, integrated public service supply mechanism in new area. Quality, level and supply mechanism of education, health care, social security and other public services are keys of successful transfer and development of Beijing's innovation resources. So Hebei should open market of education, health care in the new area to provide more abundant and higher quality public services than Beijing. Hebei should explore collaborative mechanism of social security, implement same policy, same payment standards, same guarantee level with Beijing in terms of medical care, pension, unemployment, work injury insurance and housing provident fund system. By learning international mature work visa system, Hebei should innovate public service mechanism, explore the ways of permitting all kinds personnel and their families to enjoy the basic public services according to work visa. By learning Singapore housing system, Hebei should implement housing supply and security mode dominated by public rent, low rent housing to reduce the housing cost of immigrant.

5.1.2 Carry out comprehensive S&T policy innovation and system reform

Xiong'an New Area is a national new area without any contents, the construction of S&T city must widely gather external high-end elements, especially Beijing's innovation resources, so Xiong'an New Area must do well in the fields of learning preferential policies, innovating system and mechanism and creating a policy highland of innovation development.

Hebei should actively make efforts to overlap and integrate national key regional development preferential policies. Hebei should use well the national policy of construction and development in the new area, and make efforts to overlap and integrate policies of national independent innovation demonstration area, national comprehensive reform demonstration area, national free trade zone and other high gold-containing regional development policies in the new area. Hebei also needs to select the most effective policies from related supporting policies in the country to attract high-end innovation and entrepreneurship resources.

Hebei should improve laws and regulations for the new area. By fully learning experience from Japan Tsukuba S&T city construction, Hebei should improve the laws and regulations to promote the construction of new city. Hebei could promote the state to introduce *Xiong'an New Area Urban Construction Law* involving every development and construction events, and the *Xiong'an New Area Development Plan* as a law to define functional orientation, development objectives and major tasks of Xiong'an New Area. Hebei should also introduce local laws and regulations in terms of innovation platform construction, innovation talent flow, innovation resource sharing, high-tech enterprises and S&T SMEs development, opening up and others to provide comprehensive policy preferential support to high-end and high-tech industries inand strongly promote the development of the new city.

Hebei should carry out pilot of policy innovation and system reform. Hebei should make efforts to carry out management mechanism reform of S&T research institutions in the new area, for examples, giving institutions greater autonomy in terms of personnel appointment, fund management, use of scientific research achievements and so on, improving the incentive mechanism for transformation of scientific and technological achievements in high education institutions and scientific research institutions, exploring independent legal person reform in scientific research institutions and tertiary institutions, to attract scientific research institutions settled in the new area. In the new area, Hebei should carry out reform on commercialization of scientific research achievements, for examples, establishing management procedures of disposal, approval and filing of technical intangible assets, establishing statutory benefit distribution system of official invention, state-owned intangible assets pricing system, intellectual property securitization trading system. Hebei should promote reform on existing tax settings, taxation system, implement tax system encouraging the whole society to innovation investment, for examples, adding the capital gains tax in the income tax, implementing tax credits for angel investment, allowing state-owned enterprises implement equity awards, expanding plus deducted proportion of the R&D expenditure of SMEs, allowing delay payment of income tax of scientific and technological achievements transfer. Hebei should also promote reform on investment model of science and technology R&D capital, for examples,exploring the methods of paid funding, and encouraging the elements and resources from banks, insurance, securities, equity funds and other capital markets to invest in scientific and technological innovation, make full use ofmodels of bank-government-enterprise cooperation stepwise discount, equity paid subsidies to achieve R&D capital benign cycle and preservation and appreciation. Hebei should innovate talent flow mechanism, explore talents pilot policies such as reduction of threshold of permanent residence right, relaxing the visa period, personal income tax relief and others, improve the two-way flow mechanism among university, scientific research institutions and enterprises.

5.1.3 Explore new development paths for backbone innovation carriers

Innovation carrier is an important supportive force for the construction of the national science and technology new city. For Xiong'an New Area, the construction of its innovation carriers need tomake full use of opportunity of Beijing's non-capital function dispersal and Beijing's rich innovation resources, explore new ways of cross-regional cooperation of innovation carriers, and also need to explore construction paths of new R&D institutions with market-oriented, flexible operating mechanism.

Overall replication of Beijing's backbone innovation carriers. Hebei could establish the "second Zhongguancun", "second future scientific and technological city" in the mode of "overall commission of development and management".The "second Zhongguancun" and "second future scientific and technological city" will be mainly operated, developed, and managed by Zhongguancun and future technology city. Beijing and the new area set up a joint coordination board responsible for coordinating the relevant directions, objectives and policies and other major issues of the development of carriers, jointly form bilateral working committee, responsible for settling development and construction important issues. The bilateral working committee is responsible for the joint coordination council. Zhongguancun and the future city jointly set up party committee and management committee of "second Zhongguancun" and "second future scientific and technological city" which will adapt to the management model of fully authorized, operation free from external interference.

Construct scientific and technological park in universities. The government should construct scientific and technological park in universities utilizing dispersal of Beijing's universities and R&D institutions following the mode of United States "Silicon Valley". University science and technology parks will be established mainly by backbone institutions, large enterprises or local government, taking the backbone institutions and scientific research institutions as the innovation source. On basis of industrial development and enterprises demands, those parks will dedicate to technology research and development and personnel training, and improve the park science and technology intermediary and financial services system for the SMEs incubation and collaborative management of industry-university-research.

Construct new R&D institutions. By learning the experience of new R&D institutions in Shenzhen, the government should make full use of dispersal of Beijing's backbone R&D institutions, establish new R&D institutions "operating like an enterprise" by models of "jointly input" which means the government input funds, while key research and development institutions input scientific and technological achievements, talents, and brand. New research and development institutions independently choose the research directions, establish research teams, implement scientific research management system, select the R&D models of integrating scientific discovery, technological invention and industrial development, implement management system such as contract system, hidden salary, dynamic assessment, the final phase out, risk-taking and results-sharing. The government should subsidizes the construction of institutional and scientific research facilities and the innovation teams in the forms of gratuitous support, platform construction, national special supportive facilities and special projects.

5.1.4 Strengthen collaborative innovation among Xiong'an New Area and its surrounding areas

According to the functional orientation, in future, Xiong'an New Area will gather a large number of innovation resources from Beijing to form a innovation area leading development of the BTH Region and even the country. From the perspective of the development of other areas, for a long time, there is a more obvious innovation gap among Beijing and the surrounding areas, Japan Tsukuba Science and Technology Metro did not play an obvious leading roleon the surrounding areas.By learning the above two cases, Xiong'an New Area must strengthen innovation cooperation with the surrounding areas, make full use of radiation effect to the surrounding areas, and give full play to supporting role of Beijing's innovation resources to Hebei's innovation development.

Establish a innovation chain closely linking new area and the surrounding. Hebei should encourage backbone innovation institutions in the new area to construct incubation centers and transformation bases in the surrounding areas; encourage the innovation institutions to commercialize technical research in the new area to meet the demands of the leading industries in the surrounding; support innovation institutions in the new area to establish branches in the surrounding;encourage the new backbone innovation institutions to strengthen cooperation with the surrounding innovation institutions, key enterprises, industrial basesby the modes of co-establishment, equity participation, cooperation projects to establish innovation alliances; givefull play to leading role of Xiong'an New Area in industrial transformation and upgrading and enhance the innovation level of the surrounding.

Establish unified service system among the new area and the surrounding. Hebei should encourage the construction of science and technology experts pool, databases, information bases, equipment platforms and technology markets sharing with the surrounding areas, and promote the extension of the new science and technology innovation policies to the surrounding areas to achieve free flow of innovation elements among the new area and the surrounding areas.

Box 1: Lessons of Tsukuba Science and Technology City in Japan

In 1961, the Japanese government put forward the idea of establishing a new city. On one hand, the national scientific research institutions would be moved out of Tokyo to ease the huge population and traffic pressure; on the other hand, development of science and technology and education in the city would apply technological innovation to the construction of the nation.So Tsukuba Science and Technology City came into being. The following are lessons in the construction of Tsukuba Technology City.

- First, the perfect city function is basis of attracting the population. At the beginning of the construction of Tsukuba S&T City, due to the incomplete infrastructure and single city function, the city did not have perfect living environment, so that many researchers only took it as a workplace, rather than their home. In 1985, Tsukuba, with the opportunity of the World Exposition, built a number of important infrastructures in a short time using national funds, attracting a large number of international researchers and research institutions.
- Second, the flexible institutional environment is basis of development and expansion of the new city. In this respect, Tsukuba has both experience and lessons. Tsukuba Science and Technology City improved a sound legislative system

- convince to development of high-tech industry, and many preferential policies involving real estate leasing, equipment depreciation, taxation, credit, foreign investment and others, which strongly promote development of the city. But at the same time,the government-based management model, as well as inflexible operation mechanism, led to loose linkage among industry-university-research and lowcommercialization rate of achievements.Scientific and technological advance played a limited role on the development of the city and its surrounding areas.
- Third, the excellent environment should be the main philosophy of construction and planning of the new city. Tsukuba Science and Technology City dedicated to establish a eco-city with coordinated development between human and nature. After 50 years of construction and development,existing green area in Tsukuba S&T City has reached 10,318.47hm, per capita green space reached 5,958 hm, this city has been recognized as an world famous ecological science city.
- Fourth, the key international events played an indelible role to create a development atmosphere in the new city. In 1985, the Tsukuba World Exposition became an important node in the history of Tsukuba. Tsukuba World Expo was also known as the Science and Technology Expo, the theme of which was in line with the nature of the city. The exhibition showed the world's latest scientific and technological achievements, a total of 46 countries and 37 international organizations participated in the Expo, and the admissions were totally about 20 million.The Tsukuba World Expo has greatly promoted the internationalization of the city, which has become an internationally renowned science city and has laid its place as an international scientific exchange base.

5.2 Launch multilevel pilot and demonstration in Hebei·Jingnan National Scientific and Technological Achievements Transformation Demonstration Area

In October 2016, Hebei · Jingnan National Scientific and Technological Achievements Transformation Demonstration Area was approved by the Ministry of Science and Technology, as the first batch of national scientific and technological achievements demonstration area. The demonstration area mainly consists of Shijiazhuang National High-tech Zone, Baoding National High-tech Zone, Gu'an High-tech Zone, Baiyangdian Science and Technology City, Yizhuang Yongqing High-tech Zone, Bazhou Development Zone, Great Wall Automobile Science and Technology Park, Gaobeidian International Innovation Park, Zhuozhou National Agriculture Science Park and Renqiu Development Zone and other 10 parks, forming the layout of "one area ten parks". In accordance with the requirements of *Construction Plan of Hebei · Jingnan National Science and Technology Achievements Transformation Demonstration Area* and *Outline of Coordinated Development of*

Beijing-Tianjin-Hebei, the demonstration area will focus on establishment of the industrial chain of "R&D in Beijing-Tianjin, Commercialization in Hebei", explore new models of connecting innovation elementsspillover from Beijing-Tianjin with industrial innovation demands of Hebei, formulate a number of exploratory policy in terms of cross-regional technology transactions, talents introduction, science and technology finance, finance and taxation support to achieve coordinated development in the BTH Region. According to the *Construction Plan*, on basis of the foundation of the demonstration area and the demands for the transfer and transformation of innovation resources from Beijing, we put forward proposals in terms of exploring cross-regional transfer and transformation model for scientific and technological achievements, innovating cross-regional scientific and technological achievements transformation mechanism, and improving cross-regional scientific and technological achievements transformation service system.

5.2.1 Explore cross-regional transfer and transformation model for scientific and technological achievements

Transformation of scientific and technological achievements theoretically refers to the entire process of the follow-up tests, development, application and widespread use of the scientific and technological achievements,through to the final creation of new products, new techniques, new materials and new industries.Scientific and technological achievements in Beijing include the original laboratories results and also the applied technological achievements. The demonstration area needs to transform traditional industries and develop emerging industries utilizing innovation resources from Beijing. According to the link, entity, demands and conditions of transformation of science and technology achievements, demonstration area could explore the following several cross-region transfer and transformation models for scientific and technological achievements .

Program cooperation. Hebei should encourage key enterprises such as the Great Wall Motor, Changan Automobile, Yingli New Energy and so on to promote national scientific research projects, new products and new technology projects, research key technologies jointly with Beijing backbone research and development institutions, research and development personnel and related universities, and promote technologies commercialization.

Establishment of cross-regional enterprise technology center. Hebei should support the Great Wall Motor, Changan Automobile, Yingli new energy and other key enterprises to set up technology research and development centers in Beijing, and actively utilizes Beijing's talents and innovation achievements to promote research, development and commercialization of key technologies.

Applied technology research institutes as a leading role. Hebei should focus on the leading industries in the demonstration area such as electronic information, health health new medical, advanced equipment manufacturing, new energy and new materials, energy saving and environmental protection, establish applied technology research institutes jointly with Chinese Academy of Sciences, the National Association of thousands of people and other well-known scientific research institutions in Beijing, promote high-end original scientific and technological achievements transfer into and transformation in Hebei.

Technology intermediary as a bridge between technology supplier from Beijing and demander in Hebei. Hebei should support demonstration area to establish science and technology big market jointly with Beijing, attract domestic and foreign related technology intermediaries, which will on one hand seek for technologies to meet the demands of enterprises in the demonstration area, on the other hand, promote Beijing's technologies commercialization in the demonstration area. Hebei should also encourage Beijing's backbone universities and research and development institutions to establish branches in the demonstration area to promote the relevant technology transfer into and transformation in the demonstration area.

Construction of transformation carriers. Comparing Beijing's achievements with developmental demands of the demonstration area, Hebei should give full play to space advantage, speed up the construction of comprehensive and professional pilot base, incubation base and maker space, speed up the transformation of ten parks, promote Beijing's scientific and technological achievements hatching, piloting and transformationin the demonstration area .

Industrial technology incubation. Hebei should closely track advanced technology research and development in Beijing, actively encourage Beijing's advanced technology teams to establish scientific and technological enterprises or take a stake in enterprises in the demonstration area to promote the transfer and transformation of scientific and technological achievements.

5.2.2 Innovate cross-regional scientific and technological achievements transfer and transformation mechanism

The demonstration area should carry out mechanisms innovation in the following fields to settle key issues and major obstacles of cross-regional transformation of scientific and technological achievements and to meet demands in the construction of the demonstration area.

Mechanism of construction and management of applied technology

research institutions. Hebei should establish Applied Technology Research Institutes in mode of enterprise and government co-fund. The institutes implement council and joint-stock system managed and operated like enterprises, and adopt to "one institute, two mechanism", contract research, project manager, equity incentives and other new operation mechanisms.

Mechanism of joint construction of innovative industrial parks. Focusing on ten parks of the demonstration area, Hebei should encourage Beijing's backbone R&D institutes to establish industrial bases, support the backbone research and development institutes or professional park operators to take a variety of forms to participate in construction and management of the park, explore revenue sharing mechanism.

Mechanism of application of independent innovation products. Hebei should issue key independent innovation products (technology, services) recommended directory, establish independent innovation product declaration, publishing, promotion mechanisms, organize independent innovation products supply and demand matchmaking workshop. Hebei should carry out mechanism reform on governmental procurement of the independent innovation products, use new methods of governmental procurement such as first purchase, order, the first (sets) major technical equipment testing and demonstration projects and others. Hebei should implement price deduction system for government procuring independent innovation products, set up government procurement plan for independent innovation products and gradually enhance its proportion. Hebei should carry out independent innovation product application demonstration programs to encourage enterprises to develop independent innovation products.

Mechanism of cultivation of technology transfer service institutions. Hebei should construct or introduce a number of university-enterprise joint, market-oriented investment technology transfer services institutes in the new materials, high-end equipment and other fields to meet the developmental requirements of marketization, specialization and socialization.Hebei should implement technical brokers market-based employment system.The staff in transfer enterprises can be regarded as developer of scientific and technological achievements and participate in the distribution of income distribution.

Mechanism of sci-tech finance. The Ministry of Science and Technology, the Beijing-Tianjin-Hebei governments jointly funded scientific and technological achievements transformation venture capital funds of demonstration areas, the third party is responsible for the management and operation of the fund. At the same time Hebei established SMEs credit risk compensation funds and angel investment guiding funds to speed up the transformation and commercialization of scientific and technological achievements. Hebei should actively encourage the domestic specialized technology insurance companies to set up branches in the demonstration area, encourage the insurance companies in the demonstration area to set up science and technology insurance division to start technology insurance businesses of product research and development responsibility, independent innovation products trial and others. Hebei should establish "scientific and technological achievements transformation risk compensation special funds", focusing on supporting creative, high-tech emerging enterprises with independent intellectual property rights and guiding banks to support the transformation and commercialization of science and technology enterprises by low-interest loans.

5.2.3 Improve cross-regional scientific and technological achievements transformation service system

Strengthen construction of demonstration platforms of achievements transfer and transformation. The Beijing-Tianjin-Hebei scientific and technological achievements transformation service platform would connect the Beijing-Tianjin scientific and technological achievements with enterprises in the demonstration area, provide intellectual property rights, technical achievements evaluation, patent technology transactions, capital docking and other specialized services. Hebei should encourage the parks in demonstration area to establish unified and open service platforms with obvious industrial characteristics and rational structure to enhance the existing technology transfer, technical contract registration, project consulting, technical butler services and other underlines platforms and to integrate the transformation service platforms of Beijing-Tianjin-Hebei.

Establish public scientific and technological achievements database in the demonstration area. Integrating existing intellectual property services, scientific and technological literature platforms and other data resources,Hebei should speed up the completion of the standard format of public scientific and technological achievements database, gathering massive scientific and technological achievements supply and demand information, and classifying the information according to the industries, stage, results form and other dimensions. Hebei should promote data miningof scientific and technological achievements, develop information publicizing, science and technology search and navigation services of scientific and technological achievements to meet technical demands.

Enhance the capacity of intellectual property services. Hebei should establish service system in terms of intellectual property strategy research, intellectual property management, intellectual property finance, intellectual property assessment and others to promote the rapid construction of intellectual property rights center, strengthen the enterprise IP early warning.

Promote the development of new technology intermediary. Hebei should speed up the cultivation of a number of third-party science and technology intermediary service agencies providing technology transactions, consulting and assessment, science and technology finance, research and development, intellectual property and other services. Hebei should focus on the introduction and cultivation of transnational technology transformation services, develop third-party technology transfer services to meet the developmental requirements of marketization, specialization and socialization.

5.3 Construct six major innovation alliances

Innovation Alliance is a new cooperative form among industry-university-research. Innovation alliances of Beijing-Tianjin-Hebei play an important role in optimizing allocation of innovation resources, further strengthening and highlighting regional innovation advantages and promoting innovation cooperation between Beijing and Hebei. According to the survey by Hebei Province science and technology department, most of the registered innovation alliances in Beijing-Tianjin-Hebei are involved in agriculture, which did not give full playto the regional innovation advantages and can not meet the regional transformation and upgrading demands. On the other hand, the innovation alliances face many prominentproblems in terms of weak integration, single player, ossified cooperative mechanism and unreasonable benefit distribution mechanism, so as to fail to give full play to its proper role.

In order to promote the implementation of the joint construction strategy of innovative industry with characteristic advantage in the BTH Region, the governments should focus on the establishment of six innovative alliances of renewable energy, big-data, steel, modern agriculture, bio-medicine, and high-end equipment manufacturing, which involving five key industries of electronic information and communication, high-end equipment manufacturing, biomedicine, modern agriculture, energy saving and environmental protection. These six major innovative alliances will play the role of effective carriers in establishing innovative industries with characteristic advantage.

5.3.1 Renewable energy technology innovation alliance

Establishment of Renewable Energy

Technology Innovation Alliance. This alliance consists of:

the renewable energy key technology integration innovation platform, which could be dominated by the China Electric Power Research Institute, and jointly promoted by Global energy Internet Research Institute, Research Institute of energy and new energy technology research institute, Chinese Academy of Sciences, Hebei Province Electric Power Research Institute, Beijing-Tianjin Electric Power Research Institute.This platform will strive to make technological breakthrough in the fields of development and utilization of wind and solar energy, energy storage and power grid system transformation etc., by the modes of jointly R&D and integrated innovation.

the renewable energy comprehensive utilization platform, which bases on Zhangjiakou National Renewable Energy Demonstration Area, focuses on promoting construction of coastal wind energy base and Taihang Mountain solar photovoltaic demonstration zone, promoting development, storage and transportation new technologies of wind and solar energy, implementing solar energy storage and transportation S&T demonstration projects and wind and solar energy utilization projects.

the renewable energy public service platform, which could be dominated by the National Development and Reform Commission Energy Research Institute (Policy Research), and National Renewable Energy Center (public services), and jointly established by China Renewable Energy Society, circular economy society, renewable energy Specialized Committee, National Standards Committee, China Patent Protection Association and others, the platform will focus on industry policy research and consulting, standard system establishment and technology transfer, intellectual property management, and will develop the technical road map of the BTH Region, cooperate with renewable energy innovation institutions and enterprises, connect the technology supply and demand.

the BTH Renewable energy government guiding fund, which could be co-financed by Beijing, Tianjin and Hebei, the fund will gather the dispersed governmental supporting capital in the renewable energy field, honor the technical road map, share the risks and benefits, promote the hatching, promotion and industrialization of key technology in production and application fields, and provide financial support for start-ups.

5.3.2 Large Data Technology Innovation Alliance

Establishment of Big-data Technology Innovation Alliance. This alliance consists of:

The BTH big-data key technology innovation platform, which could be dominated by China Big-data Industry Application Collaborative Innovation Alliance, jointly promoted by the university big-data research institutions and enterprises related to infrastructure layer, software layer and application service layer of big-data industrial chain.Basic tasks of the platform are formulating big-data technology industry road map and industry development standards, settling the industrial technical demands and technical bottlenecks, jointly researching & developing;

The big-data technology application innovation platform, which consists mainly of the BTH E-government Application Innovation Platform, responsible for data interoperability and sharing among industry and commerce, quality inspection, statistics, public security and other departments; the Financial Information Big-data Application Innovation Platform, which could be dominated by information department of branches of the People's Bank of China in BTH, jointly established by the local institutions under banking supervision committee, the CIRC, the Commission, responsible for interoperability of financial big-data; the BTH Big-data Trading Platform, which will focus on big-data application and system innovation to promote data information commercialization and improve the application of data information services;

The BTH big-data parks (industrial base), governments would encourage Beijing's big-data innovation enterprises transfer into and set up branches in Hebei to create big-data industrial clusters and parks in Tianjin Binhai New Area, Wuqing, Hebei Langfang, Qinhuangdao, Chengde, Zhangjiakou and other places, and to form big-data corridor in BTH Region and achieve coordinated development from dispersed parks to the whole BTH Region.

5.3.3 Iron and steel technology innovation alliance

Establishment of the Iron and Steel Technology Innovation Alliance. This alliance consists of:

The BTH steel industry key technology innovative platform, which could be dominated by Hebei Iron and Steel Research Institute, Tangshan Iron and Steel Branch of the Chinese Academy of Sciences and other steel industry scientific research institutes, established jointly by key enterprises and R&D institutions of universities and colleges including Beijing-Tianjin-Hebei Iron and steel industry energy saving and emission reduction technology innovation alliance and the national steel recycling process technology innovation strategic alliance, this platform will research & develop and commercialize the key technology, publicize major products and introduce key equipment, will also formulate technological and production standards system to promote steel industry upgrading and create green steel innovation centre influencing the world;

The BTH iron and steel technology innovation service intermediary alliance, which consists mainly of information service platform, technology brokers cooperative platform, technological and economic docking platform. And it could be jointly established by iron and steel professional science and technology intermediaries in Beijing, Tianjin and Hebei and will form a regional steel S&T intermediary services institute and network.

5.3.4 Modern agricultural technology innovation alliance

Establishment of the Modern Agricultural Technology Innovation Alliance. This alliance consists of:

The BTH modern agriculture collaborative innovation platform, consists of a main platform, which could be dominated by the National Academy of Agricultural Sciences and the three regional Academy of Agricultural Sciences in Beijing-Tianjin-Hebei, jointly promoted by the National Semi-arid Agricultural Engineering and Technology Research Center, the Northern Mountain Agricultural Engineering and Technology Research Center, the National Water-Saving Irrigation Beijing Engineering Technology Research Center and other scientific research institutions; and a sub-platform, which could be established by key technology R&D backbone institutions or enterprises to meet the key technological demands of regional modern agriculture development;

The modern agricultural technology transfer and transformation platform, which is on the basis of the construction of the Modern Agricultural Science and Technology Demonstration Zone around Beijing, and more than 100 agricultural science and technology parks in Hebei provincial 14 counties (cities, districts) adjacent to Beijing, this platform will implement agricultural science and technology demonstration projects, promote agricultural S&T achievements transfer and transformation, carry out the Beijing-Tianjin-Hebei agricultural science and technology park and major agricultural extension pilot, create agricultural high-tech application demonstration area and industrial agglomeration area. On basis of the current modern agriculture demonstration gardens, a technological application platform could be established focusing on crop germplasm innovation and breeding, chemical fertilizer pesticide reduction technology, soil quality improvement technology, pest control green agroscience, biological agents research and development, physical control and precision reduction, crop water saving technology and other key technology applications.

5.3.5 Biomedical technology innovation alliance

Establishment of the Biomedical Technology Innovation Alliance. This alliance consists of:

The BTH biomedical collaborative innovation center, which could be led by the Chinese Academy of Sciences biomedical and health research institute, and jointly established by R&D institutes of national antibiotic industry technology innovation strategic alliance, Beijing Huada gene research center, drug discovery alliance and other research institutions, national key Laboratories of protein engineering and plant genetic engineering, molecular biology and medicine, universities of Peking University Health Science Center, Union Medical College, Medical University Of Tianjin, Academy of Hebei Medical University, backbone innovation enterprises of North China Pharmaceutical Group Corporation(NCPC), China Shijiazhuang Pharmaceutical Group Co., Ltd(CSPC), Shijiazhuang Yiling Pharmaceutical Group Co., Ltd etc.. This platform will focus on settling major problems of the pharmaceutical industry; jointly train pharmaceutical industrial top-notch innovative talents in the talent shortage industries, joint construct pharmaceutical technology innovation supporting system.

The biomedical public service platform, which could be dominated by the Chinese Biotechnology Innovation Service Alliance, Beijing Pharmaceutical Industry Association, Beijing Zhongguancun Biological Engineering and the New Pharmaceutical Enterprises Association and other institutes, and jointly established by biomedical intermediary service agencies in Tianjin and Hebei, this platform will focus on construction of new drug pilot platform, Clinical research guidance center, variety research and development and transformation centers, intellectual property protection and transfer and personnel training bases.

The innovative industrial clusters in Beijing-Tianjin-Hebei, which are mainly on basis of Shijiazhuang National Bio-industrial Base, Beijing · Cangzhou Bohai New Area Biomedical Industrial Park, and Beidaihe International Health City, will attract the Beijing-Tianjin biomedical industrial resources, establish biomedical industry innovation cluster jointly with Beijing and Tianjin.

5.3.6 High-end equipment manufacturing technology innovation alliance

Establishment of the High-end Equipment Manufacturing Technology Innovation Alliance. This alliance consists of:

The BTH Rail bus technology innovation center, consists of Beijing Tianjin Hebei rail Bus Technology Collaborative Innovation Center, which could be mainly established by Beijing Track Engineering and other key laboratories, China Railway Vehicle Co., Ltd. Tangshan Rail and other enterprises, responsible for design and manufacturing technology development of key parts and high-speed motor vehicles and other advanced rail transport equipment; General Aviation Technology Collaborative Innovation Center,which could be mainly established by Beijing Aircraft/ Engine Integrated Systems Safety Key Laboratory, Key Laboratory of Structural Strength of Aircraft Engine, Shijiazhuang Aircraft Industry Co., Ltd. and others, responsible for technological development of aviation propeller, helicopter power components, large-scale axial air-cooled machine and others, development and production of Aircraft machine and components; Intelligent Robot Technology Innovation Center, which could be mainly established by Beijing Space Intelligent Robot System Technology and Application Laboratory, Tangshan special robot production base and others, responsible for technological development of control systems, gear units, servo motors and drives, sensors and end actuators and other key basic processes; and New Energy Vehicle Technology Collaborative Innovation Center, which could be mainly established by key laboratories of Beijing New Energy Passenger Car Energy Conservation and Safety, Efficient Power Transmission and System Control of New Energy Vehicles, and Hyundai Motor and Great Wall Motor and other enterprises, responsible for R&D of car low-carbon, information technology, intelligent and other core technologies and new energy vehicles key components.

The high-end equipment manufacturing services platform with functions of technical intermediaries, technical services and technical incubation and others, which could be established mainly by the backbone innovative institutions in Beijing-Tianjin-Hebei, focusing on cultivating technological transfer institutes, training and introducing technological talents, and responsible for technological achievements transfer and seeking technological resources; the high-end equipment manufacturing industry development fund could be co-financed by governments of Beijing-Tianjin-Hebei, which would provide financial services for technology innovation and innovative achievement transformation in the field of high-end equipment manufacturing.

A number of industrial clusters such as the Northern China navigation, Gu'an UAV, Handan new energy vehicles, Qinhuangdao marine engineering equipment, Tangshan rail transit, Shijiazhuang rail transit, Cangzhou laser industrial park and others, which would attract transfer and transformation of the Beijing-Tianjin high-end equipment manufacturing technology, construct industrial supporting platform for Beijing-Tianjin-Hebei high-end equipment industry technology innovation alliance.

Hebei should also improve operation mechanism of the six major alliances, mainly including two aspects:

Define roles of members of

innovation alliances. The operation of the major platforms within the innovation alliances is complementary and mutually dependent. The technical platforms play a role of bridge among the various innovation institutions, and actively jointly promote R&D of the industry forefront technology and applied technology; the technical service platforms are to improve soft environment of the collaborative innovation for the various members of the alliances to provide property rights, patent protection and technology transactions and transfer services; the fund platforms are to establish a socialized, diversified capital sources for technology research and development, incubation and transformation of innovation alliances; industrial clusters and bases are the key to the industrialization of key technologies of innovation alliances. Four types members perform their duties, complement each other to form a complete and efficient industry innovation chain.

Establish efficient innovation alliance management and operation mechanism. We suggest learning from the US manufacturing innovation alliance management and operation, establishing standardized management and efficient operation mechanism for innovation alliances, establishing management system of industrial innovation alliance, establishing cross-regional cross-sectoral Beijing-Tianjin-Hebei industrial technology innovation alliance management office, which consist of Development and Reform Commission, Science and Technology Department, Ministry of Education, Industry and Information Technology Department and other government departments, as well as Academy of Engineering, Academy of Sciences, Natural Science Foundation of the center government and three local governments. This office is mainly responsible for the identification and approval of the industrial technology alliances, the management, coordination and supervision of the construction and operation of the industrial technology alliances, and the grasp and adjustment of the development direction of the industrial technology innovation alliances.

We also suggest establishing an efficient operation mechanism for innovation alliances. Innovation alliances consist of innovation platform, service platform, fund platform, industrial base and other different types' entities. In order to integrate the members, we suggest setting up boards which was usually used by US manufacturing innovation alliances. The innovation alliances set up an independent trust board composed of representatives of members, the board could elect executive directors as leaders, responsible for the daily operation of the alliance, and elect a number of deputy directors, respectively, in charge of technical development, technology transfer, advanced manufacturing enterprises and other affairs, the members will discuss and design each proposal for the alliance development. The alliances also could have a governance committee and an executive committee. The governance committee is composed of important members, ordinary members of the alliance and representatives of small business members. It is responsible for selecting the appropriate industrial and academic representatives to form a coalition executive committee to cooperate with the board. The alliance can achieve financial independence and gradually achieve self-financing through a variety of flexible ways, such as membership fees, fee-based service activities, intellectual property licensing, contract research or product trial.

Box 2: The creation of a collaborative network of American Government-Industry-University-Institute

In March 2012, then US President Barack Obama proposed the establishment of the "National Manufacturing Innovation Network", which also be called a national government-industry-university-research collaborative innovation network consisting of many Institutes of Manufacturing Innovation (IMIs) in various manufacturing industries. By 2016, the United States has established five IMIs in the fields of the material manufacturing, digital manufacturing and design innovation, light metal manufacturing, composite materials, the next generation of electronic power manufacturing and others, in addition, four IMIs in fields of semiconductor, photon integration, clean energy , innovative fiber textile are in preparation. At August 16th, 2012, the first IMI - National Additive Manufacturing Innovation Institute (NAMII) was officially set up in Ohio, Yonston. More than 80 companies, nine research universities, six local colleges and 18 nonprofit organizations participated in NAMII. Participants also included the Ministry of Commerce and its affiliated National Institute of Standards and Technology (NIST), the Ministry of Defense (DOD), the Ministry of Education (ED), the Department of Energy (DOE), the National Aeronautics and Space Administration (NASA) and the United States National Science Foundation (NSF) and many other federal agencies.

IMI is the basic unit of Industry-University-Research integration network, each IMI will have a great autonomy, with a independent trust board composed by representative of the partners. The leader elected from executive director is responsible for the daily operation of IMI. In this governance pattern, the interests of the three major stakeholders (industry, academia and government) will be protected well.

5.4 Implement upgrading plan of Hebei's traditional industry innovative cluster

Hebei is a province with large scale of traditional industries, its resource-based industries such as steel, chemicals and building materials occupy an important position in China, Anping Wire Mesh, Qinghe Cashmere, Rongcheng Apparel, Pingxiang Bicycles, Xiongxian Plastic Packaging and other county-level characteristic industries have significant influence in national sub-industries. With China's economy entering the new normal, Hebei's development path of traditional industries depending on resource and labor force inputs are facing serious challenges from resource & environment constraint and consumption upgrading, the influence, driving force and supportive force of traditional industries are weakened. Hebei provincial innovation development of traditional industries is facing an urgent situation and arduous tasks. With the opportunity of coordinated development of the BTH, it is required to match the innovation resources from Beijing with demands of traditional industries in Hebei, implement upgrading plan of Hebei's traditional industry innovative clusters and promote transformation and upgrading and innovation development in Hebei, collaborative innovation in BTH Region.

5.4.1 Thinking and targets

Focusing on traditional industries such as iron and steel, chemicals, building materials, food, textile, light industry and others, Hebei should select a number of innovative industrial clusters which are of high technology, innovation vitality, perfect innovative organization system, excellent innovative environment and obviously agglomerate in parks. Hebei should gather Beijing's innovation resources into these clusters to form a innovation system with regional influence, increase the proportion of high value-added segments of industrial chain, cultivate backbone innovative enterprises, improve innovation service system, optimize the industry development system environment, and promote transformation of industrial clustersto new industrial clusters which are driven by technological innovation, collaboratively promoted by organizational innovation, market innovation, financial innovation and policy innovation, at last form innovative industrial clusters with high international discourse rights, technical standards, brand influence.

5.4.2 Implementation approach

We firstly divide Hebei's traditional industries into two distinct types:(1) resource-based industries such as iron&steel, chemicals, building materials and others, these industries have features of large industrial scale, large quantity of backbone enterprises, solid industrial innovation basis, are focus of provincial structural reform of supply side; (2) labor-intensive industries such as textile and apparel, agricultural and sideline products processing, plastic hardwareand others, these industries are mainly dominated by SMEs with weak innovation activities, and are the focus of sustainable development in county-level economy. We designed two different innovative cluster upgrading approaches, according to the different features and different innovation development targets of two types of traditional industries.

a. Traditional industries are suitable for such an innovative cluster upgrading approach with key enterprises as the core.

After long-term structural adjustment, traditional industries in Hebei, such as steel, chemical industry and building materials, have formed fundamentally a development pattern with large backbone enterprises as the core. The backbone enterprises have supportive force, technological leadership and radiation effect to industrial development, so it is better to select such an innovative cluster upgrading approach with key enterprises as the core for traditional industries.

Relying on the backbone enterprises of Hebei's traditional industries, the governments should construct Tangshan Iron and Steel industry innovation cluster with Hebei Iron and Steel Group as the core, Cangzhou chemical industry innovation cluster with Cangzhou Dahua Group as the core, and Handan building materials industry innovation cluster with Jinyu Group as the core to meet the adjustment requirement of industrial layout.

The backbone enterprises technical R&D institutions should establish "the BTH Iron and Steel Technology Institute", "the BTH New Building Materials Technology Institute", and "the BTH Institute of Chemical Technology" jointly with governments, universities and research institutions focusing on research and development of key and common industrial technology and commercialization of key manufacturing technology. The government could set up board of directors for each institute, members of the board should jointly confirm the contents of business, membership, intellectual property, investment, projects, funds allocation, sustainable development direction etc., to provide technical support for the development of innovative clusters and even a wider range of industries.

The governments should encourage the backbone enterprises to improve their advantages by geometric growth, complete cluster public service functions and introduce professional operators from Beijing to provide online support, life cycle management and maintenance services.

b. The county-level characteristic industries are suitable for such an innovative cluster upgrading approach with public innovative platforms as the core.

The county characteristic industries, such as Qinghe Cashmere, Anping Wire Mesh, Rongcheng Apparel, Pingxiang Bicycles and others, are of advantage of low-cost, but lack of backbone enterprises and innovation capacity, therefore, construction of innovative clusters in these industries should select such an upgrading approach with public innovative platform as the core by learning development experience of EU.

On basis of Hebei's characteristic county-level economy, the government should focus on building Rongcheng clothing innovative cluster, Anping wire mesh innovative cluster, Qinghe cashmere innovative Cluster, Daming agricultural and sideline products innovative cluster, and Xiong county plastic packaging innovative cluster.

The government should jointly with counterpart research institutions in Beijing, establish the cluster public technology innovation center (Innovation Inn) by modes of branches or co-construction, focusing on cluster technology improvement, equipment transformation, product upgrading and other common technical issues; improve industrialization of new technologies of Beijing R&D institutes, provide innovation activities information, and serve cross-regional technological transfer.

The local governments should establish cluster technology incubator base and entrepreneurship base by introducing specialized technology incubator base construction operators from Beijing, complete specialized service to provide driving force of innovation development.

The local governments should complete cluster service support system in terms of intellectual property, financial services, marketing, quality control, information services, and personnel training, by introducing professional innovation service intermediary agencies from Beijing to create an ideal environment for construction of innovative cluster.

By learning experience of innovative cluster in Japan, the local governments should establish cluster innovation development coordinating agencies with industry associations as the core. On the basis of effective connection mechanism, reasonable organization and coordination mechanism, industry associations should be responsible for research planning, overall planning, contact communication, guidance and implementation, information services, policies and regulations consulting and others jointly with cooperation of enterprises, technology research and development institutions, service agencies, etc..

Box 3: Construction and development of EU Innovation Inn

The Innovation Inn Center is one of the EU ' s programs to encourage small and medium-sized enterprises to carry out transnational technology transfer and cooperation. The network has been distributed in 33 countries, including 71 Innovation Inns which mutual support and exchange informationby Internet. It has become the most important and successful technical cooperation and transfer intermediary network in Europe.

The mission of the Innovation Inn is to support technological innovation across Europe and cross-border technical cooperation to provide a range of specialized support services for SMEs to acquire proprietary technology. The specific contents of its services include: a. Providing information of innovative activities; b. Promoting transnational technology transfer to meet the local industrial, economic and social demands; c. Promoting transnational dissemination and utilization of EU research results; d. Enhancing the technological application ability of enterprises by cross-border cooperation and partnerships; e. Providing other key services helpful to innovation and technological transnational transfer.

For effective management of IRC, each country in the European Union has a corresponding coordinating institute (National Coordinators) responsible for the implementation of Innovation Inn programs. Innovation Inns are mainly attached to public institutes, such as university technology centers, chambers of commerce, regional development agencies and national innovation institutions, most of which are co-established, the EU generally provide 45% to 50% of the funds, the rest by the cooperative units of Innovation Inns.

5.5 Actively cultivate small towns with innovative characteristics

In 2016, *Notification of Carrying Out the Cultivation of Characteristic Small Towns* issued by Ministry of Housing and Urban Development, National Development and Reform Commission and Ministry of Finance of the People's Republic of China. As the breakthrough of the new urbanization and the structural reform of supply side, construction of characteristic small town enters a new era. The state and local governments have formulated policies of construction of characteristics small towns, Zhejiang and Guizhou provinces have start off exploring development patterns before the others. In the BTH Region, obvious sub-urbanization of the two metropolis Beijing and Tianjin, and dispersal of Beijing's non-capital functions make it more compatible for Hebei to construct characteristic small towns in the regions circling Beijing and Tianjin.Beijing has formed sound innovative atmosphere and perfect innovation supportive facilities,but with the rising cost of living, innovative talents and SMEs in Beijing have a strong willing to emigrate out of Beijing. And the best destinations of innovative small and medium-sized enterprises from Beijing are regions circling Beijing which has convenient transportation.Therefore, it is necessary and feasible to construct several Hebei's innovative small towns circling Beijing to undertake innovation resources from Beijing.

5.5.1 Location and conditions of construction of innovative small towns

According to the field survey of several small towns in Langfang,

Baoding, and Zhangjiakou, we conduct comprehensive comparative analysis on the location and construction foundation of these small towns. We prefer some areas in Donghuayuan town of Huailai County, Jinglai industrial New City of Laishui County and some areas between Gu'an County seat and Gongcun Town as the best areas to construct innovative small towns.

(1) Donghuayuan town of Huailai County. Donghuayuan Town, close to Yanqing District of Beijing, one hour's drive away from Beijing Zhongguancun, has advantageous location. Transportation between Beijing and Donghuayuan is very convenient. There is an entrance of Beijing-Tibet highway in Donghuayuan Town, and in future after finishing of Beijing-Zhangjiakou Railway High-speed, there will be only 17 minutes from Beijing North Station to Donghuayuan Town. Moreover, this town which locates at the foot of Yanshan and close to the Guanting Reservoir, has excellent ecological environment. In 2016,Huailai base of China Academy of Space Technology (CAST) start to build, more key innovation institutions such as Beijing Institute of Technology, Beijing University of Aeronautics and Astronautics, Harbin Institute of Technology, Aviation NinthInstitute etc.have expressed their willing to cooperate with Donghuayuan, a batch of aerospace enterprises will enter in the town. Overall, Donghuayuan Town has superior location, convenient transportation, excellent ecological environment, good innovation development foundation, and hencehas good conditions of construction of innovative small town.

(2) Jinglai Industrial New City of Laishui County. Jinglai industrial new city which is close to Mentougou District of Beijing, five minutes' drive away from Beijing-Kunming and Beijing-Zhuozhou highway, 30 minutes' drive away from Yesanpo and Shidu scenic area, Beijing Second Airports, has good location and convenient transportation. The new city is devoted to undertake emerging industries and innovation resources from Beijing, and become a satellite city of Beijing. With the basically perfect infrastructure, Jinglai industrial new city has attracted a lot of innovative enterprises from Beijing, and has a good conditions and atmosphere to gatherBeijing's innovation resources.

(3) Areas between Gu'an County seat and Gongcun Town. This area is close to Beijing Daxing District, especially Beijing Second Airport.With the construction of the Beijing Second Airport, this area is bound to improve commuter traffic with Beijing, which will undoubtedly form more efficient and convenient transportation. Gu'an is the front of coordinated development and innovation development in county-level, cooperation with Beijing's innovation resource is ahead of other regions in Hebei. Construction of

parks with China Fortune Land Development Co., Ltd (CFLD), and cooperation of industrial technology incubators were successful. Gu'an has unparalleled conditions in terms of innovation development foundations, innovative facilities and innovation and entrepreneurship environment in Hebei.

5.5.2 Explore development path of the small town

According the experience of foreign small towns, the characteristics small town mostly is formed by two types of driving forces: external and endogenous, in particularly including patterns of talented person returning home to start businesses, continuation of family tradition, famous person driving development, grasping the opportunity of big-event, enterprise headquarters playing leading roles, emerging industry promoting development. Reviewing development conditions of innovative small town in Hebei, the endogenous driving force is relatively weak, we must develop small towns by utilizing external driving force of Beijing's innovation resources .

The East Garden small town should make full use of location advantage, deepen cooperation with China Academy of Space Technology, make efforts to introduce more CAST branches from Beijing, and then attract related firms and supporting enterprises, talents, using the brand and industrial influence of CAST.

Gu'an innovative small town should promote cooperation with China Fortune Land Development Co., Ltd, give full play to their experience of incubator establishment and operation, as well as the ability of integration of global innovation incubation resources, attract innovation resources from Beijing and other regions and improve innovation and entrepreneurship facilities and system by international standard.

Laishui innovative small town should make full use of location and ecological advantage, integrate with backbone R&D institutes and universities, actively attract large-scale R&D institutions or universities to move in or set up branches, promote gather of relevant institutions, enterprises and talents, so as to speed up construction of small town.

5.5.3 Innovate small town construction and management methods

Construction of innovative small towns should insist on the main operator model, which is guided by government, dominated by market, and participated in by the whole society.

First, give full play to the guiding role of government. The government should improve policy design to control the overall direction, improve construction system to form sound institutional environment, optimize service management to provide high quality public services.

Second, give full play to theleading role of market in construction of characteristics small towns. The government should encourage the professional city operators, specialty industry leaders, and key R&D institutions to become a small town development operator in a market-oriented and resource integration manner. The operator is responsible for planning, infrastructure construction, and introduction of foreign investment and so on.

Third, highlight extensive social participation in the governance pattern of small towns. The selection of governance entities should based on the local government and people of the town, and multi-stakeholders who have characteristics and culture associated with the small town. The nature of governance entities could be a market-oriented third parties or a permanent expert think tank or a governance alliance jointly established with a mature think tank.

5.5.4 Innovative small town supporting measures

First, improve the investment and financing mechanism.Hebei should actively make efforts to use provincial special construction funds from characteristic small towns and innovative carriers to support the construction of innovative towns. Using PPP, financial discount, direct subsidies, issuance of local government bonds and other means to attract social capital invest in innovative town construction.

Second, strengthen the land use guarantee.The county and prefecture-level city, where governance the innovative small towns, should adjust the *land use planning* and *urban and rural construction planning*, including land quota used for innovative town into the scope of urban construction land and arranging 100 acres of land for construction of innovative small towns. Hebei should encourage the demonstration town to carry out the "old house, old village, old factory" transformation project, develop wasteland and abandoned land, and support the demonstration towns to move and merge the villages, promote land adjustment. According to characteristics industries, Hebei should adjust appropriately the volume rate, green rate, construction coefficient and other control standards.

Third, optimize the innovation development environment. The government should optimize the innovative financial environment, and encourage innovative towns to develop venture capital and other financial forms; improve the innovative service supporting system, encourage the development and construction of creative space, technology market and other innovative service facilities; support transforming the existing "old house, old village, old factory" and industrial parks into innovation business facilities of "industrial housing + supporting housing", and provide appropriate financial subsidies to promote the sharing of innovative information; promote the key scientific research institutions and research centers from Beijing-Tianjin-Hebei to sever the characteristic small towns in terms of technical advice, inspection and testing, cooperative R&D, creative design, intellectual property and other services. The government should strengthen the support, science and technology departments should plan and carry out a series of scientific and technological projects in terms of industrial technology innovation, technology and cultural integration, wisdom tourism, product design and creative eco-agriculture and others which are matched with technological demands of leading industries and construction planning, give priority to support projects which meet the requirements of provincial S&T programs.

Fourth, innovate public service policy. Hebei should explore public service pilotpolicy in innovative towns taking Beijing as benchmark, and constantly improve the attraction and agglomeration effect to the innovative and entrepreneurial talents.

Box 4: Small town ' s development path : " Foreign business headquarters playing a leading role "

Formation of characteristic town leaded by the enterprise headquarters results from globalization and headquarters economy. As location of an enterprise headquarters, small town has top-level industrial status and high-end of value chain . Such as Langenthal, is the center of the global textile business headquarters, and Herzogenaurach, is the center of global sporting goods company headquarters. These enterprises have globalized branches and supplier network.Enter of headquarters can effective drive economic development and industrial structure adjustment of the town and even the surrounding areas.

First, it can promote the development of related business services. Enterprise headquarter is department of control, coordination and technological innovation, which grasp high-end resources, locate at high-end segments in value chain, produce high added value. The function of the headquarter determine the town should provide high-end business servicessuch as financial, legal, advertising and others;

Second, it can bring intangible brand effect. Headquarter can effectively enhance the local popularity, attracting professionals and gathering industries resources to form the town's leading industries.

Third, it can create jobs for the local. Herzogenaurach brought about 16,000 jobs (2011) .

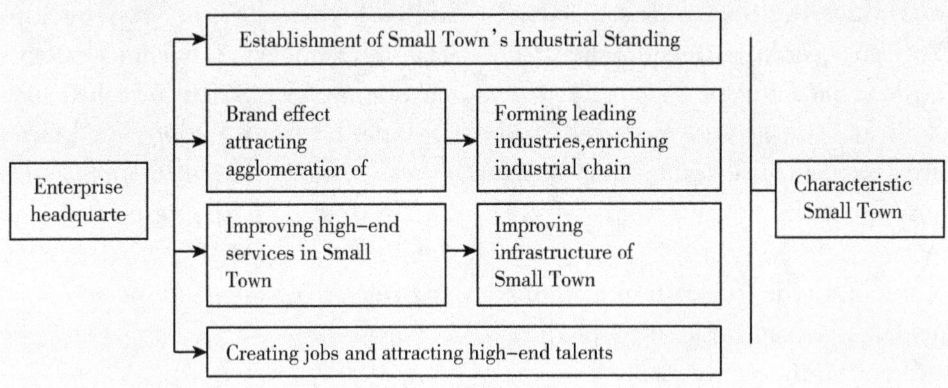

5.6 Optimize soft and hard environment supporting for S&T SMEs

In the context of the coordinated development of Beijing-Tianjin-Hebei, sound soft and hard environment is conducive to the transfer of the talent and S&T SMEs from Beijing and further to the prosperity and development of S&T SMEs. Improving soft and hard environment is an important measure for Hebei's innovation development and transformation and upgrading. The prosperity of S&T SMEs depends on a good policy environment. In recent years,Hebei Province has introduced a series of policies and measures to support the development of S&T SMEs. Hebei provincial government and related departments issued the *Opinions on Supporting the Development of Small and Medium-sized Sci-tech Enterprises* in 2013, *Science and Technology Small and Medium-sized Enterprises Growth Plan* in 2014, *Ten FinancialMeasures of Supporting for the Innovation Development of Scientific and Technological Small and Medium-sized Enterprises* in 2015, *Hebei Province Science and Technology Small and Medium Enterprises Growth Plan (2016 - 2020)* in 2016, which basically constitute the policy system supporting for S&T SMEs in Hebei. Comparing with policy system supporting for S&T SMEs in Tianjin and other regions, we conclude that there are still many gaps for Hebei, in terms of improving the support, innovation and refinement, flexible adaptation and implementation of propaganda, and propose the following three suggestions on improving the policy system, strengthening the support and strengthening policy implementation of S&T SMEs.

5.6.1 Improve the S&T SMEs policy system

Hebei Province S&T SMEs Growth Plan(2016-2020) has put forward the development targets, basic path and supporting policies about S&T SMEs, but there is not more specific policy implementation, it is recommended to improve the S&T SMEs in Hebei Proviace according to requirements of the development plan.

First, the government should introduce new fiscal and taxation policy to support the development of S&T SMEs.

Second, the government should introduce relevant innovation platform policy, such as *Regulations on Implementing S&T SMEs Growth Plan in S&T business incubators*, *Regulations on Implementing S&T SMEs Growth Plan in Engineering Technology Center* and so on.

Third, the government should introduce specific policies supporting S&T SMEs developing and researching new products, such as *Identification and Subsidy Regulations on New Products and Key Technology Products of S&T SMEs*.

Fourth, the government should introduce specific policies supporting "Stock Listing Project" of S&T SMEs, such as *Regulations on Supporting Share Reform, Listing, Domestic and Foreign Mergers and Acquisitions of S&T SMEs*.

Five, the government should introduce organization policies and implementation measures supporting S&T SMEs, such as *Regulations on Promoting Cadres Assistant to Support S&T SMEs*, *Opinions on Strengthening Performance Evaluation of the Development of S&T SMEs*.

Six, the government should introduce policies supporting transfer of S&T SMEs from Beijing and Tianjin technology or technical talents starting up S&T SMEs in Hebei, such as *Incentives to Technical Talents from Beijing and Tianjin Starting Up S&T SMEs in Hebei*, *Regulations on Supporting S&T SMEs from Beijing and Tianjin Developing in Hebei*.

5.6.2 Hebei Province should strengthen the support to S&T SMEs

First, strengthen financial support. Compared with developed provinces and municipalities, Hebei should expand scale and share of financial funds supporting S&T SMEs in each level government, expand scale of S&T SMEs development funds, angel investment guiding funds and loan compensation funds, increase the direct financial subsidies and incentives of S&T SMEs.

Second, innovate S&T SMEs financial insurance supporting model. Hebei should explore the establishment of provincial S&T policy banks which operated by market-oriented mode, issue loans to S&T SMEs in the principle of low profits. Hebei should actively promote the establishment of a venture capital alliance jointly with Beijing to attract a number of Beijing's venture capital and equity investment institutes, to form high land gathering finance, technology, industry, talent and other elements, and form a quality platform ofS&T services. By learning the experience of Guangdong, Hebei could establish 100 million yuan "SMEs financial loans risk reserve" relying on the Productivity Promotion Center, 50 million yuan "joint technology loan risk reserve" by province and prefecture level city to perfect the financing credit guarantee system of S&T SMEs. Hebei should carry out intellectual property investment and financing services, co-establish comprehensive credit model of intellectual property pledge with commercial banks in high-tech zones, private science and technology parks, professional towns and industry associations above the provincial level, comprehensively using intellectual property, assets, personal property and other asset types.Hebei should innovate intellectual property pledge comprehensive financing model, increase amount of pledge financing. Hebei should also encourage social capital to set up intellectual property risk investment platforms and tools in a market-oriented manner, and to participate capital operation of independent intellectual property enterprises.

Third, increasingly support for the development of S&T SMEs. Hebei should constantly expand financial investment in the incubator construction, actively attract the incubator professional operators to Hebei establishing new incubators and accelerators which are of normative operation, flexible mechanisms and integrating the global innovation resources; in small towns circling Beijing and Tianjin, industrial bases and various industrial parks at all levels, establish numerous professional incubators and characteristics industrial incubator bases closely integrating industry development. Hebei should strengthen the support of incubator enterprises, focusing on fostering a number of powerful, professional incubators with excellent performance, create incubator brand to lead the province incubator development. Hebei should, on basis of improving basic plant, industrial and commercial, property services, improve the incubator and accelerator service functions, improve the financial, patents, qualifications and other specialized services. Hebei should innovate incubator construction management mechanism to encourage the incubator to form a diversified ownership structure, establish stakeholder system among incubator management team, incubation enterprises, investment and financing institutions, build a incubation fund to precisely support incubation enterprises in fixed amount, regular way; explore models of compensable service, debt-for-equity swaps and stock ownership incubation; improve the incubator mode of "entrepreneurial mentor + entrepreneurship incubator + professional investment".

Fourth, improve the service of S&T SMEs. Utilizing modern information network technology, Hebei should integrate science and technology service resources from government, intermediary and the whole society, construct S&T SMEs services system achieve information amalgamation of varied services such as the determination of SMEs, government project acceptance, statistical information monitoring, policies and regulations, enterprise consulting,financing services, technology platform services and others, provide comprehensive, real-time one-stop service and technical support for government decision-making.

5.6.3 Hebei should strengthen the implementation of the policy

First, publicize policy information. Hebei should setup website interactive with S&T SMEs, timely releasing policy information, and collecting enterprises demands for policy;carry out actions of policies entering in to enterprises, comprehensively arrange and distribute policy compilation benefit the enterprises, regular organize special policy advocacy and training, publicize policy information to improve the awareness of policy information, and guide enterprises to rationally use and full enjoy preferential policies.

Second, establish S&T SMEs cadres assistance mechanism. Hebei should establish key S&T SMEs one-on-one assistance mechanism, provincial and municipal governments should organize cadres of departmental and section rank assisting enterprises in the mode of "one cadre into one enterprise for three years", focus on implementing demands survey and policy training for enterprisesto solve difficult problems.

Third, strengthen assessment and supervision on the development of S&T SMEs. Hebei should implement assessment and supervision on government leading team, departmental and section rank cadres who responsible for development of S&T SMEs; formulate special assessment and supervision methods, include this assessment into regularly assessment, annual assessment and performance assessment, the well performed cadres shall be rewarded, promoted, and the poor performed cadres shall be punished.

6. Suggestions on Hebei's utilization of innovation resources from Beijing

6.1 Suggestions on design of policy system for strengthening the utilization of innovation resource from Beijing

Fully utilizing Beijing's innovation resources is an important measure for Hebei to realize the three major strategies of transformation, innovation and coordinated development, also a major opportunity for Hebei's sustainable development. Since the implementation of the Outline of *Coordinated Development of* BTH, Hebei has achieved certain success in utilizing Beijing's innovation resources. But on the whole, due to the lack of clear thinking and tasks, unclear responsibilities division and supporting policies and measures, Hebei has not give full play to the leading role,integrate governmental and market force together, settle numerous constraints.

Effect of Hebei utilizing Beijing's innovation resources has not yet reached expectations. It is recommended to carry out policy system research and design of Hebei promoting Beijing's innovation resources more fully and orderly transfer to and transform in Hebei.

On basis of the fully analysis on intention, trend and conditions of cross-regional cooperation of Beijing's innovation resources, and requirements and foundations of Hebei's innovation development, the governments should conduct the policy top-design for Hebei Province utilizing innovation resources from Beijing, confirm the development thinking, periodical objectives, pattern and major tasks.

Hebei Province should formulate special and implementation plans, and put the specific tasks in place. According the near-term targets and major tasks in the top-design, the government should formulate special planning by types of tasks, departments, regions and major carriers.

The governments should formulate supporting policies as the instrumentality to implement the top-design policy. According to the major tasks in top-design and special plans, the governments should design finance, taxation, finance, land, talent and other policies to promote transfer and transformation of innovation resources from Beijing, study pilot demonstration policy of transfer and transformation of Beijing's innovation resource as the means of top-design.

The governments should develop "detailed rules" and "guiding rules" of national plan and policy, on basis of the effect and problem of policy implementation. In the original policy framework, it needs to further deepen and expand policies to promote transfer and transformation of innovation resources from Beijing.

6.2 Suggestions on construction of collaborative innovation interaction mechanism with Beijing

The current administrative divisions can not be changed fundamentally, we suggest that Hebei should establish collaborative innovation mechanism with Beijing as soon as possible to make full use of Beijing's innovation resources, to break the obstacles of administrative divisions, to promote the free flow of innovative elements, and to attract Beijing's innovation resources transfer to and transform in Hebei.

Establish policy interaction mechanism. Beijing and Hebei should adjust and unify innovation development plans according to their own functions and tasks which have been defined in the Outline of *Coordinated Development of Beijing-Tianjin-Hebei*. Two governments should negotiate on unified standards and qualification of talents, high-tech enterprises and SMEs, and formulate policy of mutual recognition of standards and qualifications to eliminate barriers against regional free mobility of innovation elements. Hebei should actively strive for learning and transplanting the national innovation development demonstration pilot policies of Beijing, such as comprehensive independent innovation development demonstration area, national innovation city construction, national S&T results transfer and transformation demonstration area to form a best policy environment for innovation development.

Establish resource opening and sharing mechanism. The governments should establish opening up and co-building mechanism in terms of sci-tech experts' library, information resource library, scientific research database, large-scale experimental equipment, and key technology innovative platform. Hebei Province and Beijing municipality should plan to construct large-scale scientific equipment collaborative network, sci-tech literature and technology data sharing platform, regional sci-tech experts' library and sharing network, regional technology innovation and investment and financing services platform, etc.

Establish market opening-up mechanism. On basis of the current technical exchange market, Hebei Province and Beijing municipality should plan to establish unified technology market and new technology and new products (services) procurement platform. Two governments should also support new technology and new products (services) and first major technical equipment entering into the market. Hebei should establish sci-tech projects and key scientific research projects mutual opening-up mechanism to allow R&D institutions in the two regions to participate interchangeably in key R&D programs; establish innovative coupons docking mechanism to allow R&D institutions in the two regions to buy inspection and testing, intellectual property, research and development and other S&T resources by innovative coupons.

6.3 Suggestions on improving the relevant supporting industries, facilities and system

Transfer and transformation of innovation resources has high requirements on related innovation conditions in terms of carriers construction, mechanisms, policy of destination, as well as industry chain supporting, public service level, innovative atmosphere and innovative facilities. We suggest that Hebei Province should strengthen industrial innovation supporting, facilities and system construction, to attract Beijing's innovation resources transformation in Hebei.

Step up the construction of related industrial chain. Focusing on the transformation and upgrading of traditional industries and development long-term targets of the emerging industries in Hebei, the government should carefully analyze conditions of industrial chain supporting the transformation of major S&T achievements, plan in advance and introduce relevant industrial chain projects, and create a sound environment supporting industrial development, so as to introduce continuously innovation resources from Beijing.

Step up the planning of construction of sci-tech research equipment market. Focusing on the overall layout of Hebei's innovation development, the government should formulate plans to construct comprehensive sci-tech research equipment market in the central cities, innovation agglomeration areas and innovative small towns, and construct professional sci-tech research equipment market in the hi-tech industrial parks and achievement transformation base.

Make efforts to enhance public service capacity in major region. Following the provincial new urbanization construction plan, Hebei should make efforts to improve the cultural, business, leisure, entertainment and other public service facilities to meet demands of innovative talents and enterprises; take a variety of ways to improve the education, health care and other public services. The government should explore and launch a pilot of equalization of public services in the agglomeration development areas and innovative small towns, and create a special environment to attract innovation resources from Beijing.

Actively create an atmosphere suitable for innovation development. Hebei should actively advocate respecting knowledge, advocating innovation, integrity and law-abiding, and vigorously create a good atmosphere with philosophy of pioneer, daring, innovative, competitive, tolerance failure. Hebei should deeply implement the scientific ability plan of the whole population, strengthen the popularization of science, and comprehensively improve the scientific literacy and innovation awareness of citizens; fully respect the pioneering spirit of the masses, extensively carry out scientific and technological innovation activities; publicize major scientific and technological achievements, typical innovative talents, innovative enterprises, increase the recognition of innovators, and fully stimulate the vitality of innovation and entrepreneurship.

References

[1] 蓝晓霞 . 美国产学研协同创新机制研究 [M]. 北京 : 北京交通大学出版社，2014.

[2] 张荐华 . 欧洲一体化与欧盟的经济社会政策 [M]. 昆明：云南人民出版社，2011.

[3] 曾刚 . 长江经济带协同创新研究：创新・合作・空间・治理 [M]. 北京：经济科学出版社，2016.

[4] 杨耀武 , 张仁开 . 长三角区域科技创

新政策评估及路线图研究 [J]. 科研管理，2010（5）.

[5] 沈开艳，陈建华，邓立丽 . 长三角区域协同创新、提升科创能力研究 [J]. 中国发展，2015（8）.

[6] 张仁开 . “十二五”时期推进长三角区域创新体系建设的思考 [J]. 科学发展，2012（9）.

[7] 白智勇 . 以协同创新引领京津冀协同发展 [J]. 中国高新区，2014（11）.

[8] 尹喆，周密 . 京津冀区域协同创新发展的路径研究 [J]. 现代管理科学，2016（5）.

[9] 颜廷标 . 基于中观视角的京津冀协同创新模式研究 [J]. 河北学刊，2016（3）.

[10] 皮宗平 . 长三角两省一市科技合作的现状及对策建议 [J]. 特区经济，2009（4）.

[11] 张胜，郭英远 . 破解国有科研事业单位科技成果转化体制机制障碍 [J]. 中国科技论坛，2014（8）.

[12] 陈万钦 . 促进北京科技成果向河北转化的调查与建议 [J]. 经济与管理，2016（7）.

[13] 陈俐，冯楚健，陈荣，姜东 . 英国促进科技成果转移转化的经验借鉴 [J]. 科技进步与对策，2016（8）.

[14] 刘城，林平凡 . 传统产业集群产业链与创新链融合升级的模式 [J]. 南方经济，2015（5）.

[15] 郭胜伟，刘巍 . 日本筑波科学城的立法经验对我国高新区发展的启示 [J]. 中国高新区，2007（2）.

[16] 新型研发机构成深圳科技创新的先锋力量 . 南方网，2014-9-28.

[17] 我国促进科技成果转化的若干新趋势研究 . 科学技术部火炬高技术产业开发中心网站 .

[18] 浙江科技大市场建设成效及经验 . 中华人民共和国科学技术部网站，2015-5-22.

[19] 打通科技成果转移转化最后一公里，把“金蛋”变成“金产业”的“宁波模式”. 中国宁波网，2016-10-17.

Thematic Report III

Research on Sustainable Development of Less Developed Regions in North Hebei Province

Principal Investigator: Wang Suping
Investigators: Wang Zheping, Feng Zhiguo, Yang Hongcai, Dai Haiyi

North Hebei which contains Zhangjiakou and Chengde is characterized by the widest range of poverty, the largest poverty population, and the deepest poverty in BTH Region (Beijing, Tianjin, Hebei Province). As the function area of ecological conservation and ecological shelters, north Hebei plays a key role on wind prevention and sand fixation, water and soil conservation in BTH Region. Exploring the win-win path of economic and ecological development in order to better play the function as ecological shelters while the regional economy and society is developed faster, is very important for the coordinated development of BTH Region.

The macro-economic research institution of Hebei Development and Reform Commission proposed a tentative plan of strategy of "focusing on north Hebei, constructing ecological economy demonstration plot" and a regional development framework which is consisted of industry, population, labor employment, exploitation of resources, cities and towns, and environment protection in sub report "Eliminating the poverty belt surrounding Beijing and Tianjin, improving the coordinated development of BTH Region" of Asian Development Bank (ADB) Technical Assistance Project "The Strategy of Hebei Economic Development" in 2005. Currently, it is certainly worth considering the changes and requirements of new era, deeply analyzing the underlying problems of industry development, cities and towns construction, ecological environment protection, and so on, raising the counterpart measures and policy suggestions in order to provide support to forming the win-win situation of economic and ecological development.

This project is a continuation of the former ADB project. From the point of view of making overall arrangements to solve the problems of ecology, economy and society, basing on economicand ecological sustainable development in north Hebei, this project deeply analyzes the characteristic, influencing factor, opportunity and challenge of regional development on the new era, proposes the development path, framework and key measures under the constraint of the function area of ecological conservation, and give some policy advices to the whole nation, Hebei, Beijing and Tianjin.

1. The development achievements and problems of less developed region in north Hebei Province

North Hebei has a faster development on regional economy, social progress, ecological environment protection, and infrastructure construction in the period

2005-2015 and enters a critical period of economic and social transformation, however, at the same time, there are lots of problems in the development of regional economy, society, and poverty alleviation.

1.1 The development achievements of less developed region in north Hebei Province in the past 10 years

1.1.1 A big progress in regional poverty alleviation

Since 2005, north Hebei has been listed in the key areas of poverty alleviation by Chinese government and Hebei Province. In north Hebei, 14 counties are key counties included in the national plan for poverty alleviation through development, two counties are listed in key counties included in the provincial plan for poverty alleviation through development, six counties are demonstration area of poverty alleviation surrounding Beijing. North Hebei has implemented the strategy of poverty alleviation through development, regional poverty alleviation, taking targeted measures in poverty alleviation in succession, the scope, depth and accuracy of development-oriented poverty alleviation make a big progress. There is a fast progress of economic and social development in north Hebei. The less developed situation has been improved enormously. There exist 980 thousand poverty populations living under the poverty line, with the poverty rate of 12.3% in 2015. The poverty population is shrinking substantially and the poverty rate is decreasing sharply comparing to ten years ago.In the period of 12th five-year plan, 1,465 thousand poverty people and 935 poverty villages are helped to steadily shake off poverty in north Hebei, accounting for 31.17% of Hebei. The overall strengths of poverty counties are steadily enhanced, Kuancheng Manchu Autonomous County and Chongli County are out of poverty. The income of poverty people increases continually and the living standards are improved while the poverty population reduces enormously. According to data of rural people by income quintile, the income of low-income group rural people in Zhangjiakou and Chengde in 2015 increases by more than two times comparing to that in 2005, the food and clothing (basic living consumption expenditure) decrease five and eight percent, consumer durables such as motorcycles and TV increase continually, the problem of food and clothing of poverty is solved. The people are striding towards a well-off life.

1.1.2 The strength of regional economy has been enhanced steadily

The GDP of north Hebei in 2015 is 272.22 billion yuan, 3.5 times of that in 2005, with the annual average growth rate 13.4% which is higher than that of Hebei Province. The proportion of north

Hebei GDP to Hebei Province increases from 7.7% to 9.1%. The ranking of economic aggregate of Zhangjiakou and Chengde in Hebei rise from 10th and 11th to 8th and 9th. GDP per capita is 34234 yuan, which increases by 2.3 times than that of 2005. Annual average growth rate (12.8%) is higher than that of Hebei Province. GDP per capita of north Hebei reach 85% of that of Hebei, which is 15 percent higher than that of Hebei in 2005. Government revenue of north Hebei reaches 23.069 billion yuan, 1.96 times of that in 2005, with the annual growth rate 6.95%. Saving deposits of urban and rural residents increase by more than 3.5 times from 63.154 billion yuan in 2005 to 286.934 billion yuan in 2015, with the annual growth rate 15% (see Table 1).

Table 1 Comparison of economy of Hebei and north Hebei in 2005 and 2015

	GDP(billion yuan)			Government revenue (billion yuan)			GDP per capita (yuan)		
	2005	2015	Growth rate (%)	2005	2015	Growth rate (%)	2005	2015	Growth rate (%)
Hebei	1,009.6	2,980.6	11.4	103.5	264.9	9.9	14,736	40,142	10.5
North Hebei	77.6	272.2	13.4	11.8	23.1	6.9	10,279	34,234	12.8
Zhangjiakou	41.6	136.4	12.6	7.3	13.34	6.3	9,945	30,836	12.0
Chengde	36	135.9	14.2	4.5	9.7	7.9	10,723	38,488	13.6

Resources: *Hebei Economic Yearbook* (2006, 2016), *Zhangjiakou Economic Yearbook* (2006, 2016), and *Chengde Economic Yearbook* (2006, 2016).

1.1.3 The living conditions of residents have been improved continually

The level of income and consumption have been increased substantially, living conditions have been continually improved since 2005. Per capita disposable income of urban households of Zhangjiakou and Chengde are respectively 23,841 yuan and 22,885 yuan, Per capita disposable income of rural households are 8,341 yuan and 7,923 yuan, more than 2 times comparing to that of 2005. Per capita consumption expenditure of urban households of Zhangjiakou and Chengde are 14,594 yuan and 15,636 yuan, increasing by 1.54 and 1.63 times respectively. Per capita consumption expenditure of rural households is 6,411 yuan and 6,536 yuan, increasing by 2.4 and 2.0 times respectively. Consumption structure has been improved gradually. In 2015, the Engel coefficients of rural households are 35% and 32.7% in Zhangjiakou and Chengde, decreasing by 3.6% and 9.98% comparing to that of 2005. The Engel coefficients of urban households decrease from 37.48% and 37.7% in 2005 to 27.1% and 30.8% in 2015 in Zhangjiakou and Chengde. The living conditions improve significantly. Per capita housing space of urban residents are respectively 31.86 and 29.39 square meters in Zhangjiakou and Chengde in 2015, increasing by 10.9and 7.98 square meters comparing to that in 2005. Per capita housing space of rural resident sincreases from 19.5 and 20.07 square meters in 2005 to 25.52 and 25.82 square meters in 2015. Consumer durables renew fast, while the basic demands of consumer durables such as TV, refrigerator, are already satisfied, cars and mobile phones become consumer hot spot. The number of car ownership per 100 households in Zhangjiakou and Chengde in 2015 are 21 and 17, the number of mobile phones are 143.46 and 205, which indicates that enjoyable consumption expand rapidly when basic needs of urban and rural residents are satisfied (see Table 2, 3 and 4).

Table 2 Income changes of urban and rural residents in Hebei and north Hebei

Indicator	Per capita disposable income of urban households (yuan)			Per capita disposable income of rural households (yuan)		
Year	2005	2015	Annual growth rate (%)	2005	2015	Annual growth rate (%)
Hebei	9,107	26,152	11.1	3,482	11,051	12.2
Zhangjiakou	7,714	23,841	11.9	2,329	8,341	13.6
Chengde	7,845	22,885	11.3	2,582	7,923	11.9

Notes: Data sources are *Hebei Economic Yearbook* (2006, 2016), *Zhangjiakou Economic Yearbook* (2006, 2016), and *Chengde Economic Yearbook* (2006, 2016).Per capita disposable income of rural households in 2015 is adjusted by new standard, Per capita disposable income of rural households in 2005 is measured by per capita net income of rural residents.

Table 3 Consumption changes of urban and rural residents in Hebei and north Hebei

Indicator	Per capita consumption expenditure of urban households (yuan)			Per capita consumption expenditure of rural households (yuan)		
Year	2005	2015	Annual growth rate (%)	2005	2015	Annual growth rate (%)
Hebei	6,700	17,587	10.13	2,166	9,023	15.34
Zhangjiakou	5,754	14,594	9.75	1,909	6,411	12.88
Chengde	5,946	15,636	10.15	2,180	6,536	11.61

Notes: Data sources are *Hebei Economic Yearbook* (2006, 2016), *Zhangjiakou Economic Yearbook* (2006, 2016), and *Chengde Economic Yearbook* (2006, 2016).

Table 4 Living condition changes of urban and rural residents in Hebei and north Hebei

Unit: yuan

	Engel coefficients of urban households			Engel coefficients of rural households			Per capita housing space of rural residents			Per capita housing space of urban residents		
Year	2005	2015	Growth	2005	2015	Growth	2005	2015	Growth	2005	2015	Growth
Hebei	34.6	26.1	8.5%	41	28.6	12.4%	28.4	37.7	9.3%	28.4	35.9	7.5%
Zhangjiakou	37.5	27.1	10.4%	38.6	35.6	3.0%	19.5	25.5	6.0%	21	31.9	10.9%
Chengde	37.7	30.8	6.9%	42.7	32.7	10%	20.1	25.8	5.7%	21.4	29.4	8.0%

Sources: *Hebei Economic Yearbook* (2006, 2016), *Zhangjiakou Economic Yearbook* (2006, 2016), and *Chengde Economic Yearbook* (2006, 2016).

1.1.4 The overall level of public services has improved significantly

North Hebei has continually enlarged the investment on livelihood projects since 2005 in order to improve the level of public service and let the people share the fruits of reform and development. In 2015, the fiscal input on education, health service, social security reaches 26.091billion yuan, increasing 8.24 times comparing to that of 2005. The proportion of these fiscal inputs to fiscal expenditure increases from 23.32% of 2005 to 38.21% in 2015. Education, health service and social security improve a lot. Free compulsory education is in full operation, high school education is much more popular and its quality is above medium level in Hebei Province. The gross high school enrollment rate is above 90%.Zhangjiakou is awarded the advanced unit of the "two basics" honorary title by the state council. Chengde is named advanced city of promoting balanced development of compulsory education by the ministry of education. The level of high education raises a lot. Hebei Normal University for Nationalities is co-constructed by Hebei Province and the Ministry of Education. Affiliated School of Beijing Normal University in Chengde is stated to operate.The construction of public health and basic medical care systems has made considerable progress by Zhangjiakou and Chengde. Total number of hospital beds in these two cities have been increased from 20,200 in 2005 to 39,400 in 2015, the number of public health technical persons have been increased from 24,500 to 36,300, city level co-ordination of medical insurance and immediate settlement of medical treatment in different places within the city have been completed. The standard of financial subsidy forNew Rural Cooperative Medical System (NRCMS) and medical insurance for urban residents has been raised to 380 yuan. In total of 90% rural residents are covered by NRCMS. In 2015, basic living allowances of urban and rural residents are raised to 4,770 yuan and 2,250 yuan in Zhangjiakou, while that in Chengde are 5,400 yuan and 2,800 yuan. 99% urban and rural residents are covered by social old-age insurance system, several social old-age insurance ways, such as rural mutual happiness hospital, home-based care service center for the aged in urban communities have become more and more popular. With respect to poverty alleviation, Zhangjiakou and Chengde have steadily promoted the construction of rural roads, rural drinking water security project, power grid upgrading and renovation of old and dilapidated houses. The weaknesses of public infrastructure are reduced in poverty areas. The living conditions have been improved significantly in poor villages. Rain plan and social relief have been continually implemented and developed, a large number of students from poor family have attended vocational education, and most of low-income family and five guarantees family have got aid.

1.1.5 Framework of transport facilities has been basically taken shape

North Hebei is an important region where Beijing and Tianjin develop western union and northing. In the past 10 years, the construction of transportation infrastructure, such as railway, roads, and airport has been speeded up, a modern comprehensive transportation system integrating railway, highway and aviation is basically formed. The role of north Hebei as regional transportation hub of docking Beijing and Tianjin, connecting northwest, linking northeast and directly connecting coastal area, is more and more important. The railway of Zhang-Tang, Zhang-Ji and Zhang-Shuang has been completed as scheduled, railway of Jing-Bao and Da-Qin have been upgraded, high-speed railway of Jing-Zhang has been started. Railway passenger dedicated line of Zhang-Hu, Zhang-Da, and Jing-Shen have gone well. The total mileage of railway traffic has reached 1419 kilometers. A comprehensive transportation system in which rail freight corridor is focused on national trunk channel and connecting eastern sea gate, and passenger transport network system is linked with Beijing and Tianjin and connecting "Northeast, Northwest and North China", has been basically taken shape.The total mileage of expressway traffic which externally connects Shanxi, Inner Mongolia and Liaoning, internally linked BTH has reached 1,684 kilometers. Highways of Zhang-Shi, Jing-Zang, Jing-Xin, Jing-Cheng, Cheng-Tang, Cheng-Chi, and Zhang-Cheng have been built and operated in succession. The mileage of arterial highway is 40,934 kilometers (except expressway), in which the mileage of highway above grade two is 4,921 kilometers, 12% of total arterial highway mileage. In north Hebei, arterial highway has already connected key villages and towns, important industrial base, national and provincial tourist attractions, and covered all administrative villages, constituting a versatile, crosscutting three-dimensional arterial highway traffic network. Ningyuan airport of Zhangjiakou opens five routes and links to Shijiazhuang, Shanghai, Chengdu, Guilin, Harbin, Shenyang, Dalian, Shenzhen, Xiamen, Haikou and Xian. The number of passenger throughput has increased from 24,000 of 2013 to 208,000 of 2015. The construction of Chengde airport has been finished basically and flight calibration has been completed.

1.1.6 The capacity of ecological security has been enhanced

As the function area of ecological conservation and ecological shelters, north Hebei plays a key role on ecological environment protection andwater conservation in BTH Region.North Hebei has continually enhanced ecological environment protection, water conservation, energy saving and emission reduction, prevention and control of air pollution for many years, and made a big progress on ecological environment protection, ecological attraction and environment influence continually enlarged.With respect to ecological environment construction, north Hebei has implemented water conservation project of Beijing in 21th century, paddy to dryland project, sandstorm source control program in Beijing and Tianjin, conversion of cropland to forest, promoted the forestry program cooperation of Beijing and Zhangjiakou, encouraged socialized afforestation. Forest cover rate in north Hebei has increased from 41.04% of 2010 to 47.22% of 2015, which is 16.22% higher than the average level in Hebei Province. The function of wind prevention and sand fixation, water conservation has enhanced apparently. There are six national nature reserves, nine forest parks, six new-added national experimental wet parks in north Hebei. Zhangjiakou is listed in ecological civilization demonstration areas and ecological environment protection demonstration areas, and Zhangjiakou has firstly achieved that the subsidy of function of ecological conservation area cover the whole city. Chengde is also listed in ecological civilization demonstration areas, experimental pilot of national main functional areas and water ecological civilization city, demonstration city of circular economy. Ecological space of north Hebei has gradually enlarged and the supportability of ecological products has been improved steadily. North Hebei has actively implemented the comprehensive improvement of water environment in key river basin. In period of 12th Five-Year Plan, 3781 square kilometers area of water and soil loss have been under harness, water quality of main rivers in north Hebei met the requirement of national main functional area, water quality of all drinking water sources reached the standard. Urban sewage treatment rate is 70%, water quality of all

Exit section III satisfy the standard. North Hebei also has vigorously implemented environment improvement projects, such as energy saving and emission reduction, clean energy transformation, key pollution industry governance. Energy consumption of industrial added value of enterprise above designated size in Zhangjiakou and Chengde has decreased from 2.48 tons of standard coal/10,000 yuan (Zhangjiakou) and 4.40 tons of standard coal/10,000 yuan (Chengde) in 2005 to 1.88 tons of standard coal/10,000 yuan and 1.51 tons of standard coal/10,000 yuan in 2015. There is a big progress in energy saving and emission reduction.

1.2 The problems in the development of undeveloped north Hebei Province

North Hebei has made tremendous progress in economic and social development and ecological environment protection for more than a decade. But the development gap among north Hebei and Beijing, Tianjin, especially Hebei has been enlarged. With deeply development of the coordinated development of BTH, several development problems has been emerged gradually, which restricted the sustainable development of north Hebei.

1.2.1 The gap with surrounding areas is widen, failing to develop coordinately

Comparing to Beijing and Tianjin, the disparities of economic strength, living condition and public service in north Hebei are apparent. The following part analyzes the disparities.

(1) Economic disparity has been widening. Although economic growth rate of north Hebei is faster than that of Beijing and Tianjin, because of a small base, the disparity has been continually widening since 2005. In 2015, the disparity among north Hebei and Beijing-Tianjin amounted to 3678.459 billion yuan, the number is almost 4 times of that in 2005 (970.228 billion yuan). The disparity of Revenue in the general public budget is 716.05 billion yuan, almost six times of that in 2005 (121.26 billion yuan). The disparity of GDP per capita among north Hebei and Beijing-Tianjin reaches about 70 thousand yuan, two times and 2.8 times especially than that of Zhangjiakou (35,000 yuan) and Chengde (25,000 yuan) in 2005. The economic aggregate of north Hebei is still less than one-eighth of Beijing and one-sixth of Tianjin in 2015. General fiscal revenue is less than five percent of Beijing and nine percent of Tianjin, GDP per capita is less than one-third of that of Beijing-Tianjin (see Table 5 and Figure 1).

(2) The disparity of per capita income has been enlarging. In 2015, the disparities of per capita disposable income of urban households among north Hebei and Beijing-Tianjin are about 30,000 yuan (Beijing)and 10,000 yuan (Tianjin), about two times and one

time than that of Beijing-Tianjin in 2005 (10,000 yuan and 5,000 yuan). The absolute disparity has been continually enlarging. In 2015, per capita disposable income of urban households in Zhangjiakou and Chengde are 23,841 yuan and 22,885 yuan, less than half of that in Beijing, the same as two third of that in Tianjin. Per capita disposable income of rural households are 8,341 yuan and 7,923 yuan, the same as 40 percent of that in Beijing, less than half of that in Tianjin, the level is rather low (see Table 6 and Figure 1).

Table 5 Comparison of economic and social development in north Hebei and BTH

	GDP (billion yuan)		GDP per capita (yuan)		General public budget revenue (billion yuan)	
	2005	2015	2005	2015	2005	2015
Hebei	1,009.6	2,980.6	14,737	40,143	51.6	264.9
Beijing	681.45	2,296.86	44,969	106,284	91.92	472.39
Tianjin	366.386	1,653.82	35,457	106,908	33.174	266.699
Zhangjiakou	41.579	136.35	9,945	30,837	2.104	13.299
Chengde	36.029	135.87	10,723	38,489	1.73	9.74

Sources: *Hebei Economic Yearbook* (2006, 2016), *Beijing Economic Yearbook* (2006, 2016), *Tianjin Economic Yearbook* (2006, 2016), *Zhangjiakou Economic Yearbook* (2006, 2016), and *Chengde Economic Yearbook* (2006, 2016).

Table 6 Comparison of incomes of urban and rural residents in north Hebei and BTH

Unit: yuan/ Person

	Per capita disposable income of urban households		Per capita disposable income of rural households	
	2005	2015	2005	2015
Hebei	9,107	26,152	3,482	11,051
Beijing	17,653	52,859	7,860	20,569
Tianjin	12,639	34,101	7,202	18,482
Zhangjiakou	7,714	23,841	2,329	8,341
Chengde	7,845	22,885	2,582	7,923

Sources: *Hebei Economic Yearbook* (2006, 2016), *Beijing Economic Yearbook* (2006, 2016), *Tianjin Economic Yearbook* (2006, 2016), *Zhangjiakou Economic Yearbook* (2006, 2016), and *Chengde Economic Yearbook* (2006, 2016).

Figure 1 Comparison of GDP per capita and per capita disposable income of urban and rural households in north Hebei and BTH (yuan)

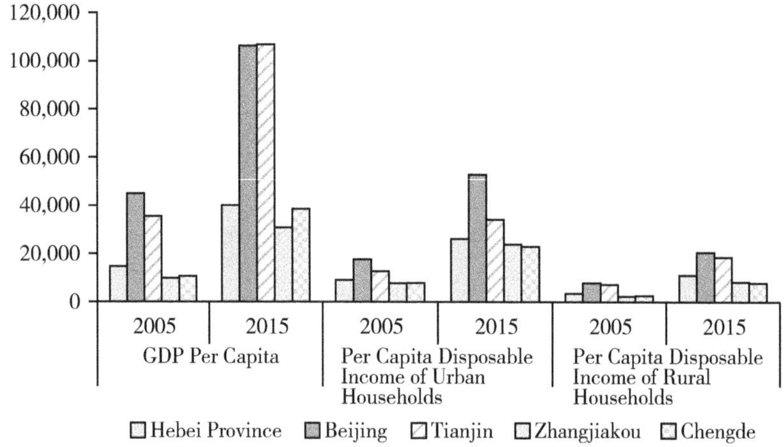

(3) The gap of public service is rather large. In 2015, the number of primary and middle school, and medical technical personnel per 10,000 persons is less than that of Beijing-Tianjin. Basic living allowances of urban residents in Zhangjiakou and Chengde are 420 yuan/month and 450 yuan/month, far less than 710yuan/month and 705 yuan/month in Beijing-Tianjin. Basic living allowances of rural residents in Zhangjiakou and Chengde are 2,250yuan/month and 2,800 yuan/month, less than one third of that in Beijing (8,520 yuan/month), about a half of that in Tianjin (6,480 yuan/month). The allowance to Road Construction for Every Village per kilometer in Beijing is 350,000 yuan, but only 35,000 yuan in north Hebei. Expressway maintenance fee per kilometer is 200,000 yuan in Beijing, however, only 20,000 yuan in north Hebei. Low public service now constrains the development of north Hebei and mobility of talents (see Table 7).

Table 7 Comparison of public service in north Hebei and Beijing-Tianjin

Unit: yuan/month, Person

	Basic living allowances of urban residents	Basic living allowances of rural residents	Minimum wage standard	Medical technical personnel per 10,000 persons
Beijing	710	710	1,720	117.48
Tianjin	705	540	1,850	—
Zhangjiakou	420	187.5	1,210-1,310	41.16
Chengde	450	233.3	1,210-1,310	51.27

Sources: Data of basic living allowances and minimum wage standard of residents are from web, medical technical personnel per 10,000 persons are calculated by the data of yearbooks.

1.2.2 Imperfect transportation infrastructure fails to support regional development

As an important node of the economic corridor of China, Mongolia and Russia (the Belt and Road), a convenient transportation infrastructure is very important for north Hebei to establish and intensify its status of transportation hub. In the past ten years, although there has been a big progress on the construction of transportation infrastructure in north Hebei, the situation of traffic block has been relieved, the varied topography, high cost of transportation infrastructure construction, such as the cost of Yan-Chong expressway is up to 0.2 billion yuan per kilometer, and limited local financial resources of undeveloped regions lead to imperfect traffic, road network density and road quality.

(1) Blocked external transportation. Despite there are many railways in north Hebei, the railways of Da-Qin, Jing-Bao and Jing-Tong belong to Sinotrans coal line, which play a small role on promoting the development of north Hebei. Transport capacity which other railways leave to north Hebei is rather restricted, failing to meet the demand of north Hebei as an important node of business and commerce logistics, there still exists serious contradiction between developed traffic and poor logistics. The framework of expressway has been preliminarily formed, but as most of expressway leading to Beijing, now the transport capacity is very tight, traffic jams and closed roads are rather serious. Some provincial roads and traveling lines which need to connect Beijing-Tianjin and play a big role on promoting the development of north Hebei, due to inconsistent planning and standards, fail to make a progress. Such as now there is a dead end highway between Zhangjiakou and Beijing which is hard to get through, 112 third class bottle neck roads cannot be effectively upgraded, the traveling line between Zhuolu and Mentougou makes tardy progress.

(2) Imperfect internal transportation. Internal transportation network density is quite low. Road density is only 0.56 kilometer per square kilometer in 2015, the same as 41.6 percent of that in Beijing-Tianjin and 57.1 percent of that in Hebei. Meanwhile, due to the limited local financial resources, the standards of highway investment, construction and maintenance are quite low, leading to the poor road quality in north Hebei.

1.2.3 Short of ecological compensation subsidy affects the construction of ecological function region

As the function area of ecological conservation and ecological shelters, north Hebei plays a key role on wind prevention and sand fixation, water and soil conservation in BTH Region. The government has continually increased investment on the ecological construction and played a key role on the improvement of regional ecological environment for many years. However, in the ecological construction process, due to the low standard of ecological subsidy, absence of ecological compensation, short of ecological management expenses, the effectiveness of ecological construction is rather low.

(1) Ecological subsidy is low. Now ecological construction of north Hebei is mainly relied on the input and subsidy of government, but the lower standard of subsidy fails to meet the demand of ecological construction, moreover, the subsidy is far below the cost of construction. In the past decades, in north Hebei, especially Zhangjiakou, the regions which located in better site condition has completed ecological environment conservation. Most of the left regions which is in bad site condition, due to poor soil, arid climate, low survival rate of sapling, plus the rising prices and high cost of ecological construction, now the ecological subsidy are far below the cost of ecological construction. According to the calculation of Huailai forest bureau, the cost of woodland was 800-1,000 yuan per mu, now the cost of the same standard afforestation rises to 3,000-5,000 yuan per mu. However, now the standard subsidy of government afforestation is only 400 yuan per mu, the ecological subsidy is much lower than the cost of afforestation. Comparing to the subsidy standard of Beijing-Tianjin, the ecological subsidy of north Hebei is lower than that of Beijing-Tianjin. In 2014, the subsidy of afforestation in Chengde is 500 yuan per mu, and that in Beijing is 2,000 yuan. The subsidy of wind prevention and sand fixation is 1,000 yuan per mu, and that in Beijing is 4,000-5,000 yuan. The subsidy standard in Chengde is only one forth to one fifth of that in Beijing. The subsidy standard has been reduced in the history of ecological subsidy development. The subsidy to the first round of returning cropland to forest is 2,000 yuan per mu in Chengde, that in the second round is reduced to 1,500 yuan per mu. The low subsidy standard severely restricts the enthusiasm and increases the difficulty of ecological construction in north Hebei.

(2) Ecological compensation is absent. As the function area of ecological conservation and ecological shelters, north Hebei has made great efforts to protect ecological environment. However, due to short of market-oriented ecological compensation mechanism, the financial burden of local government is much heavy. For example, Yangyuan County has undertook lots of ecological debts for historical reasons, in the period of the 13th Five-Year, Yangyuan County has invested one billion yuan each year for the ecological construction, and all the funds are from loans. This is a big burden to a poverty county whose government revenue is only 0.3 billion yuan. For another example, the policy of paddy to dry land has been implemented for water conservation of Beijing-Tianjin, due to short of floating subsidy mechanism

which is linked to the market grain prices, the subsidy to north Hebei is quite low. The subsidy standard was 450 yuan per mu in 2007 and increased to 550 yuan per mu in 2008. But due to changes of grain prices, the losses from paddy to dryland exceed 1,500 yuan per mu. In the Central Water Delivery to Beijing-Tianjin Project undertook by Zhangjiakou and Chengde, the subsidy standard is only 0.3 yuan per cubic meter, moreover, the subsidy is only to manual water delivery management expenses of cities and counties. The development losses brought by water conservation and protection have no yet got any reasonable compensation.

(3) Low subsequent management and protection expenses lead to unsustainable good quality of ecological environment. Now the compensation to protection expenses of collective and individual public welfare forest is 15 yuan per mu, and that of national public welfare forest is 7.5 yuan per mu, far below the protection cost (40 yuan). In recent years, most of ecological shelter forest and shrubbery built by the project of sandstorm source control program in Beijing-Tianjin, conversion of cropland to forest, do not enterthe scope of compensation of public welfare forest, therefore, there are no subsequent protection expenses to them. Based on the calculation of Huailai forest bureau, about 100 thousand mu ecological shelter forest is out of scope of compensation of public welfare forest, the number is near to 120 thousand mu public welfare forest enjoying the compensation. Low compensation and lots of forest out of the compensation scope make a negative influence on the protection of sustainable ecological environment construction.

1.2.4 High-end technology talents are too short to support industry transformation and upgrading

A number of high-end technology talents are needed to support the industry upgrading and the rising of green north Hebei. However, in north Hebei, generally, the population quality is low, personnel training and talent demand are misallocated, and technology input is not enough, which cannot support the transformation and upgrading of north Hebei.

(1) Misallocation of specialty setting and personnel training in colleges and universities and the demand of regional transformation and development.There are 12 colleges and universities in north Hebei, only 10 percent of that in Hebei. Specialties are most concentrated on medical science, agriculture, architectural engineering, normal specialty, and so on. The specialties in secondary vocational schools are focused on machining and manufacturing, information technology, animal husbandry and fishery.The specialties, which are badly needed by regional transformation and development, such as mechanical electronics, landscape architecture, ecological environment, software, new energy, tourism and

electronic commerce, are rather weak or vacant. Talents in relevant specialties are badly short and fail to meet the demand of industrial development.

(2)Small number of total talents. The proportion of R&D (Research and Development) personnel in Industrial Enterprises above Designated Size (IEDS) to the population in north Hebei is only 0.6 percent, below the level (1%) of Hebei Province. Only one expert is Thousand Talents Program scholar and one expert belongs to Hundred Talents Program in north Hebei. High-end technology talents, top innovative and entrepreneurial talents, leading talents who have independent intellectual property rights and master core technology, talents and teams who can support industry transformation and upgrading are badly short.

(3)Lack of technology investment. In 2015, the numbers of IEDS which have R&D are 78 in north Hebei, only seven percent of total IEDS, two percent below the level of Hebei Province. The expenditure of R&D in IEDS is 1.307 billion yuan, 1.5 percent of industrial added value, less than 60 percent of the average level of Hebei Province. The technology funds and investments on technology talents are not enough, restraining the capacity of technology innovation in north Hebei. Industrial Added Value (IAV) of high and new technology industryabove designated size are only 11.346 billion yuan in 2015, 13 percent of IAVabove designated size, 3% below the average provincial level (see Table 8).

Table 8 Technology investment in north Hebei and Hebei Province

	Hebei	Zhangjiakou and Chengde	Zhangjiakou	Chengde
Number of IEDS with R&D	1,388	78	42	36
Number of IEDS	15,295	1,113	564	549
Proportion of IEDS with R&D to IEDS	9.07%	7.01%	7.45%	6.56%
R&D personnel of IEDS	79,049	5,127	2,378	2,749
Internal expenditure of research funds (Billion yuan)	28.58	1.307	0.634	0.673
IAV of IEDS (Billion yuan)	1,124.5	87.28	40.47	46.81
Proportion of Internal expenditure of research funds to IAV of IEDS	2.54	1.5	1.57	1.44
Full-time equivalent of R&D personnel (person/per year)	79,452	3,102	1,597	1,505
Number of colleges and universities	118	12	6	6

Notes: IEDS means Industrial Enterprises above Designated Size, IAV is Industrial Added Value.

Sources: *Hebei Economic Yearbook* (2016), *Zhangjiakou Economic Yearbook* (2016), and *Chengde Economic Yearbook* (2016).

1.2.5 Bad soft and hard development environment cannot stimulate vigor and energy

North Hebei is not only the ecological shelter of Beijing-Tianjin but also important security shelter and moat of north Beijing, playing the role of safeguard the capital. So Zhangjiakou was opening up in 1995, 17 years later than the whole nation, leading to the low capacity of innovation and weak sense of opening.

(1) Poor government service environment. Government sectors' consciousness of streamlining administration and delegating more powers to lower-level governments and to society in general while improving regulation, and optimizing services is rather weak, the environment to respect, favor, comfort and enrich merchants is poor. Administrative examination and approval is not separated from inspection, evaluation and technical review. The coexistence of offside and absence of government function induce that the development vigor is not enough in north Hebei. The proportion of private economy IAV to GDP in Zhangjiakou and Chengde are respectively 59.07% and 63.86%, 8.66% and 3.87% lower than the provincial average level 67.73%.

(2) Lack of security mechanism for industrial upgrading elements. We still lack the incentive mechanism for industrial upgrading. The mechanism of making science and technology small and medium enterprises bigger and stronger which play an important incentive role on industrial upgrading, Green and low-carbon transformation of traditional industry, Beijing-Tianjin mutual recognition of high-tech enterprise are imperfect. Enterprise financing mechanism is inflexible, financing channel is single, co-guarantee loan of enterprise and guarantee Corporation develop very slowly, ecological environment, industrial development and industrial park construction just make a little progress. Socialized financing capacity is rather weak. Evaluation and incentive mechanism of talents, talents introduction and management mechanism, Beijing-Tianjin mutual recognition of qualification and titles of employees is imperfect, the seniority system and official-oriented thought are serious.The management of coding is rigid; the phenomenon of posts without coding is prominent, severely restraining regional innovation capacity.

(3) Inflexible industrial park management mechanism. The fruits of attracting investments are not linked with the performance-related pay of personnel. Teams with good political and professional quality who master policies, regulations and industrial development are not perfect. The guidance, assistance and agent arrangement mechanism is needed to continually improve. There are no overall planning of where projects are landing, how to share finance and tax. There still exist the phenomenon different regions fight for projects by reducing land price and raise subsidy,

inducing that industrial park fail to become bigger and stronger.

1.2.6 Income growth is slower than expenditure increase of poverty people, the quality of life is hard to improve

Hebei has made a big progress in poverty alleviation for decade, the size of poverty population has dropped dramatically, quality of poverty people's life has been improved continually, however, being restricted to variety of factors, poverty people have difficulties in increasing incomes, income growth is rather slow. Meanwhile, expenditure rigidity is continually enhanced. Income growth and expenditure increase hang upside down, some poverty families spend more than their incomes. Thereafter, all these factors influence life quality of poverty people in north Hebei.

Firstly, income growth of poverty people has been lower than average level for long term. According to the data of rural people by income quintile, per capita disposable income of low-income group rural people in Zhangjiakou and Chengde are respectively 2,336.33 yuan and 2,957.21 yuan, 2.3 and 2 times than that in 2005 (703.52 yuan and 992.36 yuan), but lower than the average growth level (3.2 and 2.4 times) in Zhangjiakou and Chengde. The gap of poverty people income and the average level has been increased from 1∶3.1 and 1∶2.5 to 1∶4.0 and 1∶2.9 (see Table 9).

Secondly, consumption expenditure rigidity has been enhanced. Income growth of poverty people is lower than the average level, but the increase of consumption expenditure is faster than average level. Per capita consumption expenditure of low-income group rural people reach 5,045.7 yuan and 5,477.6 yuan in Zhangjiakou and Chengde, increasing 3.6 and 3.1 times than that in 2005 (1,097.1 yuan and 1,344.7 yuan), and higher than average increase of expenditure (1.8 and 1.4 times), the ratio of income to consumption has been enlarged from 1:1.5 to about 1:2. Further analysis found the reason why the increase of consumption expenditure is higher is that housing expenditure is quite high and the growth is very fast, while proportion of medical care, culture and education expenditure is also large. In 2015, the proportions of these three expenditure in Zhangjiakou and Chengde are 44.97% and 42.25%, increasing 5.98% and 3.71% than that in 2005 (see Table 10 and Table 11).

Table 9 Income growth of rural people in north Hebei in 2005 and 2015

	Average income			Average income of low-income group		
	2005	2015	Growth	2005	2015	Growth
Zhangjiakou	2,198.34	9,241.22	4.20	703.52	2,336.33	3.32
Chengde	2,450.85	8,439.59	3.44	992.36	2,957.21	2.98

Sources: Household survey data of Hebei Investigation Corps of the National Bureau of Statistics.

Table 10 Expenditure increase of rural people in north Hebei in 2005 and 2015

	Average expenditure			Average expenditure of low-income group		
	2005	2015	Growth	2005	2015	Growth
Zhangjiakou	2,518.6	6,979.1	2.77	1,097.12	5,045.65	4.60
Chengde	2,869.2	6,864.8	2.39	1,344.66	5,477.64	4.07

Sources: Household survey data of Hebei Investigation Corps of the National Bureau of Statistics.

Table 11 Consumption structure changes of low-income group rural residents in north Hebei in 2005 and 2015

Unit:%

	Zhangjiakou		Chengde	
	2005	2015	2005	2015
Foods	40.47	37.86	38.96	32.66
Clothing	8.14	5.43	7.78	5.98
House	13.72	16.78	16.22	20.68
Households Facilities, supplies and services	2.93	3.2	4.22	3.6
Transportation and communication	8.07	7.78	8.77	14.07
Culture and education, entertainment products and services	18.67	14.16	9.43	9.93
Medical care	6.6	14.03	12.89	11.64
Other goods and services	1.41	0.77	1.73	1.46

Sources: Household survey data of Hebei Investigation Corps of the National Bureau of Statistics.

1.2.7 Deep poverty area is rather wide, poverty alleviation has much difficulties

Poverty alleviation has made a big progress in north Hebei; the overall appearance of region has been greatly improved. However, there are still eight counties which belong to deep poverty counties, accounting for 38% of all counties. Poverty population is 490,000 and 50% of the population in north Hebei. Theseregions locate in Bashang region and belong to mountainous region, weak ecological environment, frequent natural disasters, undeveloped transportation, lead to marginalization of the development in these regions. The proportion of poverty population and poverty rate are quite high. For example, Yangyuan county locates in mountainous area, barren land, less rainfall (Average rainfall has been only 365 millimeter for many years), poor agricultural production conditions (Average content of organic matter in soil agricultural horizon is only

13.19 g/kg, the number is lowest in Zhangjiakou even in Hebei Province), remote geographical position lead to marginalization in regional development and Yangyuan county is out of many policies of coordinated development and ecological environment protection. Sanggan River is an important branch of Yongding River, but Yangyuan County where Sanggan River flows through is out of the scope of the construction of Beijing-Hebei water conservation forest. Moreover, Yangyuan County is also not listed in the Beijing-Hebei counterpart assistance counties in Zhangjiakou and Chengde. Now there is 50,000 poverty populations in Yangyuan County. Poverty rate is 25%, 10% more than the average level in north Hebei, amounting to the poverty level ten years ago in north Hebei. Therefore, the key point and the difficulties of poverty alleviation in north Hebei lie in these deep poverty areas. Poverty alleviation policy should be continued to focus on these areas, supporting poor people to cast off poverty and get rich.

The development of north Hebei has made a big progress for a decade, the overall appearance of poverty region has been greatly improved. However, big disparity comparing to surrounding areas is the short board in the coordinated development of BTH. The main task of regional development has transformed from eliminating absolute poverty to enhancing development ability and achieving sustainable development. However, now the problems of transportation, ecological environment, talents and environment hinder high-end elements gathering in north Hebei, affecting industrial upgrading and green rising of north Hebei, decelerating the pace of building the well-off society. Some problems are even bigobstacles to coordinated development of Beijing-Tianjin and north Hebei. Nowadays, north Hebei should seize the opportunity, solve difficulties, build a long-term development mechanism, make up shortages and achieve fast development in the coordinated development of BTH.

2. Overall thoughts on sustainable development of north Hebei Province

2.1 Situations and backgrounds

Compared to ten years ago, no matter its stage of development or external environment of development, north Hebei has had significantly changes which must have profound effects on its future development.

2.1.1 Stage characteristics

At present, the north Hebei has entered a critical period of economic and social transformation. The regional development mode, motivation support, urban-rural structure and income characteristic of impoverished group has had or is having profound changes and present obvious stage characteristics.

(1) Regional development is experiencing the transition from an ecologically-constrained economy to an ecologically friendly economy. Northern Hebei, located in the windward and upstream area of Beijing and Tianjin, is an important ecological shelter, playing the roles in ecological service and food security as "reservoir", "vegetable basket" and "back yard garden" for Beijing and Tianjin. Previously, the development of north Hebei had been severely restricted by ecological requirements. The conflict between regional development and ecological protection was very sharp. The problem how to meet the needs that "the government need a good ecology, the local needs a good development and the people need profit at the same time" has not been solved. Recent years, with the situation that external constraints became more strict,relying on its ecological advantages, north Hebei have searched out an eco-friendly development path. Therefore, the north Hebei is experiencing the transition from an ecologically-constrained economy to an ecologically friendly economy. First, relying on its ecological advantages, renewable energy, cultural tourism, health-enhancing leisure, fitness sport, big-data, cloud computing and other eco-industries in north Hebei, with a rapid development in an enlarged scale, have bloomed into an important drive of local economic development and become important engines of industry transformation. Second, relying on its good ecological environment, north Hebei has established a set of undertaker and platform near the capital such as Huailai County, Zhuolu County and Luanping County with beautiful environment, full function and prominent features for quality factors of Beijing and Tianjin. The concentrating effect of production factors has begun to emerge and the new poles of economic growth has formed. Third, relying on distinctive location and transportation advantages, in July 2015, the city Zhangjiakou joint with Beijing has succeed in winning the right to hold the next Winter Olympic Games. Therefore, Zhangjiakou has become an important part of BTH coordinated development. Its notability and influence have been substantially increased. The steps of non-capital function dispersal in Zhangjiakou even the north Hebei has been accelerated. It's regional economy and position will continue to go up. Forth, with the further headway has been made with ecological mechanism reforms and continuous ecological input has been put for many years, the ecological environment benefits has begun to emerge: Qiansongba Woodland in Fengning Manchu Autonomous County has finished the first cross-regional carbon emission trade program in China; Chongli City has become the only national first period carbon sink city in north of China. The value of eco-

production has been achieved. It has also fundamentally solved the regional problem that ecology was intertwined with poverty in north Hebei, which laid foundations for making lucid waters and lush mountains become invaluable assets.

(2) Industry development enters the transformation stage from resource-dependent industries to green and low-carbon industries. For a long time, resource-based industries such as the steel industry and the mining industry dominated the north Hebei's economy. For example, the total output value of mineral products and further processing industries in Zhangjiakou, and ferrous metals from the mining, smelting and rolling industries in Chengde accounted for 1/3 and 2/3 respectively of enterprises above designated size in northern Hebei. In recent years, resource-dependent industries have gradually shrunk because of improvements in ecological environment management, especially the implementation of the "6643" project. The north Hebei has strengthened more efforts to phase out the industries such as steel, cement, building materials and mining industry and shut down the pollution factories and cutting overcapacity. During the 12th Five-Year period, steel production capacity was cut by 6.24 million metric tons and iron production was cut by 7.61million metric tons in north Hebei. The output proportion of the ferrous metal rolling industry in all manufacturing industries dropped from 40.11% to 30.13%. Zhangjiakou was entitled "one of the first period cities for the trail of green transformation and development" by the Ministry of Industry and Information Technology. At the same time with the substantial reduction on the conventional resource-based industries, north Hebei has given priority to develop emerging industry such as new energies, new materials, advanced manufacturing and modern service industries, regarding them as the important task of supply-side structural reform and entering the transformation stage to green and low-carbon industries. As for the manufacturing industry, the north Hebei has built up a number of key projects such as Volvo engines and automobile manufacture, BAIC Foton Motor Xuanhua truck-mounted concrete pumps, Qizhi dairy company, wind and photovoltaic storage and transmission. The industries such as equipment manufacturing, automotive vehicles and accessories and food processing have had more contribution to the economy. The scale of high-tech industry such as advanced manufacturing, newenergyand electronics information has been expanded. In 2015, the value created by the high-tech industry rose to 11.346 billion, increased by once than that of 2010, with an annual average growth of 15.61%. The value created by new energy in Zhangjiakou rose to 10.2% of enterprise above designated size industry. Huai'an industrial parks has become one of the first batch of emergency industry demonstration

parks. As for modern service industry, the development of culturaltourism, e-commerce and modern logistics has been accelerated. In ten years, celebrated tourism brand has been built up such as Zhangbei County Grass Skyline, Chongli County skating and Rehe County Royalty Hunting Garden. The income of tourism service has had an annual average growth of more than 33.5%. E-commerce platform Alibaba has developed rapidly. The provincial e-commerce trail in Kangbao County has built up "first-tier, multi-quality, multi-platform" system. In the period from 2005 to 2015, service industry contributed 40.46% of economy growth in north Hebei. It has become the new growth areas with more function as a "stabilizer" for economic growth and "accelerator" for structure adjustment.

(3) Population migration continues the trend of "Two Minus and One Increase". In these ten years, influenced by regional living environment, job opportunity, level of income and other factors, population mobility of north Hebei continued the trend of ten years ago: local residents moved out of north Hebei, migrated from rural area to urban area, and from Bashang region to Baxia region. These migration trends, increasing the urban population, decreasing the rural population and population in Baxia region, can be concluded as the "Two Minus and One Increase" pattern of population migration and distribution. What's more, because of the constant improvement on transportation and information, the migration speed has been increased than that of ten years ago. In 2015, the household population in north Hebei amounted to 8,460,800. It was 509,000 more than resident population. Emigrant population was up to 6.73%. Because of emigration, the population in north Hebei increased slowly and it showed a trend to go down about the account of the population of Hebei Province. In the period 2005-2015, the resident population in north Hebei increased from 7,550,000 to 7,951,800 and rose by 5.32% which is far less than the average increase of Hebei Province. The portion of the entire province was dropped from 11.02% to 10.71%. When a large population emigrated, the speed of rural-urban migration also increased. From 2007 to 2015, the population of urban area in Zhangjiakou and Chengde had increased from 914,000 to 1,113,700 and from 505,500 to 683,400 respectively (the data was estimated based on the 1% of population sample). Zhangjiakou had listed as a big city. The priority position as a central city was lifted and the combined effect of central city had gradually appeared. From 2010 to 2015, the resident population in the towns of north Hebei increased by 461,700 from 1,750,700 to 2,212,400. The resident population in the countryside decreased by 993,100 from 6,470,700 to 5,477,600. In Bashang region, the population gradually decreased. The population of the six

counties Zhangbei, Guyuan, Shangyi, Fengning and Weichang decreased 33,600 from 1,617,000 to 1,583,400.

(4) Main income sources of peasants shift from agriculture work to off-farm employment. Limited by the low level of urbanization, undeveloped city economy, the secondary, and tertiary industries job opportunities, a large amount of labor force had to work in conventional and inefficient agriculture sector. The number of employees in the primary industry was higher than the other two. Agriculture was the main source of farmers' income. With the rapid urbanization, growth of secondary and tertiary industries has been speeded up, accelerating the transfer of labor force from agriculture industry to manufacturing and service industries. People's wage has increased rapidly. At the same time, the reform of property right systems has accelerated the right circulation of agricultural land and forest land. The profit linked mechanism "enterprise+cooperative+farmer" has gradually formed. Farmers can "get rent" by circulating the land management right, "become shareholders" by inputting their poverty relief funds, "earn wages" by working on location, " gain dividend" by collectivizing resources like land and become a shareholder of cooperatives. All of these pattern has emerged and farmers' income sources have tended to be various. The influence of system reforms has gradually appeared. Farmers' transfer payment has increased. According to statistics, the proportion of agriculture operating income in Zhangjiakou and Chengde dropped from 43.77% to 37.6% and from 30.72% to 22.38% respectively from 2010 to 2015, both of the two cities dropped by more than 8%. Personal income proportion from secondary and tertiary industries (including wage, transfer payment and property income) has increased by 6.17% from 56.23% to 62.4% and by 8.35% from 69.28% to 77.63% respectively(see Table12).

Table12 2010-2015 structure change of farmer per capita income in north Hebei (%)

Indicators	2010		Indicators	2015	
	Zhangjiakou	Chengde		Zhangjiakou	Chengde
Farmers' net average income per person	100.0	100.0	The per capita disposable income of farmers	100.0	100.0
Wage	42.90	59.04	Wage	42.46	62.30
Agriculture operating income	43.77	30.72	Net agriculture operating income	37.60	22.38
Net property income	2.50	3.42	Net property profit	1.64	1.89
Net transfer payment	10.83	6.80	Net transfer profit	18.30	13.44

Source: a rural area residences survey from Survey Office of the National Bureau of Statistics in Hebei.

(5) Urban construction enters the transformation stage from simply scale expansion to attaching equal importance to scale and quality. The ten years from 2005 to 2015 is a critical period for urban construction and development in north Hebei. Zhangjiakou and Chengde has grabbed the historical opportunities such as new types of urbanization and "three-year reconstruction" and worked hard on city construction. The city scales have enlarged while urban frameworks have expanded. At the end of 2015, Zhangjiakou administrative reorganizing proposal was passed by State Council of the People's Republic of China. The central cities were expanded from three groups of town to five groups, with the area expanded from 868.96 km^2 to 6,377.81 km^2. The urban district area rose from seventh largest to first in Hebei Province in terms of size. Its population increased from 1,113,700 to 1,754,200 and rose to fourth in the province. Urban built-up area in Chengde expanded from 97 km^2 in 2010 to 112 km^2 in 2015. The scale of central cities enlarged while urban functions and carrying capacity were gradually improving. The construction of infrastructure and public service equipment such as urban roadside green-land, underground pipeline network, wastewater reuse and internet communication has been accelerated. The service function such as trade and shopping, public health and medical services, culture and entertainment, leisure and fitness has been improved. Zhangjiakou has become the first "National Forest City". Chengde has successfully built up "National Garden City" and has been entitled "China Top Ten Leisure Characteristic City". All towns have completed construction of sewage treatment facilities and central disposal for garbage.The "production, education and urbanization" integrated development pattern has been generalized to the entire province. A livable and workable environment has formed. The construction of Smart Cities, the integration of "the three networks"(the telecommunication network, the television broadcast network and the Internet) has been accelerated. As a result, Chengde has been in the list of provincial "Smart City trial cities". The level of digital and network-based city framework has been significantly improved. The digitization of city planning and management, intellectualization of infrastructure, and the accessibility of public services has been well promoted.

2.1.2 Development Opportunities

(1) Zhangjiakou will join Beijing to hold the 2022 Winter Olympic Games, which will make its notability and influence substantially increase. It has given new drivers for the expansion of opening up in Zhangjiakou, and even other cities in north Hebei, forming new media for the two wings pattern of Zhangbei County and Xiong'an New Area's coordinated development and bringing new opportunities to accelerate BTH world-class metropolitan cluster

construction .

(2) In the 13th Five-Year period, Chinese national government will launch a series of policy arrangements on ecological civilization construction and mechanism reforms. These reform measures will accelerate marketization and improvement on the diversified compensation mechanisms of ecological conservation, take ecological advantages, realize the value of ecological products and achieve green development in north Hebei.

(3) In new era, Chinese government has implemented the national poverty alleviation project which has provided comprehensive and multifacetedpolicy and financial support on infrastructure construction, industry development, ecology preservation and public services. It is supposed to speed up the pace of poverty reduction in north Hebei Province, and provide policy support for establishing a well-off society in this region.

(4) With the promotion of coordinated development in BTH Region, transportation integration was the first to have a breakthrough. The interurban transportation from Beijing and Tianjin ring to Zhangjiakou and Chengde has begun to construct one after another. The seventhring of Beijing will be opened to traffic. The capacity of Zhang Cheng airport has been improved. The gradually completed transportation system has paved the way for accelerating the development of north Hebei.

(5) In the 13th Five-Year period, the acceleration of energy structure adjustment and power mechanism reforms nationwide will promote the development of renewable energy such as wind, solar and pumped storage to enter a golden age and provide support for fostering new mainstay industry, accelerating industry transformation and achieving green development in north Hebei.

(6) With the background of coordinated development in BTH Region, the removal of non-capital functions from Beijing, relying on the ecological environment with blue sky, lucid waters and lush mountains, will create opportunities for north Hebei to undertake some functions of scientific research, education and medical service, culture and sports, and to develop health care and elder care, leisure tourism and culture creation industries.

2.1.3 Challenges

(1) The functional orientation of north Hebei is the ecological preservation area of the BTH Region. It requires to give priority to improve some functions of ecological protection system, water conservation, tourism and leisure and supply of green products, and to build up BTH ecology security barrier and national ecological civilization demonstration zone. The enhancing on regional ecology position and function will raise higher requirements for north Hebei to change development

mode and integrate the concept of green development into the whole process and all aspects of modernization.

(2) With the deep promotion of coordinated development in BTH Region, north Hebei's development of ecological society has been significantly improved. Compared to the rest region of the province, constrained by the weaker supporting capacity to economic development and less satisfactory infrastructures, north Hebei is at a disadvantage in the competition of undertaking non-capital function transfer and attracting productive factors.

(3) Growing pressure from regional ecological environment preservation makes achieving industry transformation and green development become a urgent need. Exit mechanisms of traditional industries driven by administrative power didn't coordinate with emerging industry promoting mechanisms, which will threaten the transformation of economic growth mechanism.

(4) Fragile ecosystem and lacking resource in north Hebei lead to the problem that the poverty issues in this region are very severe and poverty reduction is costly. Meanwhile, achieving a comprehensive well-off society is faced with severe problems due to unsatisfactory public services, infrastructures and ecological construction.

2.2 Development ideas

In the future, enhancing development capacity should be the strategic focus for sustainable development; creative coordinated development should be the strategic beginning for sustainable development; restructuring ecological regional development should be the strategic underpinning for sustainable development; achieving full values of ecological products should be the strategic approach for sustainable development, optimizing the development environment should be a strategic guarantee for sustainable development, making north Hebei become a win-win situation for the economy and the ecology demonstration zone.

2.2.1 Enhance self-development capacity

Continuously enhancing regional development capacity is the real solution to eliminate regional poverty in north Hebei, and narrow the development gap with surrounding areas. The core of strengthening regional development ability is to foster and develop new emerging strategic underpinning industries. At present, the conventional resource-based industries, limited by the resource environment and market, has a trend of downturn. On the contrary, emerging ecological and green industries have a good momentum. Whereas they are still small-scale, short-chain and low-level. Therefore, it is urgent to expand industrial scale, extend industrial chain and improve industrial level, so as to offset the gap originated from economic downturn, and stimulate sustainable and stable development.

2.2.2 Innovative coordinated development mechanism

Northern Hebei Province, adjacent to Beijing and Tianjin, is the key area in the implementation of the coordinated development strategy of BTH Region. The region has had multiform and multichannel cooperation on ecology management, industries joint and targeted aid. However, at present, limited by the framework arrangement, normalized and institutionalized mechanisms have not yet been formed in terms of regional coordinated development and counterpart-assistance between north Hebei and Beijing-Tianjin. The historical opportunities brought by the strategy of coordinated development in BTH Region, should be seized. Therefore,at the same time with the government playing the leading role, it is necessary to play the enterprises' main role, to innovate market-oriented mode, to explore coordinated development mechanism and to improve the ability and level of coordinated development in the fields of ecological environment protection, industrial and trade cooperation, non-capital function dispersal, personnel training and communication, infrastructure construction and so on.

2.2.3 Reconstruct regional development framework

Oriented as an important water conservation functional area in the BTH Region, the special ecology function orientation requires regional development to regard expanding supply of ecological products and enhancing regional ecology function as the premise. But at present, north Hebei is far below requirements of ecological conservation in terms of land use structure, industrial development system, urban development layout and ecological construction. Therefore, in the process of north Hebei development, it is necessary to speed up the construction and adjustment in terms of a land use structure consistent with the ecological function, a green industry system consistent with the ecological and economic win-win pattern, an urban-rural development system consistent with the carrying capacity of resource and environment, and ecological protection system consistent with the requirements of ecological protection, in order to meet requirements of the water conservation functional area.

2.2.4 Realize the value of ecological products

Achieving full values of ecological products is an important guarantee for ecological civilization construction and an important aim for promoting ecological civilization mechanism reforms. Northern Hebei, as an important ecological shelter, plays important roles on persevering water and preventing wind(sands), providing high-quality organic products and services for the BTH Region. Because ecological products and services is complex and diversified, it's difficult to precisely identify people who benefit from production of these environment-friendly products and services. Despite receiving certain compensation from central government, the value of eco-products is still far from being fully recognized. Therefore, it is necessary to accelerate the exploration of effective and diversified mechanisms for the value realization of eco-products and services, aiming at making lucid waters and lush mountains become invaluable assets and reaching a win-win situation for the economy and the ecology.

2.2.5 Optimize the development environment

The essence of optimizing the development environment is to build the core competitive advantages of regional development. The aim of preserving and improving the development environment is to increase the competition chips. Compared to other areas of BTH and developed coastal cities in China, except having advantage on ecological environment, north Hebei has poorer soft and hard environments for development, especially shows on undeveloped infrastructure construction, a less complete system of industries, lacking of guarantee of advanced factors and undeveloped public services, which lead to north Hebei in a disadvantageous position. Therefore, it is necessary to strengthen infrastructure construction, enhance the overall quality of the population and the labor force, improve support for innovation and entrepreneurship, and reshape the business environment to build the core competitive advantage of regional development.

2.3 Strategic task

In the future, north Hebei will enter a critical period of achieving sustainable development. Northern Hebei should focus on constructing win-win situation for the economy and the ecology demonstration zone and continually strengthening regional water conservation function. At the same time, the area should accelerate construction of a land use structure, a green industry system, and a development layout of urbanization and ecological protection system consistent with the ecological function development. It should also comprehensively enhance regional development capacity areas and narrow the development gap with surrounding.

2.3.1 Construct the land use structure consistent with the ecological function

The construction of ecological and water conservation functional zone in north Hebei provides high quality ecological environment and ecological services. It has to have two conditions: on the one hand, it has to have sufficient ecological space; on the other hand, it has to maximum the ecological benefits in per ecological space unit. Especially, sufficient ecological space is the premise and fundamental.

From the general condition of the north Hebei, grasslands and forests area add up to 3,847,000 hectares, ecological space accounts for more than 50% of total area so ecological space is relatively sufficient. But for some areas,ecological space is unbalanced distributed and land use structure is unreasonable,especially it can be seen in Chengde and Zhangjiakou. Chengde has relatively sufficient ecological space accounting for 63.4% of total area in the city; whereas Zhangjiakou's ecological space is severely insufficient and only accounted for 36.4%, 15% lower than the entire area. At the same time, land used for building, cultivated land, plantation land and other farming land account for 35.8% with a relatively higher land reclamation rate(see Table 13).

With a further analysis, Bashang area in Zhangjiakou, except grasslands and forests, the territorial development area is almost 580,000 hectares, accounting for more than 42% of Bashang area. Among them, cultivated land has 490,000 hectares , accounting for up to 36%. Bashang area is one of the most vulnerable areas of ecological environment in Hebei Province. Natural calamities such as sandstorms and droughts happened frequently. Furthermore, intensive development and land reclamation strongly interrupt the ecological environment. All of these exacerbated the vulnerable ecological environment, bring the threat of desertification and alkalization to the land.

Therefore, in order to improve the ecological protection function, Zhangjiakou should adjust its land use structure, decrease the quota of cultivated land and increase quota of grasslands and forests to form a new regional land use structure dominated by ecological land. Comprehensive considering regional ecological status and land use base, based on current land use structure, the area, especially for Bashang area, should continue the "Grain for Green" program, sharply decrease cultivated land and increase grasslands and forests to achieve the grasslands and forests area's proportion changing from current 36.5% to 50%. At the same time, the proportion of cultivated land should be adjusted to 12%. The land use structure of Chengde should be maintained. After the adjustments, the ecological land use space dominated by grasslands and forests will account for 65%, cultivated land will account for 10%, the other use land including plantation land, other farming land, land used for building and unused land will account for 25%(see Table 14).

Table 13 Study on the use of land in north Hebei in 2015

Unit: 10,000 hectare, %

	Less developed regions in north Hebei		Chengde		Zhangjiakou	
	Area	Proportion	Area	Proportion	Area	Proportion
Total area	762.8	100.00	394.9	100.00	367.9	100
Cultivated land	133.2	17.46	40	10.13	93.2	25.33
Plantation land	27.9	3.66	13.6	3.44	14.3	3.89
Wooded land	344.5	45.16	234.5	59.38	110	29.90
Grassland	40.1	5.26	16.0	4.05	24.1	6.55
Other farming land	13.3	1.74	5.1	1.29	8.2	2.23
Land used for building	28	3.67	11.9	3.01	16.1	4.38
Unused land	175.8	23.05	73.7	18.66	102.1	27.75

Source: provided by Zhangjiakou and Chengde.

Table 14 North Hebei ecology-dominated land use structure in mid and long-term

Unit: 10,000 hectare, %

	Zhangjiakou				Chengde		North Hebei			
	Before adjustment area	Before adjustment proportion	Before adjustment area	Before adjustment proportion	Area	Proportion	Before adjustment area	Before adjustment proportion	Before adjustment area	Before adjustment proportion
Total area	367.9	100.00	367.9	100	394.9	100	762.8	1	762.80	100
Cultivated land	93.2	25.33	44.15	12	40	10.13	133.2	17.46	84.15	11.03
Grasslands and forests land	134.1	36.45	183.95	50	250.5	63.43	384.6	50.42	434.45	56.95
Other land	140.6	38.22	139.80	38	104.4	26.44	245	32.12	244.20	32.01

Source: provided by Zhangjiakou and Chengde.

2.3.2 Construct a green industry system consistent with the Ecological and Economic Win-Win Pattern

Taking the road of win-win situation for the economy and the ecology not only can we construct a good ecological conservation function zone, but also it is the requirement and inevitable choice to accelerate getting rid of regional poverty. The area should follow the approaches-industrialization of ecological construction and greening of industrial development, put efforts to build up the green industry system which takes big ecological industry as an advantage, led by renewable energy industry and be characterized with big data industry.

(1) Forster the ecological industry and create industries with advantages of benefiting and enriching people. The biggest advantage is the good ecological environment. In BTH, fog and haze is difficult to deal with in a short time. As a result, fresh air, healthy water and green food have become scarce resources chased by more and more urban residents. Adjacent to Beijing and Tianjin, north Hebei is the first choice for residents from Beijing and Tianjin to relax, keep fitness and healthy. The area should stand on the base and advantages of ecology, establish the "ecological+" thinking, integrate and amplify the natural ecology with the characterized resources such as hot springs, ice and snow, culture agricultural products, vigorously develop big ecology industries which provide amusement, entertainment, health care, fitness services for the urban residents of Beijing and Tianjin, create well-known leisure and health care brands. First, ecotourism. Following the all-for-one tourism concept, the area should deeply mine unique resources, and vigorously shape the four major brands: the skiing and hot springs, Inner Mongolia, folkways appreciation, history and culture to create a international tourism destination which based on Beijing and Tianjin, facing North China even the whole world. Second, leisure and health care industries. Relying on the quality resources such as natural oxygen bar, hot spring and genuine medicinal materials, the region should construct a large batch of health industry park, and health care and elderly care bases, promote combined medical and elderly care service to become an influential health industry gathering place in China. Third, forestry. The region should actively explore marketization afforestation and ecological forest development pattern, develop and strengthen ecology management and protection services including the protection forest management, forest fire prevention and anti-epidemic, forest and grass breeding series, and ecological workers training. Fourth, agriculture and agricultural sideline product processing industry. Taking the opportunity of holding the Winter Olympics and aiming at the high-end consumer market, around the meat and milk, grapes,vegetables,

potatoes, fruits, edible fungus, eggs and other agricultural products and their deep processing, the region should regard "quality, organic, characteristics" as its direction, put efforts to build a number of modern agricultural industrial park and first-class facilities, first-class standard, modern agricultural industrial park and agricultural products processing enterprises with first-class equipment, the most strict standard, and the best means of detection to create the "Olympic food supply base".

(2) Strengthen the high-end equipment manufacturing industry and create a regional economic development support industry. Advanced devices manufacture is an important direction for industry transformation and upgrading. The machinery manufacturing industry in north Hebei has relatively strong industrial technology foundations. In recent years, under the background of the coordinated development in BTH Region, high-end equipment manufacturing, represented by automobiles and components, has shown a good development trend. The area should rely on the good development foundation, focus on the automobiles and components, special equipment, energy saving and environmental protection equipment, accelerate the extension of industrial chain, building new heights for emerging equipment manufacturing. First, automobiles and components. Following the idea of the whole industry chain, the region should rely on the existing core components and parts projects, gradually expanding to large parts, automobile and automobile related service industries, speed up the gathering of automobile enterprises and driving the research and development, logistics, commerce and trade, services and other related enterprises. Second, the machinery equipment manufacturing industry. Relying on the existing development foundation of the coal machinery and construction machinery, the region should accelerate the development toward the sophisticated and specialized, speed up the development of public safety and emergency equipment, general aviation and aerospace components, aerospace accessory equipment wind and equipment, energy-saving environmental protection equipment, numerical control machine and other emerging equipment industries, to foster the formation of machinery and equipment manufacturing new advantages; Third, intelligentialize and servitize equipment manufacturing. Accelerate the "Internet +" collaborative manufacturing, promote cloud computing, Internet of things, intelligent robots and other technologies in the production process, and strive to improve the equipment manufacturing industry digital and intelligent level. Focus on improving the functions and value-added of products, the region should actively develop service-oriented manufacturing, promote integration between equipment manufacturing

and service industry, promote the transformation of enterprises to the "manufacturing+service" mode, guide enterprises to strengthen research and development, design, sales and other service sectors, to achieve value-added services.

(3) Strengthen the renewable energy industry, build leading industries with green development. Vigorously develop renewable energy industry is an inevitable choice to comply with the trend of world energy reform and to ensure energy security. Especially for the serious atmospheric pollution situation in BTH Region, it urgently needs to accelerate the development of clean energy, change the coal-dominated energy consumption structure. Northern Hebei has rich wind and solar energy resources, also have certain advantages on biomass energy, geothermal energy and water resources. In recent years, with the support of the relevant policies of the Chinese government, the development of renewable energy in the north Hebei is in the ascendant, showing a good momentum. In the future, the area should seize the favorable opportunity of the construction Zhangjiakou National Renewable Energy Demonstration Area, focus on the promotion of taking in and applying electricity, and the trans-regional power outside transmission in this area, eliminate the restriction of institutional mechanisms as the key issue, and rationally and orderly develop various types of energy sources, to ensure the healthy development of renewable energy and to make renewable energy a leading industry in the production and lifestyle reforms in the region. First, development field. The area should, under the premise of controlling the rate of abandoned wind and abandoned light in 5%-10%, promote rational and orderly development of wind and solar resources, continue to expand the scale of new energy installation. Recently new energy power installation scale reached 30 million kilowatts, it will reach 5,000 million kilowatts in long run. It will truly become the new energy power output base of the BTH Region. Second, the absorbing field. According to the requirement of new energy power consumption proportion recently in north Hebei is less than 15% of total social consumption, and not less than 30% of the long-term demand, the region should promote the renewable power electricity to be first to consume; actively promote regional solar roof project, accelerate the high-rise building renovation and popularization of solar heating system; promote solar heat gathering, electric heating, geothermal heating, hot dry rock heating, seasonal heat storage, biomass heating and other projects, expanding the winter coal-fired alternative scale. Third, the export sector. Creative on inter-provincial (urban) electricity trading mechanism, promote renewable energy power to trade online in BTH and even greater area. Fourth, promote integration development of "internet+energy", supported by big data, Internet of

Things and energy storage technology, use the operation mode "self-produce and self-use, connect to internet by the rest electricity and adjust the electricity net", construct all kinds of distributed energy resource, and explore and develop smart energy system.

(4) Developed big data industry and create characteristic industry with inspiration of new momentum. With the development of internet and mobile internet technology, big data industry has a bright development perspective. It and its derivative industries will create and produce a lot of new industry status and value-added services, becoming a stimulus key point for industry transformation and upgrading. Because of its natural cool climate and clean air, north Hebei become the first choice for enterprises to set up data base. For now, the place has gathered a lot of famous enterprises such as Alibaba Group, Soshare and China Electronics Corporation. In the future, following the industry development approach "data storage-data analysis-data application", the area will attract a lot of big data and related industry enterprises, and will build up development bases of new emerging big data industry in north China. First, build up interactive data centers. Relying on the development base already had, based on the Zhangbei cloud computing industry base and Chengde Zhongguancun (China's Silicon Valley) big data core entrepreneurship park, the area should promote to construct cloud computing data centers and data backup centers for core industries, enterprises and public departments so that the big data storage bases will be built up; Second, develop and strengthen big data industries. With the requirement of serving industries, enterprises and public services in BTH, the region will attract, gather and develop a lot of enterprises with good quality such as big data, Internet of Things, Mobile Internet, e-commerce and call center; third, foster big data equipment manufacture industry, take in computer terminal manufacture enterprises, support the development of cloud computing terminals such as Internet of Vehicle products, wearable devices, smart mobile phones, tablet computers, develop data center device manufacture industry such as huge storage, New Generation Network, computer room equipment and New architecture server; forth, develop big data software industry, enhance cooperation with Zhongguancun technology hub, develop a lot of basic software and applications such as platform resource management, cloud security protection, big data storage, data mining and analysis so that give software support for the development of big data industry.

2.3.3 Construct urban-rural development system consistent with the carrying capacity of resource and environment

The ecological environment in north Hebei is vulnerable. It is easy to be devastated by human and difficult to recovery. The land that can be developed and utilized is less than 30% of the total land. The harsh natural conditions and degenerated ecological environment lead to that the limited the population carrying capacity of the area is difficult to support local residents' living and development. The orientation as water conservation functional area in the BTH Region will strengthen the rigid restraint of space developing scale and distribution. Comprehensively considering about population scales, migration trends, infrastructure and ecological requirements, the area will set up a urban-dominated population distribution pattern and a town scale structure with three main parts: central cities, towns and counties, major small towns in the future.

(1) Form an urban-dominated population distribution pattern. In the coming five years or more, the population migration in north Hebei will continually the trend that move to outside and to towns. With the acceleration of urbanization and construction requirements of ecological conservation function, the migration may further accelerate. The population distribution pattern of urban and rural will change from rural-dominated to urban-dominated. In 2015, the urbanization rate in north Hebei was up to 49.8%, 2.2% higher than that in 2014. If develops in the same speed, it will be up to more than 60% by 2020; in ten years, north Hebei will enter the later stage of urbanization and its speed of urbanization will be slowed down. If the annual increase rate count as 1%, then the urbanization rate will up to more than 70% by 2030.

(2) Build up the "three-main-parts" town scale system. Recent years, influenced by rural tourism development, characteristic tourism villages development, returning migrant workers' business set-up and the high barrier of entering central cities, the migration from rural to towns shows trends stable increase in central cities, rapid increase in towns and counties and speed-up increase in major small towns. Take Zhangjiakou as example, in the period from 2010 to 2015, population increase of central cities, towns and counties, major small towns account for 0.32%, 0.83% and 5.88% of the city population. See Table 15. In the coming 5 years or more, with the continually narrowing gap between urban and rural area development and promotion of beautiful village construction, small towns are still the main receivers for rural population migration, and rural population migration will follow the trend of recent years. Based on present trend of population growth, three types of urban population scale will be similar at 20%-25% of total population. The distribution pattern of urban population that central cities, towns and counties, major small towns divided population into three part will be formed. Considering Bashang plateau area is national development-restricted area with special ecological position and vulnerable ecological environment, local governments

should develop county towns as the center population gathering area; in Baxia area, county towns and major small towns can be viewed as population growth poles.

Table 15 The change of the urban population accounting for the total in Zhangjiakou City recently

Unit: %

	Central city population		County population		Organic town population	
	Proportion	Growth rate (%)	Proportion	Growth rate (%)	Proportion	Growth rate (%)
2010	24.91	In five years, it increased by 0.32 percentage points at a rate of 0.06 percentage points per year	15.60	In five years, it increased by 0.83 percentage points at a rate of 0.17 percentage points per year	4.66	In five years, it increased by 5.88 percentage points at a rate of 1.18 percentage points per year
2011	24.93		15.16		6.33	
2012	24.97		15.18		7.48	
2013	24.98		15.39		8.58	
2014	25.08		16.11		8.90	
2015	25.23		16.43		10.54	

Source: Provided by Zhangjiakou and Chengde.

(3) Accelerate the proper concentration of dispersed rural population. Combining with the relocation of poverty alleviation in the new era, the construction of beautiful countryside, and the development of rural tourism and distinctive towns, following the principles of planning guidance and voluntary participation of the masses, we should orderly promote the rural population in areas,which have poor living conditions, fragile ecological environment and frequent natural disasters, to transfer into the earth dam and the mountain basins and the scattered distribution of natural village population to the central village. Also according to the deployment of urbanization, we should speed up the construction of housing for immigrants, complement the public service facilities such as drinking water, travel, electricity and communications, and overall push forward the ecological restoration and protection and the development of green industries for the out-migration areas.

2.3.4 Construct ecological protection system consistent with the requirements of ecological protection.

Around the construction of water conservation functional areas, we should set up ecological protection systems for forests, grasslands, wetlands and soil and water conservation and improve the system for water and energy conservation and intensive use in accordance with local conditions, thus providing ecological and environmental support for the green rise in north Hebei and the coordinated development in BTH Region.

(1) Improve the forest protection system. Focusing on the ecologically fragile areas such as desertified land and serious soil erosion, we will step up efforts in comprehensive harnessing and build an ecological system consisting of the windbreak and sand fixation at the junction of Hebei and Inner Mongolia, the dam-farming protection net, the water conservation zone along the dam and the mountain water and soil conservation network, and expand forest area to give full play to the ecological functions of forests.

(2) Improve the grassland ecological system. With the principle of grass-livestock balance, according to the type of grassland and production capacity, we will rationally formulate a system of banning grazing, delaying grazing and rotational grazing, check the carrying capacity of grassland to fully realize the grass-livestock balance. For the grasslands with poor living environment, serious degradation and unsuitable grazing, we will implement enclosure and grazing prohibition and the policy of ecological reward on Bashang grassland, thus gradually restoring grassland ecological function.

(3) Improve the wetland ecosystem. With the guidance of restoring the historical ecological function of wetlands, famous wetlands in historical period shall be comprehensively restored. We should appropriately increase the proportion of ecological water use in the wetlands which disappear or are shrinking due to lack of water resources, make ecological water supplement and rescue wetlands that degenerate in the middle and lower reaches of the river, and promote returning farmland to wetland and returning grazing to pasture in dam area, thus gradually restoring the original wetland ecological environment.

(4) Improve soil erosion control system. Focusing on the protection of Beijing-Tianjin water source areas, we will promote the soil and water ecological management in the Yongding River, Chaobai River and Luanhe River in accordance with the mode of "enclosure governance in the upstream, development governance in the midstream, and level terrace construction in the downstream", and accelerate the ecological restoration of abandoned mines to further improve the soil and water erosion restoration models in different types of topography and erosion types.

(5) Improve water resources development and utilization system. Focusing on building a water-saving society, we should speed up the construction of a water-saving production and living system based on the principle of "strictly controlling the total water consumption, drastically reducing agricultural water use, controlling industrial water use, fully guaranteeing urban and rural domestic water use, and appropriately increasing ecological water use", so as to constantly improve the efficiency of water

resources development and utilization and optimize the structure of water resources development and utilization.

(6) Improve energy development and utilization system. Taking the clean transformation of energy system as the guide, according to the idea of "strictly controlling the total amount of energy, reducing coal consumption and developing clean energy" and relying on the existing development foundation, we should actively promote the pace of clean energy development and utilization including wind energy, solar energy, geothermal energy, pumped storage, biomass energy and natural gas, thus making the clean energy as the main energy source in the region by 2030.

3. Significant measures to achieve the sustainable development in less-developed regions in north Hebei Province

3.1 Speed up the construction of water conservation function area; explore ways to achieve the value of ecological products

3.1.1 Formulate ecological construction investment standards due to the needs and local conditions

The division of administrative area led to hang upside down phenomenon of input standard and construction condition in the ecological construction in north Hebei and Beijing-Tianjin, that is, Beijing and Tianjin have good site conditions and high investment standards, while the site condition is poor in Hebei Province, and the investment standard is low. In order to promote the ecological integration and protection of the BTH Region, we must break the administrative barriers. That needs to explore and establish a long-term mechanism for regional ecological construction and protection that is consistent with input standards and construction conditions, matching input scale with ecological status, and integrating ecological benefits with protection responsibilities, and establish BTH water conservation function area construction fund considering co-financing by the Central Government and the BTH governments to undertake regional ecological construction and protection, gradually leveling regional ecological input standards.

3.1.2 Explore the establishment of inter-regional land occupation and forest compensation mechanism

The less-developed areas in north Hebei have always taken on the important task of "keeping water, blocking sand and preventing wind" for BTH Region. The Program Outline for the Coordinated Development of the BTH Region strengthens the ecological function and status of this region, and proposes to build a ecological function area with complete ecosystem, relatively good environmental quality and abundant water resources, thus providing ecological security for the coordinated development in BTH Region. Over the years, the Chinese Government has continuously increased its investment in ecological construction in this region and effectively deterred the deterioration of the ecological environment. However, due to the arduous tasks of ecological construction in north Hebei under the new situation and the lack of a long-term ecological construction and protection mechanism, it is unsustainable to rely solely on the ecological construction mode invested by national finance. In order to fundamentally solve the problem of "the state should be ecological, the local areas need to develop, and people want to become rich", it is urgent to innovate the ecological construction and protection investment mechanism. Therefore, on the basis of absorbing the current balance of cultivated land requisition and compensation in Hebei Province, we should explore the implementation of increasing ecological land while occupying cultivated land between ecological functional area and key development zones or optimized development zones. And taking the northern part of Hebei Province as a pilot, pioneer tests should be conducted in advance. While other key development zones or optimized development zones in BTH Region account for one mu of cultivated land, we should invest to construct an additional mu of ecological land for the north Hebei region. The following two options can be considered: First, enterprises need to pay a certain percentage of ecological construction tax to obtain land quota, government departments should set up a management institutions for ecological construction fund to manage funds, which will be partly used directly for ecological construction such as returning farmland to forest and grass. And these funds will also be partly used for expenses of farmers land revenue guarantee and post-management under rules of market-economy and supervision of the relevant departments; second, enterprises, according to quantity of the land occupied, should directly purchase the same amount of the ecological construction land in the north Hebei, and pay seedling fees, labor costs and management fees and so on. The above two solutions can not only solve the insufficient funds for ecological construction to ensure the sustainability of ecological construction, but enhance the ecological security capacity in BTH.

3.1.3 Improve the long-term mechanism of ecological compensation

At present, on the mechanism of compensation for ecological protection, both the Chinese government and the Hebei provincial government have promulgated corresponding opinions and made arrangements for carrying out ecological protection compensation and improving its compensation mechanism. As an important water conservation area and ecological barrier area in BTH, it is urgent for the north Hebei to explore and establish a long-term mechanism of ecological compensation and actively carry out ecological protection and compensation practices in accordance with the spirit of the relevant documents and the regional actual conditions, so as to explore the path and provide experience for pushing forward the realization of the value of ecological products and promoting the ecological beneficiary and protected areas to achieve benign interaction.

(1) Actively promote horizontal ecological compensation pilot. At present, the BTH has not carried out horizontal ecological compensation in the true sense. Even the pilot trial of Tianjin-Hebei water environment compensation conducted in 2016 is only a joint effort to control the water environment for controlling the cage fish culture of Pan-Da Reservoir. Thevefore, it is a long way from compensating for losses suffered due to the transfer of the right to use resources, the loss of the right to development, and the implementation of ecological and environmental standards that are higher than those in other regions. Seizing the opportunity that the state strengthens ecological compensation mechanism, we should actively promote the BTH ecological compensation pilot to accelerate the development of impoverished ecological regions and provide experience for other similar regions that can be copied and promoted. Taking Chaobai River Basin as a pilot, we should actively promote Beijing-Tianjin water resources compensation, determine the water resources compensation standards, methods and ways based on the allocation of basin water use rights, and provide reasonable compensation for the upstream areas while ensuring the water demand in the downstream areas.

(2) Expand the scope of public welfare forest compensation gradually. The north Hebei has played an important role in conserving water resources for Beijing and Tianjin, maintaining soil and water resources, resisting disasters, purifying air, improving climate, carbon sequestration and oxygenation, and biodiversity. Taking the core area of Fengning as an example, the total value of ecological services that can be produced in a total area of seven million mu of forests in the county is 19.5 billion yuan every year (based on the 8th national forest resources verification data), of which a total value of water conservation is 4.8

billion yuan, conservatively reaching up to more than two billion yuan of the annual water supply value for the downstream . At present, about 2/5 of the existing forestland of more than 50 million mu in north Hebei is not included in the compensation range of public welfare forests, seriously affecting the local ecological benefits of forestry. Therefore, all natural forests and man-made forests in the north Hebei should be designated as public welfare forest of Beijing-Tianjin water conservation area. Ecological forests under construction or constructed in the future will all be included in the management of public welfare forests after reaching a certain standard, and will all be included in the support range of the central government's ecological compensation fund for forest ecological benefits.

3.2 Accelerate the construction of high-level platform, build a green transformation carrier

3.2.1 Create a platform for the opening up of the Olympic Games

Beijing and Zhangjiakou jointly bid for the 2022 Olympic Winter Games, which is a major strategic opportunity to rewrite the history of economic and social development in Zhangjiakou and even in the north Hebei. The Olympic Winter Games is not only a large-scale and world-wide sports event for Zhangjiakou, but also builds a platform for the opening up in Zhangjiakou and even in north Hebei. It is of great significance to strengthen international exchanges and cooperation, attract foreign investment, and comprehensively enhance the level and energy level of Zhangjiakou's opening up to the outside world so as to promote the transformation of regional development concept, mode and momentum. Therefore, taking the Olympic Games as the leading platform for regional open development, we should accelerate the construction of an open development environment that is in line with international standards, painstakingly shape the Olympic city brand, comprehensively promote the city's international reputation and influence, speed up the promotion of international economic, technological and cultural exchanges, and actively attract foreign advanced concept, capital and talents, so as to promote the development of open economy in the region.

(1) Enhance the internationalization of Olympic cities. In accordance with the world's vision and international standards, we will improve the internationalization of public service facilities in the main urban area of Zhangjiakou and Chongli Division, and build an international business hotel, foreign restaurant and entertainment, high-end medical service facilities and international convention and exhibition center with a high standard to comprehensively enhance foreign hospitality. In accordance with

international standards, we will improve local laws and regulations, perfect the international legal consultation mechanism, establish a unified service window for foreign personnel, and create a service platform of foreign investment management, so as to provide convenient services for overseas people pass visa and business investment. We will strive to create an international language environment and implement bilingual sign projects in public places. That needs to promote multilingual information navigation systems in public transport, hotels, shopping centers and hospitals in the main urban area and Chongli Division, and speed up the formation of a team of high-quality foreign service talent. Keeping up with the international trend, we should give full play to the ecological low-carbon and historical and cultural advantages, and establish the unique brand image of Zhangjiakou ecology, low-carbon, fashion and passion.

(2) Create high-level international exchange platform. Relying on the high-end convention and exhibition facilities in Chongli Division, we should actively seek to host or undertake the Olympic Summit, Economic Development Forum, China Urban Development Forum, the International Forum on Renewable Energy and other international forum activities to build the East Davos. We should make good use of the Olympics Winter Games to promote Zhangjiakou and Chengde to join hands in introducing a number of international sports events and large-scale cultural activities with high international reputation and brand influence; attract the establishment of international organizations with Zhangjiakou and Chengde as the main office or regional office for international exchanges; jointly organize a group of regular investment promotion conferences in north Hebei, especially investment promotion activities aimed at European and American countries; explore the formation of "internationally renowned entrepreneurs club", and organize well-known entrepreneurs to carry out exchanges and cooperation and investment home inspection in north Hebei.

(3) Create an open economy Relying on the Olympic Games, we should exert the advantage of low-carbon ecology history and culture, and focus on the introduction of advanced talents, technologies and concepts to strengthen cooperation with transnational sports culture, energy conservation and environmental protection, advanced equipment manufacturing, business services and other industries and enterprises, so as to strive to introduce a number of multinational corporations headquarters, regional headquarters, research and innovation centers, procurement and marketing centers and manufacturing bases. We should try our best to develop the characteristic product brand. That needs to embed more local famous products into the humanities, Olympics, ecology

and low-carbon concepts focusing on biology, medicine, electronics, fur, household appliances, energy conservation, environmental protection and agricultural by-products, thus cultivating a group of internationally renowned brands to promote the famous brand of the north Hebei to the world.

3.2.2 Establish a green development demonstration platform

At present, with good ecological environment and resource conditions, the north of Hebei Province has been successfully listed as a national ecological civilization demonstration area, a demonstration pilot city for the construction of national main functional areas, a national demonstration area for renewable energy development, and a pilot city for green transformation and development of national industry. Therefore, the north of Hebei Province is given the top pilot rights and some policy support in the industrial transformation and upgrading, the construction of ecological civilization, strategic transformation of energy and other aspects, thus building a demonstration platform for the regional green development. Taking these national pilot demonstration platforms as an opportunity, we should actively carry out pilot demonstration in institutional innovation, mechanism innovation and system innovation focusing on crucial areas and key links, so as to explore a green growth path suitable for the characteristics of the north of Hebei Province.

(1) Actively carry out various pilot demonstrations. Focusing on the construction of various national pilot demonstration areas, we should speed up formulating relevant implementation plans, make relevant matching rules, and strictly implement the target division of responsibilities in order to provide the basis and guarantee for the construction of pilot demonstration area. In the process of building pilot demonstration areas, according to the facts, we must actively explore and try out practical measures, ways and paths to address the serious problems of the system, institutional obstacles and policies in a spirit of daring to be the first. We should truly combine the national level planning with the actual situation of the region, and implement the policy orientation of the country.

(2) Strive for national policy support. Building various types of national pilot demonstration areas is to boldly test in relevant fields to explore replicable and propagable experience and modes for the development of relevant fields. Objectively, it will face the constraints of the current institutional mechanisms and policies. For example, the construction of Zhangjiakou national renewable energy demonstration area faces the system constraints such as the original energy development planning, renewable energy trading and the formation of renewable energy electricity price, as well as the policy obstacles

in the construction land and passage construction. We can do nothing if relying solely on the local government to solve these problems, but it is urgent for the country to give relevant policy support. Therefore, in the process of building all kinds of pilot demonstration areas, governments at all levels in north Hebei should pull out lists of institutional mechanisms constraints, policy barriers and financial bottlenecks encountered, and actively communicate with relevant parties and strive for the support of national departments through various channels, so as to create conditions for smoothly promoting the construction of pilot demonstration.

3.2.3 Create a new growth pole for urban development

The two central cities, Zhangjiakou and Chengde, are important platforms for population transfer, industrial upgrading and regional Promotion.They are important carriers for improving the image of thecity, expanding open cooperation and integrating into the urban agglomeration of BTH Region. They are the important engines for regional transformation and green development in the future. However, due to the influence of natural topography, there is a serious shortage of the reserve space for the development of the two cities. The central city of Chengde is located along the Wulie River, while the central city of Zhangjiakou is located along the Qingshui River. They both have limited space for urban expansion. Zhangjiakou adjusted the administrative divisions in 2015, which included the original Xuanhua County, Wanquan County and Chongli County into the urban category and Yanghe New District is currently under construction. However, on the one hand, Wanquan and Chongli are relatively far away from the main urban area and have a weak foundation for development, so they are difficult to play a leading role in a short period of time. On the other hand, Yanghe New District is only 30 square kilometers, so it is difficult to undertake the task of expanding urban space and optimizing urban functions. Therefore, it is urgent to learn from the experiences and practices of other cities in Hebei Province. We should select the appropriate relatively open area around the central city to build a modern new city with high-end functions, facilities and industries, thus creating a new growth pole for the development of central cities.

(1) Plan to construct Xuanhua New District. It is suggested that the new district should be selected in the triangular area surrounded by G7, Xuanda Expressway and Zhangshi Expressway, covering Xuanhua City and Shalingzi Town, Chunguang Township, Hezixi Township, Ta'erchun Township, Yanghenan Town, Houjiamiao Township and Gujiaying Town. The area is about 2,000 square kilometers. Located in Zhangxuan Basin, this area has sufficient space for development

with its open flat terrain; located in three high-speed encircling area with the main urban area in the north and the Xiahuayuan District in the south, the district, which has a number of high-speed railways, provincial roads and planning inter-city railways, is a necessary place for the northwest to enter Beijing and has excellent traffic conditions. This region has a relatively better economic basis. Yanghe New District is a demonstrative base of renewable energy achievements and a new city of science and education that Zhangjiakou makes efforts to establish, where now the infrastructure framework has basically taken shape and a number of high-end service enterprises and advanced manufacturing enterprises have been introduced. Xuanhua urban area is an old industrial base with a solid industrial foundation, which now has over 300 thousand population. And in recent years, the surrounding countryside like Jiangjiatun and Ta'ercun have developed rapidly in suburban agriculture and modern service industries such as sports and health, leisure and pensions, cultural tourism. In the future, according to the requirements of building an Olympic city and leading the regional transformation, Xuanhua New District will speed up the development of high-end equipment manufacturing industries such as snow sports equipment, renewable energy equipment, engineering equipment, special purpose vehicles and spare parts and modern service industries such as business exhibition and headquarters economy focusing on Xuanhua urban area and Yanghe New District; and other cities and towns, relying on the existing foundation, accelerate the development of leisure and entertainment, sports health and suburban tourism and other service industries in response to the needs of high-end consumer groups in Beijing and Tianjin. We will plan to construct the urban light rail connecting the main urban area, Xuanhua New District, Xiahuayuan District, Wanquan District and Chongli District, so as to promote the traffic integration between urban areas.

(2) Plan to construct Luanping New District. It is suggested that Luanping New District should be selected in the river valley between Zhangbaiwan Town and Luanping County with an area of over 600 square kilometers, covering Zhangbaiwan Town, Datun Man Township and Luanping Town. Located in the Luanhe River valley, this district is suitable for urban and industrial development with its open and flat terrain, and it's a rare region around the main urban area. There are national road 112, provincial road 353 and 354 and Jing-Tong Railway with convenient traffic conditions. Having Luanping Economic Development Zone and Zhangbaiwan New Industrial Demonstration Zone in this region, it has sound industrial foundation in the fields such as electronic information, food medicine, new building materials, etc. In the future, based

on the requirements of constructing international tourism city and enhancing the visibility and influence of the city, the Luanping New District will focus on the development of high-end service industries such as cultural creativity, technology research and development and business exhibitions relying on its profound historical and cultural heritage, and vigorously develop advanced manufacturing industries such as new materials, bio-pharmaceutical, green food, energy conservation and environment protection with park Industrial upgrading. And we will build a group of landmark buildings that showcase the cultural characteristics of Chengde and organically integrate the mountain, water system, green space and open space with the city to create an international tourist city with its natural ecological atmosphere, historical and cultural aura, and characteristics of that time. At the same time, in accordance with the standards of urban expressways, we will actively promote the upgrading of the existing national highway, smooth the traffic roads in the new district to the main city and the new district to Luanping mouth of Daguang Expressway, in order to build an important support area of the international tourism city and an important growth pole for green growth in the New District.

3.2.4 Promote industrial upgrading supporting platforms

In a decade, great progress has been made in the development of the park in north Hebei, thus forming a group of representative industrial parks such as Zhangjiakou Economic Development Zone, Xishan High-tech Zone, Chengde High-tech Zone, Shuangluan Economic Development Zone, Luanping Economic Development Zone, Weichang Modern Agriculture Demonstration Zone, Zhangjiakou Saibei Management District National Modern Agriculture Demonstration Zone. That supports the growth of regional economy, and drive the rural residents out of poverty and getting rich. Overall, however, the existing industry clusters or industrial parks are still dominated by traditional resource-based industries and are more concentrated in the manufacturing sectors, which is incompatible with the objective requirements of regional green development and transformation and upgrading. At the same time, modern agricultural demonstration parks are small in number and scale and low in grade, which is incompatible with the urgent requirement of vigorously developing the modern agricultural economy in north Hebei and speeding up getting rid of the regional poverty. To this end, efforts should be made from the following two aspects to accelerate the construction of an industrial platform and make it an important engine for promoting green transformation in the region.

(1) Create an "upgraded version" of industrial park development. We should eliminate high-pollution and

high-emission industries in the park which do not meet the functional orientation of water conservation area, and promote the green transformation of traditional industries such as chemical industry, building materials, machinery, food and so on. At the same, we should strictly control the project admission, and formulate industry entry standard system, and accelerate the development of green industries such as high-end equipment, big data, green food and natural mountain spring water by comprehensively considering factors such as industrial relevance, resources and environment friendliness and economic benefits, so as to promote clean production and recycling transformation among enterprises in the park, and promote the recycling and green development of the park. We should abandon the no-focus development mode of "one county, one park". But in accordance with the principle of "concentrating efforts on major issues," we should focus on the development of central city parks, surrounding county parks around Beijing and Tianjin, transportation hub county parks and valley basin county parks, and give support to land quota and funding arrangements. We should support enterprises in the park to extend the production and manufacture into upstream and downstream sectors, and speed up the introduction of research and development design, technological innovation, intermediary services and other enterprises, so as to improve the industrial chain and enhance the competitiveness of the industry. Drawing on the advanced experience, we should carry out new modes of operation and management such as "giant department", "cooperation operation" and "overall trusteeship", and explore new mechanisms for personnel identity, position management and income distribution to fully stimulate the vitality of the park.

(2) Promote the extension of scale and the improvement of quality in modern agricultural demonstration zone. Based on the regional advantages and highlighting the characteristics of the north Hebei, we will speed up the development of agricultural demonstration zones of plant cultivation, high-efficiency fruit and ecological tourism with the principle of "ecology, high-end, specialization, large-scale" to strive to upgrade more existing municipal parks to state-level parks on the existing basis. Drawing on the development mode of Xingchun of Luanping County and Xiaoguan Village of Yangyuan County, we should combine the growth of enterprises, the development of parks and the poverty alleviation of farmers, so as to support the growth of agricultural leading enterprises with the help of poverty alleviation funds and financial capital, and promote the development of modern agricultural parks by leading enterprises, and realize the employment of rural labor force and farmers; poverty alleviation by the

development of parks. At the same time, the agricultural leading enterprises and cooperatives participating in poverty alleviation should be given priority to the preferential policies such as direct subsidies for ecological special industries, subsidized loan interest subsidies, land circulation subsidies, loan guarantee awards, and labor transfer training subsidies. And we should encourage and guide farmers to promote the transfer of land contractual management rights to new types of agricultural operators such as large growers, family farms, farmer cooperatives and agricultural enterprises through such forms as subcontracting, renting, exchange and assignment, and equity cooperation, in order to create conditions for the large-scale agricultural operation and the construction of a modern park. We should guide the agriculture park to develop its third industry relying on industry to promote the integrated development of the three industries, extend the industrial chain of agriculture, and improve the conversion rate and added value of agricultural products, so that we can promote the deep integration of agriculture and tourism, education, culture and other industries, thus achieving the development of agriculture from single production to ecological and life functions.

3.2.5 Build functional dispersal undertak-ing platform

International experience shows that the characteristic town is an important carrier and realization form of the outward spread of the functions of central cities in the era of post-urbanization. At present, there has been the prototype of innovative town around Beijing, Tianjin, Shanghai, Hangzhou and other metropolitan cities. Adjacent to Beijing, the north of Hebei has the unique advantages of developing characteristic towns with its excellent regional conditions and good ecological environment. Especially the built intercity transportation accelerate the pace of urbanization in north Hebei and Beijing-Tianjin which provide good conditions for the rise of characteristic town. Therefore, based on the advanced experience both at home and abroad, and combining with the regional industrial characteristics, cultural heritage and ecological endowment, the north Hebei will build characteristic towns with the integration of industry, city, people and culture, taking the sites along Beijing-Zhangjiakou Intercity Railway and Beijing-Shenyang Passenger Line as key points, the construction of high-speed rail new city as the main carrier and the undertaking of capital functional dispersal as the main direction.

(1) Construct characteristic town according to the local conditions. In Yu County, Jimingyi, Weichang County, Pingquan and other deep culture regions, we will strive to build international cultural tourism towns which can experience history and

culture and highlight cultural creativity and design theme; in the regions with rich health resources such as hot spring town, Chinese medicine planting base, wine growing base and spring water areas, we will create Beijing North leisure and recreation towns highlighting the theme of health where we can enjoy the environment of landscape resources; In the surrounding areas of the central city or around Beijing and Tianjin which has convenient transportation, regional advantages, better foundation, we will forge innovative and entrepreneurial towns highlighting the characteristics of different industries with high-end elements of agglomeration; Other areas should also tap the advantages of resources, and highlight the regional characteristics, so according to local conditions, we will create a batch of fashion sports town, photovoltaic town, big data town, royal hunting town and so on.

(2) Adhere to a high starting point planning. Learning from the advanced experience of Zhejiang, we should accurately grasp the connotation and extension of the town. That suggests we should abandon "big and complete" industrial orientation but strive to be "special and strong", abandon the "disperse and weak" functional system but strive to "get together and close", and abandon "large and wide" urban form but strive to be "fine and beautiful", abandon the "old and stiff" system design to strive to be "live and new." We will make the connection between detailed rules of characteristic town and relevant plans such as economic and social development, land use, urban construction, industrial development and ecological environment protection, so that we can meet the needs of the construction of characteristic towns and coordinate with the overall development of the region.

(3) Make innovation in management models of specialized towns. Drawing on the operation mode of China Fortune Land Development Corporation in Gu'an of Langfang province, we will give full play to the flexibility, autonomy and innovation of enterprises participating in market competition to operate the development and construction of characteristic townships as a whole project. And the enterprises should raise funds, attract investment, infrastructure construction, talent introduction and so on. We can also draw lessons from the mode of Yunqi town of Hangzhou, closely focus on the needs of entrepreneurs and give play to the leading role of private leading enterprises to build the foundation of innovation and entrepreneurship and public service facilities, and make relevant supporting services by the government to attract entrepreneurs to invest, thus jointly creating a industrial ecological chain of government leading, private enterprise to guide and entrepreneurs to invest.

(4) Improve public service level. Referring to the practice of Xiong'an New Area, in accordance with the principle of connection with Beijing's

public services, we should study to formulate the connection with education, medical care and social security system of Beijing to gradually level the gap in public service, thus creating conditions for functional dispersal and population shifts. Drawing on the construction experience of intelligent town, we should build perfect digital infrastructure and public service facilities to improve infrastructure service capabilities. And we need to strengthen the construction of road greening, ecological isolation zone, green corridors and forest, to build a beautiful system of ecological landscape and enhance the comfort and livability of small towns.

3.3 Optimize the capacity of public services and increase public service supply to form a public service system appropriate to population distribution and demands

3.3.1 Optimize the configuration structure of public service resources in line with population distribution and demand

Now, the resources of public services in north Hebei, especially of high-quality public services, are mainly concentrated in central cities and counties. According to the above analysis on the development trend of population transfer and urbanization, small towns in the future will become the major places carrying on rural migrants, and will form a three-point distribution pattern with the central cities and counties. Therefore, it is necessary to speed up the establishment of a suitable public service configuration structure.

(1) Adjust and optimize public service resource allocation system. High-quality public resources such as medical, health, education and culture in central cities and counties should further extend to other areas, especially some small towns far away from central cities and counties should establish additional health care, cultural and educational institutions to speed up the construction of public service facilities and meet the basic public service needs of local residents.

(2) Innovate public service resource allocation mechanism. We should establish a system that staffs of public institutions in central cities, counties and grass-roots take turns to go to the grassroots periodically, and give policy support to personnel in public institutions at the grassroots level on such aspects as wages, welfare standards, professional promotion, and cadre promotion. Meanwhile, we should strengthen the connection of public service institutions such as health care and education with Beijing and Tianjin, and explore to extend the go-to-grassroots system to Beijing-Tianjin and north Hebei, in order to enhance the level of public service of north Hebei.

(3) Optimize public service resource allocation form. We should actively develop the "Internet + public service" mode to strengthen the construction of public service facilities at the grassroots level, especially at the township level, comprehensively upgrading the level of information, and simultaneously promote networking and data sharing of relevant agencies in counties, central cities and even Beijing and Tianjin and actively promoting telemedicine, Internet diagnosis, and Internet education, to create conditions for meeting the needs of grass-roots public services.

3.3.2 Optimize the supply structure of public service resources in line with population structure and demand

The north Hebei is close to Beijing and Tianjin, so it is obvious that its population and labor force transfer to the outside region. Since the population transfer mostly concentrated in young and middle-aged, the proportion of middle-aged and elderly residents is higher. In 2016, the proportion of people aged 60 and above was 21.07%, higher than the average level of the province by two percentage points. Considering that this region will become a well-known recreational pension base in northern Beijing and the proportion of seniors coming from outside region, especially from Beijing, will increase, this proportion may further increase. Therefore, it is urgent to establish an old-age medical security system that is appropriate to the population structure. At the same time, the labor force in north Hebei is generally poorly educated and its production skills are scarce. In particular, the lack of employment skills and ways of getting rich for the poor have become important constraints on poverty alleviation and regional development. There is an urgent need to establish a skill training system that is appropriate to enhance the employability of the workforce. Moreover, some endemic diseases in north Hebei, such as Kashin-Beck disease, Keshan disease, have long plagued local residents, so it is urgent to improve the medical and health service conditions. In view of this, it is necessary to optimize the supply structure of public services from the following three aspects:

(1) Improve the level of pension services. We should innovate the diversified supply mechanism for pension services, speed up the introduction of domestic and international health and pension service institutions, and actively explore the cooperation ways with the governments, enterprises and non-governmental groups in Beijing and Tianjin. Also we need to plan and construct pension service institutions with large-scale, chain-orientation and branding in counties around Beijing and Tianjin such as Huailai, Zhuolu, Chicheng and Luanping. This measure can expand the provision of pension services and meet the needs of pension services at different

levels. We should speed up the integration of health care and pension, and establish a sound business cooperation mechanism and referral green channel in medical institutions and pension institutions, so as to build a service mode in which pension, attendance, rehabilitation and hospice services connect with each other. We should strengthen joint cooperation with Beijing-Tianjin pension institutions to strive for the establishment of regional medical centers, branch offices, cooperation in medical treatment, specialist collaboration and cooperation in pension institutions, and fully draw upon the experience of Langfang Yanda Hospital to establish barrier free access for the transfer and renewing of Beijing-Tianjin medical insurance.

(2) Improve vocational skill training system. We should carry out precision skill training. Focusing on the actual development and market demand in north Hebei, we provide employment skills training and outbound labor training to migrant workers who need to shift employment, carry out job skills upgrading training for on-the-job migrant workers, carry out demonstration training on rural entrepreneurship and skill-rich leaders, undertake a new type of professional farmer training for peasants engaged in agricultural production and services and entrepreneurship training for farmers with entrepreneurial conditions and entrepreneurial needs. We should promote collaborative construction to speed up the human resources information sharing platform of north Hebei and Beijing-Tianjin and improve the regional labor employment policies to join each other so as to build and share a base for public employment and training. We need to strengthen the guidance of science and technology, and give full play to the role of agricultural extension service cloud platform and 12316 agricultural information service platform. And we shall set up service stations of science and technology at county, town and village levels to promote the activities of special commissioners to the countryside and timely solve the problems in peasant labor production.

(3) Improve endemic disease prevention and control system. We need to further improve the comprehensive prevention and control system. For Keshan disease in north Hebei is still not completely eliminated, the local health administration departments step up monitoring and evaluation, actively promote the implementation of comprehensive prevention and control measures in the ward to further establish and improve the Keshan disease patient files; poverty alleviation departments focus on helping the impoverished families because of Keshan disease which established card for archives. We should actively carry out scientific research, give full play to the centralized advantages of medical research institutions in Beijing and Tianjin and carry out multi sectoral, interdisciplinary joint technical research

to strive to launch a number of suitable for the prevention and control of Keshan disease in north Hebei, and establish prevention and control technology transformation demonstration sites to gradually spread throughout the country.

3.4 Further improve the precision of poverty alleviation due to local conditions and people

3.4.1 Strengthen the guarantee function of social assistance policy for the poorest population

At present, the population of poverty-stricken people in north Hebei, who are incapacitated by their ability to work, is large. In 2015, the rate of poverty was as high as 12% due to illness and disability, while the proportion of people aged 60 and over in the impoverished population in Zhuolu County of Zhangjiakou accounted for as high as more than half. However, the current targeted poverty alleviation policy stipulates that the poor can enjoy the poverty alleviation loan discount policy, for the special disadvantaged groups such as those aged 60 and above who have lost their ability to work, the banks will not provide loans. As a result, on the one hand, poverty alleviation funds can not be spent and on the other hand, those who have the ability to work and who have financial needs are hard pressed to make loans so that the effect of alleviating poverty is greatly reduced. Therefore, it is necessary to increase the intensity of targeted poverty alleviation efforts, accurately identify such groups of destitute people and strengthen the guarantee function of social assistance and other policies, so as to achieve stable poverty alleviation as soon as possible.

(1) Intensify the medical assistance. We need to strengthen the recognition and management for people of medical security assistance, further reduce the hospital charges or cancel the reimbursement starting line, and increase the proportion of reimbursement assistance such as hospital reimbursement for serious illness insurance, inpatient medical assistance and medical aid for inpatients with major diseases. Thus, we will gradually include rehabilitation programs and non-public accidental injuries in the coverage of medical insurance, and comprehensively improve the medical assistance for the destitute groups. At the same time, learning from the advanced experience of Shandong Province, the government should purchase commercial supplementary medical insurance for the poor and organize the medical aid network for the difficult groups.

(2) Improve the level of living security. We should perfect the social assistance standards and price adjustment dynamic adjustment mechanism and improve the standards of minimum living allowance and the support for special difficulty to ensure

that the protection standard has always been coordinated with the level of economic and social development. And we should improve the temporary assistance system. For the family that is still very difficult in life after the assistance, they can further apply for temporary assistance.

(3) Guide social charitable aid. We need to take various forms of twinning help in poverty-stricken group of families, advocate enterprises and public institutions to donate money for the poor, establish village volunteer service station, carry out pair rescue activities such as "one-to-one" "the public help one" and "one help one" to provide regular services for destitute families.

3.4.2 Speed up the poverty alleviation in deep poverty areas by comprehensive policies

Carrying out poverty alleviation in deep poverty areas is a "hard bone" that is the most difficult to get rid of in the new era and a tough battle for winning the poverty alleviation. Under the precondition of upholding the basic strategy of targeted poverty reduction and alleviation, we will help people increase confidence in their own ability to lift themselves out of poverty, and see that they can access the education they need to do so by comprehensively policies. And we will intensify targeted poverty alleviation, give more concentrated support to those areas in deep poverty, and take more effective measures to truly eliminate poverty.

(1) Increase the concentration of support for deep poverty areas. We will focus on the deep poverty areas in such fields as the investment in poverty alleviation, industrial development, photovoltaic poverty alleviation, ecological protection, public services, land use protection and financial support so as to ensure that the newly added funds for poverty alleviation are mainly used in areas with deep poverty, the projects are mainly located in these areas, and the measures are mainly concentrated in areas of deep poverty. In detail, it is necessary to increase the funds for deep poverty areas which should be higher than the regional average on the basis of ensuring the integration of various types of agriculture-related funds.

(2) Strengthen the policy extension to marginalized and deep poverty areas. We need to adjust the implementation scope of the current BTH eco-construction protection project and include all counties in north Hebei into it. The current counterpart assistance mechanism in Beijing and Tianjin should be adjusted. And considering the factors such as the overall county poverty, ecosystem integrity, the conclusion of historical origin, we should re-adjust the counties to arrange counterpart assistance and include all counties in the north Hebei into the scope of Beijing-Tianjin counterpart assistance, meanwhile ensure the greatest poverty area to get the most help.

(3) Improve targeted assistance mechanism in poor areas. For poverty-striken counties, each county should clearly have a provincial leader in charge of guiding and arranging a direct provincial bureau, an economically strong county (city, district), a province-owned large-scale enterprise and a financial institution to jointly help them; for poverty-striken villages, each village must have one provincial directorate-level cadre to contact a provincial directorate working group and a privately-run strong enterprise in the urban area to help them; and for poor families, we will arrange one provincial or municipal cadre in each family to have a counterpart assistance.

4. Policy recommendation

4.1 Recommendations on nation level

4.1.1 Better ecological compensation policy

(1) Establish long-term mechanism of water resources compensation in BTH. It is recommended that the Chinese government should coordinate Beijing and Tianjin to provide financial-based water compensation for the upstream areas based on the water quality of warehouses (Guanting Reservoir, Miyun Reservoir and Pan-Da Reservoir).

(2) Set up construction fund of BTH water conservation function area. It is recommended that the Chinese government should coordinate with Beijing, Tianjin and Hebei, jointly financed by the Central Government and the three places, to set up a fund for the construction of the BTH water conservation function area, and give priority to supporting the construction in the fields of water conservation, ecological protection and restoration, environmental pollution prevention and control, and circular economy development, as well as ecological environment monitoring and regulatory capacity-building. In addition to the financial fund from the central government and BTH, the fund sources can also draw a certain percentage from the transaction income to enrich the fund accounts, combining with the market-oriented process of eco-products.

(3) Accelerate the legislation on ecological compensation. It is suggested that the Chinese government should promulgate relevant laws as soon as possible so as to promote the ecological compensation between the upper reaches and the lower reaches, the ecological benefit area and the ecological protection area to the law level, and regulate the ecological protection and compensation with the legal system.

4.1.2 Further improve infrastructure development legislations

(1) Cancel the local matching funds for state-funded public projects. The Program Outline for the Coordinated Development of the BTH Region suggests that the local supporting facilities should be canceled in concentrated contiguous destitute area counties and key counties for national poverty alleviation and development work outside the areas, and below the county level. Due to the relatively low level of overall development in north Hebei, only the four counties of Kuancheng, Xinglong, Huailai and Zhuolu do not belong to the contiguous destitute counties or the national key counties outside the areas. However, since all four counties are adjacent to Beijing and Tianjin, there are many public welfare projects such as transit traffic and water conservancy projects. At present, the annual financial revenue of Huailai County with the best economic strength is only about 1 billion yuan, and the supporting pressure is relatively large. Therefore, it is suggested to cancel the supporting funds for the public welfare projects arranged by the state in the counties and sub-counties.

(2) Increase the proportion of subsidies for local infrastructure projects. Due to the backward economy and weak local financial resources in north Hebei, the task of infrastructure construction such as local traffic roads and water conservancy is still heavy in the future and it is difficult to rely solely on local financial resources. It is recommended that the Chinese government should step up subsidies for local infrastructure projects such as village roads, drinking water projects in this area referring to the development strategy of the western region.

4.1.3 Increase the support for renewable energy development policy

The north Hebei has the unique conditions for the development of renewable energy. In particular, Zhangjiakou City is the only one demonstration area of renewable energy approved by the State Council, and has great potential in the development of renewable energy and energy transformation. However, the current institutional mechanisms and policies are hindering the rapid development of renewable energy. Suggestions:

(1) It is recommended that apart from the land use of office buildings, booster stations and paved plant roads listed as construction land in the photovoltaic power generation project in north Hebei, the occupation of land by photovoltaic modules should not change the nature of the original land. Photovoltaic poverty alleviation is an important way of poverty alleviation and development in poor rural areas. However, at present, the land for photovoltaic is regarded as construction land by the land departments and

the procedures for transferring land for construction must be handled. This stipulation greatly limits the development of photovoltaic power generation projects. In fact, the use of photovoltaic land does not change the nature of the original land, in which photovoltaic modules rely on steel to support, so the construction of photovoltaic power generation project will not destroy the land, and will not form a permanent land. The space below the array of components can still use for agriculture, fishery, forestry and animal husbandry production, and it is an important form and carrier of multi-energy complementarity, prolific integration and the improvement of the comprehensive efficiency of land use. At the same time, photovoltaic modules have a positive effect on water and soil conservation and reduction of evaporation in arid and semi-arid regions. Therefore, it is recommended that in solar power projects, only areas used for office building, transformers and paved plant roads may be listed as Construction Land. Land use nature may not be changed in areas occupied by solar power panels.

(2) Carry out independent target for photovoltaic development in north Hebei. The current distribution of photovoltaic indicators at various levels from country to local regions cannot meet the development needs of regional renewable energy. Taking Zhangjiakou alone as an example, in 2016, the city only applied for 550,000 kilowatts indicators for photovoltaic poverty alleviation. According to this pace, the cumulative PV indicators will be only three million kilowatts by 2020, which is far from the newly added target of six million kilowatts in the 13th Five-year Plan period. Therefore, it is suggested that photovoltaic land use should be listed independently in Zhangjiakou and even in the north of Hebei Province from the perspective of building a national demonstration area for renewable energy and promoting energy transformation in the BTH Region.

(3) It is suggested that Zhangjiakou City should be listed as national power system reform pilot. At present, our country has entered a comprehensive pilot phase of power system reform. It is suggested that Hebei Power Grid should be listed as national power system reform pilot to speed up the energy supply-side reform with electricity price reform as the core and to gradually liberalize the power transmission and distribution market, thus creating conditions for improving the proportion of power supply in the renewable energy power supply system in Zhangjiakou and even in north Hebei.

4.2 Recommendations for Hebei Province

4.2.1 Create exit mechanism for resource-based industries

Driven by the joint efforts to control air pollution and construct the ecological conservation functional area in BTH Region, Hebei Province proposed that by 2020, Zhangjiakou City will build "no mine city", "no steel city" and "no coal city", and Chengde City build a "coal-free city", so that the northern part of Hebei Province gets into trouble of accelerating the loss of traditional impetus and lacking new motivation. It is suggested that the Hebei Provincial Party Committee and Provincial Government speed up the construction of coordination and linkage mechanism for the withdrawal of old industries and the cultivation of new industries. While ensuring the withdrawal of resource-based industries, Hebei Province should accelerate the cultivation of emerging industries to ensure the smooth transformation of old and new kinetic energy.

(1) Support the transformation of resource-based industrial enterprises. For mining enterprises, we need to support them to greatly develop mountain photovoltaics and combine the mine rehabilitation with photovoltaic poverty alleviation, and give protection in terms of index allocation, priority access to the Internet, land use indicators and bank loans. For the iron and steel enterprises, we should support their transformation from manufacturing to service, and strive to expand into the fields like research and innovation and Internet finance. And we should formulate policies to encourage steel enterprises to shift excess capacity to foreign countries, so as to guide them in improving the quality and efficiency of overseas investment.

(2) Set up a new industry development fund in north Hebei to change the original land use. It is suggested that the government of Hebei Province set up a fund for the development of new industries in north Hebei, which allows resource-based industrial enterprises to buy their shares for withdrawing from the land and attracts other social capital to enter. This will be used for the development of original vacated land and encourage it to develop high value-added industry projects such as high-end manufacturing, business exhibition, technological innovation, cultural and creative industries. And the government will give preference to project approval, environmental assessment and taxation.

(3) Give priority to the coordinated development of Beijing-Tianjin-Hebei industrial transferred projects. In promoting the connection and cooperation with Beijing-Tianjin industry in Hebei Province, priority should be given to projects suitable for regional functional positioning to be introduced to the north of Hebei.

(4) Properly handle related items. In light of Hebei Province's solution to the overcapacity of steel, we should properly handle assets accounting, creditor's rights and debts and other matters, properly place laid-off and unemployed workers to realize re-employment for training them, in order to ensure a smooth transition.

4.2.2 Create mechanism for achieving full values of ecological products

Rich in ecological resources, the north Hebei has piloted the project in such areas as regional water resources compensation and forestry carbon sequestration transaction. Under the background of carrying out the system reform of ecological civilization throughout the country, we should further deepen the system reform of ecological civilization to promote the realization of the value of ecological resources and products.

(1) Promote the establishment of a national carbon trading market. With the help of abundant forestry resources and abundant forest reserves in north Hebei, we should accelerate the establishment of a carbon trading market. It is suggested that the Hebei provincial government should intensify its communication with the national forestry department to set up a national pilot platform for carbon trading in Hebei Province, and formulate plans for trading volume and quota allocation of carbon-permit based on the national unified framework to promote the construction of the carbon sequestration market.

(2) Set up a sound forestry property mortgage system. We will further promote forest tenure rights system reform, clear and perfect the forestry property rights system, and promote the forest land resources right. On this basis, we will set up forestry property mortgage guarantee fund in Hebei Province, in order to provide guarantee for promoting forestry property mortgage and create conditions for revitalizing the forestry resources and achieving the forestry ecological value.

(3) Explore to carry out water rights trading system. We should explore to establish water resources asset property system jointly with Beijing and Tianjin. That needs us to determine the subject, objects, conditions, procedures and other contents of the right to use water resources and implement the use and benefits of water resources into water users. Thus, water assets property system is gradually formed with clear ownership, well define power and responsibility and regulation efficiency. On this basis, we also should explore to establish water rights trading market to carry out different forms of water rights transactions in different levels, promoting the optimal allocation of water resources.

(4) Improve emissions trading system. On the basis of drawing on the experiences and lessons of emission trading in the past, we should improve the management methods of the paid use and trading of pollution emission rights, and study to determine its transfer standards. We will start the initial verification of emission rights of existing sewerage units in an all-round manner and timely begin to collect use fees for emission rights in such key industries as electricity, steel, cement and glass, and other sectors will

gradually implement the paid use of emission rights.

4.2.3 Improve connected rural development planning mechanism

Countryside is the key and difficult point in the development of north Hebei. In recent years, with further promotion of "agriculture, rural areas, and farmers" and development of poverty alleviation by the Chinese government, the focus of the policies of the state and Hebei Province has shifted down and the measures for supporting the development of "three rural" are very intensive. However, since various tasks belong to different departments, to a certain extent it weakens the overall support for the development of "three rural". To this end, it is suggested that at the provincial level in Hebei, the overall coordination and guidance of the north Hebei should be increased to form a join force.

(1) On the basis of integrating various existing plans, we will formulate and implement a plan for rural development. We need to carry out a systematic review of the planning of the construction of the beautiful countryside, the development of characteristic towns, the development of leisure agriculture and global tourism, infrastructure construction, the comprehensive management of small watersheds, the economic development of ditch and other fields involving agriculture and rural areas. On this basis, we should formulate plans for rural development and define areas and fields for key development in combination with the regional ecological carrying capacity and development foundation, so as to make the existing plans be seamlessly connected and lay the foundation for the overall development of the area.

(2) Innovate rural development and construction mechanism. We should actively introduce modern tourist enterprises, cultural enterprises and agricultural enterprise groups in the surrounding areas such as Beijing and Tianjin and set up development and construction companies in north Hebei to support and encourage local villagers to invest in the form of land, homesteads and labor services or buy shares to invest the tourism development in the whole rural area and the construction of characteristic town and modern agricultural park. And the government is responsible for the investment in public service facilities and infrastructure services.

(3) Organize and concentrate various types of support funds in rural areas. For the areas where the government is responsible for investment, the funds of the state and relevant departments of Hebei Province shall be integrated according to the plan, and concentrated on the key areas determined by the planning in accordance with the existing channels. Thus, we can avoid the no-focus situation, give full play to the join force of funds of the central and provincial departments and strengthen the examination and supervision over the use of various funds.

4.3 Recommendations for municipal governments of Beijing and Tianjin

4.3.1 Strengthen personnel training and labor employment training to the north Hebei

It is suggested that we should make full use of the current counterpart support channels in Beijing-Tianjin and Zhangjiakou-Chengde region and increase labor force training and employment assistance in north Hebei, in view of the problems such as the low quality of labor, the mismatch of professional setting in regional colleges and universities and the development needs and the shortage of qualified personnel in north Hebei.

(1) We will further expand counterpart assistance. At present, Beijing-Tianjin counterparts involved 15 counties in north Hebei, so it is suggested that Beijing and Tianjin extend the scope of counterpart assistance in personnel training and labor training to the whole north part of Hebei to enhance their own "blood making" capacity, considering that other counties also face the problem of lack of high-end talent and low-quality workforce.

(2) We will carry out the targeted training for professional talents. In response to the urgent need for the professionals in such fields as machinery manufacturing, electronic information, new energy, sports and leisure, health care, medical and nursing, it is proposed that Beijing and Tianjin organize related institutions and research institutes to increase their precise support through orientation training, personnel exchanges and scientific research cooperation so as to meet the needs of qualified personnel to the maximum extent.

(3) We will strengthen labor service connecting and cooperation. In terms of promoting employment and targeted poverty alleviation, it is suggested that Beijing and Tianjin establish a labor service cooperation training base with the north Hebei, and carry out "order training" for the demand of workers in enterprises, in order to export qualified rural labors for Beijing and Tianjin.

(4) We will increase the assistance for employment training of enterprises in north Hebei. It is suggested that Beijing and Tianjin actively carry out a variety of ways like school-enterprise cooperation, regional cooperation and sending students to the countryside, to conduct skill training on the needs of all kinds of labor workers in the north of Hebei on the basis of their own educational advantages.

(5) We will establish a platform for interoperability of labor resources information system, which proposes that unified system of post information collection and publication, employment introduction, teaching management and certificate issuance should be

established in Beijing, Tianjin and north Hebei so as to realize the sharing of labor resources and labor information resources.

4.3.2 Create and improve unified certification system

With the further development of the coordinated development in BTH Region, the industry tie-in and market exploration between north Hebei and Beijing-Tianjin continue to increase. However, the quality of the administrative division and the recognition (certification) system of qualification has brought a lot of inconvenience for corporate investment home and market integration. Therefore, it is suggested that the municipal government of Beijing and Tianjin, in collaboration with the relevant government departments of Hebei Province, formulate a unified certification (recognition) and quality standard system on the basis of thoroughly examining various types of qualification authentication, qualification accreditation, inspection and quarantine standards and quality standards, to merge the original cross-over projects in the three places and clean up those that are not in line with the actual development, thus creating the conditions for the talent exchange, vocational education, business investment and market development in the three places.

4.3.3 Expedite road development connecting Beijing, Tianjin, and surrounding counties

At present, although the counties in north Hebei around Beijing and Tianjin is adjacent to Beijing, the traffic linking with Beijing and Tianjin are not smooth due to the low level of the Beijing-Tianjin roads or heavy traffic load on the existing roads. In order to further promote coordinated development in Beijing-Tianjin region, the vast majority of counties around Beijing and Tianjin have already planned a number of construction projects for upgrading and connecting with the Beijing-Tianjin roads. For example, the projects, such as Zhuolu-Beijing road to be planned by Zhuolu, the redevelopment of county road water lines to be planned by Huairou, the reconstruction of national road Xingyang Line and the reconstruction of provincial road Shiyou, need the support and cooperation of Beijing and Tianjin. Beijing and Tianjin municipalities should deploy agencies to strengthen connection in areas involving the Beijing, Tianjin, and Hebei to develop road construction and renovation plans. Following unified development standards, the municipalities should push for county road improvement or road construction.

References

[1] 刘娟 . 我国农村扶贫开发的回顾、成效与创新 [J]. 探索，2009（4）.

[2] 朱小玲，陈俊 . 建国以来我国农村扶贫开发的历史回顾与现实启示 [J].《生产力研究》，2012（5）.

[3] 张亮，赵邦宏，张润清 . 河北省贫困区域状况及扶贫开发战略分析 [J]. 保定学院学报，2014 年 1 月 第 27 卷（1）.

[4] 刘颖，梁立华 . 环京津落后地区扶贫发展对策研究——以张家口为例 [J]. 经济研究导刊，2014（13）.

[5] 武振钧，闫晓燕，尚继文，李琳 . 关于构建河北省"大扶贫"格局的建议 [J]. 职大学报，2012（1）.

[6] 毕树广 . 环京津张家口地区贫困成因及对策 [J]. 农业经济，2011（6）.

[7] 韩春 .《中国农村贫困的新特征及反贫困对策研究》. 特区经济，2010（3）.

[8] 黄海燕，王永平 . 新阶段贵州农村贫困特征与反贫困策略调整 . 贵州农业科学，2010，38（7）.

[9] 兰传海 . 环京津贫困带扶贫开发研究 . 经济研究参考，2015（2）.

[10] 程联涛 . 我国贫困地区区域特征及扶贫对策 . 贵州社会科学，2014（10）.

[11] 任红燕，申潞玲，任虎成，秦作霞 . 山西省新阶段农村贫困特征及致贫成因分析 . 山西农业大学学报，2013（12）.

[12] 李仙娥，李 倩 . 秦巴集中连片特困地区的贫困特征和生态保护与减贫互动模式探析 . 农业现代化研究，2013（7）.

[13] 汪霞，汪磊 . 贵州连片特困地区贫困特征及扶贫开发对策分析 . 贵州社会科学，2013（12）.

[14] 王敏 . 我国农村反贫困政策变迁及效果评价 [J]. 劳动保障世界，2012（10）.

[15] 马玉芳，沙景华 . 环京津贫困带问题研究 [J]. 首都经济贸易大学学报（双月刊），2016（7）.

[16] 何芬，赵燕霞 . 美、日促进集中连片特困地区减贫的经验借鉴 [J]. 世界地理研究，2015（12）.

[17] 成福伟，张月丛 . 基于能值分析的京津冀生态支撑区绿色可持续发展评价——以河北承德为例河北大学学报（哲学社会科学版）[J]，2016（7）.

[18] 李荫樾，王贤斌 . 农村扶贫开发政策的变迁与启示 [J]. 现代化农业，2014（7）.

[19] 河北省出台支持环首都扶贫攻坚示范区及阜平发展政策 . 长城网 .2013-02-16.

This book is the result of a co-publication agreement between China Financial and Economic Publishing House (China) and Paths International Ltd (UK).

Title: Study on the Coordinated Development of Beijing-Tianjin-Hebei
Advisory Group of Experts of ADB Technical Assistance Project: TA-9042 PRC
ISBN: 978-1-84464-688-3
Ebook ISBN: 978-1-84464-689-0

Paths International Ltd

Published in the United Kingdom
www.pathsinternational.com

www.ingramcontent.com/pod-product-compliance
Lightning Source LLC
LaVergne TN
LVHW082054290326
834995LV00004B/19